The Inner City

Architects' Year Book XIV

Editorial Advisory Committee

Jane Drew
Theo Crosby
David Lewis
Dennis Sharp

The Inner City

edited by Declan Kennedy and Margrit I Kennedy

Paul Elek   London

FOR NORA, ANNE AND ANTJA

© Paul Elek 1974

Published by Elek Books Ltd
54-58 Caledonian Road London N1 9RN

Printed by Unwin Brothers Limited,
The Gresham Press,
Old Woking, Surrey

ISBN 0 236 15431 1

In the same series edited by David Lewis

The Pedestrian in the City (1965)
Urban Structure (1968)
The Growth of Cities (1971)

CONTENTS

Acknowledgments

THE INNER CITY is the fourth of the Architects'
Yearbook series to be devoted to a single subject.
The previous three, *The Pedestrian in the City,
Urban Structure* and *The Growth of Cities,* were
edited by David Lewis. As in these three books,
most of the articles here have been specially written.
However, as the acknowledgments below show,
some have been reprinted, expanded or adapted from
previous publications.

The editors may have changed, but the previous
editor, David Lewis, eased the transition by sharing
the pains of conceptualizing this volume. We wish
to thank him also as a contributor, as member of the
advisory board and as a friend. Thanks are also due to
Theo Crosby, Jane Drew, Maxwell Fry and Dennis
Sharp, in recommending subjects, authors and topics,
and contacts.

The following have kindly permitted a reprint of
articles and illustrations originally published by
them: the Greater London Council for 'Living with
Traffic' which was published in 1973 as a result of
public discussion among the inner-city residents
of London; Steven J Kidder and Alyce W Nafziger
of the Center for Social Organization of Schools,
Johns Hopkins University, USA, who compiled the
*Proceedings of the National Gaming Council's
Eleventh Annual Symposium,* Baltimore 1972, from
which we reprint Ervin Bell's 'U-DIG' Game, a
Tool for Urban Innovation'; *Ekistics* (Greece) for
C A Doxiadis' article, 'Order in our thinking: the
need for a total approach to the anthropocosmos',
which appeared in their 200th issue, for an expanded
version of Aditya Prakash's 'Rehri — the mobile
shop of India' and S G Thakurdesai's 'Sense of
place in Greek anonymous architecture'.

Few articles have been written in pure isolation.
There are acknowledgments many authors would
like to include; some will be necessarily omitted
through lack of information on the editor's part,
but we join with van Ginkel Associates in thanking
the Transportation Section, City Planning, the
Department of Highways of the Transportation
Administration, and the Regional Plan Association
(all of New York) for assistance in the preparation
of their contribution. John Wiebenson's design and
explanation of 'A public information system for
Adams–Morgan streets' was part of a project,
funded by the D. C. Commission of the Arts,
directed by Topper Carew, with graphic consulting
by Tunney Lee and Jack Patrick of 'The New
Thing'. The editors also acknowledge John Allpass
et al., *Urban Centres and Changes in the Centre
Structure,* Copenhagen 1968, as the source of the
diagrams at the beginning of their article.
Photographs for the editors' introduction were
provided by J Jenicek, K Plicka, Landeshauptstadt
Munchen (these taken by Erika Groth-
Schmachtenberger and Christl Reiter),
Fosa Photoservices, Lagos; for Ernest Erber's
article by Louis B Schlivek; for John Kinard's
article by the Anacostia Neighborhood Museum;
for Ed Berman's article by Min Hogg and the Save
Piccadilly Campaign; for Mike Franks' article by
John Dougil and others; for David Lewis's article
by Jay Bee Studios, Cinema 76, Balthazar Korab
and Eugene L Edwards. In addition Dietrich Worbs
would like to thank his translator E W Teichmann
and the publisher of the illustrations reproduced
here from H Kulka, *Adolf Loos — Das Werk des
Architekten,* Vienna 1931.

The editors wish to thank Judy Barricella, Pittsburgh,
and Bärbel Kirchner, West Berlin, for their typing
assistance; and especially our publisher's editor,
Janet Haffner.

7

CHRISTOPHER ALEXANDER — English architect, planner, mathematician; Director of the Center for Environmental Structure, Berkeley, California, USA; author of *Notes on the Synthesis of Form,* 1964 (with Serge Chermayeff); *Community and Privacy: Toward a New Architecture of Humanism,* 1963; also wrote the prize-winning essay *A City is Not a Tree,* 1966.

ERVIN BELL — American architect, founder and editor of *The Architectural Index,* now Associate Professor of the College of Environmental Design, University of Colorado.

ED BERMAN — Harvard graduate and Rhodes scholar, now Artistic Director of Interaction Trust, an organization interested in making the arts more relevant to local community life, sponsored by the Arts Council of Great Britain; Chairman, Save Piccadilly Campaign.

CONSTANTINOS A DOXIADIS — President Doxiadis Associates, consultants on the development and ekistics; Chairman, Board of Directors and President, Athens Technological Institute, Greece; author of numerous articles and books, among them *Architecture in Transition,* 1963; *Between Dystoria and Utopia,* 1966; *Emergence and Growth of an Urban Region, The Developing Urban Detroit Area,* 1966; and *The Two-Headed Eagle,* 1972.

ERNEST ERBER — American planner and Director of Research and Program Planning for the National Committee against Discrimination in Housing, Inc., Washington, DC; he taught at the Urban Studies Center at Rutgers State University, and is a member of the graduate faculty of Pratt Institute, Department of City and Regional Planning; editor of the book *Urban Planning in Transition,* 1970.

RAY A FRIEDEN (architect) and BRUCE D MANN (economist) — were post-graduate Peace Corps volunteers in Iran when they completed a study of Kerman for the Ministry of Interior, Teheran, Iran. Their contribution to this book is a section of their report *An Urban Model for Non-Overdeveloped Nations,* 1971.

MIKE FRANKS — English urban planner, employed first by Liverpool's City Planning Department and then, after private practice, in the multi-disciplinary Covent Garden Development Team, London.

van GINKEL ASSOCIATES — planners and architects, Montreal, Canada; their innovative work covers regional planning for Malaysia; educational planning for the Province of Quebec; airport planning and design for several countries; the design of the pedestrian precinct and minibus for Midtown Manhattan; they also acted as consultants for the Montreal Metro and World Exhibition.

THE GREATER LONDON COUNCIL — came into being with the decision of the British Parliament to amalgamate the central boroughs (LCC) with the surrounding metropolitan area under one administrative authority.

SARA ISHIKAWA — architect and member, with Christopher Alexander, of the Center for Environmental Structure team for the development of *A Pattern Language which Generates Multi-service Centres,* 1969

SHUN KANDA — Japanese architect, presently an instructor in environmental design at Harvard University; also taught at the Boston Architectural Center, and collaborated with Jose Luis Sert, and Benjamin Thompson, Cambridge, Mass.

DECLAN KENNEDY — Irish architect and planner, Professor of Urban Infrastructure, Technical University, West-Berlin, Germany; Assistant Editor of *Ekistics;* taught at Darmstadt Institute of Technology, West-Germany; School of Architecture, Dundee; and the University of Pittsburgh, USA.

MARGRIT I KENNEDY — German architect and planner, practised in Germany, Scotland and America; former member of Urban Design Associates, Pittsburgh; research fellow in planning and urban simulation/gaming at the Graduate School of Public and International Affairs, University of Pittsburgh, USA.

JOHN R KINARD — founder and Director of the Anacostia Neighborhood Museum of the Smithsonian Institution, the world's first intermediary museum, in Washington DC, formerly with the Office of Economic Opportunity on the Eastern Shore of Maryland and with 'Operation Crossroad Africa' in Tanzania, Kenya, and Zanzibar.

DAVID LEWIS — Andrew Mellon Professor of architecture and urban design, Carnegie-Mellon University, Pittsburgh, USA, 1963-68; taught at Yale 1969 and 1970; author with Hansmartin Bruckmann of *New Housing in Great Britain,* 1961; editor of the last three *Architects' Year Books;* founder-partner, Urban Design Associates, USA.

ADITYA PRAKASH — Principal of the School of Architecture in Chandigarh, India. His report on mobile shops is based on a larger study in that city and in Ambala, conducted in 1971, and assisted by Pallah Muderjee and Amar Puri.

RICHARD RIDLEY — partner in 'Octoberman', an architectural, planning and graphic design firm in Washington, DC, working in the fields of housing, transportation, city planning, campus planning, and special interest planning; since 1971 Assistant Professor of Architecture, Howard University, Washington, DC.

MURRAY SILVERSTEIN — writer/designer and member with Christopher Alexander of the Center of Environmental Structure team. Author of *Dorms at Berkeley* (with Sim van der Ryn, 1966).

PETER F SMITH — British architect and psychologist; Queens' College, Cambridge 1952-57; general architectural practice 1957-61; doctoral research, Manchester University 1961-63; lecturer, Department of Architecture, Sheffield University since 1965; sole principal Ferguson Smith & Associates.

JOHN L TAYLOR — Director of the Sheffield Centre for Environmental Research and Senior Lecturer in the Department of Town and Regional Planning, University of Sheffield, currently a visiting Nuffield Social Science Fellow at several environmental simulation research centres in USA and Western Europe. Also former editor of the Salzburg Congress on Urban Planning Bulletin, joint editor of two Cambridge Education Monographs on Instructional Simulation Systems, and author of *Instructional Planning Systems,* 1971; co-author with Rex Walford of *Simulation in the Classroom,* 1972, and editor of *Planning for Urban Development,* 1972.

S G THAKURDESAI — Indian architect who won the Michael Ventris Memorial Fund 1959 for Architecture; he studied and worked with Jose Luis Sert, Jackson & Associates in Cambridge, Mass, and is presently teaching in the Department of Architecture, California Polytechnic, San Luis Obispo, USA.

JOHN WIEBENSON — former Professor of Architecture, University of Maryland; now in private practice, advocate planner and architect, in Washington DC; designed Resurrection City in 1968.

DIETRICH WORBS — German architect and planner, scientific assistant at the Central Archives for University Planning at the University of Stuttgart, 1969-70; associate to the Planning and Information Center (HIS) at the University of Freiburg, 1970-71; founder-partner Development Planning Associates, Stuttgart/Berlin 1971.

8

DECLAN KENNEDY
MARGRIT I. KENNEDY

9

Two extreme positions among urbanists and urbanites are now clearly identifiable. On one hand there are those who believe that the city or rather the inner city as we know it is a decaying relic of the past and will be abandoned soon. On the other hand we find those who see the city as a democratic unit between the neighbourhood and a national government. An example of the first group is Melvin Webber. His 'The Post-City Age',[1] was published in 1968, when it had become clear that many American renewal efforts were gigantic failures in inner city reconstruction. The second view typified by Robert Dahl's 'The City in the Future of Democracy'[2] in 1967, spread the notion that political power and resources for the cities are crucial to democratic government. A number of political scientists now argue that only a greater share of political power can help the city solve its problems.[3] They hold that nations are too small and egoistic to solve the global problems of survival, and too large and removed from cities to prevent urban problems from rapidly approaching catastrophic dimensions.

The options open to us according to these theories are quite different, though neither questions the fact that we are going to have 'urban areas'. The first presents us with the problem of how best to remove the corpse called the 'inner city', infested with the worst urban ills. According to the other the inner city could again become the heart and focal point of the surrounding region, a centre of political activity, cultural, social and economic life, similar to its historic predecessor, the medieval city state.

The purpose of this book is to explore some of the consequences of contradictory demands made on inner cities: to uncover the reasons for their growing complexity and discuss various revolutionary approaches. It will also indicate that what happens to the inner city ultimately depends on the will of the people, the 'dominant paradigm', or inherent cultural values of a given society, different social subgroups, or the number of individuals ready to 'love it or leave it'.

An exact definition of the inner city, the central business district (CBD), or city centre, which can be applied to more than one city does not exist. However, most cities contain a 'core' area with high density developments, specialized and overlapping functions, and a lower density 'frame' in which CBD functions are mixed with residential uses, or other non-central activities.

The difference between the two zones is marked, and sometimes openly hostile. Whether the core expands and impinges upon adjoining communities or whether it contracts because of the evacuation of industrial premises and offices (thus inviting vandalism and decay) — it presents a constant threat to its immediate neighbours.

In the late fifties and early sixties, discussion about inner city problems was heated. Traffic congestion, decay, the moving out of business establishments, industry and the wealthier part of the population were soon to be experienced in all the major cities of the world. The year zero for the inner city seemed to be in sight; the blight of the inner city was making headlines in newspapers; and scholars of all the pertinent disciplines issued their analyses for what had happened and what should be done about it. Urban renewal programmes became the hope of the people trapped in the cities that something would happen and a turn for the better was in sight. Only a few years later 'urban renewal' had become a dirty word, symbolizing empty and expensive highrise apartments in a sea of poverty and deprivation, vacant buildings and sites, and the inevitable stories of displacement of the poorest and most powerless in the nation.

It became more and more evident with every new failure that the problems of the inner city were far more complex than anybody had foreseen. First and foremost, inner city problems were not always problems of the inner city alone. For example, to solve traffic congestion in the inner city, planners found that they had to go to the source of the problem in the lower density suburbs. Here, clustered by race, income, class and education, some citizens found that the socio-cultural values placed on amply space and two cars could be realized.

In other words, the thrust of the search for solutions to inner city problems not only had to go further towards micro- and macro-levels of inquiry, but also toward disciplines originally concerned with quite different subject areas: anthropology offered the possibility of discovering micro-level 'qualitative' data, filling in the gaps left by that brand of sociology which was oriented towards quantitative research tasks; political science and economics became increasingly important in dealing with the questions and relationships between power, wealth and underlying national goals; behaviourism and psychology, whether quantitatively 'biased' or not, greatly increased our understanding of the interaction between human and environmental systems.

City planning offices began to employ community planners, social workers, and systems analysts. And architects not only began to concern themselves with

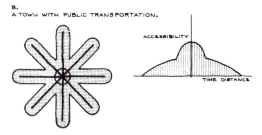

A.
A TOWN IN THE PEDESTRIAN- BICYCLE- AND HORSEDRAWN CARRIAGE PERIOD.

ACCESSIBILITY

TIME DISTANCE

B.
A TOWN WITH PUBLIC TRANSPORTATION.

ACCESSIBILITY

TIME DISTANCE

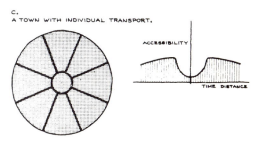

C.
A TOWN WITH INDIVIDUAL TRANSPORT.

ACCESSIBILITY

TIME DISTANCE

Accessibility to the centre: different transportation modes and settlement patterns.

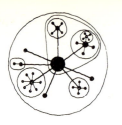 

the functions of the human brain, but also with the social and cultural values, interests and needs of their clients; the relationship between aesthetics and pyschology, and ways to order the complexity of human settlements (see Doxiadis', Smith's and Worbs' articles).
Basically, architecture grew beyond architects, and

Above: The development of relationship between the inner city and its city-region.

Below: Munich, plan of one of the pedestrian precincts in the historic core.

architects have grown beyond architecture. Inter-disciplinary teamwork, it seemed, was working best, where all team members had a multi-disciplinary background with one part of their education relating specifically to urban problems. A reflection of this can be found in this book, as most articles here deal with areas of overlapping concern between architecture, planning and other disciplines. Many focus on user involvement, information, and participation, reflecting some of the major single changes in the attitude of architects and designers toward their work in the last decade. These changes will be particularly crucial in the design, redesign or maintenance of inner cities, where one-way decision-making has in the past resulted in the grossest inequities. Today more and more architects see themselves as 'horticulturists' of community processes and individual self-expression in the sense David Lewis describes in 'A Community Determines What Its Centre Is.'
An attempt to systematize the pattern of development in the relationship between the inner city and outlying districts on a world-wide basis is difficult. The amount and quality of research that has been carried out in different countries varies widely. The American 'model' is probably the most clearly de-

fined. The 'concentric zones hypothesis' postulated by Burgess[4] and supported by Hoyt[5], was further sustained by what Alonso[6] calls the 'more-land-but-less-accessibility' phenomenon. Both theories have worked in the same direction: the continuous outward migration of the wealthier parts of society. However, the reasons are different. The concentric zones hypothesis is the spatial equivalent of the filtering process or trickle-down theory of the housing market according to which new houses are built only for the well-to-do, but in time pass on to those with lower incomes. Thus the wealthier absorb most of the depreciation costs before the house is handed on. The emphasis was on 'newness', and it was expected that the simple outward movement of high income to the suburbs could be reversed through urban renewal, clearing the decaying part of central cities and replacing it with new and more expensive housing.
Recent investigations, however, have suggested that the peripheral position of the rich may be a result of their preference for lower density rather than new-ness of the building.[7] Ample space is preferred over shorter journey-to-work; and accessibility has become an 'inferior good' as the wealthier substitute it

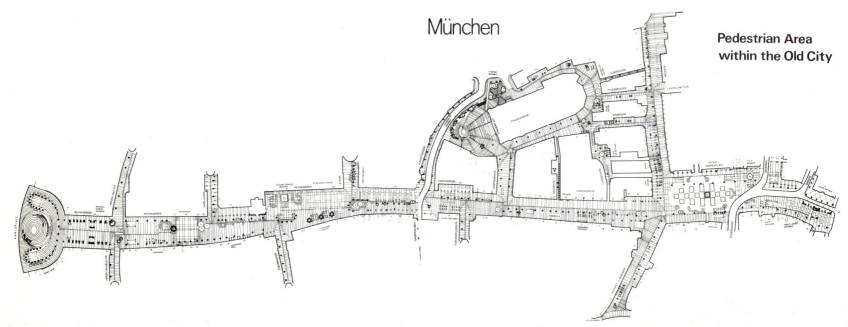

München

Pedestrian Area within the Old City

Above: Etching showing the Marienplatz in 1840.

Below: The same in 1972.

with more land.

Ernest Erber in his contribution to the present volume takes this argument one step further. He holds that it is not only ample space but *also* the shorter journey-to-work which attracts the rich to the suburbs since business establishments, industry and large corporations have moved in the same direction. This further draws middle and upper income groups away from inner city locations. The inner city becomes the territory of the poorest social groups and an eroding tax-base aggravates the difficult struggle of the centre to offer a viable living environment.

In Europe, where for historical reasons towns and cities were dense and living space in them costly and tight, the 'concentric zones hypothesis' has never been quite as simply applicable as in North America. Although some outward movement of the rich has undoubtedly taken place, several factors have contributed to the maintenance of the inner city as an urban and regional centre:

— first and foremost there is a cultural and historical attitude quite unlike the American, namely that cities are the place of civilization, of urbaneness;

— European cities have, in general, more status and political power and resources;

— land has been a limited resource all through history, and land-use regulations were adopted early to restrict outward growth as much as possible;

— lastly there are two factors that seem to mutually reinforce each other: (a) the relatively greater expense of owning and operating a car, and (b) the existence of relatively efficient inter-urban and intra-urban public transport. These have meant fewer highways cutting through inner-city land, fewer parking spaces taken up by private automobiles, and a higher degree of accessibility to the inner city for all income groups.

As a result of the increasing concern with rehabilitation rather than building new communities, and the widespread provision of pedestrian precincts linked to mass transit systems, life in the city centre has become more attractive in recent years.

In Munich the completion of underground and mass transit lines allowed the conversion of two main traffic arteries in the inner city to pedestrian malls. They are not only shopping areas but major focal points for recreation and cultural life in the metropolitan area. Historical monuments, fountains, restaurants, cafes, cinemas, theatres and museums form a continuous chain of attraction, beauty and enjoyment. At night facades, fountains, and monuments are illuminated, on sunny days people will sleep, relax, and loiter amidst the colourful landscaping.

The average width (20 metres) of the Neuhauser/Kaufingerstrasse, in the beginning, gave reason to believe that it would be hard to fill this space with life and make it attractive. Just the opposite turned out to be true. Statistics before and after the completion of the pedestrian precinct show that the number of passers-by had nearly doubled. (From 7200 per day in 1966 to 120,000 per day in 1972.)[8] However, not everybody in Munich was in favour of the one-directional support of the inner city. Many professionals and citizens publicly criticized the city planning office for its pre-occupation with an 'outmoded centre-ideology', and its neglect of planning for the city as a whole. At its present stage of growth, it seemed to them, the city should be directed toward decentralization rather than centralization. To create more attractions like the pedestrian precinct, according to Peter Bode, would finally 'choke the city in its own dynamic'.[9]

The intricacies of different traffic modes, and the separation of pedestrian and vehicular traffic, have to be viewed in the wider context of the urban area. Long range and short term measures are necessary to renew existing communication systems which no longer function properly.

Nowhere is the breakdown of these systems more evident than in the heart of the wealthiest city in the world — Midtown Manhattan. The van Ginkel plan — revolutionary, given the traditional American aversion to walking — separates pedestrian and vehicular traffic and deals with some solutions which can be realized immediately, but which are compatible with the larger framework of long-term plans.

World Fairs, Expos, or Olympic Games may present a chance for frustrated planners to tackle inner-city traffic problems. Seattle, Montreal, Mexico City, Tokyo, and Munich are showpieces for the use of technical and organizational knowledge. The critical question however is whether these accomplishments will serve to make the city as a whole more habitable and humane.

Urbanization, mainly in the developing countries, will reach unprecedented dimensions during the next decades. The question therefore arises: can any lesson be learned from what happened in the more developed countries during the last hundred years? Can the fate of the cities, now medium-sized, or small, which will become the inner cities of tomorrow, be a happier one than their European, North American or Japanese

counterparts? The answer seems to depend more on the political wisdom and courage of those in power than on technical know-how.

In most developing countries the enormous migration from rural to urban centres has created the most formidable problems in form of unplanned squatter settlement along the urban fringe. In South America squatter settlements mostly occupy marginal land.[10] They spread along river valleys, mountain tops or unused grounds in concentric rings, linear strips or any other development form. Outmigration of wealthier parts of the population is prevalent in some but not in all South American cities. Where it happens, similar consequences as in North American inner cities can be observed.

In 'New Influences on Persian Cities', Frieden and Mann show how the intimate and functioning human scale now existing in urban centres there may be preserved in the face of contradicting demands for modernization. Their conclusions, mainly to ban all incompatible uses — private traffic, large-scale developments — from the core; to provide for development areas outside the inner city; and connect the new and old centres by an efficient public transportation network, are similar to those advocated for European and American cities with a functioning historic core.[11]

Whether this solution can work depends to a great extent on how it is sold to the public, and whether people want to buy it in any guise. In this respect Persia may not be greatly different from England, Germany or North America.

The report 'Living with Traffic' explains some of the old Greater London Council's proposals for new parking patterns, commuting behaviour, and transit efficiency. It followed a paper called 'Traffic and the Environment', which was a request for feed-back from the public. Traffic solutions as a matter of vital importance for London's wellbeing, would have to be financed and used by every citizen. The GLC therefore decided that public comment on it would not only help the Council to

Opposite: Foliage and water fountains in the Marienplatz, the Richard-Strauss-Brunnen, and Karlsplatz, Munich.

Above: Lake Havasu City, a new city in the desert of Arizona, built and sold by private enterprise.

Below: Shopping area in Ibadan, Nigeria.

13

determine which actions to take, but also influence other public authorities combined under its jurisdiction. Often it is after the critical downfall of attempts to involve the user, or solicit user comment, that information is made available to the lay person. However good a design or a conclusion from years of research may be, it will have little avail, if the message does not penetrate to those whom it is meant to serve. Reams of research documents are useless to those who have neither the time, the formal education nor the inclination to grapple with them.

Richard Ridley and his 'Octoberman' group tried to overcome the communication gap between the professional and the interested citizen by using comic book techniques to convey the message: as mediators between the concerned neighbourhoods and the city council they achieved the relocation of several metro stations in Washington, DC and a change in parking requirements, according to community standards.

The question of accessibility to information is closely linked with the question of choice. Before people can enjoy the diversity of the inner city and use the choices open to them they have to be aware of them. There are many ways to increase public awareness of options open to each individual. John Wiebenson suggests the use of street signs and urban spaces in a more effective communicative way. John Kinard, Director of the Anacostia Neighbourhood Museum, has dispersed and readjusted the functions of the museum to deal with the needs of minority groups and the educationally disadvantaged.

In their 'Collection of Patterns which Generate Multi-Service Centers' Christopher Alexander, Sara Ishikawa and Murray Silverstein prove that the social and design aspects of information dissemination and self-help concepts can be systematically combined. Their set of generic principles can be related to any similar task in inner city poverty areas.

Just as the very concentration of options in the inner city creates more than the sum of the parts so does the very concentration of poverty or ills become an ill in itself or an additional evil. The two 'synergisms' of glamour and decay side-by-side, without the softening effects of a transitional zone, certainly have contributed to the 'image of brutality' in connection with the inner city. This may be the reason why poverty in the suburbs or rural areas has received far less attention. The ultimate goal in our preoccupation with inner city poverty is to eliminate it. However, even at this level of analysis things are not as simple as they seem. John Seely who lived in one of the Chicago Slums said about it:

' . . . no society I have lived in before or since, seemed to me to present to so many of its members so many possibilities and actualities of fulfilment of a number at least of basic human demands: for an outlet for aggressiveness, for adventure, for a sense of effectiveness, for deep feelings of belonging without undue sacrifice of uniqueness or identity, for sexual satisfaction, for strong if not fierce loyalties, for a sense of independence from the pervasive, omnicompetent omniscient authority-in-general . . . These things had their prices of course — not all values can be simultaneously maximized. But few of the inhabitants whom I reciprocally took 'slumming' into middle class life understood it, or, where they did, were at all envious of it. And, be it asserted, this was not a matter of 'ignorance' or incapacity to 'appreciate "finer things''. It was merely an inability to see one moderately coherent and sense-making satisfaction system which they didn't know, as preferable to the quite coherent and sense-making satisfaction-system they did know . . .'[12]

Later studies like Ulf Hannerz' 'Soulside'[13] offered a similar description of a slum street which is by no means totally negative.

There may be under what we perceive as decay, dirt, and poverty, a way of life which does not exist anywhere but in the inner city. It may be that the attraction and richness of inner cities depends on the contrast of wealth and poverty, beauty and ugliness, and the overlap of the legal and the illegal. All this may in fact far more adequately represent the inherent qualities of human life and growth than the equalizing similarity of suburbia.

To create the kind of richness and potential which we inherited in our inner cities in a new community is far more difficult than to define and separate different functions clearly. Walking through the new towns of Europe or America the lack of choice and spontaneous interaction is blatantly apparent. Aditya Prakash's plea for the legalization of the *rehris* (mobile shops) in Chandigarh, springs from a similar consideration. Looked down upon, as an element of ugliness and disorder, Prakash argues that planners with public authority should rather recognize the *rehris'* vital importance in the development of the city and their potential for increasing choice and adding a sense of urbaneness in an 'artificial' new environment. Life in most new communities could be greatly enriched by allowing, if not sponsoring, the 'Happening of Selling and Buying' to take place in a less organized manner.

The social costs of eliminating traditional behavioural settings in new communities or renewal areas are hard to measure. Of vital importance to Japanese life, for instance, is the concept of *hiroba*, a flexible space-time interface between the public street and private house. A study of Japanese city-planning, and civic legislature, however, shows a lack of reference to this expression of community life. Shun Kanda points out that, in contrast to western cultures, public political and religious ceremonies do not exist in Japan. It is therefore understandable that public squares and plazas which often form the focal points of attention in our inner cities are absent. The street itself is the setting for community life. Festivals and mass gatherings usually take a processional form, which is facilitated by the flexible traditional Japanese architecture with its paper, wood or bamboo screen walls, allowing private spaces to be temporarily converted into a community space. Characteristically the term 'space' does not exist etymologically. Thus *hiroba* signifies an 'experiential place' rather than a physical entity, a public spatial expression which in Japan is possible only through individual and public participation in creating a living environment.

As a result of the mild climate in Greece, forms of outdoor living and socializing developed, which are impossible under more extreme conditions. Thakurdesai on these pages analyses this unique European concept of space and its use. In existing public places, a high number of political and social life is made possible by opening buildings, shops, and coffeehouses in a particular angle to the *plateia*. In contrast to the Japanese concept the outdoor space is the most important place for life in Greece and no indoor space is considered in the same way. But similarly the problem is whether these cultural values are sufficiently understood and whether they can be reflected in building ordinances and planning regulations, or whether it will be left to chance how the *plateia* will be maintained, rehabilitated, renewed, or restructured. There is no question that the replacement or change of inner city fabric is physically and socially disruptive. Just how much has to be done to clear the decaying parts and how much can be done to save the coherence of the total system often becomes a matter of critical balance. The contributions on Covent Garden and Piccadilly can be seen as significant not only for London's but any metropolitan core surgery.

In this last decade one new technique which will, hopefully soon, allow planners to take the 'soft' factors into account has entered into the planning

15

and design professions: this is urban simulation-gaming. Environmental simulation laboratories in America now experiment with different groups of people, in what could best be termed a mixture of on-going education and urban planning and design, to pre-test different planning alternatives and design styles, open decision-making and the interaction and communication of different ethnic and socio-economic groups.

Games have always been a means by which people have built abstract models of their relationships to the natural, supra-natural, social, and man-made environment.[14] Urban simulation-games, in this context, may be seen as representing our way to build a model of the complex and dynamic social systems of today.[15] To fully understand the multiplicity of forces impinging on the inner city or any urban decision-making process, mainly in a democratic arena, our sequential communication forms of writing, reading, and lecturing are insufficient. Richard Duke[16] therefore describes urban simulation-gaming as a new language, which more adequately than our existing languages conveys a complex or overlapping reality. The explosion of new games in the last few years bears witness to our urgent need for for this new communication form.

John Taylor and Ervin Bell share some of their experiences in this new field, which indeed may contribute more to solving inner city problems in the future, than our present design and participation methods.

If the city as a symbol reflects societies' most fundamental self-images and aspirations, the survival or elimination of the inner city will reflect the diversity of cultural values of different societies. The inner city now exists as a fragment of history in a time of unprecedented change and impatient demands to conform to these changes. Beset by conflicting claims and counterclaims it has become the arena of the most powerful and most powerless. It can be charming and exhilarating, monstrous and depressing. Whether the synergism of inner city life is a relic of the past and can be substituted by new modes of

Above: Prague, Lobkovic Palace below the castle (18th century).

Below: Holle Centre, Essen, Germany. Model of design concept (by Seidensticker and Budde) for multi-use structure in the inner city.

communication and transportation, and whether telephones, picturephones, and cable television will replace face to face contact is unclear. The fact that the enormous increase in telecommunication parallel-ed an enormous increase in travel via car, rail, and air in recent years may indicate that the traditional forms of human interaction have been stimulated rather than substituted by technological advances in communication and that these amazing new possi-bilities may indeed reinforce the traditional richness and coherence of our inner cities.

Towers, unfunctional but symbolic expressions of power and centrality in the city as symbol.

Above: Pittsburgh, Pennsylvania, one of the few re-built inner cities in America.

Below: Prague, the capital of Czechoslovakia, one of the most beautiful inner cities in the world.

Are we indeed building our new centres according to medieval models?

Notes

1   Melvin M Webber, 'The Post-City Age' in *The Conscience of the City*, pp. 1-20, ed: Martin Meyerson, New York, 1970.

2   Robert A Dahl, 'The City in the Future of ' Democracy', in *The American Political Science Review,* pp. 953-970, December 1967.

3   *ibid.,* also see
Robert T Norman, 'Government for an Urbanizing World: an Example from India', pp. 435-440, in *Ekistics 205*, Vol. 35, Dec. 1972.

4   Ernest W Burgess, 'The Growth of the City', in *The City,* eds: R E Park and E W Burgess, Chicago, 1925.

5   Homer Hoyt, 'The Structure and Growth of Residential Neighborhoods in American Cities', p. 116, Washington, D.C., Federal Housing Administration, 1937.

6   William Alonso, 'The Historic and the Structural Theories of Urban Form: Their Implications for Urban Renewal', pp. 227-231, in *Land Economics,* Vol. XL, No. 2.

7   *ibid.*

8   *München: Fussgaengerbereiche in der Altstadt,* Baureferat der Landeshauptstadt München, 1972.

9   Peter M Bode, 'Erstickt München an seiner Dynamik? pp. 122-124, in *Zenterale Fussgaengerbereiche,* compiled by Karl Assman, Dokumentation, Münchener Bauforum 3, Munich, June 1969.

10 John C Turner, 'A New View of the Housing Deficit', pp. 115-125, in *The Growth of Cities,* ed: David Lewis, London, 1971.

11 Margrit and Declan Kennedy, 'The Regeneration of Regensburg', pp. 150-172, in *The Growth of Cities,* ed: David Lewis, London, 1971.
Hans Blumenfeld, 'Criteria for Urban Form', pp. 434-436, in *Internal Structure of the City,* ed: Larry S Bourne, New York, 1971.

12 John R Seely, 'The Slum: Its Nature, Use, and Users', p. 10, in *Journal of the American Institute of Planners,* Vol. 25, No. 1, February 1959.

13 Ulf Hannerz, *Soulside: Inquiries Into Ghetto Culture and Community,* New York, 1969.

14 Omar Khayyam Moore and Alan Ross Anderson, 'Some Principles for the Design of Clarifying Educational Environments', pp. 571-613 in *Handbook of Socialization Theory and Research,* ed: David Goslin, Chicago, 1969.

15 Margrit Kennedy, 'Education and Urban Planning as Congruent Events', pp. 74-80 in *Proceedings of the National Gaming Council's Eleventh Annual Symposium,* compiled by Steven J Kidder and Alyce W Nafziger, Report No. 143, The Johns Hopkins University, Baltimore, Maryland, 1972.

16 Richard D Duke, 'The Language of Gaming', pp. 52-59 in *Proceedings of the National Gaming Council's Eleventh Annual Symposium,* op. cit.

17

THE INNER CITY IN THE POST-INDUSTRIAL ERA:

A STUDY OF ITS CHANGING SOCIAL FABRIC AND ECONOMIC FUNCTION

ERNEST ERBER

Central cities of industrialized nations are undergoing far-reaching changes that call into question the continuation of their historic social forms and economic functions. Though this transformation is most pronounced in American cities, where it is further complicated by factors of race, there is considerable evidence that the trend is world wide. This study examines the new urban forms and functions by focusing upon American cities as the most advanced examples. The reader, utilizing his knowledge of urban development within his own geographical purview, should be able to identify those aspects of the American pattern that serve as international prototypes, as distinct from those that are uniquely American. The author is prompted to avoid definitive judgments on the implications of his thesis for the rest of the world by an awareness that his first-hand familiarity with urban conditions is limited to the American scene.

The population of the central cities of the USA, as recorded in the 1970 Census, was exceeded for the first time by that of the so-called suburban rings; 62.2 million inhabitants in the central cities compared to 74.9 million in the 'suburban rings'. These two groupings together totalling 137.1 million, compose the population of the nation's metropolitan areas. The later term is used here, and throughout this paper, as synonymous with Standard Metropolitan Statistical Areas (SMSAs) as officially designated by the Bureau of the Census. In addition to the metropolitan population, the 1970 Census recorded 63.2 million persons living outside of SMSAs, mainly in cities under 50,000, towns, villages and rural areas.

The changes affecting central cities are both quantitative and qualitative; the impact of each being reciprocal. Quantitative change is the more conspicuous, because, in part, it is the more measurable, both by eye and by statistics. Qualitative change (in the sense of essential nature and characteristics) eludes definitive description; necessarily, in this case, an analytic process. The latter, unavoidably based on interpretative judgment, is always subject to challenge by a series of alternative explanations. As long as the latter proceed from the same quantified data, debate might illuminate but rarely convince. Validation must await observation of unfolding events. In this sense, this study's thesis, largely predictive by projection, will be confirmed or refuted by the accumulation of data that traces currently faint trend lines so boldly as to be beyond debates.

Quantitative change, mainly in the proportions of population and employment located in central city as compared to its suburbs, is more frequently noted and subjected to comment than are those qualitative changes that involve distribution of urban functions. The latter are characterized, mainly, by the high proportion of traditional functions of the central city that have been duplicated in its outlying growth areas, obliterating classic distinctions in the roles of the city and its suburbs. As a consequence, the very terms 'central city' and 'suburb' no longer suffice to describe the new reality, either as to form or function. The central city has, in effect, become the *inner city* and the urbanized areas beyond its boundaries have become a new, *outer city*. The changed role of the inner city, and the new spatial pattern and socio-economic function of the outer city, constitute two variants of the same phenomenon: the metropolitan areas as a new form of human settlement.

In keeping with the thesis of this paper that the social and economic transformation of metropolitan areas has not only created new forms and content, but has altered the *nature* of the relationship between inner city and the urbanization that develops beyond its boundaries, the terms 'central city' and 'suburb' will be used only within the historical context of the period, mainly before 1950, when the current relationship had not yet emerged. The search for the proper nomenclature for the urban phenomenon of settlement beyond the city's borders has occupied scholars, mainly sociologists and urban geographers, for a long time, beginning with the efforts of Graham Taylor in 1915 and Harlan Douglas in 1925 to define 'industrial suburb', 'residential suburb' and 'satellite town'. Rapid urbanization outside of central cities after 1950 rekindled scholarly preoccupation with this matter, mainly in the work of Amos Hawley, Leo F Schnorre, Sylvia F Fava, William M Dobriner and Herbert J Gans.

The term 'inner city' acquired a generally accepted meaning in the literature that denoted those portions identified with function and pathologies characteristic of the modern industrial city. These characteristics predominated in the central portion of cities, but in theory could, and in practice often did, encompass the entire city as a political jurisdiction. Given this meaning, 'inner city' was useful in distinguishing various parts of the city by function and population types. Those parts of the jurisdicational city in which central city characteristics did not predominate, shared many features, often most, with suburbs rather than with the inner city. In turn, some portions of the suburbs had more 'inner city' characteristics than typically suburban ones.

1. Overview: The metropolitan area as a new form of human settlement

As is true of society's structural and functional changes generally, the transformation of the central city and its suburbs into a new metropolitan form was triggered, and continues to be propelled, by technological changes. Though the latter includes an extensive list of inventions, the internal combustion engine is the single, most important catalytic agent in the transformation from the city/suburb arrangement to modern metropolitan forms and functions. Widespread affluence, itself a product of technological advances that increased productivity at a faster rate than population growth, facilitated mass ownership of personal transportation in the form of the automobile. The latter, together with the motorbus, created new home/job linkages that freed the labour force from fixed, right-of-way carriers designed to serve travel within the classic central city and to and from its residential suburbs. The motor truck, in turn, freed manufacturing, construction, servicing and distribution from locational dependence upon similar fixed routes for movement of goods.[1]

National affluence also permits an increasing number of people to afford a middle-class life style that includes a high degree of mobility in exercising options as to residence. Consumers' choices as to life style are reflected, in turn, as majority opinions in the decision-making process of government; influencing such critical areas as the allocation of resources for highway construction, the granting of local 'home rule' in regulating land use and construction, and the provision of federal income-tax deductions to ease the cost of home ownership.

Hoboken, New Jersey. High density at the core of the New York Region, where dwellings are tightly packed around the harbour, in New York City, Newark, and Hudson County, N. J.

Technological change and the life-style choices of growing affluence combined to create the spatial pattern of the outer city. The latter is characterized by low-density spread of population and the highway-oriented, discontinuous 'scatteration', mainly in low-rise structures, of a wide range of productive, service and administrative functions previously confined to central cities.

The economic base of the outer city is increasingly independent as a consequence of its inclusion of substantial primary employment, i.e., production of goods and services for the national and world markets. This trend serves to undermine the historic symbiosis between central city and classic suburb, in which the city served primarily as a job market and the suburbs primarily as a housing market. By 1968, only 50% of the jobs in the New York Metropolitan Region were located in New York City, along with 43% of the Region's labour force.[2] Conversely, the outer city contains 50% of the jobs and 57% of the labour force, the difference reflecting roughly, the margin of outer-city residents who commute to inner city jobs over the number of inner-city residents who work in the outer city, the so-called reverse commuters.

The classic, residential suburb, as distinguished from satellite industrial town,[3] contained only such non-residential uses as satisfied local needs for convenience goods and services. The central city supplied the rest. The contemporary outer city in comparison, provides, in greater or lesser degree, aspects of almost every urban activity associated with the central city. Manufacturing remains the major base for primary employment, though the former grows as a much

Far left, top: Subsidized housing on Manhattan's West Side. In foreground, Frederick Douglass public housing project; in rear, Park West Village, middle-income subsidized housing.

Far left, below: Playground, Frederick Douglass public housing.

Above left: Lower Manhattan. High density at the core of the New York Region where jobs are heavily concentrated.

Left: Steelwork for new buildings rises behind the demolition of old tenements on Lower East Side. Something usually must be torn down before anything new can be built in the Region's old cities.

smaller rate than does non-manufacturing employment. In 1971 it represented about 1 out of 4 jobs in the New York-Northeastern New Jersey area. However, less than half of the manufacturing jobs were in New York City. Its total of 735,000 manufacturing jobs represented a decline by about 100,000 such jobs since 1960. Though office employment, especially corporate headquarters, continue to favour the inner city, office floor space also continues to multiply in the outer city. Regional Plan Association's projection of about 1.4 million more office jobs in the New York Region by the year 2000, assumes that they will be equally divided between the inner and outer cities.[4]

Secondary employment, i.e., production of goods and services for the local population, has been estimated by economists on a rule-of-thumb basis to be a ratio of two jobs in secondary employment to one in primary employment. There is evidence that rising living standards, reflected in the growth of consumer spending for services, has increased the ratio in favour of secondary employment, especially in the more affluent outer city. The latter presents an attractive market for every type of enterprise that caters to American middle-class consumption, with the result that outer city residents find a decreasing need to visit the inner city, except for the small percentage who find local art exhibits and concerts an inadequate substitute for the inner city's cultural attractions.

The population characteristics tend to show different proportions for inner and outer cities in the categories of race, income, occupation, schooling, value of dwelling unit occupied, percentage of home ownership and tenancy, welfare dependency, car ownership, household size and composition, etc. Urban society's social stratification and racial segration is expressed in this inner/outer dichotomy on a geographical scale never approximated by past segregation within the central city.

It is the contrasting racial composition of inner city and outer city which underscores most heavily the potential for conflict and civil disorder. The trend toward increasingly black inner cities and white outer cities continues unabated. While the percentage of whites in the populations of the outer cities of the US metropolitan areas remained substantially unchanged between 1960 (95.5%) and 1970 (95.8%), the inner cities became increasingly black during the same decade, going from 18% in 1960 to 24% in 1970. Additionally, other ethnic minorities, Mexican-Americans, Puerto Ricans, Orientals and American Indians, increased their numbers in the major cities.[5]

The significance of this new dimension in racial separation in the United States lies in the related concentration by social class, occupations and income levels. In addition to being a rejected subcultural grouping in American society, the racial and ethnic minorities are composed overwhelmingly of the victims of the industrial system and urban conditions; the unemployed, the low-paid, the lesser skilled, the minimally schooled, the chronically ill, and generally, those most in need of public assistance. Those better-paid manual occupations for which the predominant skill levels of the minority labour force are suited (mainly in manufacturing) tend to be precisely the ones to be declining in the inner city and increasing in the outer city, if at all.

Next to contrasting population 'mixes', the most-striking difference between the inner city and the outer city is in physical form. The outer city is designed to accommodate the automobile, in comparison to the inner city's historic dependence upon public transportation, a pedestrian radius, and the elevator. The outer city has evolved an urban form that uses the highway as a basic point of reference in site selection for retail centres, industrial clusters, office buildings, hotels (re-named motels), motion picture theatres, churches, hospitals, colleges, restaurants, etc. Structures are low rise and occupy a small percentage of their land area, much of which is devoted to automobile parking. Pedestrian access is not expected and design does not facilitate it. If there is validity to the contention of environmental psychologists that structural mass, form, and height and the openness of space affect our behaviour patterns, certainly the sharp contrast between the respective man-made environments of the inner and the outer city must further accentuate difference in human responses that are already fostered by the respective status consciousnesses of the inner and outer city's inhabitants.

As more of the functions once performed only in central cities are now duplicated in the outer city, if not pre-empted by it, the two parts of the metropolitan areas are cast increasingly in adversary roles. These involve competition for desirable private sector facilities and confrontation and conflict over state and Federal resource allocations. This dichotomy is sharpened by the growing contrast in population composition of inner city and outer, expressing differing needs and making competing claims upon the public purse; a situation fraught with the threat of civil disorders that could further reduce the interdependent inner/outer linkages and even rupture those that are minimally essential to health and safety, unless state or Federal intervention protects them.

The extent of this dichotomous development is more pronounced in the large metropolitan regions, with New York probably the most advanced case. Size is related to rate of change largely as a consequence of the factor of distance (more accurately: travel time) as a prime cause of decentralization of functions. Where the scale of the metropolitan region causes employment to be divided into a number of geographically circumscribed labour markets, served by coordinate housing markets, it facilitates the trend toward an outer city that is increasingly self-sufficient, and an inner city with a narrowing economic and social role. The link between the region's size and the extent of metropolitan transformation is not, however, absolute. Susceptibility to change is affected also by the functional 'mix' of the area's economic base, i.e., manufacturing, distributive, administrative, resort, etc., with some types being more vulnerable to the inner/outer dichotomy than others. Change is also influenced by the region's natural features; the manner in which topography and the contours of land and water either encourage low-density spread or inhibit it.

The age of a city also influences its degree of susceptibility. Cities that were to experience most of their growth after 1920, adapted to the automobile far more successfully than cities that had peaked by then; viz. Los Angeles compared to Boston. As a consequence of this variety of influences, some metropolitan areas in the population range of 500,000 undergo change in the direction of the new urban forms more rapidly than others in the range of 1,000,000. Of a national population of 203,211,926 in 1970, residents of metropolitan areas, as defined by the Bureau of the Census, comprised 140 million, an increase of 17% from 1960. This increase was almost entirely in the outer cities, since the total for inner cities showed a very slight gain. However, were the impact of these socioeconomic changes to have serious political consequences only in the nation's metropolitan areas with populations of one million or more, the results would be profound for the nation as a whole, because such areas serve as vital administrative, communications, and transportation hubs. Additionally, they contain over 80 million persons, 40% of the nation's population.

Change is not a new phenomenon in the history of the city, as any student of Max Weber[6] or Lewis Mumford[7]

can profess. Until the emergence of the metropolitan region,[8] with its dichotomous inner city and outer city, however, urban form, throughout its many-centuried functional evolution remained essentially the symbiotic relationship between city and suburb, a pattern traced back to ancient times.[9] This form was carried to its apex in the modern city as shaped by the industrial revolution. The altered role of the contemporary inner city, however, is a product of the post-industrial era,[10] characterized by the declining proportion of the labour force engaged in manufacture, or in manual occupations generally. Metropolitan centres in Western Europe, Japan and Australia also reveal many characteristics of the new dichotomous urban form first identified in American metropolitan growth. Other characteristics, however, remain uniquely American. Which of these are truly indigenous to American cultural patterns and political institutions, and which reflect American prototypes of conditions likely to be replicated abroad, requires further investigation.

2. An alternate concept of the inner city

Before examining the changing functions of the inner city, it is necessary to consider an alternative concept of its place within the metropolitan phenomenon; a view that represents conventional wisdom on the matter.[11] This is the theory that the entire metropolitan area is merely the traditional city enlarged; that the changes are merely quantitative, not qualitative. It sees the metropolitan areas as merely the central city overflowing its political boundaries and growing organically beyond them. It contends that political boundaries are essentially irrelevant in dealing with phenomena that is basically social and economic in character. In viewing the metropolitan area as the 'real city', to use George Romney's[12] term, the old central city, or most of it, is seen as fulfilling the function previously identified with the traditional inner city area, i.e., the central business district, adjacent wholesale and storage areas, and the highest density residential areas.[13] What were once the city's outlying residential neighbourhoods are, in this view, beyond its limits in the form of suburbs. This school of thought sees the relationship between the inner city and its outlying parts as still essentially symbiotic. It seeks to build upon this interdependence to overcome governmental fragmentation through 'trade offs'.

This theory fails to explain the changed urban forms wrought by the impact of technology upon the distribution of population and functions. It were as if

electricity, the automobile, electronic communications, the airplane, assembly-line production, and the shift from predominance of blue-collar to white-collar employment have had no effect upon urban social and economic structure and function. The acceptance of the metropolitan area as 'a new form of human settlement' has meaning only if it is viewed as a successor, not only to the earlier urban/rural relationship that explains the rise of the city based on its agricultural hinterland, but also to the city/suburban relationship based on the employing role of the city and the residential role of the suburb. The central city as a political entity has no relevance viewed from one aspect of the problem, but is overwhelmingly important from another. Whether the old central city continues to be demarcated by political boundaries or not, it remains a distinctive urban form, affected by the metropolitan transformation of which it is a part. The central business district, the density of structures, the type of housing, the street pattern and widths, the underground utility network, and the nature and distribution of community facilities are all interwoven functionally with specific groups of people, both daytime and night-time populations. This complex physical, social and economic interrelationship is not dependent upon the maintenance of the city's political boundaries. Its replacement by metropolitan government might have some long-range effects, to the extent that it affects the balance of power among socioeconomic groups that compose the metropolitan area. The old central city, however, would survive essentially as the inner city, distinctly different in all those respects described previously as contrasting with the outer city. Its role within a unified metropolitan government would evolve differently only in certain respects from that of the central city as a separate political entity; again, depending on the distribution of political power within the metropolitan government.

This is illuminated by the changing history of annexation. There was a time when suburbs sought to be annexed by their central city because it brought an extension of city services; central cities, meanwhile, viewing it fiscally sound to gain additional ratables through such annexation. Today, annexation revolves around the issue of white political dominance. Annexation of the suburbs is viewed as a means of shoring up control of the central city by whites in the face of the threat posed by an increasing black population. Suburbs likewise view annexation in terms of the white/black power struggle and often oppose it to avoid involvement.

'The distribution of political power' . . . that is the heart of the matter. Its importance can only be understood when the city (or the metropolitan area, for that matter) is viewed as a functioning unit of society. Society is people, and the man-made environment of streets and structures have importance only as they serve people; rich or poor, white or black, landlords or tenants, taxpayers or welfare recipients, blue-collar workers or white-collar workers, in-commuters or out-commuters, motorists or transit riders. Viewed from this perspective, the political boundaries that separate the inner city from the outer city can be overwhelmingly important in that they significantly affect the distribution of political power between groups with conflicting interests.

It is not accidental that despite prodigious efforts on its behalf over twenty-five years, metropolitan government shows little evidence of becoming a widespread reality. Outer city inhabitants have seen no advantage to merging with the inner city and were alert to many distinct disadvantages. As racial minorities gain in numbers and political power in the inner city, they also see more disadvantages than advantages in metropolitan government. Continuance of the political boundary between the inner and outer cities assumes, if anything, increasing importance to key groups on either side of it as the distinctive social characteristics of the inner and outer cities become more apparent. The cry of 'home rule' on the lips of the outer city homeowner is echoed by the inner city inhabitants' call for 'community control' now copied by other inner city ethnic groups.

Insofar as the course of development can be influenced by public policy at the municipal level, and insofar as the quality of liveability can be affected by development policy and the allocation of local revenues, political power and, consequently, jurisdictional boundaries are critically important to various classes of citizens. It determines what can be built where; who pays how much in taxes; whom the police protect and whom they harrass; where school district boundaries are drawn and the quality of education they provide; whether civil rights laws affecting equal access to housing and other urban opportunities are enforced or overlooked; whether subsidized housing is built or not, whether expenditures for ecological or aesthetic concerns have priority over those for health or welfare facilities.

In the light of both (a) the uniquely different urban forms and functions of inner and outer cities and (b) the political boundaries as jurisdictionally crucial in policy and resource allocation decisions, it is patently invalid to hold that the metropolitan area is simply an organic expansion of the old central city, and that the latter plays the same role today within the metropolitan area, i.e. the 'real city', that the inner core played within the central city of an earlier period. What makes an examination of the inner city's role so critically important is, precisely, that it is changing from that played by the 'inner city' in a previous period and that this change is not only a matter of scale, but of function and social fabric.

3. The changing function of the inner city

What will become of the previously-designated *central* city, now the inner city of the conglomerate metropolitan area? Will it continue to have a function? If so, what will it be? Or has changing technology and the life styles of increasing affluence rendered the inner city obsolete — socially, economically and physically? Will it continue to decline in population and activities while new growth rings extend the outer city, very much as a tree trunk rots out at the core while adding growth brands at the outer edge? Is the Geddes-Mumford[14] prediction of necropolis as the last stage of the modern city's life cycle reserved for the inner city? Or can 'urban renewal' change the physical structure of the inner city to accommodate functions now being lost to the outer city? How is this adaptation to be accomplished? Is the redesign of the inner city to accommodate the automobile by adaptation of outer city form? Can the inner city have a future only at the price of transformation to the low densities and openness of the outer city?

The search for answers to these questions might well begin with an examination of the function of the central city in the past. Though these have changed from time to time throughout history, they found their rationale in the factor of centrality.[15] Each city served its hinterland and benefitted from central location within it, usually measured in time/distance translated into transportation costs.[16] The function of the ancient city as *palace* (administration), *market place* (exchange of goods and services), *citadel* (security, law, order) and *temple* (worship, art, music, learning) were available to the greatest number of hinterland inhabitants by virtue of the city's centrality. The craftsmen and mercantile capitalists of the Middle Ages exploited the lengthening trade routes to the degree that their city enjoyed the advantages of centrality. It was in the modern industrial city, however, that the value of centrality was developed to its highest point.

The industrial city was a child of the industrial revolution; a term which describes, essentially, the social and economic consequences of the invention of the steam engine. The latter not only powered the factories, but drove the railroad trains and steamships that brought the raw materials to be consumed for energy (mainly coal) and those to be processed, and that distributed the finished products to the markets of the nations and the world. Centrality now related primarily to sources of raw materials and markets for finished goods. The central 'point of contact' in this in-flow and out-flow process was where rail, water and labour supply came together most efficiently. It was usually a waterfront site (since water was needed for boilers, cooling, and industrial waste disposal) served by rail. Around it were crowded the densely-built housing for factory workers, concentrated within relatively confined areas as dictated by the need to be within walking distance of their place of work. To the historic functions of palace, market place, citadel, temple, workshop, and counting-house, the modern industrial city thus added the factory, railroad centre and that unique type of drab, densely-crowded housing for industrial workers that became its hallmark.[17]

Within the industrial city, the inexorable logic of centrality produced the modern central business district, and within it as benchmark, the high value intersection. The latter became the point of reference in rationing degree of centrality of location through the price mechanism of ground rent. The premium placed upon centrality, and the price placed on advantageous parcels, resulted in efforts to maximimize returns by intensity of use, resulting in extremely high percentage of coverage of lot by structure, and construction to as great a height as the technology of building and of vertical transportation would permit until the dangers to public health, order and welfare eventually resulted in public regulation of density and height through zoning and building codes.

The intolerable pressure of city residents in need of living space was relieved by the invention of electrically-driven intra-city transit, originally in the form of the tram or trolley car. Electric power modified the centralizing influence of the steam engine, initially by permitting factory workers and central business district employees to live at greater distances from their jobs as the trolley lines opened up new areas for residential development, since identified by an urban historian as the 'streetcar suburbs'.[18]

In a number of cities, specifically those favoured by

locations that continued to permit expansion of economic opportunities and foster concomitant population growth, the residential areas tapped by trolley also became overcrowded and faster methods of transit were introduced, in the form of electrically-driven trains on their own rights-of-way, above or below the congestion of street traffic. These elevated and subway lines brought additional areas into residential use within approximately the same travel time to central locations as experienced by trolley riders from more close-in neighbourhoods.

Commuter railroad service brought even more distant areas within relatively the same travel time range of the city's centre by tapping areas beyond the city limits and creating the residential suburbs. However, rail-fares, in contrast to intra-city transit, were based on distance travelled and, at a minimum, far exceeded the amount customary for the average wage earner to pay in going to and from work. Rail fares had the effect of filtering out all but the higher income brackets. As the latter concentrated in the suburbs, they created a pattern of housing relatively more expensive than found in most city neighbourhoods, resulting in 'peer group' communities, identification with which conferred status upon their inhabitants. In time, suburbanites took steps to assure a continuation of the peer-group environment, including protection of their property values, by using local land use and building controls to exclude residential construction deemed likely to attract those with incomes below the levels considered acceptable locally.

There are several observations to be made on the growth process by which the modern central city diffused its population through a succession of ever more rapid transit:

1. Though the population was diffused, the centre of the city remained the point of reference in measuring desirability of location in accord with the principle of centrality. As a consequence, a density gradient extended from the central business district to the most distant suburbs.

2. Though improved transportation spread the population over an increasingly wide area, it remained centre-oriented. As a matter of fact, improved transportation increased the labour market for centre city employers and the customer potential for it purveyors of goods and services. (This was the high tide of 'downtown' department stores, theatres, etc.)

3. The city's functions remained, relatively speaking, centrally located. The exceptions were manufacturing and bulk goods handling. The latter sought the neces-

sary amount of space for an expanding scale of operations in the areas where land was less expensive but yet was served both by rail lines, to handle freight shipments, and transit lines, to provide access for the needed supply of labour.[19] Manufacturing that required a relatively small amount of floor space per employee or unit of production, and was not dependent upon rail sidings, remained closer to the central business district to take maximum advantage of centrality for labour supply and external economies. The substitution of electricity for steam as energy gave an increasing number of manufacturing categories independence from rail as a source for coal; with the development of trucks (the earlier models of which driven by electric storage batteries) the freedom from rail ties increased. However, the need to be accessible to labour supply kept them near the city's transit hub.

4. The central business district, manufacturing 'ribbons' along rail lines, the old 'close-in' high-density neighbourhoods, the trolley car residential districts and the commuter suburbs were in symbiotic harmony, governed by the travel time rhythms of pedestrian radius, trolley trip, rapid transit and commuter railway. They were the products of the city's organic growth process, which unfolded in keeping with functional interrelationships.

The city's historic accretion of function is now seen as a film being run in reverse as the inner city divests itself of some functions and carries on others at a reduced scale. Manufacturing, the last function to be acquired, is the first to depart. Prior to the industrial revolution, there were few large cities, usually no more than one in each nation of Western Europe. These served as the centre of government, seat of learning, major market place, etc. Will the inner city revert to these functions in the post-industrial age? How many such cities are needed? If New York plays such a role, is there a need for Boston and Philadelphia? If Chicago plays such a role, is there a need for St Louis, Detroit and Cleveland? What is the future of a predominantly industrial city in the post-industrial era?

The major in-depth study of the changing function of the central city in the post-war period was the New York Metropolitan Region Study directed by Raymond Vernon of Harvard's Graduate School of Public Administration for Regional Plan Association, Inc., completed in 1960.[20] The study charted the transformation of the New York Region from its earlier city/suburb symbiosis to the new metropolitan form. 'The fact that employment trends and population trends do not diverge markedly in most sections of the Region sug-

gests a number of things,' concluded Vernon. 'It casts doubt on any image of the Region as a giant cluster of human activity held together by a great nub of jobs at the centre . . . it affords a picture of a Region in which the centripetal pull is weakening. This, in turn, means a further modification of the over-simplified picture of the Region as a ring of bedroom communities in the suburbs emptying out their inhabitants every morning to the central city. Incomplete and misleading as that picture is today it promises to be even more misleading in the decades ahead.[21]

The Vernon study documented the strong outward movement of manufacturing and wholesaling from inner city to outer city, with a levelling of retailing in the inner city, while growing in pace with an exploding population in the outer city. Offsetting these losses in the inner city, according to Vernon, would be continued growth of office employment in the central business district, though its share of office functions would be proportionately less as office buildings were constructed in the outer city. Vernon's findings underscored the transition of New York City to a primarily administrative centre. Developments since 1960 have borne out Vernon's analysis. The trends he identified hold true, generally, for all major American cities. Of all jobs added between 1959 and 1967 in five large metropolitan areas, 70% were outside of the central city. In a study of ten metropolitan areas, the outer cities were found to gain heavily in manufacturing (79%), retail trade (78%) and wholesale trade (68%), while the inner city gained in service, finance, insurance, real estate and government employment. '. . . State and local government agencies . . . represent the most rapidly growing major field of employment in the country and one heavily concentrated in cities.'[22]

Between 1959 and 1967, New York City lost 70,000 blue-collar jobs in manufacturing, while the rest of the metropolitan region gained 140,000. By 1968, 57% of the region's blue-collar jobs were located outside New York City. At 733,000, the 1971 factory job total in New York City reflected a net loss of 96,000 over the past two years. Some 216,000 jobs were lost since 1960 compared to a loss of 92,000 between 1950 and 1960.[23]

This accelerating pace of declining employment in manufacturing raises the question as to whether it is likely to remain operative until New York City has lost *all* manufacturing employment, or whether there is reason to believe that factory jobs will stabilize at a reduced figure. The Vernon study examined factors that cause some manufacturers

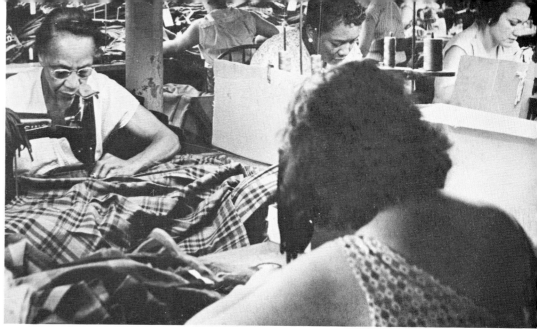

Above: Sewer repair man in Manhattan. The large numbers of rural blacks and Puerto Ricans who have migrated into older cities of the Region since the beginning of World War II possess few urban skills and usually find themselves in the lowest-paying jobs.

Above right: Workers at Frilly Pleating Company in Manhattan's garment district, many of them rural blacks and Puerto Ricans.

Right: Line of people waiting for interviews at Harlem Welfare (now Social Service) Center.

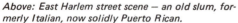

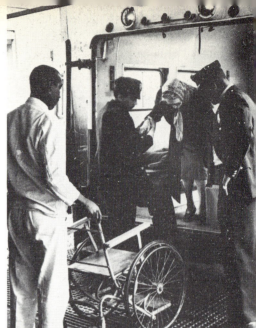

Above: East Harlem street scene — an old slum, formerly Italian, now solidly Puerto Rican.

Above right: Old lady being helped out of ambulance at Harlem Hospital. Increasingly, the inner city's population is made up of older people and members of minority groups.

Right: Spanish church sign on old synagogue in Tremont area of the Bronx. Since the mid-1950s blacks and Puerto Ricans have spread out from established slums into many middle-class white areas throughout the city. (1920 is street number, not date).

Opposite: Puerto Rican girls in the bedroom of an East Harlem tenement.

Far right, top: Typical apartment house, Tremont area of the Bronx, one of the continually changing neighbourhoods in the city.

Far right, below: Abandoned apartment house, typical of many to be found in changing neighbourhoods of New York City. This one in the Brownsville section of Brooklyn.

to leave the inner city and others to remain, including space needs, external economies, land cost, congestion, wages, freight and taxes. The factors of space needs, Vernon found, caused larger establishments to leave the inner city while dependence upon external economies caused smaller ones to remain. The study charted the loss of manufacturing employment caused by competition from lower-wage areas of the nation, especially the South, reflecting the high cost of living in the New York Region and the resulting relatively high-wage levels. Such losses to other parts of the United States were more than offset, however, by the increase in manufacturing employment in the New York area's outer city, where wages tended to equal those of the inner city when averaged for all types of industries or occupations. (The *average*, however, conceals extreme differences in wage rates in certain industries or occupations.)

The study's emphasis on the Region's high wages relative to some other parts of the United States obscured the point, critically important to an examination of whether all manufacturing will leave, that the inner city has held a sizable pool of low-paying jobs by virtue of its sizable low-wage resident labour supply. In October 1969, some 451,000 full-time (30 hours per week or more) jobs in New York City paid less than $90. per week.[24] In manufacturing such low wage jobs were found mainly in the clothing, toy, jewellery, novelty, leather, electrical equipment and textile-mill products industries. (In non-manufacturing, they were concentrated in retail trade, restaurants and personal services). Since the outer city has no comparable pool of poverty-level labour, those industries dependent upon it remain tied to the inner city. In the division of manufacturing establishments between inner and outer cities, it would appear, labour-intensive, low-wage industries will be located in the inner city.

Vernon's study relied heavily on the factor of centrality in projecting the growth of office space in the inner city, predominantly in its central business district. He based this assumption on the advantages of centrality in (a) assembling large office work forces, (b) in face-to-face contact in conducting executive-level business negotiations and (c) in the external economies provided by highly-specialized business services (management consultants, attorneys, advertising agencies, brokers, printers, office machine maintenance, etc.)

The firmness of Vernon's projections on office employment in the inner city remains debatable (and is debated intermittently, especially when a major cor-

porate headquarters moves to the outer city or the construction of a new inner city office building is announced). Vernon himself attached several caveats to his office-growth projection. One was the future effect of the increasing length and cost of the commuting journey from the outer city residence of office employees to the central business district, affecting especially the supply of 'literate women' to fill secretarial and clerical positions. (When Vernon wrote this, black and Puerto Rican young women had hardly begun to be visible in central offices.) His other caveat was on the possible impact of electronic data processing and communications on face-to-face contact in corporate decision-making.[25] This induced him to speculate on the possibility that large administrative offices would emulate manufacturing firms which had split off production and storage operations for removal to the outer city in an earlier period, while keeping decision-making, sales, and other face-to-face contact functions in the centre. 'This amoeba-like behaviour' had not shown itself as a strong trend by the late 1950s, but Vernon did note that 'central offices also have shown some expansion of employment in the suburban counties.[26]

By 1965 Regional Plan Association was recording growth rates of office space outside of New York City of 27% in the inner ring counties, 26% in the intermediate ring and 14% in the outer ring. This compared with a 5% growth rate in the central business district. Since the latter represented 54% of the region's office floor space, it represented overwhelmingly the single largest addition of office floor space of the foregoing locations.[27] RPA tended to dismiss the importance 'of a few office buildings on isolated, campus-type sites in the suburbs' that had been 'widely publicized'. Six years later, however, RPA was hedging its projected growth of Manhattan office employment with a warning that 'corporations will continue to take the easier route of finding their own vacant site 'if planned clustering was not facilitated and Morris D Drawford, Jr, its Board Chairman, was noting RPA's concern with the inner cities' 'burden of poverty and crime', slow renewal processes and lack of image.[28]

The predominant position of office employment in the national economy is beyond dispute as the United States becomes more definitively a post-industrial society. 'The United States economy passed from the predominance of agriculture (1860) through the predominance of manufacturing (1860 to 1940) to the currently emerging dominance of the service sector in accounting for the greatest amount of

employment and contribution to gross product. The coming decade promises to reflect the observable trends of the past. The industries which display the greatest potential for growth are all service industries (finance, insurance and real estate; services and civilian government), while three of the four which are projected to decline (agriculture, transportation and warehousing, textile-mill products and mining) are extractive or manufacturing industries.[29] Knowing this only heightens the anxiety over the unanswered question of whether the principle of centrality has been vitiated for office location; it does not answer it. The answer lies imbedded largely in as yet missing empirical evidence that (a) face-to-face contact can (or cannot) be substituted for by closed circuit television, (b) that large staffs of 'literate women'[30] can (or cannot) be assembled as easily in the outer city and (c) that those who supply the external economies will (or will not) be available when and where needed in outer city.

Beyond these questions are others: if it feasible to divide a major corporate office into a decision-making and external contact component and a 'back office' production component? If so, which types of industries have a greater susceptibility to such a bifurcated set-up?

There is impressive evidence that many top flight corporations have decided to experiment with an outer city location for their headquarters far more than was indicated to be likely in RPA's 1965 reference to the phenomenon. At that time General Foods, Union Carbide, International Business Machines, American Cyanimid, and a few other corporate giants were the conspicuous pioneers in outer city headquarters operations. Since then a growing number of other 'big name' corporations have joined them: Ingersoll-Rand, Allied Chemical, Pepsi Co., Reinhold Publishing, Stauffer Chemical, Inter-Continental Hotels, American Can, Olin, Uniroyal, Borden, Corn Products, Avon Products and Western Electric. RCA announced a move and then postponed action. Many less well known firms, some in *Fortune's* magic '500 largest' list, have also made the trek from inner city to outer city.

The phenomenon is US-wide, maybe even worldwide. Second rank cities, i.e. major industrial centres whose *administrative* role is limited to relatively confined regional hinterlands, such as Detroit, Cleveland and St Louis, prove especially susceptible to movements of manufacturing corporation headquarters beyond the municipal limits of such cities. When an executive says that his company is taking space in

St Louis, he is likely to mean Clayton, Mo., located in its outer city. Clayton has 40,000 office employees and only 16,000 residents. Southfield, Michigan occupies the same role in relationship to Detroit. Even in modern, bustling Atlanta, headquarters to the Old South, 'office parks' in the outer city attract a formidable roster of regional offices of national corporations.

The accumulation of empirical evidence of corporate office movement to the outer cities of American metropolitan areas documents a trend that can no longer be dismissed as episodic. On the other hand, the evidence does not suffice to conclude that centrality is no longer a factor in the most efficient location of all types of administrative functions. However, it is now possible to extract some broad, preliminary conclusions from the evidence at hand and to advance some hypotheses and conjectures about some of the more specific aspects of the phenomenon.

1. A sufficient number of major corporations now operate successfully from headquarters in outer cities to remove this choice of location from the experimental stage, as well as placing it beyond explanations that categorize it as 'special type, 'eccentric' or 'capricious'. The advantages and disadvantages of such location of headquarters can now be observed and studied. The argument for centrality that rested on sufficient labour supply, face-to-face contacts, and external economies has been overcome by the example of workable solutions in outer cities.

2. The ability to collect a sufficient number of clerical-level employees in an outer city location is affected by the number of corporate offices that cluster in one area. However, the continuing population growth of outer cities, consisting largely of middle-class households that have traditionally supplied the required office personnel, largely female at the clerical level, provides an expanding office labour supply that is likely to be commensurate with expanding demand generally. The automobile, the preponderant mode of travel to work in outer city offices, permits the assembly of work force from relatively long distances and, thereby, enlarges each corporate office's labour market to include a sizable portion of outer city. In 1963, automobile travel represented 80% of all trips to work locations in the outer city of the New York Metropolitan Region.[31] A study of white-collar employment in Westchester County in 1970 revealed that the number who commuted into the county almost equalled the number of Westchester residents who commuted out, and that the in-commuters were drawn from a wide-flung market area that included substantial numbers from Western Connecticut, Putman County and Rockland County.[32]

3. Face-to-face contact in the conduct of corporate business has proved manageable for executives in outer city locations though with some strain on organizational capabilities involved in the logistics of planning executives' time and travel scheduling. It should be noted that the preponderant flow of communications involved in business management is *within the corporation.* This does not benefit necessarily from centrality of location. Those communications which involve exogenous interaction (banks, brokers, advertising agencies, accountants, special counsel, government, etc.) requiring face-to-face contacts tend to be foreseen and largely capable of being deliberately arranged events, rather than chance, improvised, or emergency encounters. The outer-city based executive is, of necessity, a highly mobile operator and trips to the central business section of his metropolitan area are interspersed with those to other parts of the country or abroad. An outer city corporate headquarters is almost always supplemented with an inner city adjunct office that specializes in external contacts. The president of the company invariably has a second office in the inner city.

This arrangement is in keeping with the growing flexibility in corporate structure and operational procedures necessitated by increasing diversity of product and/or services produced and marketed by each corporation, the extreme expression of which is the conglomerate, with its collection of utterly disparate types of businesses. The trend is toward decentralized responsibility for separate divisions of corporate enterprises with much 'flying in' to headquarters for consultation when the telephone proves inadequate, or 'flying out' to product division headquarters by the president or other top executives. In the light of the degree of mobility required of corporate executives for internal coordination, travel to the inner city for external contacts (to arrange for a bond issue, negotiate a contract with a parts supplier, etc.) imposes no undue hardship.

The maintenance of both inner city and outer city offices by corporations has led to a wide variety of practices in placing certain functions in one or other location. As consequence, the very term 'headquarters' becomes less informative as to what functions are housed there.

When Xerox Corporation, for example, moved their 'headquarters' from Rochester to Stamford, Conn. (within New York's outer city), it involved only some two dozen of the very top executive team and included, in all, only 168 employees. They deliberately sought to separate their think-tank, decision-making echelon from the 'work-horse' departments, which remained in Rochester. Corporations moving from the inner city to the outer city have every incentive provided by consideration of cost and personnel recruitment also to move their 'back office' operations, which are relatively unrelated to external contact. When Allied Chemical moved from New York City to an outer city location in Morris County, it involved 1,200 out of 1,600 on headquarters staff. Its Fibres Division, consisting of 200 employees, and an additional 200 in other divisions remained in its Times Square Tower.

4. The extent to which corporate offices in outer city can avail themselves of external economies depends in large measure upon a sufficient concentration of offices within a locality to induce supportive services to also locate there. Business services cover a wide range of types; from patent lawyers to office cleaning. The more highly specialized services are less likely to locate in outer cities, though it is conceivable that they will find it advantageous to have brand offices near major concentrations of corporate offices. Purveyors of office supplies, office machine maintenance services, etc. are invariably already in or close to outer city localities chosen for corporate offices. A sufficient number of the latter will cause such suppliers to expand and/or multiply.

5. Corporate offices in the outer city show a tendency to cluster in the form of relatively loosely grouped sites relating to transportation linkages to the inner city's central business district via road and rail and to other national and global centres via air. However, the emergence of such corporate office nodes in any specific part of outer city *is dictated primarily by adjacency to a traditional residential concentration of corporate executives,*[33] and only secondarily, though necessarily, to transportation facilities required to assemble the work force.

The largest corporate office node in the New York Metropolitan Region has emerged in the form of a belt stretching roughly from the White Plains, NY area to the Stamford Connecticut area, a distance of about 13 miles. Westchester County (NY) and Fairfield County (Conn) have historically contained the most prestigious 'bedroom' suburbs inhabited by New York's top corporate management. It is this that has initiated corporate office moves to this area. Its rail, road and air facilities made it feasible. It is not premature to conclude from this order of criteria governing corporate office locations, that it is a forlorn hope to expect executives to move their residence to a renewed inner city, when the evidence indicates that they are more apt to move their corporate offices to the outer city where they reside. The fact that high-income communities in other parts of New York's outer city have proved far less potent in attracting corporate offices is attributable, largely, to the income sources of their richest inhabitants. Long Island's famed North Shore estate areas are inhabited typically by 'old wealth', more likely to be represented on the boards of corporations than in active management. The newer, more fashionable communities on Long Island with high-income residents draw these mainly from commercial enterprises (wholesale, retail, services) or manufacturing of non-durables (textiles, clothing, publishing); neither of which finds it feasible to separate corporate headquarters from live operations that require centrality of location by reason of external economies and customer or other face-to-face contact. New Jersey's communities that have concentrations of high income residents, such as Short Hills, Montclair, Ridgewood, etc., have been preferred, historically, by those who work in Lower Manhattan's financial district, mainly in banking, the stock market, insurance, etc., activities that continue to be highly dependent upon centrality of location.

6. The argument that corporate offices will remain in central business districts because the latter provide for daily social functions (lunch at the club, etc.) that are an integral part of the executive's way of life seems not to hold up when tested against actual conditions of life at outer city headquarters. Top executives can still make the rounds of familiar peer-group haunts on those days that business brings them to their inner city offices. Outer city corporate offices have executive dining rooms as well as certain restaurants and country clubs where the corporate brass congregates. Executives of outer city corporations testify to increased social visiting to each other's homes. Since this involves their wives, it appears to be in keeping with the growing enlightenment on the role of women current in the business world, and the reduction of emphasis on masculine social rites, such as the 'men-only' clubs. In contrast to the latter, the outer city country club has long ago evolved from a businessmen's golf course to a family recreational centre for the rich, with activities for all age groups.

7. The place of air travel in the life of the contemporary generation of corporation executives gives great importance to home and office locations with regard to an airport. Executives who fly in and out of the Westchester County Airport are within 15-30 minutes of both their homes and their offices. It permits them to crowd more working hours into travel days and makes possible one-day trips to most cities of the United States and Canada, with return home in time for dinner.

Our knowledge of outer-city advantages is still not sufficient to permit detailed identification of all types of corporations for which the move from inner city to outer city is feasible. It would appear from the foregoing that most of the corporate giants that resemble those already operating from outer city locations *can* emulate them, if they choose to do so. It is also clear that many administrative functions cannot disregard the factor of centrality and must of necessity remain in the inner city's business district, at least, given the current state of communications technology. The vast majority of the nation's 500 largest corporations have their headquarters in central business districts; 125 of them in New York City alone. If movement to the outer city is a practical option, what is likely to cause them to do so?

Reasons for moving corporate offices to the outer city, as they appear in a composite of announcements by spokesmen for companies making such a move, are divisible into references to outer city advantages and to inner city problems.

Allied Chemical's vice-president emphasized outer-city living conditions as an aid to attracting young scientists who seek good communities and quality schools for growing families. Others referred to closeness to airports; still others to the consolidation of scattered divisions under one roof.

Inner-city problems mentioned most frequently are rising rates and rentals, lack of suitable space, poor commuting and traffic congestion. However, where the press was able to get anonymous statements from company personnel, these stressed crime, corruption and the increasing black population, especially as reflected in lower echelon help.

New York City's Economic Development Administrator (Ken Patten) attributed decisions to leave the inner city to 'social distance': 'The executive decision-maker lives in a homogenized community, ethnic and class community,' he continued. 'Increasingly his employees in the city are from communities very different in class and ethnicity. The decision-maker can't relate to the city kid: that kid doesn't look the same as him. It's an older generation in charge trying to re-establish a setting that seems to be more comfortable, more the old way.'[34] Later, he became more specific and was quoted as saying that 'many executives are uneasy with the tensions and strains of the city and the black and brown faces among their workers.[35]

An insurance executive in Detroit who asked not to be identified is quoted as stating that the vice-president of a prominent corporation moving to the outer city told him 'that they wanted to move for one reason—to get rid of low echelon workers, like file clerks and typists. These days those workers have to be black.'[36] Other sources refer to the low competence of available clerical help. In a 1970 survey of 103 corporations employing one-fifth of the work force in New York City, the Economic Development Council, a business-based group, asked them to list the principal adverse factors in recruiting clerical manpower. 'First on the list by an overwhelming margin was the school system's inability to produce enough people with the necessary skills in reading, mathematics and writing.'[37]

New York is, of course, a very special city. It is the business capital of the United States; in measure also the business capital of the Western Hemisphere, if not of the Western World. New York is Wall Street (stock exchange), Broadway (entertainment), Madison Avenue (advertising, publishing, mass media) and Lincoln Centre (performing arts). It is unique among American cities in the volume and diversity of specialized services that cannot be performed presently without a high degree of the type of personal interaction possible only from an office in the central business district. It is the nation's primary research and development centre. It is headquarters of the largest foundations and the leading non-profit 'public interest' or 'good cause' organizations. It has the nation's only recognized 'Intellectual Establishment'. It shares with Washington, New Orleans and San Francisco the ability to attract large numbers of tourists and conference attendees from the rest of the country and from abroad, supporting a vast hotel, restaurant, taxicab and entertainment industry. The inevitable loss of much of the rest of New York's production employment and the possible loss of much of its corporate headquarters employment, would still leave the inner city with many functions that would secure New York's pre-eminence among the nation's cities. But the loss of substantial amounts of white-collar jobs in addition to the on-going loss of blue-collar jobs, could prove decisive in inaugurating changes in the inner city's economic base and accelerating changes in its social fabric that could prove catastrophic. Though the economic functions of the inner city can be examined apart from its social fabric, the two are, of course, integrally related and changes in either have a reciprocating effect. The changing characteristics of New York's population, especially with regard to class and race, will have a decisive effect upon its economic base. If this is the prospect for New York's inner city, it will be more crushingly the case in most of American's other major cities, which lack New York's substantial list of unique functions. Some of them are already undergoing transformations that are more rapid and consequential than New York's.

4. The changing social fabric of the inner city

Almost five million whites, largely skilled and middle class, migrated out of the inner cities of the United States between 1960 and 1970. Their loss was balanced by an excess of births over deaths and the in-migration of some 1,337,000 Negroes and other minorities, largely from rural area.[38] Racial minorities also supplied one third of the natural increase. This continued a pattern of massive demographic change in inner cities begun in the late 1940s.

Though some professionally mobile blacks also moved to outer cities, the 1960 racial ratio of 95.8% white and 4.2% black, remained virtually unchanged.[39] The black proportion of inner cities, however, increased from 14% to 19% during this decade, Considerably greater increases were recorded in the largest of them: New York, Chicago and Los Angeles gained almost 700,000 Negroes through in-migration alone between 1960 and 1970, the equivalent of 28% of their 1960 black population.

The natural increase of blacks in inner cities also exceeded that of whites by 21.6% to 8.6%, using each race's population total for 1960 as the base. Because the white population of inner cities contains higher proportions of older and unattached persons, their crude birth rate is even smaller in relation to blacks than the margin nationally. In metropolitan areas of 2 million or more, the natural increase of whites in inner cities was only 4.7%, while that of blacks remained constant.

Metropolitan area's white population growth took place only in the outer cities, which accounted for 80% of the increase for the nation's metropolitan area. In-migration and natural increase added 15.6 million whites to the population of outer cities and on 1.1 million blacks.[40]

Negroes now constitute the majority in Washington, D.C. (71%), Newark, NJ (54%), Gary, Ind., (52.8%) and Atlanta, Ga. (51.3%). Cities in which Negroes exceed 40% of the population are Baltimore, Md. (46.4%), New Orleans, La. (45%), Detroit, Mich. (43.7%), Wilmington, Del. (43.6%), Birmingham, Ala. (42.0%), Richmond, Va. (42.0%), and St Louis, Mo.

40.9%). These latter cities are all likely to have black majorities by 1980, while Chicago, Philadelphia and Cleveland are projected to reach the 50% mark not many years later. If other non-whites are added to the Negro population figure, the combined percentage increases sharply for a number of larger cities. There are over one million Puerto Ricans[41] in New York City, constituting 13.4% of the population. The combined Negro-Puerto Rican percentage of New York's population was 36.8% in 1970 and is projected to top 50% by 1985.[42] In view of New York's loss of one million whites in each of the last two decades, this projection might prove to be too conservative.

What is the significance of the expected emergence of black and Spanish-speaking majorities in a dozen or so of the largest cities in the United States within a decade or two? The mere fact that Americans of African and Latin American descent will outnumber those of European descent would not, of and by itself, be very significant. Its profound implications can be discovered only if read against (a) the grim heritage of three centuries of unresolved race relations between an advantaged and dominant majority and a disadvantaged and oppressed minority; (b) the new found pride, self-reliance and militancy of blacks in asserting their determination to be equal, not only in legal rights, but in power and status; (c) the combined character of the blacks' struggle as both racial group and social class, and (d) the institutional inelasticity of white society in the face of minority pressures to share in power and wealth. The profound significance of 'black cities' therefore is that they will be inherited by their new majorities at a time of heightening consciousness of both whites and black with regard to the status and income implications of the blacks' challenge to white dominance, and the consequent use as leverage of the power of numbers and the moral weight of a formal majority to exact concessions as the price for the continued functioning of a white-dominated central business district in a black-dominated city.

A fuller comprehension of the significance of black majorities in major cities requires an understanding of the singular impact of blacks upon the urbanization process in the post-industrial era. It is necessary to establish at the outset that (a) blacks are uniquely different from previous strands woven into the city's social fabric by virtue of the latter's intrinsic nature as a component of a white racist society, hitherto geared to the assimilation of whites only, and (b) that the economic mechanisms that operated to as-

similate immigrants from rural areas in the cities of the industrial age are increasingly deficient in the cities of the post-industrial era. In short, the city responds to non-whites differently than to previous immigrants, and has been transformed functionally from what it once was.

To view the Negro as only another in the historical succession of newcomers to the city from rural life is to misread the empirical evidence of the contemporary urbanization process, or to do violence to it by forcing it into a Procrustean bed of historical theory.[43] When the city functioned as the vortex of industrial society it sucked in the raw material of human resources as required by the economy; disciplining, regimenting and instructing the newcomer in 'urbanism as a way of life.'[44] Wherever capitalism appeared it created industrial cities that fattened upon the consumption of the surplus rural population. American's earliest factories drew their levies from the sons and daughter of farmers, beginning with Yankees from the soil-poor farms of New England. In the post-Civil War decades this role was assumed increasingly by European immigrants who reached the shores of America in mounting waves that reached their crest in the decade of 1901-1910, when over eight million arrived. The Negro had been on the American urban scene for several generations before this hot-house growth of industrial cities, but he stood apart from it. As the tide of industrial prosperity lifted successive strata of city dwellers to higher social and economic status, the Negro was kept confined to pre-industrial occupations specially designated by white society as 'black man's work', and to segregated tightly-drawn residential districts, the now notorious black ghettos.

Negroes entered industry in significant numbers only during World War I, when a manpower vacuum was created by the nation's effort to meet the economic demands of 'total war', requiring for the first time a fully mobilized 'home front'. These new opportunities for blacks initiated mass migrations from the rural South, where 90% of all Negroes lived as late as 1900, to northern and midwestern cities. The old ghettos burst their bonds and blacks in desperate search of living space exploited cracks and crevices in the white resistance to gain footholds in new parts of cities and soon expanded them into additional ghettos.

The period between World War I and the Depression of the 1930s marked the first stage of large-scale urbanization of Negroes in northern cities. It was also the period when black urban life styles took form, marked by the emergence of Harlem and its black institutions as a prototype for urbanizing blacks in the rest of the country.

The period was ushered in with inter-racial violence; race riots in Chicago and East St Louis took high tolls in life, injuries and property damage. The riots were essentially mob violence by whites accompanied by the reappearance of the Ku Klux Klan as a mass movement aiming to 'put the nigger in his place', i.e. to deny him the residential mobility and employment opportunities the city had provided all previous immigrants.

Though Negroes were pushed out of many areas of employment gained during the war, they did keep some significant footholds, as in steel and meat packing. The sharp curtailment of immigration from abroad by imposition of Federal quotas unfavourable to Southern and Eastern European countries created new opportunities for blacks in low-wage industries during the rapid economic expansion of the middle 1920s. Mass unemployment during the depressed 1930s reduced to a trickle black migration from the South to the cities. Millions of unemployed whites now shared the hard and uncertain life of urban impoverishment that is the constant lot of a high proportion of blacks. The latter benefited from the New Deal's emergency welfare schemes inaugurated to relieve suffering among the jobless. Blacks continued to depend on government support when whites found jobs as employment rose in response to rearmament for World War II.

A demand by blacks for the same job opportunities, dramatized by a threatened march on Washington, wrung from the Federal Government a Fair Employment Practices Act, which, aided by World War II labour shortages, opened most basic industries to blacks, including many occupations in which they acquired specialized skills. Black migration from the South to the cities was renewed and soon became a torrent. Though some found shelter in the government's temporary housing for war workers, built near munitions plans and shipyards, most blacks crowded into confined ghetto quarters, living under desperately difficult conditions.

As the war ended, agriculture in the South cut back production and accelerated mechanization, displacing farm labourers with mechanical cotton pickers and other labour-saving devices. The displacement of blacks from agriculture was one aspect of the overall technological revolution that reduced the entire farm population of the nation, without regard to race or section of country. The US farm population dropped from 32 million in 1920 to 10 million in 1970.

Most rural whites, however, either owned farms or were tenant farmers who owned equipment. They were able to liquidate their assets to enter other enterprises or, at least, to buy a home in an area of their choice. Blacks were largely farm labourers or sharecroppers whose extremely small cash income precluded accumulation. The plunging decline in farm employment consequently set them adrift as impoverished refugees. Harsh discrimination in employment and housing in the South gave them few opportunities to re-establish themselves in their native states, except in the ghettos of the larger cities (Atlanta, Birmingham, Memphis, New Orleans, Richmond, Norfolk, etc.) Prospects for employment and housing seemed better in the North and West, and millions of black refugees from the South's shrinking agricultural economy headed for such cities as Washington, Baltimore, Philadelphia, Newark, New York, Chicago, Cleveland, Detroit, St Louis and Los Angeles.

The torrent of black migration to the cities became a steady feature of demographic change in the United States as displaced blacks in the 1950s and 1960s moved out of the South at an average annual number of about 150,000 totalling 4.5 million between 1940 and 1970. Only 53% of all Negroes lived in the South by 1970, with only 6% of Negro males in the labour force and 2% of females working on a farm. In that year 74% of the total Negro population lived in metropolitan areas as compared to 68% of the total white population, with 58% of all Negroes in inner cities as compared to 28% of all whites. (In 1950 the comparable figure had been 44% for Negroes and 35% for whites).

The mass movement of Negroes into the largest inner cities coincided with the mass exodus of whites to the outer cities. The transition was facilitated by a push/pull rhythm in which some whites were pulled out of inner city by the lure of outer-city life styles, while their white neighbours who stayed behind felt 'pushed' out later by the growing black population. In actuality the moves were probably more indirect; someone somewhere in the inner city moved to the outer city and precipitated a chain of moves that created a vacancy in the racial transition belt around the spreading ghetto. Vacancies in such transitional areas are invariably filled by black families desperately seeking to improve their housing, rather than whites, who have more options to choose from.

Since most housing in outer city is more expensive than most housing in inner city, those making the outward movement must meet an income test. This determines that the movers to outer city are, on the whole, in

higher income brackets, more remunerative occupations, and, generally, at a stage in their family cycle where they have children and some savings. Insofar as ethnic backgrounds can be correlated to these factors, the outward movers in the earlier part of the 1940-1970 period, were more likely to be white Anglo-Saxon Protestants, or second or third generation German, Irish or Jewish[45] households, and, increasingly, in the latter part of the period, of Southern and Eastern European stock. The less affluent of the white ethnic groups have no choice but to remain in the inner city. They seek to keep intact one or more of their traditional ethnic neighbourhoods, anchored around churches or other institutions.

Income is next in importance to race — and integrally related to it — as a determinant of inner city's social fabric. Income is the monetary expression of the gap between the races created during three centuries of slavery, discrimination and segregation and expressed in occupation, employment/unemployment, education, health, welfare dependency, savings and other forms of wealth, family stability, and similar indices of status in our culture. This pervasive gap causes race to denote also social class in urban demography. (The Negroes' disadvantaged position is shared in varying degrees by Mexican-Americans, Puerto Ricans and American Indians).

In 1970 the median family income of Negroes and other races was 61% that of whites, a considerable gain since 1958 when it was 51%.[46] Since it had been as high as 57% in 1952, the continued narrowing of the income gap is not to be viewed as an automatic process. In 1970, for the entire United States, 32% of all Negroes and other non-white races received incomes below the government's poverty level (about $4,000 for a family of four), while only 10% of whites were in this bracket. Poor families of all races composed 13.4% of the population of inner cities as compared to 7.2% of outer city. The third most important determinant of the inner city's social fabric is the age distribution of the population.

The latter tends to concentrate the elderly in the inner city. This is caused by the departure of younger white families to outer cities, leaving the elderly in inner city neighbourhoods where many own homes and most have social and other ties. In 1968, whites over 65 years of age composed 13% of all white residents of inner cities and only 8% of all white residents of outer cities. Poverty among whites is concentrated among the elderly (22.4%) compared to blacks (8.8%), The majority (58.1%) of elderly poor live alone or with non-relatives.[47]

Race, low income and advanced age are becoming the dominant characteristics of the inner city's social fabric. As a consequence an increasingly high percentage of the inner city's population lives there without the historic rationale of a productive role in the city's economic functions. Many came to the inner city as refugees from technological revolution in agriculture, and stay on as trapped victims of the transition from industrial to post-industrial society. Their rationale becomes increasingly the measure of security afforded by such housing as they occupy and the availability of health and welfare supports, however wretchedly inadequate. As noted previously, manufacturing, which provides the greatest number of jobs that require minimal training, is declining in inner cities and being partially replaced in most of them (entirely in a few) by office employment. Left behind in the inner city is a growing labour supply that is structurally unemployed by virtue of the geographic mismatch between jobs and skills and/or the 'skills gap' between manual skills and office manpower needs.[48]

Though the number of non-white persons in the labour force who have adapted to the manpower needs of post-industrial society is growing, mainly by virtue of the greater schooling of the young who enter the labour force, they face both the persistence of job discrimination and the competition of white youth advantaged by both education and the sophistication, 'contacts' and greater familiarity with the world of office employment. Though 46% of the black and Puerto Rican entrants to the labour force in the New York Metropolitan Region between 1960 and 1968 were classified as 'white collar', high unemployment rates for young people persisted in poverty areas of the inner city.[49]

After an analysis of low incomes among New York's black and Puerto Rican households. Regional Plan Association projects this dubious future for them:

'For a variety of reasons, not of their making and over which they have virtually no control, these latest arrivals, unlike earlier in-migrants, seem to be trapped in a vicious cycle of poverty. To enable them or their children to extricate themselves from this morass, economic growth per se will probably need to be supplemented, at least in the medium run (say, over the next decade) by a whole range of supplementary measures carried out in part by the private sector but substantially underwritten by the public sector. 'The income forecasts have as their premise that Negro and Puerto Rican households will have no greater difficulty in achieving middle-income status than predecessor in-migrants of other backgrounds, i.e. the forecasts assume that the whole population will share in rising income. It is recognized that this has not been true for Negroes in the past. This, then, is more in the nature of a challenge than a prediction. If this assumption is to prove valid, it will require deliberate and forceful public policy measures.'[50]

During the five years since this was written, the evidence is not encouraging for RPA's premise. Quite the contrary is the case. Economic decline, municipal and state fiscal crises, and social disorganization have weakened the ability of the private sector, of government and of community self-help programmes to carry out prescribed 'supplementary measures'.

5. Growing social disorganization in the inner city

The narrowing of the inner city's economic functions and the weakening of its social fabric have placed strains upon the ability of its institutions to discharge responsibilities with expected efficiency and quality of performance, and have subjected group and interpersonal relations to stresses that foster fears, anxiety and outbreaks of violence. The overall effect has been a growing social disorganization. It is manifested in poverty, unemployment, welfare dependency, family instability, crime, drug-abuse, health care deterioration, housing shortages and abandonment, school under-performance, public transportation decline, pollution, ugliness, dirt, municipal services curtailment, and threatening municipal bankruptcy. The 1970 Census showed that the trend toward concentration of persons with incomes below the poverty level in the inner cities continued, with 13.4% of their population in this category.[51] It also revealed that the gap had widened since 1960 between the median income of those living in the inner cities and the median income of those in the outer cities.

The swift rise in unemployment in the United States caused by the economic recession that began in 1969 was felt more severely in inner cities than in outer, despite the large amount of the recession-susceptible manufacturing industry located in the latter. The unemployment rate for white persons 16 years and over in 1970 was 4.9% in inner cities compared to 4.5% in outer cities, and for Negroes 8.3% in inner cities and 7.4% in outer. New York City's job total declined by 184,000 during 1970 and 1971, while it was increasing by 600,000 nationally. New York City's unemployment rate rose from 3.5% in 1969, to 4.6% in 1970, and then to 6.7% in 1971, exceeding the national rate of 6.0%.[52]

Unemployment was much higher among young members (16 years to 19 years) of the inner cities' labour forces, reaching 14.3% for whites and a catastrophic 31.8% for blacks. In the poverty areas of inner cities joblessness among black youth reached 40%, not counting those out of school but not actively looking for work. Sar A Levitan and Robert Taggart III, in a study of the job crisis for black youth, analysed its consequences: 'The fact that 40 percent of all black teenagers in urban poverty areas are currently unemployed cannot be isolated from such societal ills as rising crime and civil unrest, although the relationships between employment and other social problems cannot be easily established. Careful studies have indicated a significant positive correlation between juvenile delinquency and unemployment. The relationship between illegitimacy and economic opportunity has not been demonstrated, but it is plausible that some women view welfare as the only means to independence when employment opportunities are limited. Finally, there is the fearful possibility that in this time of rising expectations the sudden and drastic increases in ghetto unemployment will lead to another and more severe round of urban riots. Thus the problems of black teenagers are carried over to the rest of the community. The ever-increasing numbers of idle and undirected inner city youths add to the deteriorating quality of urban life.'[53]

Older workers are unemployed for longer periods than are younger workers and earn less when working: the earnings of the 55-64 age group being only 86% of those of the 35-44 age group. Though the unemployment rates of older workers in the labour force tend to be lower, a high percentage of this age group is no longer actively seeking work and, therefore, technically no longer in the labour force.[54] In 1970, 10.3% of whites aged 45 to 64 years in inner cities were no longer in the work force, and 15.2% of Negroes and other minority races were in this category.[55]

A study of the manpower problems of poverty areas in New York City revealed that official unemployment rates are deceptively conservative for such areas. Though only 4% were found to be 'officially' unemployed during the period of July 1968 to June 1969, as many as 15% of all males between 20 and 64 years old were not actively looking for work, another 7% were working part-time and not seeking full-time work for various reasons and an additional 7% were employed at full-time jobs that paid less than $65 a week. The composite of these categories adds up to

Below: The cutting edge of new development in southern Middlesex County, about 45 miles from Times Square.

Opposite, above: Suburban development in Paramus, New Jersey, about 15 miles from Times Square. Density of about six houses to the acre typical of early 1950s subdivisions.

Opposite, below: Large-lot zoning in northwest Bergen County — Wyckoff or Mahwah. Today, most of the vacant land in the Region zoned for residential use is zoned for single-family homes on lots of ½ acre or larger.

Far right, top: Suburban school in Waldwick, New Jersey. The main object of large-lot zoning is to hold down the number of school children and thus control spiralling school taxes, which are the greatest burden faced by the Region's local governments.

Far right, below: This is one of three 19th-century schools still in use in Newark, New Jersey, an example of the inequities among school districts under a system which relies chiefly on local property tax for school support.

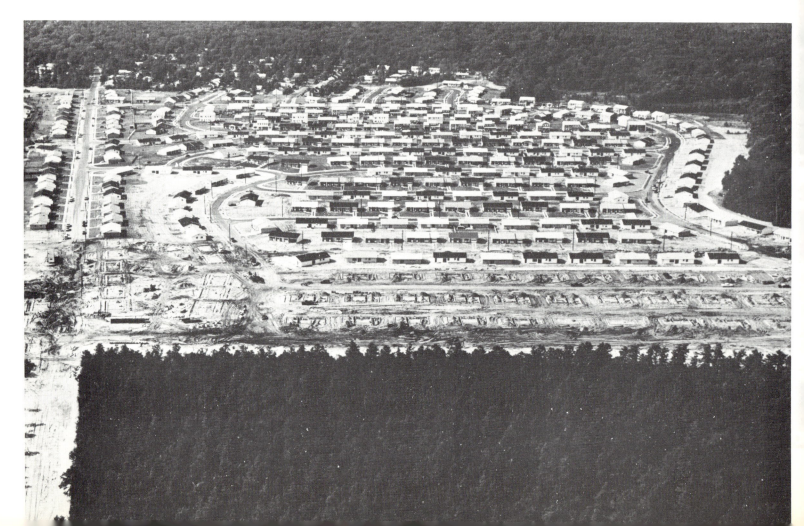

fully one third of all males between 20 years and 64 years of age in abnormal work situations.[56]

The high percentage of New York's labour force that is unemployed or underemployed is reflected in the large-scale dependence upon public welfare, which reached the total of 1.25 million in 1972, or over 15% of the city's population, or one in six inhabitants. Of this number, about 133,000 were the 'working poor', those receiving welfare payments to supplement their low wages. Of the city's 348 health districts, 62 had more than a third of the population on welfare, 33 had over 40% of the population on welfare, and 7 had over 50%. Some 770,000 persons have been added to the welfare roles since 1965, expanding the known poverty areas and creating new ones in previously self-sufficient and stable neighbourhoods. A mapping of location and density of welfare recipients in New York City in 1965 and in 1971 is not unlike x-ray photographs that record the spread of malignancy in a healthy organ. 'While there is a national spotlight on the expanding welfare problem here ' reports *The New York Times,* 'other big cities such as Baltimore, Philadelphia, St Louis, and San Francisco, have proportionately about the same number of welfare clients as New York does and Neward has many more.'[57] A study by the Federal Government's Health, Education and Welfare Department early in 1972 indicated a trend toward welfare recipients being more representative of the low income population as a whole. The report stated that 'more welfare families had unemployed fathers in the home, more lived in big cities and fewer were black.' They also pointed out that welfare recipients were tending to be younger, healthier, better fed, and better educated than ever before.[58] Poverty and the operational procedures of the welfare system have combined to destroy the traditional family unit among a great number of the poor. The federally-financed and locally-administered programme of Aid to Dependent Children has placed a premium upon fatherlessness. Since the presence of a father with some earnings decreases the chances of public assistance, there is a strong incentive for the father to desert for the benefit of his family, or to be reported as having 'disappeared' in order to augment family income. It also provides the mother with a measure of financial independence of the father and encourages creation of households headed by women maintaining liaison with a man or succession of men. Fully 70% of all individuals receiving welfare assistance in New York City are in the Aid to Dependent Children category, almost entirely mothers and children in fatherless households.[59]

Urban society and especially the inner city has proven highly susceptible to drug abuse. The sordidness and frustration encountered by the poor tempt an increasing number, especially the young, to seek 'relief' and 'happiness' in the temporary euphoria provided by narcotics. 'According to the best estimates, there are approximately 150,000 to 250,000 active heroin addicts in the United States, perhaps half of whom live in New York City'.[60] According to the President's Report to the White House Conference on Drugs in 1969, there were 180,000 addicts in the country; 60 to 70% were black, Puerto Rican or Mexican American, 85% were male and an estimated 25% under the age of twenty-one.

The inner city has been the main locus of the increasing crime that afflicts urban life in the USA and shows crimes to be increasing at a rate of approximately 11% per year since 1967. 'Most serious crimes occur in big cities. The Crime Commission pointed out that a third of all robberies and a fifth of all rapes occur in cities of more than one million population. Most surprisingly, therefore, the city crime rate is higher than the suburban rate and far higher than the rural rate.' The growing violence is reflected in police fatalities, with 100 deaths in 1970. The fillings of police officers indicate an annual rate of increase of 50%.[61]

There is a high degree of racial correlation between offenders and victims in most categories of crime. Except for robbery, the victim and the offender are likely to be of the same race. In a study of crimes in 17 major cities, it was found that Negroes were the victims in 70% of homicides, 68% of aggravated assaults, 60% of rapes, 40% armed robberies and 38% of unarmed robbery. Negroes were the assailants in 73% of homicides, 74% of aggravated assaults, 71% of rapes, 85% of armed robberies and 81% of unarmed robberies.[62]

Fear of crime has become a major factor in influencing the development of the inner city. Because of the high incidence of minority involvement in crimes, whites have come to identify crime with poverty. The increasing visibility of colour in the inner city causes whites to consider it increasingly dangerous territory, not only for residence, but as a place of work and business. This negative image of the inner city affects location decisions of both households and business institutions. A study by the National Industrial Conference Board mentioned fear of crime as one of the reasons why corporate personnel now resist being transferred to New York City, once considered a highly desurable plum.[63] Once the focal point for health services, the inner city faces an increasing crisis caused by the shortage of medical personnel and

deterioration and obsolescence of facilities. 'The apparent reluctance of young doctors to settle where they think crime, school and neighbourhood problems are acute is sharply reducing the number of physicians practising in Brooklyn and the Bronx and is causing serious concern among medical authorities', reports *The New York Times*. The president of the Bronx County Medical Society is quoted as describing the situation as 'critical, and his counterpart in the Brooklyn society as saying, 'we are going to have to do something soon or face very grave consequences.' Waits as long as two months by private patients seeking an examination are reported in both boroughs. Private practitioners have virtually disappeared from poverty areas, and inner-city hospitals, desperately short of funds, report a growing inability to attract American-educated medical school graduates to serve as interns. The Bronx Medical Society reports crimes against doctors making calls resulting in injuries. Brooklyn suffered a 23% loss of physicians between 1950 and 1969 while experiencing only a 6% loss in population. Westchester County, in New York's outer city, experienced a 87.8% gain in physicians during the same period, as compared to only a 41.9% increase in population.[64] The Lyons Family Health Center was created in Newark several years ago to encourage private practitioners to provide inner-city services. Its administrator reports that 'ten years ago there were 60 physicians with offices on Lyons Avenue, now there are only eight.' The centre has induced doctors and dentists to give several hours a week for less than their normal fee to provide for some 1,300 patients per month. Some of the practitioners are quoted as valuing the opportunity to see inner-city residents because the poor continue to suffer from ailments not encountered among their outer-city patients.

Housing in the inner city is adversely affected by a disinclination of capital to invest in inner cities, except for special locations that provide a market for luxury apartments. The result is a failure to maintain the least profitable units in the existing stock and their eventual abandonment and removal from the market, and construction of new housing only with government subsidies.

A study of housing in seven cities 'produced extensive evidence that entire neighbourhoods housing hundreds of thousands of central city dwellers are in advanced stages of being abandoned by their owners.[65] The study cites as causes housing obsolescence, the magnet of suburban residential and industrial development, increased tax rates and declining municipal services, erratic code enforcement and urban renewal programmes. . . .' The process that ensues is described: 'at the same time that the market is exploited, perceived or threatened racial change accelerates disinvestment, first by the mortgage money market and second by owners. Real estate can no longer be sold or refinanced at competitive rates. Deterioration spirals as maintenance declines. Neighbourhood flight accelerates, first by investors and then by the socially mobile, until only the poor, the aged and the severely deprived remain. The crisis ghetto emerges; abandonment is virtually completed.'

This process is reflected in two separate sets of statistics. The first is population data that reveals densities in the heart of slums as the poor move out of the worst blocks, usually beset by breakdown of services and dominance by drug addicts who congregate in abandoned buildings. The second is housing conditions data that reveals an increase in central cities for Negro households living in units with complete plumbing facilities, from 79% in 1960 to 95% in 1970.[66] This gain represents the abandonment of the worst units in the core of the slum and the spread of the ghetto to absorb surrounding blocks of substantial housing.

Approximately 80,000 new and converted dwelling units were added to the housing stock of New York City between 1965 and 1968. However, some 100,000 units disappeared from the stock during this time, 'enough to house a population of almost 300,000. Thus, in the last few years, while the number of households in the city has continued to increase, the number of homes has actually declined.' The result is a worsening shortage of units; New York City's vacancy rate is now under 1%. 'Long lists of families — currently 135,000 — await public housing, and musty tenements, obsolete 50 years ago, are still rented.[67]

Three-fourths of all Federally subsidized housing is located in inner cities. Much of it is undergoing destruction that is more convincingly indicative of the social disorganization of inner cities than any other phenomenon. Many of the housing projects built in the 1950s and early 1960s have become uninhabitable because of poor design, inferior construction, erratic management policy, misuse of property by occupants, vandalism and crime. While the case of the Pruitt-Igoe project in St Louis is nationally notorious, it is only an extreme case of the deterioration of much of the public housing of inner cities. The Pruitt-Igoe project has been the subject of debate as to whether to demolish it or invest over $30 million in its rehabilitation. The occupants of the Stella Wright Project in Newark have recently petitioned the city's Housing Authority to relocate them and raze the buildings. They contend that the project was badly designed and has become uninhabitable.

Beginning in the mid 1960s the Federal strategy in housing the poor shifted from publicly-owned housing to co-operative and other forms of non-profit ownership under the 221(d) (3) scheme and, subsequently, the 236 scheme. These provide for federal subsidies to lower mortgage costs. Beginning in 1970, defaulting of obligations became widespread and the federal government found it necessary to foreclose and assume ownership. Many of these projects suffer not only from financial distress, but have become uninhabitable and are being vacated. Vandalism and crime are cited as driving out the low-income inhabitants for whom such housing marked a significant upgrading of accommodations.

Foreclosure and government ownership has also been widespread in the single-family ownership programme for low income families (Section 235), largely as a result of fraud by real-estate brokers and collusion by government appraisers. Houses with defective heating, plumbing, wiring, roofing and/or structural defects were purchased by the operators of such fraudulent rings and sold at many times their value to poor people with government subsidies of mortgage payments.[68] Confronted with the need to invest sizeable amounts of money to make the houses habitable, the new owners simply 'walked away', leaving them to the Federal government. The latter already owns some 5,000 single family homes in Detroit alone, and testimony at hearings in that city disclosed that it might cost the government $200 million by the time it has closed out the foreclosure operations and repossessed the properties.

The housing feature writer for *The New York Times,* John Herbers, reports that 'in the long run, some authorities believe, Federal ownership could have a beneficial effect, especially if the central cities continue to become a wasteland. If accumulated in large plots the land could be employed for a number of purposes, from building parks or new communities to homesteads. But all of this runs counter to the philosophy of the current Administration and to the present trend against more centralized control.'

Herbers notes that 'there are (housing) failures in the suburbs, too, but not nearly as many. The suburban ring constitutes the new city and has a stability that can overcome failures in construction and management.[69] The inner city's growing social disorganization has taken its toll in the schools. These have been assessed as oscillating between tedium and turbulence, with lowered quality of education as an ever present condition. In five studies of the inner city schools, all agreed that they were inferior to those of the outer cities. In inner-city schools pupils lagged in reading and other achievement tests, their teachers tended to be less qualified, the expenditure per pupil was lower, the buildings were much older, the classes were larger, the schools were more racially concentrated by whites or blacks, depending upon the neighbourhood, and drop-out rates were very high.

The increasing success of minority populations in achieving 'community control' of local schools has, as yet, not demonstrated any significant improvements. Big city schools continue to be the focal for strife, riots, strikes, racial incidents and vandalism. Teachers complain of increasing difficulty in maintaining order. School administrators and teachers opt for early retirement in the face of seemingly insurmountable problems.

Public transportation, the circulatory system that built the inner city and remains indispensible to the life of the large ones, is suffering from financial problems that frustrate efforts to modernize and rationalize their operations. Buses and trolley-cars are victims of the traffic congestion caused by private automobiles that clog inner-city streets never designed for the automobile. Mass transportation improvements that command the highest priorities are those designed to carry outer-city residents to and from inner-city business centres. Though intra-city transit riders remain numerous, they lack political weight at the federal level, the only effective source of funds for transportation.

The current concern with pollution of air and water places heavy burdens on inner cities to upgrade disposal practices to meet the exceptionally high standards required for dense population areas. The growing public awareness of ugliness and dirt reflect badly on American inner cities with a tradition of scandalously unkempt 'housekeeping', both on public streets and private property. The growing mass of impoverished inner-city dwellers consider a high priority public concern with these matters to be almost a mockery when they lack essentials for living with minimum convenience and comfort. The deterioration of the inner city's environmental conditions and street level appearance is a physical reflection of its growing social disorganization.

The inner city's ability to cope with the problems that threaten to overwhelm it is severely constrained by its

limited resources; specifically, revenues to meet municipal budgets that grow in proportion to the concentration
of poor people within its borders. Education, health,
welfare, housing and public transportation are municipal
services that increase in cost in direct ratio to the number of inhabitants generally, but especially in ratio to
low-income residents. The burden placed upon inner-
city government by the accumulation of the disadvantaged, with all their attendant problems, comes at a
time when the inner city's tax base is eroded by outer
city competition for industrial and commercial ratables
and luxury apartment houses.

Asked whether big cities are really on the verge of
bankruptcy, public finance economist, Dr Dick Netzer,
answered, 'Yes, you could say that — if you mean they
have run out of money to finance services that people
consider essential. That, of course, is different than
bankruptcy in the legal sense. Very few cities, even in
the depths of the depression in the 1930s, defaulted
on the debts they owed bondholders. But now, for the
first time in many years, cities are finding they can
keep going only by making large-scale reductions in
personnel — and that means cutting services. Netzer's
prescription for the financial ills of inner city governments is massive infusion of funds for health, education, welfare, housing and transportation.[70] The
rationale for such expenditures from the US Treasury
tends to be shifting from past emphasis upon the inner
cities' vital importance to the welfare of a nation, to
current emphasis upon the role of the inner cities as
habitat for the nation's disadvantaged — the poor, the
black, the elderly, the addicted — and their claim
upon the national revenues as keepers of the nation's
unwanted people.

6. The struggle for power and resources in the inner city

The civil disorders that swept through the major cities
of the United States between 1964 and 1968 marked
a turning point in racial and class relations in urban
society. Blacks emerged as a power-conscious political
block, no longer content to assert legal arguments for
individual equality, but organized to demand a share
of power as the leverage for access to resources to
improve living standards. The emergence of black
power consciousness, triggered the same aspirations
among other disadvantaged groups; Puerto Ricans,
Chicanos, Indians and, lately, the inner city 'white
ethnics', i.e., Italian, Polish and other immigrants
and their descendants who continue to live in inner
city enclaves largely because they cannot afford to

join their more affluent compatriots who have migrated to the outer city.

The changed mood of the inner city was noted by the
Commission on the Cities in the 1970s: 'But if material conditions in those ghettos, *barrios,* and white
ethnic working-class neighbourhoods that we visited
in the course of preparing this report are a cause for
much discouragement, the state of mind on the
streets is a cause for some hope. People are angry.
Perhaps they are angrier, even, then they were four
years ago. But their anger no longer seems to be the
helpless kind that can express itself only by smashing
and burning. We heard only a little talk of burning.
'The most disturbing point most of those we spoke
with made was that they had no faith at all in the
system — the government and the private wielders
of power — as a protector or a provider. This dis-
enchantment has plunged many into cynicism or
apathy or despair. But in others it has inspired a new
tough pride, self-confidence, and determination. Every
place we visited we found at least a hard-headed cadre
who knew that the people will have to rely on themselves for much of whatever they get — on their own
intelligence and courage, their own imagination and
ingenuity, their own patience and resolution and rage.
We found an attitude on the streets that people will
receive from the system only what they have the
cleverness or strength to obtain. We found people
banding together, speaking the language of brotherhood, and reaching for the levels of power.'[71]

The powerful motor force driving the new alignment
of powers in the inner city, however, is not a vague
'language of brotherhood', but rather the heightened
race-consciousness, pride and militancy of blacks.
It were as if the white man's magic of chicanery and
wiles, alternating with resort to brutality as the occasion required, had suddenly lost its hold upon the
minds of American blacks. Self-hatred has been replaced by hatred for the oppressor, identified, with
increasing exposure of detail, as the white-dominated institutions that conspired for over three centuries to both exploit and exclude blacks in a thousand
ways, large and small. The existence of a conscious,
outraged and militant population of formidable proportions in the inner cities of the United States,
moving toward majority status in a number of the
largest, is a social and political reality of overwhelming
importance, not only to the inner cities, or their outer
rings, but to the nation as a whole.

Few whites have assimilated the significance of the
new level of consciousness achieved by the blacks'
struggle for status in American society. Whites still

read 'equality' in constitutional terms of 'equal protection of the law,' when blacks see it with simple and
majestic logic as closing the gap between the races in
every facet of American society; income, wealth,
education, occupations, ownership, public office,
corporate control, health, housing, mobility, communications, choice and self-determination as to culture
and life styles. Well-intentioned whites fail to realize
that the gap can never be closed by increasing the
crumbs from the white man's table in proportion to
his growing affluence. The black man wants no less
than to sit at the table as an equal. The black man's
struggle for equality has, therefore, only begun. The
overwhelming significance of this realization for the
inner city is that it is destined to serve the blacks of
urban America as crucible for forging the weapons
of power and as bastion from which they can be wield-
ed. This process is already under way. The future of
the inner city will largely be determined by the
black's struggle for equality as they now define it. Its
outcome will decide more than the fate of the inner
city; it will decisively affect the outer city, and, consequently, the future of American society.

The outcome is still unclear. American society is no
less racist than when so described by the Kerner
Commission five years ago. The massive study of
employment practices affecting race by Professor
Orley Ashenfelter, based on employers' returns covering some 26 million workers, concluded that 'it was
also shown, however, that relative educational attainment could explain no more than one-third of the
difference between the occupational positions of
Negroes and Anglos.'[72] Two-thirds of the difference is
explained by racial discrimination. Closing the education gap, therefore, does not close the occupational
and income gaps. In 1969, the median income of
Negroes with four years of high school was $6,192,
while that of whites with only one to three years was
$7,812.[73]

To the extent that blacks make progress in narrowing
the gap between the races, whites somewhere will feel
the consequences; preferential hiring, 'quotas',
'busing' for quality education for blacks, subsidized
housing outside the ghetto, open enrollment, black-
owned business opened with federally-underwritten
loans, increased taxes for increased health and welfare
services, black teachers and school administrators,
patronage for black politicians, etc. The conflict
dramatized by white resistance to public housing in
Forest Hills and by white votes for George Wallace's
opposition to busing signalizes the stiffening of white
resistance to closing the gap at their expense. Since

it cannot be closed at anyone else's expense, it becomes a struggle to 'keep the black in his place.' Spanish-speaking or other disadvantaged minorities, not to speak of white ethnics, show no readiness to accommodate to the blacks' assertion of power. Each group seeks to hold and possibly expand its access to political power, employment, housing and community facilities, especially schools. The first weapons to be forged in this crucible by the blacks will be the political skills necessary to make the accommodations required for coalition-building when one has less than complete power. With 40% of black teenagers out of school and out of work, and police harrassment unchanged, there are bound to be developments beyond the control of any politically-conscious leadership, regardless of skill. With liberation from the white man's psychic domination has come the contempt for whites and their institutions, which serves many young blacks as moral sanction for private restitution of wealth. The alienated and embittered black youth that gave rise to the Black Panthers and urban guerilas, typified by Rap Brown, will loom large as a factor in shaping the future of inner cities.

7. Some prospects for the inner city

In a brilliantly perceptive inquiry as to the fate of inner city as long ago as 1942, José Luis Sert asked *Can Our Cities Survive?*[74] The failure to make the city livable Sert declared thirty years ago, causes people 'to abandon their over-crowding neighbourhoods for a "quiet home" in remote suburbs, undeterred by hours of uncomfortable travel back and forth. Industry, too, moves out — to cheaper land, to regions of lower taxes, to convenient sites on rail sidings or side roads. *The city is breaking up.* Such dispersion of great cities know neither control nor planning. It is provoked by urban chaos itself, and is facilitated by modern means of transportation.' Sert's question can be framed with data and insights not available to him, even if it cannot be answered definitively. The data and insights contained in the foregoing pages seem to suggest that, akin to Netzer's observation that cities do not go bankrupt literally, cities do not simply die and vanish. The inner city is likely to survive for this historical epoch, but with vastly changed functions, and, if form follows function, then with changed form also.

Firstly, it will continue to exploit the advantages of centrality, even if only to hold a bedrock residue of those functions that pay a heavy penalty in efficiency if located peripherally: central banks, utilities, information media, communications, governmental administra-

tion, highly specialized services and top-quality arts. Secondly, it will have advantages in holding labour-intensive, low-productivity, low-earning, manufacturing industries by virtue of a resident, low-wage labour force that is subsidized by supplementary welfare, food stamps, public transportation, public housing, and socialized medicine. It is quite possible that these establishments will be duplicated in outer city by others who will produce a more standardized product, with greater capital investment in equipment for a more durable and larger market. The point being made here is that a level and type of manufacturing activity might survive in an inner city uniquely adapted to its advantages, but not in direct competition with establishments in the same or similar industrial category located in the outer city. Thirdly, it will function as the urban reservation for the poor, the minorities, the social-problem families and individuals. Here American society will house and feed its 'misfits'; those who do not measure up to the white, middle-class standard of success. The nation will pour billions into the maintenance of inner cities. It will pay for welfare, health, education, 'made work', transportation, housing, recreation, entertainment, policing, and an army of ethnic retainers serving as a colonial elite and bureaucratic liaison between white society and the inner city.
Outer city and inner city will live side by side, each with its set of functions. Those of outer city will express traditional society; private enterprise, corporate dominance, tax revenue producing, home-owning, white, middle-class inhabitants. Those of inner city will express western compromise between the economic realities of post-industrial society in a free enterprise, non-planning, pluralist, individualist nation and the Christian ethic which rejects euthanasia or genocide of an unneeded and unwanted population as solutions.

What holds our metropolitan society together? What is the reality beneath the oft-repeated assurances that inner and outer cities are really one; that they are interdependent; that they cannot survive if parted? Is it the daily movement of commuters from one to the other? This would appear to be a slender link since they hold only a small percentage of the total jobs in a metropolitan area (about 8% of the New York Regions's eight million jobs).
Is such a racially, socially and economically separated metropolitan region workable? Its workability is not conceivable within a democratic society. But democracy itself might be the victim of the effort to *make it work*. Washington, DC is both first major US city with

a black majority and the first American city whose residents have been deprived by a 'no knock law' of the ancient Anglo-Saxon sanctity of the home from search without warrant. The police state erected over the inner city would eventually engulf the nation. Inner city as a reservation for the poor and the racial minorities would be an invitation to civil war. Defiance and rebellion by its inhabitants could lead to Attica on a massive scale. A glimpse of such a nightmare is presented in the possible fate of inner city described in the Report of the Commission on the Causes and Prevention of Violence.

'Between the unsafe, deteriorating central city on the one hand and the network of safe, prosperous areas and sanitized corridors on the other, there will be, not unnaturally, intensifying hatred and deepening division. Violence will increase further, and the defensive response of the affluent will become still more elaborate.'[75]

How elaborate they are becoming can be seen from this prototype outer city fortress:

'One new subdivision under construction outside Washington, DC, offers maximum security for all residents. The sixty-seven high-cost residences in this 167-acre project will be individually guarded by electronic alarms and closed-circuit television units. The entire development will be surrounded by two fences, broken for entry at only two points, both with guardhouses. Residents will be telephoned to approve visitors. The two miles of fencing will be surveyed by a closed-circuit television system and fortified by hidden electronic sensors. All residents will carry special credentials for identification.'[76]

Responding to these grim forebodings, one industrialist, the chairman of the National Urban Coalition, Sol M Linowitz, warned Americans: 'One thing is clear: Our society cannot indefinitely endure the tensions created by a nation half ghetto and half split-level. As we look about us and see the chaos in city after city, as we listen to the voices of frustration and anger and despair coming from the citizens who are trapped in those cities, as we read the bleak statistics of our failure to right the wrong of racism, there is danger that the United States may be on the verge of tearing itself apart.'[77]
Though this warning is based on chilling realism, it should not be misread as prophecy of the inevitable. Massive infusion of money into the inner cities, especially a score or more of the largest, can buy

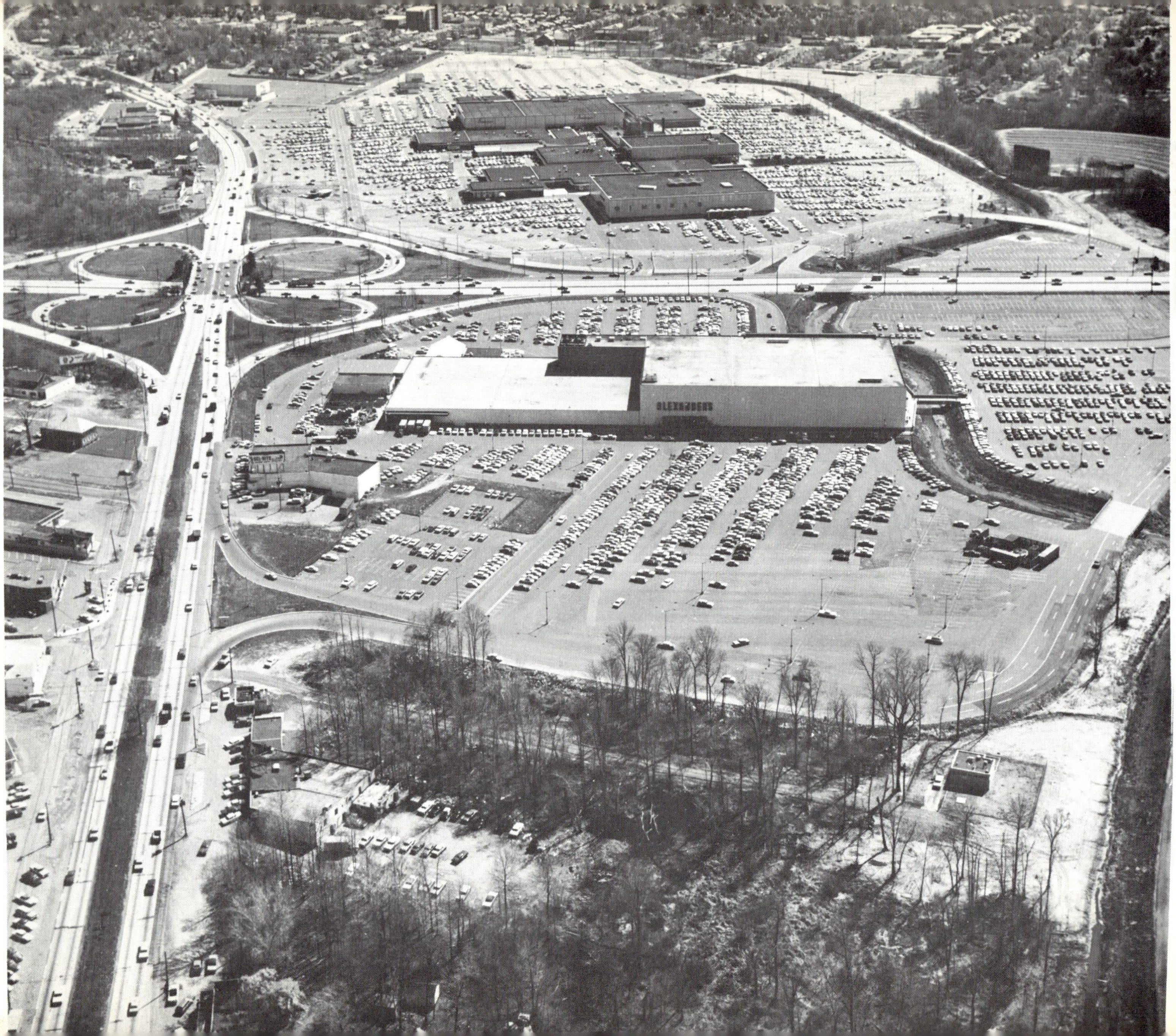

Above: View across parking lots from Alexander's to Gimbels, in Paramus, New Jersey.

Left: A cloverleaf in Paramus, New Jersey, Alexander's in foreground, and behind it the Garden State Plaza with Gimbels and Bambergers and over a hundred smaller shops. A spread-out automobile world.

Above right: Sign on wall of Alexander's department store, Paramus branch, under construction in the early 1960s. As white middle-income families moved from cities to suburbs, major shopping and services followed.

Right: Printing plant of Wall Street Journal in lower Middlesex County, New Jersey. As industry moves out of the cities, plants seeking more space are encouraged to settle in municipalities seeking tax ratables that send no children to school.

time by assuaging the discontent and placating the outrage of selected strata of critically-placed inhabitants of inner cities. If one or two decades of such bought time are used constructively by society to reverse the trends toward an extreme dichotomy between inner and outer cities, these two forms of urban settlement might again become complementary and each would eventually be inhibitated by those who were there by free choice based on life-style preferences, rather than fears and constraints that make for concentrations of racial, social and economic homogeneity. But such reduction of extreme differences between inner and outer populations involves, of necessity, a levelling down of peaks and levelling up of valleys on the metropolitan area's social terrain. This assumes wisdom and far-sightedness on the part of the advantaged that has been rare in the history of human affairs.

Notes:
1 The relationship of function to space is a source of great difficulty, not only in nomenclature, but in substantive analysis of metropolitan phenomena. This is illustrated clearly in Gans' critique of Wirth's seminal, and now classic,'Urbanism as a way of life'. (Gans: 'Urbanism and Suburbanism as Ways of Life: A re-evaluation of Definitions, in *Neighborhood, City and Metropolis,* eds. Robert Gutman and David Popenow, New York, 1970). Melvin M Webber's challenging view of urban functions freed from traditional territorial concepts is also illustrative of the problems involved. Donald L Foley provides insights into the nature of the problem in his effort to integrate function and space. See Melvin M Webber, Donald L Foley, et al, *Explorations Into Urban Structure.* Philadelphia, 1967. Hans Blumenfeld distinguishes the 'modern city'

Far left, above: The Ford Assembly Plant, which moved from Edgewater, New Jersey (a ferry's ride away from Harlem) to Mahwah, New Jersey, 30 miles out in Bergen County, in 1955.

Left, above: Workers coming out of the Ford Plant in Mahwah, New Jersey. A third of them (mostly blacks and Puerto Ricans) still live in the older cities of the Regions's core, and travel a long distance to work by car, often in car pools.

Left: Even offices are moving out of old city downtowns onto suburban campuses, including a substantial number of corporate headquarters like these of Allied Chemical in Morris Township, New Jersey.

from the 'modern metropolis' by pointing out that the urban form has 'undergone a qualitative change, so it is no longer merely a larger version of the traditional city but a new and different form of human settlement.' He notes, in the same essay, that 'the emergence of a basically new form of human settlement is an extremely rare event in the history of mankind.' *The Modern Metropolis: Its Origins, Growth, Characteristics and Planning;* pp. 61-2, MIT Press, Cambridge and London, 1967.
2 Regional Plan Association, *Linking Skills, Jobs and Housing in the New York Urban Region.* New York, March 1972. Mimeographed. This report quantifies the highly complex factors of a mismatch of skills available in the labour force and the skills required in the labour market as well as the mismatch in location of jobs and labour force between inner and outer cities. In RPA's computation, the outer city includes such large satellite cities as Newark, Jersey City, Paterson, Bridgeport and New Haven, and many lesser ones.
3 Graham Taylor's study (*Satellite Cities,* New York, 1915) focused on the emergence of what were mainly 'company towns'; large-scale manufacturing enterprises, often involved in industrial processes that constituted nuisances in high density areas of cities, which were located along major railways several miles beyond the city limits. Harlan Douglas (*The Suburban Trend,* New York, 1925) sought to describe employing suburbs, as distinguished from residential ones. A summary of more recent studies is contained in Schnorre, 'Urban Form: The Case of the Metropolitan Community', reprinted in *Neighborhood, City and Metropolis,* op. cit. Satellite towns vary in their origins and main characteristics. In New England, many satellite towns were founded at the site of water power in the early decades of the industrial revolution. The location of others was influenced by canals and other inland waterways. Many were the commercial centres of farming areas.
4 Regional Plan Association, *The Second Regional Plan: A Draft for Discussion,* p. 49, New York, 1968).
5 Data from the 1970 Census on minorities other than Negroes is not available for the nation as a whole at this time of writing. However, the Puerto Rican population of New York City increased from 602,000 in 1960 to 1,051,200 in 1970. United States Commission on Civil Rights, *Demographic, Social and Economic Characteristics of New York City and the New York Metropolitan Area,* p. 4, (Washington, DC, February, 1972. Mimeographed).
6 Max Weber, *The City,* New York, 1962.

7 Lewis Mumford, *The City in History,* New York, 1961.
8 The emergence of the metropolitan area and the division of functions between inner and outer cities was foreseen and described with remarkable accuracy by H G Wells some seventy years ago. 'Enough has been said to demonstrate that old "town" and "city" will be, in truth, terms as obsolete as "mail coach". For these new areas that will grow out of them we want a term, and the administrative "urban district" presents itself with a convenient air of suggestion. We may for our present purposes call these coming town provinces "urban regions."' 'The Probable Diffusion of Great Cities', a chapter in Wells' *Anticipations of the Reaction of Mechanical and Scientific Progress Upon Human Life and Thought,* p. 67, New York and London, 1902. His views might have been influenced by that first great urbanologist, Charles Booth, a contemporary of Wells and a fellow-Londoner. See Harold Pfautz, ed. *Charles Booth on the City: Physical Pattern and Social Structure,* Chicago, 1967.
9 A letter, written in cuneiform on a clay tablet, addressed to King Cyrus of Persia in 539 B C by an early suburbanite extols the virtues of that life style. 'Our property seems to me the most beautiful in the world. It is so close to Babylon that we enjoy all the advantages of the city, and yet when we come home we are away from all the noise and dust.' Ivar Lissner, *The Living Past: 7,000 Years of Civilization,* p. 44, New York, 1957.
10 'A different, more subtle structural change has been the transformation of the economy into a "postindustrial" society. The weight of the economy has shifted from the product sector to services; more importantly, the sources of innovation are becoming lodged in the intellectual institutions, principally the universities and research organizations, rather than in the older, industrial corporations.' Daniel Bell, 'The Year 2000 — The Trajectory of an Idea', *Daedulus,* Journal of the American Academy of Arts and Sciences, Summer, 1967, pp. 643-644. Also see Bell's 'The Post-Industrial Society', Eli Ginzberg, ed. *Technology and Social Change,* pp. 44-59, New York: 1964.
11 'The Metropolitan Community of Today is a way of life, one might even say a civilization. It is the city "writ large".' John C. Bollens and Henry J Schmandt, *The Metropolis: Its People, Politics, and Economic Life,* p. 57, New York, 1965.
12 George Romney, Secretary, U S Department of Housing and Urban Development, is currently attempting to foster inner/outer co-operation in urban programmes by popularizing the term 'Real City'

(capitalization his). 'I apply that term to our metropolitan areas — where more highly populated cities have spilled over their legal boundaries and spread their people beyond into the surrounding countryside.' Address to the Metropolitan Area Planning Council's Regional Growth Conference, Boston, January 28, 1972.

13 Gans, in his critique of Wirth (see Note 1), divides the central city into and 'inner city' and an 'outer city'. He contends that Wirth's description of urbanism as a way of life is based essentially on characteristics identified with the inner city. Gans sees the 'way of life' of his 'outer city', i.e. residential neighbourhoods within the central city, as much closer to the way of life of the 'suburbs'. Gans' observations are valid. Developmental trends, however, are diminishing the significance of his 'outer city' as the characteristics of Wirth's 'inner city' encompass so much of the rest as to become the functional and social format of the entire central city. (There are, of course, wide variations in different cities because of varying patterns of municipal boundary law as they affect annexation.) Gans sees his 'outer city' and 'suburbs' as essentially the same in function because he sees them as residential appendages of his 'inner city', failing to assess their respective roles as employment locations. His 'suburbs' (my 'outer city') have become more self-sufficient in terms of a balance between resident labour force and local employment than is the case with his 'outer city'. The latter is far more dependent for employment upon the core of the central city and continues in a symbiotic relationship to it to an extent that is no longer true of areas beyond the city limits.

14 See Mumford's 'Brief Outline of Hell' in his *The Culture of Cities,* New York, 1938. Also see his chapters on 'Suburbia — and Beyond' and 'The Myth of Megalopolis' in *The City in History,* New York, 1961.

15 For a summary of theories of urban land development relating to the factor of centrality see F Stuart Chapin, *Urban Land Use Planning,* New York, 1957. Included are descriptions of salient contributions by Homer Hoyt, Ernest W Burgess, Walter Firey, R D McKenzie and other scholars prominent in this field. Omitted is reference to Robert M Haig and Leo Grebler, two giants whose studies provided new insights that led to the formulation of laws of urban land development and, consequently, a measure of predictability. Robert M Haig, *Major Economic Factors in Metropolitan Growth and Arrangement,* pp. 19-43, New York: Regional Survey, Vol. I. Leo Grebler,

Housing Market Behaviour in a Declining Area, New York, 1952.

16 Walter Christaller, *Central Places in Southern Germany,* Englewood Cliffs, NJ, 1966. Originally published in 1933. Also: Donald J Rogue, *The Structure of the Metropolitan Community,* Ann Arbor, 1949.

17 Mumford, *The City in History,* op. cit., pp. 446-481. Also see Blake McKelvey, *The Urbanization of America, 1860-1915,* pp. 35-72, New Brunswick, NJ, 1963.

18 Sam Bass Warner, Jr, *Streetcar Suburbs: The Process of Growth in Boston, 1870-1900,* Cambridge, Mass., 1962.

19 Haig, op. cit., pp. 33-40.

20 Published in nine volumes, with a technical supplement by Harvard University, Cambridge, Mass. during 1959 and 1960.

21 Raymond Vernon, *Metropolis 1985,* Cambridge, Mass., 1960.

22 *Manpower Report of the President,* pp. 89-90, Transmitted to the Congress, April 1971, Washington, DC.

23 *Regional Labour Statistics Bulletin,* Number 30, December 1971. US Department of Labor

24 New York Urban Coalition, *The Working Poor: The Problem of Low-Wage Workers in New York City,* New York, September 1970.

25 Vernon, op. cit., p. 126.

26 Ibid., p. 124.

27 Regional Plan Association, pp. 116-117, *The Region's Growth,* New York, 1967.

28 'The Office Boom Jolts the Planners', *Business Week,* January 23, 1971. Also: 'The State of the New York Urban Region', address by Crawford to 42nd Anniversary Dinner of Regional Plan Association, February 16, 1971.

29 Jack W. Carlson, Benjamin G. Dvais, and Robert Raynsford, *Necessary Manpower Adjustments in the United States Economy During the 1970s.* Washington, September, 1970. Mimeographed.

30 Vernon's term. *The Changing Economic Function of the Central City,* p. 56, New York, 1959.

31 Tri-State Transportation Commission, p.19, *Measure of a Region,* New York, 1967.

32 Economic Consultants Organization, Inc., *The White Collar Labor Market in Westchester County, 1971-75,* p. 7, White Plains, NY, 1970.

33 Ken Patton, New York City's Economic Development Administrator, was quoted in *The New York Times* of February 2, 1969, following his negotiations with officers of 12 companies that were 'reviewing'

their office location in New York, 'that the complaints he heard from chief executives were highly personal — they had no desire to live in the city and are frustrated with commuting by railroad or bus from New York New Jersey and Connecticut suburbs. When these executives talk to me they said 'I've had it with the cocktail parties and the opera, I don't need it any more'. In a feature article in *The New York Times* of November, 28, 1971, Melvin Mandell writes that 'observer have long noted that the new sites chosen by firms very frequently turn out to be just a few miles from where the chief executive has his home.'

34 op. cit.

35 'The Roadblocks in the Trek to Suburbia', *Business Week,* April 17, 1971, p. 60.

36 *The New York Times,* April 28, 1971.

37 *The New York Times,* Dec. 6, 1970.

38 Dr George H Brown, Director, Bureau of the Census, US Department of Commerce, Statement to US Commission on Civil Rights, Washington, DC, June 14, 1971. Table 6.

39 Negroes represented 4.5% of outer city population in 1970. Ibid., p. 2.

40 Ibid., Table 6.

41 US Commission on Civil Rights, op. cit.

42 Regional Plan Association, *Linking Skills,* op. cit., p. 9.

43 Oscar Handlin's, *The Newcomers — Negroes and Puerto Ricans in a Changing Metropolis,* Cambridge, Mass., 1959, suffers from the author's persistence in trying to evaluate racial minorities with concepts drawn from the acculturation experience of European immigrants. Morton Grodzins, *The Metropolitan Area as a Racial Problem,* Pittsburgh, 1958, reveals an incomparably superior comprehension of race in the American urban setting.

44 Louis Wirth, 'Urbanism as a Way of Life', *Neighborhood, City and Metropolis,* op. cit.

45 The suburbanization of Jews in some cities has been so extensive that one writer refers to Cleveland as the 'city without Jews'.

46 The significance of this narrowing of the gap has been exaggerated by some urbanologists, such as Daniel P Moynihan ('The Schism in Black America', *The Public Interest,* Number 27, Spring 1972). Commenting on this phenomenon, a Bureau of the Census study observes that 'Negro families whose incomes about equalled that of whites comprised a relatively small proportion of all Negro families in the United States . . . An important part of the explanation of the narrowing gap between white and Negro

incomes is the working wife . . . Young Negro families in which only the husband worked were making only about three-fourths as much money as comparable white families in both 1959 and 1970.' ('Differences Between Incomes of White and Negro Families by Work Experience of Wife and Region: 1970, 1969, and 1959.' Bureau of the Census, US Department of Commerce, Current Population Reports, Series P. 23, No. 39, December, 1971).

47 *The Poor in 1970: A Chartbook,* pp. 10 and 42, Office of Planning, Research, and Evaluation, Office of Economic Opportunity, Washington, DC.

48 Regional Plan Association, *Linking Skills,* etc. op. cit., pp. 2-5.

49 'More than four out of every ten teenagers reported no work experience during the year preceding the survey interview.' 'Poverty Area Profiles', p. 7, Urban Studies Series, No. 13, Oct., 1969, US Dept. of Labor.

50 Regional Plan Association, *The Region's Growth,* op. cit., p. 110.

51 'Report on National Growth 1972' p. 22, Report of the President to the Congress of the United States, February 1972.

52 *The New York Times* report on April 20, 1972 quoting Herbert Bienstock, director of the Middle Atlantic Regional Office, Bureau of Labor Statistics, US Department of Labor. Mr Bienstock corrected preliminary figures in an earlier release (December 1971) which listed New York City's loss during 1970 and 1971 as 106,000. According to the earlier rèport, 'New York City, with 56% of the area's jobs, accounted for better than 80% — 72,000 out of 84,000 — of the area's job cutbacks in 1971.' Regional Labor Statistics Bulletin, op. cit., No. 30, December 1971.

53 Sar A Levitan and Robert Taggart III, Background Paper in *The Job Crisis for Black Youth,* pp. 29-30, The Twentieth Century Fund Task Force on Employment Problems of Black Youth, New York, 1971.

54 Bureau of Labor Statistics, The Employment Problems of Older Workers, Bulletin 1721, Washington, DC, 1971.

55 *Manpower Report of the President 1970,* op. cit., p. 87.

56 Poverty Area Profiles, op. cit., pp.5-6

57 April 10, 1972.

58 *The New York Times,* February 2, 1972.

59 In the Bureau of Labor Statistics study of New York poverty areas (Bedford-Stuyvesant, Central Harlem, East Harlem, South Bronx) it found 'that more than four out of every ten households were headed by women — nearly half the Negro and one-third of the white and Puerto Rican households had female heads.' *Poverty Area Profiles,* op. cit., p. 7.

60 Commission on the Cities in the '70s, *The State of the Cities,* p. 90, New York, 1972. The Commission was assembled by the National Urban Coalition. Senator Fred M Harris and Mayor John V Lindsay served as co-chairmen.

61 Ibid., p. 75-80.

62 National Commission on Causes and Prevention of Violence, as given in *The Social and Economic Status of Negroes in the United States,* p. 103, Bureau of the Census, US Department of Commerce, jointly with Bureau of Labor Statistics, US Department of Labor. Washington, DC, 1971.

63 *The New York Times,* December 10, 1969.

64 Ibid., December 6, 1970.

65 The Center for Community Change and The National Urban League, *The National Survey of Housing Abandonment,* New York, 1971.

66 *The Social and Economic Status of Negroes,* op. cit., p. 91.

67 US Commission on Civil Rights, op. cit., p. 25.

68 US Commission on Civil Rights, *Home Ownership for Lower Income Families: A Report on the Racial and Ethnic Impact of the Section 235 Program,* pp. 33-39 et passim, Washington, DC, 1971.

69 January 2 and 13, 1972.

70 'Why Cities Are Going Broke'. *US News and World Report,* February 22, 1971.

71 *The State of the Cities,* op. cit., pp. 6-7.

72 Orley Ashenfelter, *Minority Employment Patterns,* 1966, Prepared under contract with W E Upjon Institute for Employment Research for US Equal Employment Opportunity Commission and the Office of Manpower Policy Evaluation and Research of the US Department of Labor, Washington, DC.

73 *The Social and Economic Status of Negroes,* op. cit., p. 34.

74 José Luis Sert and Congress Internationaux d'Architecture Moderne, *Can Our Cities Survive?* Cambridge, 1942.

75 *To Establish Justice, to Insure Domestic Tranquility.* Final Report, Washington Superintendent of Documents, US Government Printing Office, 1969.

76 Robert Gold, 'Urban Violence and Contemporary Defensive Cities', p. 152, *Journal of the American Institute of Planners,* May 1970.

77 *The State of the Cities,* op. cit. Foreword.

Ernest Erber's paper on *The Inner City in the Post-Industrial Era* is part of a larger work to be published in the winter of 1974-75, tentatively titled 'The New Racial Separation—The Metropolitan Jobs and Housing Mismatch and Its Racial Implication'. The work is an outgrowth of a study sponsored by the National Committee Against Discrimination in Housing and funded by the Carnegie Corporation of New York, a foundation.

NEW INFLUENCES ON PERSIAN CITIES

A CASE STUDY OF KERMAN, IRAN

RAY A FRIEDEN & BRUCE D MANN

Change in Iranian cities is no longer slow and moderate. New and international technological forces, similar to those affecting cities all over the world, require almost instant responses, and most of the larger cities in Iran are now independent and rich enough to respond to these demands. When the response to change was a slow and incremental process, new developments could easily be integrated within the existing city structure. When the process of change involves rapid and large-scale decisions, it becomes increasingly more difficult to provide for new development within the context of the historical city.

The historical element

In her early history the main reasons for urbanization in Iran were economic. Cities gradually became production and market centres, trading regionally and internationally.

The transportation technology of the time, the human being and the beast of burden, is the key to understanding the physical development of these cities. International and regional trade was carried on by camel caravans. To participate in trade meant that the city had to provide facilities for receiving these animals, housing their owners, and storing their goods. The form developed was the *caravansarai*. Traders and shops were located in or around the *caravansarais,* and eventually this developed into a bazaar.

The bazaar became the centre of the city. The inhabitants of the city were dependent on the bazaar for almost all their needs. This meant that virtually every house in the city had to have pedestrian access to the bazaar. The result was a compact residential area surrounding the bazaar and served by a pedestrian circulation system, the *kutchée*.

The *kutchée* system was more than just a circulation system. *Kutchées* were not built very wide, for they needed only to cope with the traffic of humans and

sometimes animals. Because of this the high walls bounding the *kutchée* (defining the house beside the *kutchée)* provided shade. Thus, even for the hottest part of the day the *kutchée* was usable. Because of this shade and the lack of other open spaces nearby, the *kutchée* became a recreation space for children, and a social space, mainly for women (who could not go to teahouses or loiter in the bazaar).

The old Persian city, then, was a compact, single nucleus city. The bazaar was the nucleus surrounded by housing, usually in a circular fashion. Because of the transportation technology available the city retained a completely human scale. This type of urban settlement has two serious shortcomings. The first disadvantage can be called the growth radius. It would be impractical for the city to grow much larger than a walking distance radius from the centre. The second disadvantage is the relative inflexibility of the transportation/circulation system.

The development of vehicular traffic

The growth radius and inflexibility of the *kutchée* system are the traditional infrastructure with which the new technologies come into conflict. For example, it is assumed that every household in the city will shortly own a car and that access needs must be honoured. Furthermore with better and cheaper vehicular access the economic base of cities as regional and national production centres will grow rapidly. As a result modern city planning in Iran has endeavoured to overcome the disadvantages of the traditional infrastructure by widening the *kutchées,* slashing new streets through the old city for access and breaking the growth radius of the pedestrian circulation system.

The irrationality of planning Iranian cities totally by vehicular criteria is that cities are lived in by people, not cars. Giving vehiclular access to older sections of cities destroys the existing pedestrian circulation system, the *kutchée* recreational areas, the general public open spaces, and impinges on a long-established social system.

Moreover a vehicular system in the old cities is destructive and expensive. It is destructive in two senses. First, to convert a pedestrian *kutchée* system into a vehicular system requires widening the *kutchées*. This means that house owners facing the *kutchée* must destroy their existing walls and set them back closer to their homes. Generally, after the *kutchée* has been sufficiently widened for vehicular access, the land values of the lots bordering the *kutchée* increase. Then the land owners must pay the city an increased tax

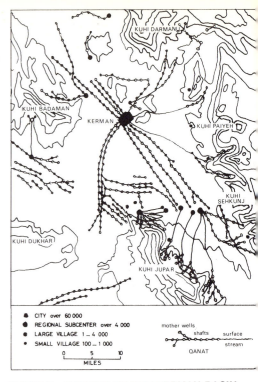

KERMAN - QANATS OF THE KERMAN BASIN
from CITY AND VILLAGE IN IRAN by PAUL WARD ENGLISH (19

based on the new land value. In many cases this results in the owner selling the land to a developer who then constructs a multi-story apartment building. A multi-story dwelling unit destroys one of the basic needs in Persian housing, privacy. This can, and usually does, become a cycle, leaving behind the poor who cannot afford to move and the apartment dwellers, a relatively transient group in Iranian society. It is difficult to re-establish the sense of neighbourhood that before was so important to the inhabitants of the area.

The vehicular system is also destructive in the sense that it requires more of the area's resources than the

*Right: Multi-level caravansarai in Tabriz bazaar —
now used for manufacturing.*

46

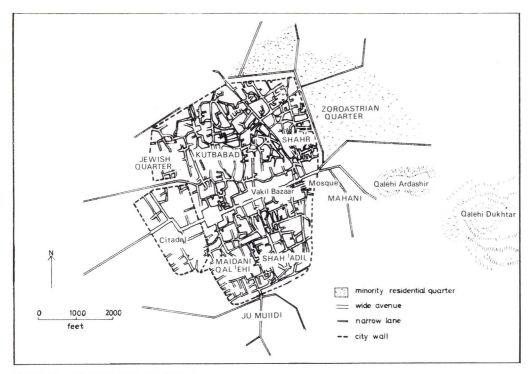

KERMAN - NINETEENTH CENTURY
from CITY AND VILLAGE IN IRAN by PAUL WARD ENGLISH (1966)

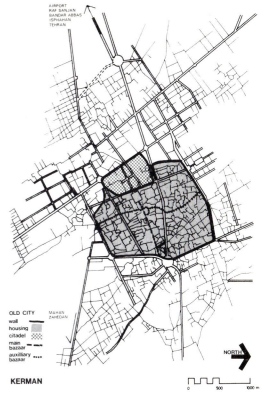

KERMAN

Far left: The continuous bazaar at Kerman — a view from the roof.

Left: A typical kutchée in Kerman. Note also the wind tower, used for relieving the extreme summer heat by gathering the breeze and bringing it into the house, usually over a pool of water.

existing pedestrian system. *Kutchées* must be widened; housing lots must, therefore, be smaller. Usually the widened *kutchée* must be paved; this reduces the number of options for the use of the city budget. Existing recreational and social spaces are eliminated; new spaces must be developed for these activities. Most importantly, an existing viable circulation system is replaced by one that is costly to maintain and in the long-run not viable.

Our reason for questioning the new planning is that it can only be a short-term solution. In fact the short-term may be very short indeed. As the experience of large cities not only in Europe and the United States but in developing countries demonstrates, the problems of servicing the private car (streets, parking, fuel and repair stations, etc.) can be enormous and, of course, increase as the numbers of cars increase.

The basic fallacy of the new planning is that once the city decides to provide an infrastructure for private automobile use it is then rational for individuals to purchase and use cars. This starts the cycle. As more and more people buy cars the city must continually expand the infrastructure to meet peak load demands. With cars people can live further from the centre of town. As the city spreads out, more people buy cars. The costs of the infrastructure and its maintenance increase. The cycle continues and the costs increase further.

The public cost of providing the infrastructure is just one part of the total cost of private car use. There are non-monetary costs of equal importance, as well as many indirect monetary costs which are paid by everyone but which benefit private car owners. Large numbers of cars in a city cause air and noise

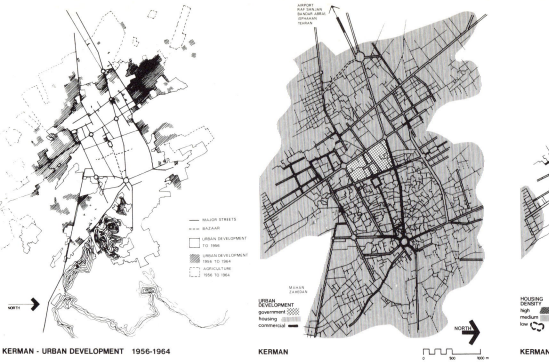

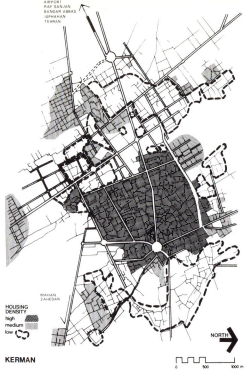

KERMAN - URBAN DEVELOPMENT 1956-1964

- —— MAJOR STREETS
- ----- BAZAAR
- ☐ URBAN DEVELOPMENT TO 1956
- ▨ URBAN DEVELOPMENT 1956 TO 1964
- ⫶ AGRICULTURE 1956 TO 1964

NORTH →

KERMAN

MAHAN
ZAHEDAN

URBAN
DEVELOPMENT
government ▨
housing ▥
commercial ▬

NORTH →

0 500 1000 m

KERMAN

MAHAN
ZAHEDAN

HOUSING
DENSITY
high ▦
medium ▥
low ⬭

NORTH →

0 500 1000 m

pollution problems. The costs for these are paid by everyone breathing dirty air and suffering high noise levels. People pay the costs of congestion by wasting their time sitting in traffic jams. There is also the problem of safety. This cost is paid in the form of human lives wasted.

In some countries the trend toward total vehicular systems is now being reversed. Large cities in Europe, for example, are trying to re-establish areas based on the needs of the pedestrian and to restrict the use of the automobile. The problem is now to transform this historical Iranian model in order to incorporate the current needs for growth and expansion and yet maintain the advantages of the historical city.

A planning alternative

Our recommendations are based on three main considerations. First the traditional neighbourhoods of Persian cities, developed over a long period of time,

remain extremely relevant to present cities and there is little reason why they cannot continue to form the basis for residential development in the future.
Second, the bazaar, as a social, physical and economic entity, remains a viable focus for cities, and with the traditional residential areas is capable of forming a basis for Persian city-centres in the future.
Finally, these two elements, the bazaar-city centre and the residential neighbourhoods must be closely linked by a public transportation and communication system which provides the growing city with the traditional proximity patterns. In the old cities the only form of transportation was pedestrian and most citizens had roughly the same degree of access to all parts of the city and their travel was free. The modern public transportation service should also offer free, comfortable and convenient service from any point in the city to any other.
Recognizing the fact that modern cities will continue to grow far beyond the limits of pedestrian travel as

they have already done, urban development must provide a motorized public transportation service to enable citizens to move freely through the city. The ownership and use of private vehicles cannot be excluded, but the city must provide, as an alternative, an efficient system of mass transit.
Our planning alternative is based on pedestrian areas (five to ten minutes' walking radius) linked together by this public transport service.
There are three kinds of areas. The first is a single city centre, served by the transportation service and directly linked to all other areas by bus every five to seven minutes. Secondly, neighbourhoods around this centre are primarily pedestrian and contain a smaller centre for convenience goods and services. Each centre is connected by bus to all other neighbourhood centres and to the city centre. Third are also ex-urban areas reserved for large-scale uses, such as warehouses and production processes incompatible with residential environments.

The residential neighbourhoods designed for pedestrians (as opposed to the automobile) are perhaps the most radical departure from current Iranian planning practices.

The density of these neighbourhoods is roughly that of traditional Persian housing. This density is required in order to have a public transportation service that is truly efficient. The efficiency of such a service is inversely proportional to the number of stops it must serve. Planning should strive to minimize the number of stops (while serving the same size of population). This goal can only be realized if people are clustered together in the vicinity of well-defined poles or centres which can then be served by buses.

Iranians have, over long centuries, developed housing and neighbourhood types of high densities which are perfectly adapted to the Persian style of life and the local conditions of climate, geography, etc. The housing system which has resulted from this development is the walled, inverted compound and the narrow pedestrian *kutchee*. It is this system which we are proposing for our planning alternative.

At the centre of the neighbourhood is the bus stop and the local shopping centre, a kind of *bazaarché* (small bazaar). This local centre serves all of the daily needs of the people. The existence of such a centre does not exclude the possibility of smaller concentrations of commercial facilities within the neighbourhood, but it does give a focus for these kinds of facilities and for the neighbourhood. Also in the centre are stores which do not serve daily requirements but which find it possible to operate successfully outside of the bazaar (city centre) due to the high concentration of residential facilities near the neighbourhood centre.

The neighbourhood centre is not restricted to commercial activities. It is open to any activity which wishes to locate there, subject of course to certain restrictions on the size of the centre itself. We would hope that many kinds of activities would locate there to avoid the high costs of the city centre and to take advantage of modern telecommunication links. Such a decentralization, especially of work places, will tend to make the public transportation service more effective by distributing peak period loads throughout the city. It will also make it possible for employees to live quite close to their jobs without giving up good homes.

The neighbourhood centres are also good locations for a variety of public facilities, especially schools,

A view from above: typical housing in Kerman.

51

libraries, clinics, etc. Schools to high school level would be especially welcome here as the problems of sending children to nearby schools are far less than to schools scattered throughout the city. There is also a gain in safety, since children going to local schools would not be obliged to cross any major streets or compete with vehicles in any way.

While we have been talking as if the neighbourhoods are entirely pedestrian, such is not the case. Few existing *kutchées* are really too narrow for vehicles, although sharp corners in the high-walled *kutchées* can effectively prevent vehicles from entering every part of the *kutchée* network. Furthermore, vehicles are necessary, for the incapacitated, for emergencies, and the delivery of bulky or heavy objects. But vehicular use of *kutchées* should be restricted by law and by physical design. Residents of these areas are not prohibited from having cars, they are simply obliged to park them on the edge of the neighbourhood so that its real density of people can remain high.

Indeed, these neighbourhoods are not seen as having particularly well defined boundaries. Rather, we are simply giving a principle for urban development. People who want to walk and take advantage of the free bus service should be permitted to live close to bus stops and to facilities which obviate the necessity of a car. They should not be obliged to walk further than necessary because a neighbour is using several square metres of ground to park his car and because the city has used hundreds of square metres for larger streets to accommodate more cars, thus decreasing the net residential density of a neighbourhood. But as one gets farther from the centre, the desire for a car will increase and people should be permitted to own them. Housing densities in these neighbourhoods will be lower since space can be used for parking and streets.

The bazaar city centre is the other major part of our planning alternative. It is, like the other urban nodes, a pedestrian area permitting the concentration of a large number of facilities very close to bus stops. It must also be a complete centre, offering to every citizen all of those goods, services and facilities not available to him in his neighbourhood centre. It is well-connected to the rest of the city by direct bus routes to each centre so that travelling to the modern bazaar city centre will be as convenient tomorrow as it was fifty years ago.

The contents of this new city centre must, by necessity, be limited to those activities which deal primarily with people. These include retail sales, retail services, showrooms, offices of professionals, administrative offices which are responsible for contacts with the general public, hotels, restaurants, social and religious facilities, for example. Not permitted to locate in this area are those activities and facilities which do not deal with the general public. Warehouses and factories whose goods are not always sold directly to the public are to be located outside the city.

Administrative offices whose chief functions are internal as opposed to dealing with people should also not be located in the centre. Modern methods of administration together with modern telecommunications systems make such separation of functions possible. All activities requiring constant vehicular access should be outside the city centre. This should, in fact, become a basic zoning criterion. There must be no large-scale access for the delivery of goods, but only machine servicing facilities. A car sales office, for example, can be in the bazaar-centre, but its garaging repair department must be in the ex-urban service centre.

The centre is to be primarily a pedestrian area with vehicular paths to service the various activities. The vehicular system should be clearly subordinated and removed from the pedestrian system. Such clear separation permits greater efficiency in both systems. The pedestrian circulation system should take its cue from the bazaar. It should be spacious but not so large as to be overwhelming. It should be covered, well-ventilated and well-lit. It should be provided with good paving and should be cleaned regularly (and designed to make such cleaning easy). The system should include places to rest, for example, gardens or squares.

The vehicular service system should be designed to permit use by taxibar-type vehicles only and should be provided with numerous loading and holding areas. Wherever it crosses a pedestrian way, speed control devices should be installed to insure the safety of pedestrians.

The city centre is what ties all the parts together. All the traditional activities of the old city centre should be preserved there and an area for new functions should be provided. For most Iranian cities the core of the city centre will be the bazaar. This provides a vivid link for the city with its past. More importantly, using the bazaar takes advantage of an existing facility.

The main problem in developing the bazaar city centre complex is integrating the activities in the bazaar and on the street. Currently, the street is more visible and accessible than the bazaar because of the

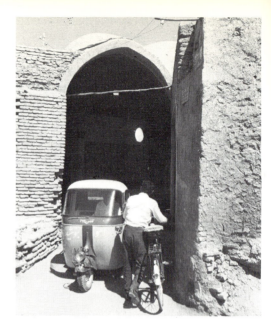

Modern form of material transport — taxibar — leaving via an auxiliary exit of the Kerman bazaar.

omnipresent car. However, if people can be encouraged to use the public transportation system rather than their private automobile, this imbalance can be corrected. The bazaar, after some restoration work, can become an interesting place to walk in and regain visibility over the street. By carefully considering the access requirements of the stores in the bazaar and modifying the existing system of access to the bazaar, this problem should become negligible. There is no reason why, with careful planning, the bazaar and street cannot work together to provide an active, viable city centre.

The working criteria for the main street network are relatively clear. Its only task is to interconnect all of the city nodal points for the bus service. A subsidiary network branches off the main system at points between neighbourhood centres to provide vehicular access to the peripheries of the neighbourhoods. These secondary networks are also locations for the homes of car owners. The main system should be carefully designed to get maximum use out of the streets and to separate people from vehicles. For example, by prohibiting parking on public main roads, one source of great danger (people getting out of and into their cars) is eliminated.

Another way in which this planning alternative preserves city streets for public transportation is by placing those facilities requiring access for large trucks in an ex-urban service-storage-manufacturing centre. Thus one major reason for congested streets would be eliminated. Also, machine services are in the ex-urban centre and do not contribute to congestion, traffic or pollution in the city.

Our planning alternative rests on the premise that the inhabitants of the city can be encouraged to abandon their cars in favour of public transportation for city travel. This premise cannot be lightly regarded. Few public bus systems have ever been successful at getting people to give up their cars.

There is a difference, however, between what we suggest and the average public urban transit system. We suggest a public service transit system, not a public system interested in how much revenue it gets. Our argument is essentially that since the city must grow larger than a walking distance radius, the people of the city need some form of transportation. The choice is between private transportation with all its problems, or public transportation which tries to avoid these problems. The main disadvantage of public transportation is that for any given individual it is less convenient than a private system. We believe, however, that this problem can be overcome.

A public transit system is inconvenient because it does not go to the rider's house. People who ride buses must walk to the nearest stop to find a bus. To minimize this problem we suggest that no house should be more than 3-5 minutes' walking distance from a bus stop.

Another inconvenience of a public bus system is waiting for a bus to arrive. To correct this partially, we suggest that enough buses be in operation on all routes so that the waiting time at any stop is never more than 3-5 minutes for off-peak hours. Further, all stops should have clean shelters with some available seating.

Always a problem for public bus systems is deciding on the price to charge for the service. We recommend that enough buses be available so that everyone who wants to ride can be accommodated at price of zero. (Furthermore, for this price no one should have to stand in the bus.)

We also recommend that special lanes or streets be allocated only for bus traffic. This will guarantee quick delivery of passengers to their destinations. The routes of the bus system will be concentrated on connecting the neighbourhood centres and the city centre. Ideally, each neighbourhood will have its own bus routes to the city centre. Some routes to connect the neighbourhood centres will evolve as demand arises.

Operating and maintaining a bus system with a zero price, like the one we have suggested, is a problem. The system needs money to operate it; buses, personnel and maintenance are not free. Since the bus system is a public service and the whole community will benefit from its successful operation, we suggest that part of the cost be covered from the city budget and the rest from the special interest groups which derive a particular advantage. Perhaps the largest group to benefit will be the retailers in the city centre. A special urban transportation tax should be levied on them to help pay for the bus system. The bus system, by reducing traffic in town, will provide a benefit to those people who still prefer to use their own cars. These people should pay a special annual urban transportation tax also. Further, all facilities provided for the private car, such as parking lots, should help pay for the cost of the bus system. From all these sources enough money should be available to provide the city with the kind of bus system we suggested.

The idea of financing a public bus system with a zero user charge is in fact exactly the same as the financing of the infrastructure needed for private vehicles. When new streets are built or old streets are repaired, the financing comes from a special tax on the land which benefits from the improvement and from the city budget. No charge is levied directly on the users of the new or improved street. We suggest that this model be applied to the public service bus system, since it is a part of the entire transport system of the city and more relevant and useful to a much larger proportion of the population than is the private system. Since a public transportation system requires far fewer streets than a public-plus-private one, expenditures on streets will be much less and the surplus can support the public bus system.

The urban model which we have proposed is a step towards avoiding a whole series of problems which the unrestricted use of the automobile and truck generate. Iran will sooner or later be forced to solve these problems. The sooner she begins, the cheaper and less disruptive will be the solution.

Preserving the enormous richness of traditional inner city activities, and allowing the city to expand and assume new functions, generates a continuing crisis and presents seemingly insoluble contradictions. Only bold and thoughtful actions like the planning alternative discussed here can maintain the viability of the Persian city as a whole.

Note: This article is taken from a report on the City of Kerman, Iran, prepared by the authors while they were serving as Volunteers with the American Peace Corps in Iran. The authors wish to express appreciation for the cooperation given them by their co-workers in the General Technical Office of the Ministry of Interior, Teheran, especially Engineer Yazdan Hooshvar and Engineer Bahram Sadri. In the City of Kerman, a special note of thanks must go to the staff of the Provincial Engineering Office — Office Director Engineer Safy and Peace Corps Volunteer Peter Forster; to the Office of the Mayor of Kerman; to the Kerman Office of Traffic Police; and to the Office of the Governor-General of the Province of Kerman. In Teheran, also, the Office of the American Peace Corps should be mentioned, especially Esfandiar Bahrampour who, as Field Officer, encouraged and supported this project. All errors — in fact and conclusion — are the sole responsibility of the authors.

MOVEMENT IN MIDTOWN

van GINKEL ASSOCIATES

54

Contemporary society depends on a multitude of systems — the post office, the telephone company, the delivery of goods, commuter trains, building construction, garbage collection — most of which no longer function properly, or occasionally cease to function altogether. Nowhere is the breakdown of these systems beginning to be more in evidence than in the heart of the wealthiest city of the world — Midtown Manhattan.

Nowhere else do utilities, transportation and services function under such great stress and with such precarious margins of tolerance; and since most systems operate under hypertension, the possibility of a chain reaction is not unimaginable. The cumulative effect of overloaded systems is felt by millions of New Yorkers whose daily life is a long sequence of hypertension, frustration and wasted energy.

The task of dealing with congestion in Midtown Manhattan, therefore, has considerably broader implications than those of increasing traffic flows and assigning more space to pedestrians. The real task is to make the city habitable and humane.

The systems we are continuing to build are self-limiting and we are near the end of that limit. Remedial measures are of two kinds — those which require a very large expenditure of money and a long period of realization and those which can be effected quickly and require little money. This article deals with solutions some of which can be realized immediately, but which are compatible with the larger framework of long term plans. The inefficiencies of transportation, communication, utilities and services can not however be resolved by short range measures. Many of the systems will have to be renewed in order to achieve a desirable level of effectiveness.

Short term measures, therefore, should be directed principally at creating oases in which dependency on present systems is reduced, making possible the redesign and replacement of these systems.

Midtown Manhattan contains areas of incredible densities. Added to the traffic which they generate is the massive through-traffic which results from the location of Midtown on Manhattan Island.

The present study proposes to ease congestion by adjustments to the existing street system which will tend to separate traffic of different characteristics and thus, among other things, increase roadway capacity; and by increasing the priority accorded to short range movement within Midtown. The latter involves the closing of a number of streets and avenues to general vehicular traffic. These closures have a wider implication than that of their immediate function, which is to increase pedestrian space and provide a convenient local minibus service.

The purpose of the 'pedestrian street' is manifold. Planting of trees and vegetation will replenish oxygen in the air and will reduce noise levels. The wide walkways, the separation from fast vehicular movement and the slower pace, will stimulate relaxation while shopping or strolling during lunch hour. These streets also form the beginning of a network which will facilitate the movement of emergency vehicles. Ultimately, underground services can be concentrated here, thus removing one disruptive element from the major streets — that of underground works and street repairs.

We feel that the measures which are proposed can be a realistic point of departure for the more ambitious and long range reorganization of Midtown in the manner that befits the center of the world's greatest city.

Circulation

The grid system of Midtown streets and avenues was designed many years ago for an entirely different scale of development than has since occurred. As buildings have risen higher the number of employees and residents has increased, generating increasing numbers of cars and trucks to serve them. But the streets and sidewalks and the way in which they are used have remained the same. The result is unbearable congestion, noise and stress — and massive inefficiency and costs to the city and its inhabitants. This is evidenced in the commuter's frustrating daily struggle to get to and from work; the fact that over 75% of the employees in Manhattan choose to go to work by public transit despite the unbearable service; the fact that the levels of some pollutants are seven times higher in Midtown than in the rest of the City; and the fact that many planners and politicians are suggesting that the automobile be banned completely from Midtown. Congestion in Midtown is legend.

A major requirement for improving the performance of the existing grid is to balance north/south movement with east/west movement. Historically, Midtown development and movement has been predominantly north/south (on the avenues).

Along the avenues the quality and kind of development is relatively cohesive. Along the streets, however, it changes from block to block — from good quality residential on the east to high-rise office buildings in the east central area to four- and five-story tenements, warehousing and empty lots in the west. Even now when concentration of land use on the east side is so intense that land costs per square foot are ten or more times what they are on the west side, the east continues to develop while the west lies dormant.

Circulation routes are heavily imbalanced in favour of north/south movement. Only three of the streets are as wide as any of the avenues and the north/south public transit lines greatly outnumber the east/west ones. This is logical in terms of the geography of Manhattan, but not in terms of Midtown. More traffic is drawn onto the avenues than the adjacent streets can handle. Journeys across Midtown are hampered not only by the congestion this creates on virtually every street, but also by the traffic using the avenues for through movement between north and south Manhattan.

The streets in Midtown are characterized by a number of problem areas which further increase the imbalance with avenues. These include point congestion caused by irregular intersections and dead-ending; conflict with street delivery and supply vehicles; poor connections of bridge and tunnels to the street system; use of west side streets as valves for overcrowding in east side streets (which will no longer be possible if the west side develops to the same degree as the east side); conflict of pedestrian movement with automobile and truck traffic and with parking; and under-utilization of the widest streets which are now two-way.

Circulation can be improved, congestion can, in large part, be eliminated and Midtown can be made more livable through a series of simple measures. There are, however, many things which cannot be done. Automobiles cannot be totally eliminated — no realistic substitute will be available for a long time to come. On the other hand, the capacity of the grid cannot be increased to meet the continually increasing demands of the automobile — demands which in New York City are potentially limitless. But whereas the grid cannot

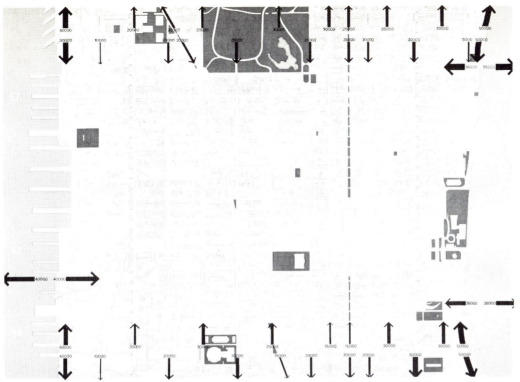

WHERE TRAFFIC GOES PRESENTLY
— NUMBER OF VEHICLES ENTERING AND LEAVING DAILY

island seeking out those streets that are momentarily less congested than others, causing more turning movements and conflict with delivery vehicles and pedestrians.

Where through traffic should go

Traffic moving north and south on the avenues at present can be divided into three categories:

— through traffic with origin and destination outside Midtown
— traffic with either its origin or destination in Midtown
— internal traffic with both origin and destination in Midtown

Through-traffic should be diverted to the periphery *(below)*. In order to do this it is necessary to reorganize expressway movement. The expressways must be de-

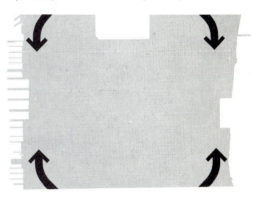

be changed significantly, we can change the way in which it is being used — by clarifying which traffic is and is not essential to Midtown and by delineating the routes for traffic flowing in and out through the area. By optimizing the use of streets and avenues and reconciling the many different types of demands placed on them, congestion can be relieved, movement can be speeded and the human need of places to walk and rest and enjoy can once again be satisfied.

Where traffic goes presently

At present all avenues in Midtown carry through traffic as well as local traffic. All streets are filled to capacity not only by traffic seeking to gain essential access to development along them but by traffic filtering off the

avenues travelling from one side of the island to the other *(above)*.

Because there are no routes around Midtown that are significantly faster than the internal avenues, traffic fights its way through Midtown. At peak periods the expressways and the avenues both are overloaded and between peaks the situation is only slightly improved. A great deal of through traffic uses routes at the centre of Midtown such as the Central Park Drives, Sixth and Seventh Avenues, or Fifth, Madison, Park, Lexington and Third Avenue. But this is also the area of the highest concentration of local traffic. Consequently through traffic is slowed, local traffic is hampered and the result is continued congestion.

Similarly, because there are no routes that afford fast crosstown movement, traffic tends to zig-zag across the

signed as two-part routes — a bypass with no connections to Midtown, and a feeder route with connections to major crosstown arterials, linked to the bypass north and south of Midtown. This will provide a desirable route around Midtown for traffic that otherwise would pass through it, and the streets and avenues will thereby be relieved for Midtown use.

Where traffic should leave and enter

Traffic leaving and entering should be routed in such a way that the point of entry of a vehicle to Midtown is as close as possible to its destination, and likewise its exit is as close as possible to its origin. Trips to and from entries and exits should be made on streets and avenues specifically designed and regulated to handle this traffic rather than by filtering through the grid.

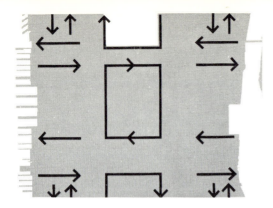

This requires relating entry and exit points to an arterial network of streets and avenues which provides good distribution over all Midtown *(above)*. Journeys between origins and destinations within Midtown should be as much as possible on the arterial network to leave the local streets free from through traffic whenever possible. The location of this arterial network should:

— deliver traffic to within two or three local streets of its destination
— prevent the necessity or desire for traffic to use local streets as short cuts.

Major traffic routes — proposed

An arterial network has been defined as shown *(above right)* to divert traffic travelling between north and south Manhattan around Midtown, to connect the bridge and tunnels directly with the expressways in order to avoid unnecessary loading of the grid, and to distribute traffic from one part of Midtown to another by means of express arterials. The major streets — 34th, 42nd and 57th — are made one way in order to smooth flows and more than double their capacity. Central Park drives are closed permanently in order to discourage through traffic from using Sixth and Seventh Avenues. Central Park South and Central Park West are one way, forming a loop to carry traffic around the park and simplifying flows at Grand Army Plaza and Columbus Circle. Traffic lights on Third, Fifth, Eighth and Ninth Avenues are timed to discourage through traffic.
All exits and entries on the FDR drive are closed, except those connecting with the arterial network. A new bypass expressway to carry through traffic is construc-

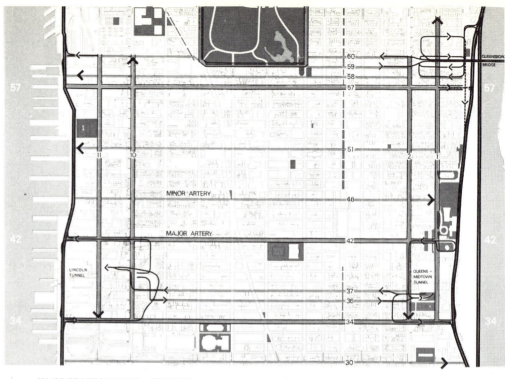

MAJOR TRAFFIC ROUTES — PROPOSED

ted on landfill in the East River, which can be developed for parkland and residential use. Revenues from this development can pay for construction of the expressway.
The network thus formed will leave the majority of streets free for access to development and other local uses.

Major traffic routes — immediate solution

The first stage in the implementation of this network is shown *(opposite)* 34th, 42nd and 57th Streets, Central Park West and Central Park South should be made one way. Traffic regulations, parking and stopping limitations, turning restrictions and traffic light timing, should be designed to favour flow on the arterial streets and avenues and discourage unnecessary traffic on the local streets. First and Second Avenues and Tenth and

Eleventh Avenues act as the major north/south arterial in the first stage, diverting traffic to the periphery prior to construction of the new expressways. The majority of these changes involve little or no expenditure and all can be implemented immediately.

Public transit and the 48th street connection

There are now five north/south subway lines in Midtown *(page 58)*: on Eighth, Broadway, Seventh, Sixth and Lexington/Park, and cross-town lines at 42nd, 53rd and 60th. These lines and the commuter train service at Grand Central and Penn Stations are the principal means of travel to work of Midtown employees. A new subway is being constructed on Second Avenue; new train stations have been proposed at a Metropolitan Transportation Center and the converted Penn Station freight line.

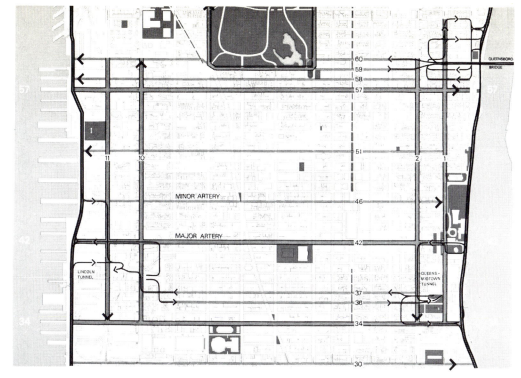

MAJOR TRAFFIC ROUTES — IMMEDIATE SOLUTION

The area of highest density of employment is between the Grand Central complex and Rockefeller Center. The subway system brings people to the edge of the high density area but there are no lines within it. The heavy use of the Times Square/Grand Central shuttle, which runs from two of the north/south subway lines to the southern edge of the highest employment density area demonstrates the need for distributor movement to take people from the subway and rail commuter lines to their places of work.

Bus service in Midtown, like subway service, is essentially north/south with lines on all the avenues except Park and Twelfth. There are cross-town bus loops at 66th, 59th, 57th, 49/50th, 42nd and 34th. The 49/50th Street bus route is well located to supply the need for secondary distribution across town, but fares are too high and the service too slow to serve this function.

A new rapid transit line is to be built along 48th Street *(page 58)*. This line is envisaged as a connection between existing north/south lines and between places of work across the island. Proper design of this connection could serve as a means of correcting deficiencies of the public transit system in providing for distribution within Midtown. 48th Street links the United Nations area; Grand Central — the terminal point of commuter rail service and the centre of the highest job concentration in Midtown; Rockefeller Center and the new office building developments along Sixth Avenue; Times Square — the focus of tourist and entertainment activity; and the theatre district.

In addition to the proposed Superliner Terminal at the foot of 48th Street and the proposed convention Center, a new development is planned for west Midtown. Consisting of residential and commercial areas

with office buildings along 48th Street from Eighth Avenue to the waterfront, this will radically alter the pattern of Midtown development. Development until now has been concentrated on the east side and along the avenues. Development of the west side will provide a valve for the pressures of office space demands and will give increased significance to the requirement for east/west movement, particularly along 48th Street.

48th Street is in an excellent location to serve as a spine which connects major areas of activity in Midtown. Apart from the rapid transit line, a bus loop system can be developed in conjunction with neighbouring streets so that the 48th Street area becomes a corridor across Midtown.

Movement along the 48th Street spine is of three types:

— long trips for which subway is appropriate;
— trips of one block or less which is the scale of pedestrian movement and for which additional pedestrian space and amenity is required;
— and trips within the spine which require a small scale movement system such as minibus.

These systems, designed to work together, can provide excellent distribution for the heart of Midtown and the same concept can be expanded through all of Midtown where required.

The proposed rapid transit line along 48th Street should extend from New Jersey to Queens for maximum efficiency and maximum impact on cross town development. This would provide direct connection from the proposed New Jersey S. T. O. L. Port and Railway Terminus, and from the Queens residential areas. Conversion of the Penn Station freight line on the west side to commuter rail service, with a station at 48th, would further increase the effectiveness of the 48th Street line.

Trips within the spine itself, however, require a different type of movement system — one that is simple to get on and off, capable of frequent stops, scaled physically to pedestrian movement, with low fares, and easily manoeuverable. The ideal system to meet these requirements would be service by minibus — small vehicles holding twenty to thirty passengers with small engines emitting very little noise and pollution. Installation of minibus service on 48th implies an entirely new character for the street. It should be redesigned to reinforce its new function — as a pedestrian and pedestrian movement street. This can best be accomplished if it is closed to automobiles, and sidewalks are widened and landscaped.

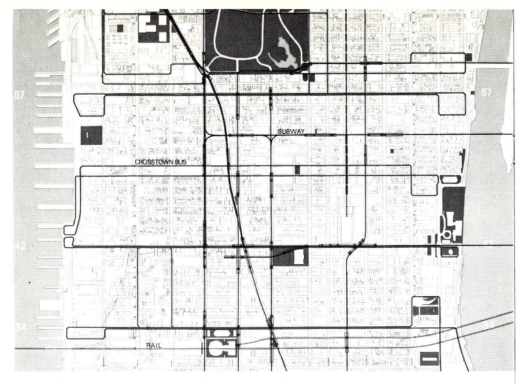

EXISTING PUBLIC TRANSIT AND CROSSTOWN DISTRIBUTION

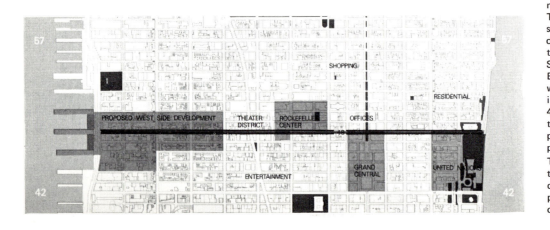

Pedestrian

In a highly concentrated area where the demand on movement systems is as great as it is in Midtown Manhattan, provision must be made for relief from the general high intensity of use. The stress created by the levels of noise, constant activity and movement which are particularly intense in Midtown must be offset by areas of low level activity, places to walk and relax, vehicle free precincts and trees and grass.

Areas of intense land use have the greatest requirement for pedestrian ways simply because they have the greatest number of people, the most completely manmade environment and the most noise.

The area of most intense land use and the highest employment density in Midtown (Grand Central complex to Rockefeller Center) has virtually the same ratio of pedestrian space as any other part of Manhattan but the concentration of people is ten or more than in most parts of the city. The result, as confirmed by the pedestrian study of the Regional Plan Association, is overcrowding of the existing pedestrian areas. Existing pedestrian space is deficient in quality as well as quantity. Sidewalks are narrow, noisy, dirty and overcrowded. Pedestrian concourses are all underground, hence windowless, and are usually dark and dirty. Subway stations are exceptionally squalid and must be cleaned opened up to light and air and designed in accordance with the needs of human beings.

Bryant and Central Parks and the UN Plaza are located near the high job density area, but are too far from the highest job concentrations for lunch-hour trips to the park. The construction of mid-block arcades, especially in central and west Midtown will aid movement and provide useful and pleasant pedestrian space. There is however a crucial need for more pedestrian space immediately, especially in the area of highest density *(opposite)*. The redesign of Madison and Lexington between 42nd and 57th Streets; of 48th and 49th Street between Lexington and Eighth Avenues; and Broadway between Herald Square and Lincoln Center will answer this need. With this network, every point in east Midtown (between Second and Eighth Avenues, 40th to 60th Street) is within 4 minutes walking distance from either a park or a pedestrian street. This provides the opportunity for relief from the noise and pressure of traffic.

To reduce conflict between pedestrians and traffic, the interface between the two should be defined as clearly as possible. This requires reinforcement of the place of the pedestrian in Midtown through the creation of a continuous pedestrian network which is as inde-

pendent of other traffic as possible.
The following elements of a potential pedestrian network already exist in Midtown:—

— Rockefeller Center Concourse
— Times Square subway station and the Port of New York Authority Terminus
— Bryant Park subway station, Herald Square and Penn Station
— Grand Central complex
— Central Park, Bryant Park and the United Nations Plaza
— Lincoln Center
— Subway stations and concourses

The use of 48th Street, Madison, Lexington and Broadway for pedestrian movement, would connect all of these elements into one continuous network. This system would be supplemented by widening sidewalks on Fifth Avenue and by closing Fifth Avenue during the weekend for strolling, shopping and sightseeing on foot.

48th Street

48th Street passes through the heart of both the existing and proposed Midtown concentrations (Grand Central complex, Rockefeller Center and west Midtown) in addition to the United Nations, the proposed Convention Center and passenger ship terminal and the two waterfronts. The rapid transit connection will attract people within these areas onto 48th Street so that this street will have a very large number of pedestrians, making it very desirable to reserve the use of the street for pedestrians and minibuses only *(next page).*
A number of pedestrian ways now exist or are planned within the blocks between 48th and 49th Streets. There are two of these through-block connections between Madison and Lexington, the access road to Rockefeller Plaza, the planned shopping concourse in the new Rockefeller Extension and others are proposed. Consequently, the blocks between 48th and 49th become very desirable for further pedestrian development. In order to strengthen 48th as a pedestrian street and create a pleasant precinct for shopping and resting, 49th Street and 48th Street should be closed from Lexington to Eighth. Because of the ongoing construction of the Rockefeller Extension west of Sixth, immediate closure should be limited to the section east of Sixth.

Broadway

Broadway is a major shopping and tourist street. Its

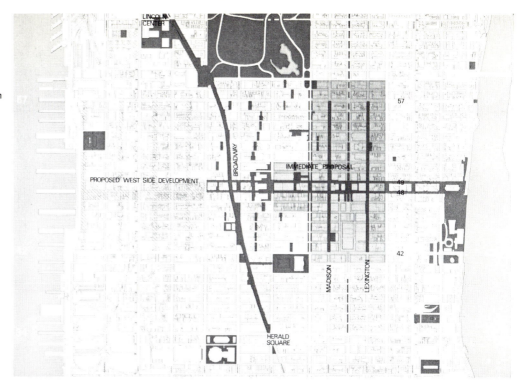

PROPOSED PEDESTRIAN STREETS
— SHOWN WITH EXISTING AND PLANNED MAJOR OPEN SPACE

historic and visual character evoke a strong image — in which lies its attraction for tourists. It forms the spine of the threatre district and connects Lincoln Center, Central Park, the Coliseum, Times Square and Herald Square where some of the major regional stores of New York City are located. In addition, Broadway passes through areas of high job concentration west of Rockefeller Center, and through the garment district. When west Midtown is developed, Broadway will lie in the middle of the west and east Midtown concentrations.
Since it is the most highly accessible area by subway a large number of people will change from the north/ south subway lines to the east/west minibus lines and 48th Street rapid transit line in the Broadway area. For Broadway to be exploited to the maximum, its full width from Lincoln Center to Herald Square

should be designed for people on foot.

Madison and Lexington

Madison and Lexington have a variety of thriving retail stores. These are the type of stores that could make a pedestrian street work — coffee shops and snack bars, clothing, jewellery and gift shops, etc. These avenues are narrow enough that they can be designed to the scale of the pedestrian and building along them is more related to the sidewalk than to the movement along the street. Madison and Lexington are both 'extra' avenues in the grid — flanked by short blocks that encourage walking *(over).* Along with Park Avenue which is already landscaped and Fifth Avenue with widened sidewalks and trees, Madison and Lexington as pedestrian streets would provide a substantial pedestrian precinct precisely where it is required — in

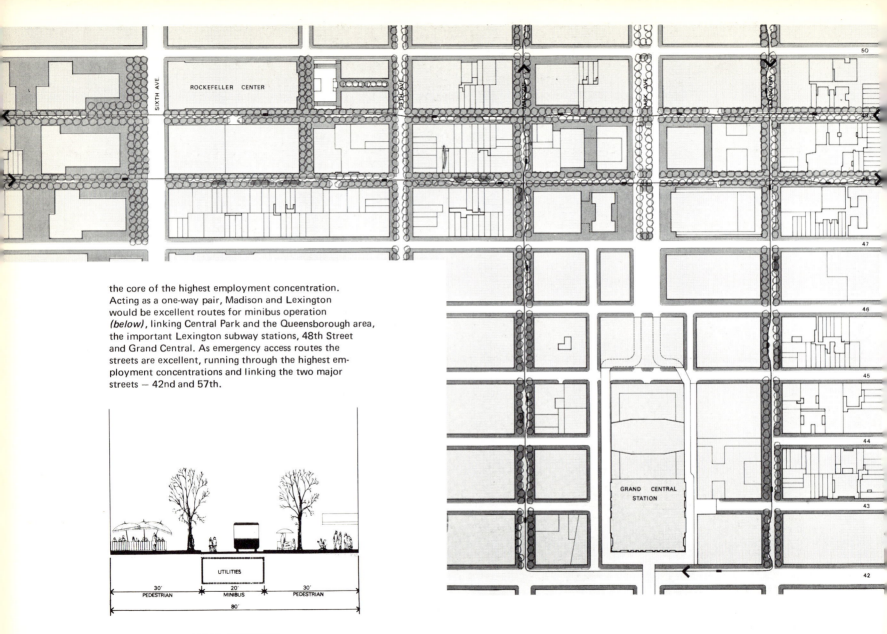

SIXTH AVE

ROCKEFELLER CENTER

FIFTH AVE

MADISON

PARK AVE

LEXINGTON

50

49

48

47

46

45

44

43

42

GRAND CENTRAL STATION

the core of the highest employment concentration.
Acting as a one-way pair, Madison and Lexington
would be excellent routes for minibus operation
(below), linking Central Park and the Queensborough area,
the important Lexington subway stations, 48th Street
and Grand Central. As emergency access routes the
streets are excellent, running through the highest employment concentrations and linking the two major
streets — 42nd and 57th.

UTILITIES

| 30' PEDESTRIAN | 20' MINIBUS | 30' PEDESTRIAN |

80'

MADISON AVENUE SECTION

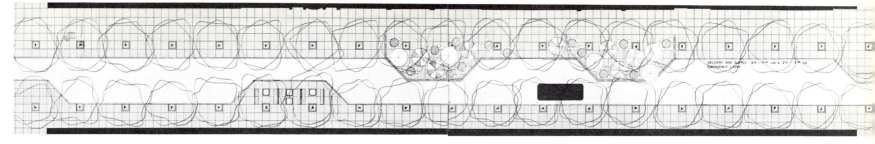

48TH STREET PLAN — FIFTH TO MADISON

Introduction of these streets as pedestrian ways would have an enormously beneficial effect on the highly concentrated office areas which flank them and on shopping in Midtown.

Fifth Avenue

The temporary closure of Fifth Avenue on Earth Day and the subsequent weekend closures indicated the real value of a pedestrian street in Midtown. Fifth Avenue traditionally has been the street closed for parades. It is one of the most beautiful streets in the world, with such landmarks as the Public Library and Bryant Park, Rockefeller Center, St. Patrick's Cathedral and nationally known stores, culminating in Central Park.

It is a wide and ceremonial avenue — and in this lies its strength and beauty. The scale of the avenue itself and of the buildings which border it bespeak considerable formality. It needs a commensurate scale of movement, whether of traffic or people, in order to be alive as a working urban street. This can be achieved by maintaining traffic on Fifth Avenue,

while widening and improving the sidewalks and planting trees along the street to increase its amenity for pedestrians.

Closure of Fifth Avenue is proposed during summer weekends for strolling, shopping, and sightseeing when the pace of activity in Midtown is less intense.

Minibus

Creation of a network of pedestrian streets provides an opportunity to solve many of the problems of circulation and movement in Midtown which have until now been pre-empted by demands on the use of the street surface by automobiles. The streets forming this network are ideally located for minibus service. Minibuses provide assistance to the pedestrian for trips which are longer than desired or enjoyed on foot, yet which require the convenience and economy of walking. Consequently, minibuses should follow the major pedestrian

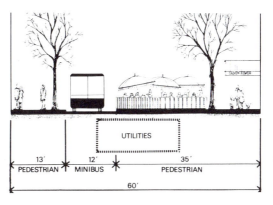

48TH STREET SECTION

routes — the desire lines being the same — and be available at the places where pedestrians will congregate (above).

The character and quality of the minibus itself and of minibus service should be consistent with that of the pedestrian street — casual, restrained and convenient (left). They should be comfortable, easy to get on and off, with ample seating and standing space for twenty to thirty passengers. They should have large windows which can be opened in the summer, to take advantage of the pleasant environment of the street (below). Since the buses are inexpensive to operate, fares can be low — five to ten cents — or they can be free. On a fare system, transfers between regular buses or subway and the minibus should be allowed. Minibuses have been successfully operated in other cities on this basis.

The minibus network (next page) should connect the following elements along the proposed pedestrian streets:

— Stations of the north/south subway lines
— Grand Central Station
— Places of work in east Midtown, the highest concentrations being the Grand Central complex and Rockefeller Center
— Future places of work in central and west Midtown
— Other elements along the 48th Street corridor, such as the proposed Superliner Terminal and Convention Center, the west Midtown office spine, the proposed north exit to Grand Central Station, Times Square, the Theatre District, the commuter rail station of the converted Penn Central Freight Line and the Metropolitan Transportation Center (LIRR, connection to Kennedy Airport)
— Shopping areas along Madison and Lexington, Herald Square and 42nd Street, Rockefeller Center and 57th Street
— Existing parks and public open space: Central Park, Bryant Park, the United Nations plaza, Lincoln Center, Times Square and Herald Square

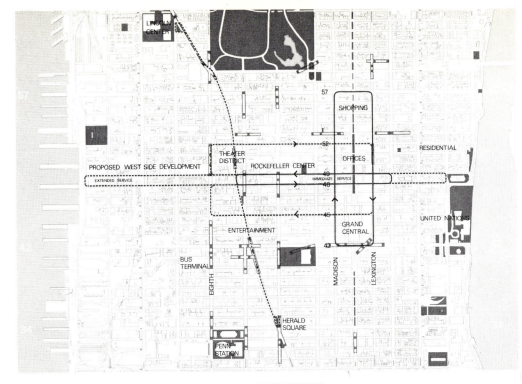

MINIBUS LOOPS — SHOWING CONNECTION WITH SUBWAY STATIONS

— Future pedestrian areas such as the pedestrian deck of the proposed west Midtown development and the concourse between Sixth and Seventh Avenues

48th/49th Loop

This loop should be implemented immediately. In conjunction with the Madison/Lexington loop it connects the majority of the foregoing elements, and provides crosstown service between subway lines and places of employment. In addition, tourist oriented service should be provided on these streets between Times Square and the United Nations. These could be minibuses taken from the regular routes at off-peak hours and decorated to indicate their special function.

Madison/Lexington Loop

This loop also should be implemented immediately. It would serve passengers moving north and south between Grand Central Station, the subway lines and their places of work. It would also serve tourists and shoppers from 42nd Street, Grand Central Station, Madison, Lexington, Park and Fifth Avenues and Central Park.

Broadway

This line would mainly serve shoppers and tourists and would increase accessibility to the other elements of the pedestrian network. Because of the varying traffic and service conditions along its length it cannot be implemented immediately.

Route flexibility

Since the functions of the various routes are different, the levels of service required throughout the day will vary. The 48th Street loops need a very high frequency during rush hour and a lower frequency during the rest of the day. The demand on the Madison/Lexington loop will be relatively constant throughout the day. The tourist and shopping routes need more buses afternoons, evenings and on weekends. This will allow flexibility in switching buses between routes so that fewer buses will be required to maintain a high level of service Routing also can be flexible, changing as the demands become apparent and as new development takes place.

Emergency systems — fire, police and ambulance

There is an immediate requirement for a network of emergency routes in Midtown which will allow emergency vehicles to travel as quickly as possible to the scene of an emergency. At present, with undifferentiated streets, vehicles rely on traffic allowing them priority. During heavy traffic, it is sometimes impossible for traffic to move to the edge of the road to allow the emergency vehicles to pass, and in Manhattan this is a critical weakness in the priority system. An emergency system is therefore required in which the streets always allow the passage of emergency vehicles, for example:

— The transport modes on the emergency streets must be such that even when the street is operating at maximum capacity, it is possible for an emergency vehicle to pass unimpeded.
— The streets must never be loaded to such a capacity that the passage of an emergency vehicle is prevented.

The emergency routes can be either exclusive to emergency vehicles; have the volume of traffic restricted; or the modes of traffic restricted. Nowhere is the volume of emergency traffic such that an exclusive right of way is justified. It is unrealistic to consider controlling the volume of traffic on Midtown streets to such a level that emergency vehicles could be guaranteed a clear passage.
The third alternative, restriction of traffic mode, can be the basis of a solution. Even when crowded it is possible to clear bus and pedestrian streets. Therefore, the pedestrian and bus-only streets should be considered as the major elements of the emergency network.
Design of these streets must take into account the requirements of emergency access. Adequate width must be allowed for at least one fire truck to pass to a fairly high speed, or two vehicles to pass in opposite directions if slowed down. In practical

terms, this means that trees, seats and barriers of any kind should be placed to allow direct movement of emergency vehicles and there should be visual and aural warning to pedestrians of the approach of a vehicle. Present warning devices on the vehicles are sufficient, provided that there are no visual obstructions. Sufficient space must be available for pedestrians to take refuge as the vehicle passes. This can be assured by marking the through route differently from the rest of the street (different paving, for example). Adequate width should be provided on the streets for buses to pull over to one side to allow the vehicle to pass.

The emergency/pedestrian system should be implemented gradually as opportunities arise. Closure of 48th Street to all traffic except buses and limited delivery can be the beginning of the system. The street is ideal for cross-town movement between the highest concentration areas. Broadway closed to all but limited delivery access will act together with 48th to make an emergency framework running north/south and east/west. Madison and Lexington Avenues, closed to through-traffic also, should be incorporated into the network, providing emergency access to the highest concentration area.

Delivery and supply

Midtown

Circulation of delivery and supply vehicles in Midtown poses entirely different problems than does circulation of automobiles. Many different types of goods each with its own size, time and handling requirements, must be transported to every part of the area each day. Unlike most automobiles, delivery trucks usually make many stops, necessarily spend a great proportion of their time at the curbs, often double parked, and constitute the only available mode for their purpose. The 1:30 p.m. Regional Plan Association Skycount found that trucks constituted 37% of all moving vehicles and 57% of all parked vehicles. Furthermore, considering that the parking and manoeuvring space for a truck is often equal to that of 2–3 cars, and that intra-Manhattan trucking is characterized by a very low load factor, their disproportionate importance in traffic flow is obvious. Not only do truck deliveries have an adverse effect on traffic circulation, they infringe on pedestrian movement both at sidewalks and crosswalks, are heavy polluters, noisy, and wear hard on the road surface. Obviously, alternative means must be found to move goods in Midtown.

Development of efficient means of delivery and supply

in high density downtown areas is long overdue. The City Planning Department's proposed freight study is timely and should provide the background data necessary to implement improvements in the system of delivery and supply. It is essential, however, that it provide guidance for immediate and short term measures and that it be designed as a developmental tool rather than purely as an instrument of analysis. In order to provide a frame of reference for this aspect of the study, a comparison and initial evaluation has been drawn between those modes presently available and those with development time in the near future. Two areas require immediate attention and can be used to test new systems — the garment district and the proposed pedestrian streets.

No alternate modes that could replace trucks on a wide scale presently exist, even if the political, operational and economic problems of changeover could be solved. Means should therefore be employed to regulate the use of existing trucks in order to increase their efficiency and decrease their adverse effects on street use. In areas of intense use, such as the garment district, and in specific areas where existing trucks are incompatible with other street uses, as in the proposed pedestrian streets, it is possible that small-size modular vehicles could operate on the street surface carrying goods to and from nearby transfer docks (above).

Such a system could be operated either as a concession or by individual operators depending on the area and extent of application. A single concession service seems most appropriate in the pedestrian streets whereas the size and complexity of the garment district and the firmly entrenched interests of truckers would likely dictate a multi-operator arrangement in the area. The advantages of developing a new modular vehicle over using existing small vans and pick-up trucks is that containerization of goods would become realistic, leading to savings in curb-stop time, reduction of truck bulk and control of loss and pilfering. The vehicle could be specifically designed for the urban core situations in terms of manoeuvring, engine size and gearing, noise and pollution control and multiple use (eg for passengers). It is imperative that such a vehicle be developed for use in high density downtown areas and New York should lead the way in supporting its development.

The only reasonable alternative to the modular surface vehicle is an overhead track vehicle system, several of which are now operative in the United States. Although these have not been applied as yet to urban delivery and supply their mechanical and systems capability has been proven in industrial and airport applications. This

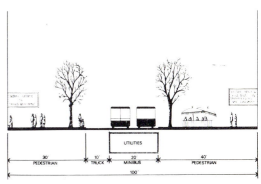

BROADWAY SECTION

type of system is most appropriate to high intensity areas where fixed routes do not constrain, where building form can be adapted to the goods transfer requirements, or in new developments. In Midtown, where the fixed constraints of utilities, grid and building form are already so great it is unlikely that fixed systems could have any more than limited application. In the west Midtown development grade separation is possible, so truck or other surface vehicle delivery would be most appropriate. In the garment district, however, a fixed track system could be feasible providing costs can be reasonably recovered.

Garment district

The garment industry remains in Manhattan because of low rents, tradition and complex inter-relationships between the segments of the industry. Over the past few years some few firms have moved out to other areas but most have stayed. Rents are now very near the limit that many manufacturers can afford to pay but most firms choose to remain and pay rather than suffer isolation from suppliers, jobbers or other manufacturers. Removal of the industry to another location has been proposed by others as a means of solving the internal physically restrictive problems of the industry and of eliminating the congestion caused to Midtown circulation. Complete removal over a short period of time would be extremely costly to the city and to the industry. Many changes and disruptions would be created in the industry which could lead to disaster for many firms. Gradual removal is more realistic but would have to be effected with extreme care in order to have least adverse effects. This would require a long term study of the operation of firms

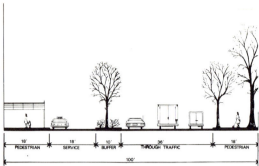

CENTRAL PARK SOUTH SECTION

and their inter-relationships, economic factors, legal factors and replanning of the area. In short, removal of the industry or of any substantial segment of the industry, is a long range alternative. For a period of at least twenty years, the problems of the garment industry and Midtown must therefore be solved together.

Solution of the chaotic traffic situation in the garment district cannot wait on long term plans. Nor can it wait on development of technology or even long range study. The problems are immediate, and immediate solution must be found.

Any solution must pay for itself. Subsidy by the city is as unrealistic as the hidden subsidy now paid in the blocking of traffic and the use of sidewalks and curbs for loading and sorting. Five alternatives present themselves:

— Enforcement of off-street loading and unloading, each business providing docking facilities on it own premises
— Truck docks constructed within each block, rentable for loading, unloading and sorting on a per hour basis.
— One centrally located avenue closed to through traffic within the garment district and developed either as an in-street docking area, or with arcaded building frontages for docking and possibly warehousing.
— Developing the blocks between 36th and 37th Streets as loading, unloading and transfer facilities.
— A transfer depot could be built west of the garment district — near Tenth or Eleventh Avenue or over the freight yards.

These alternatives should be evaluated in terms of fore-

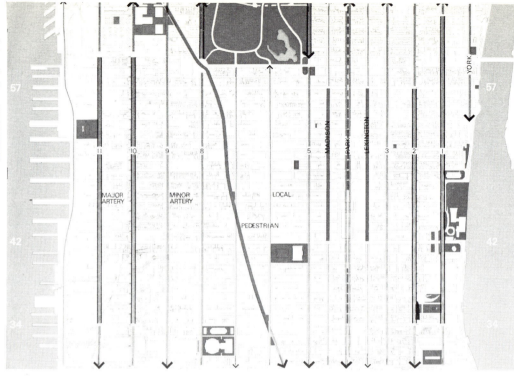

AVENUES CLASSIFIED

cast costs, recovery of costs, benefit to circulation and effects on the garment industry. Criteria can be developed and applied quickly in order to gain a clear view of priorities for further study. The proposed OMPD study of the garment district should examine these alternatives with a view to immediate implementation of the most desirable and should leave detailed analysis for secondary study.

Street classification

The existing streets and avenues of Midtown work together as a system. Within this system a hierarchy of use has developed, defining the demands on traffic regulation, street or sidewalk widening, stopping requirements, etc. In broad terms, streets and avenues now function as:

— major arteries
— minor arteries
— local streets

Streets with a similar position in the hierarchy form a series of grids of different size to serve different functions in the circulation/delivery system.

The problems of the existing system are a result of deficiencies in the hierarchy:

— the hierarchy as it exists is not as clear as it should be, which gives rise to the overlapping of functions (arteries serving also as local streets for example), with a reduction of efficiency for both functions.
— There is an imbalance between the categories in the system, for example a shortage of collector/distributor streets, and as a consequence other streets carry a function to which they are not suited. This

65

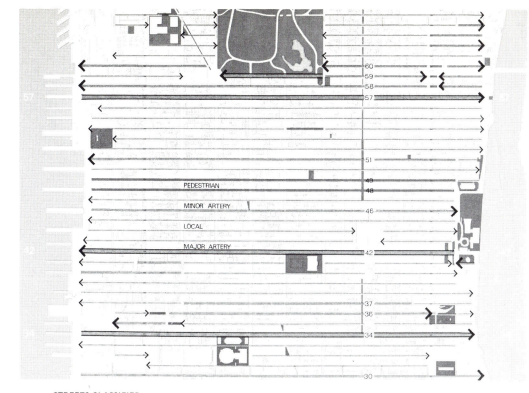

PEDESTRIAN

MINOR ARTERY

LOCAL

MAJOR ARTERY

STREETS CLASSIFIED

imbalance extends down the hierarchy as far as pedestrian movement, where there is a lack of streets assigned primarily to pedestrians and a shortage of sidewalk space.
— The different categories are not well related to one another with respect to geography or to land use.

These deficiencies can be corrected by creating a clear, balanced hierarchy of streets and avenues related to the pattern of land use in Midtown. This can be done by strengthening or altering the function of existing streets and avenues *(left and above).*

Major arteries

A large meshed grid of high capacity roads is necessary, adjacent to, but not within the areas of high land use concentration and traffic generation, to connect these areas with each other and with the entrances and exits to Midtown. These should be one way roads for maxi-

mum capacity and to facilitate turning, with progressive traffic lighting timed to long cycles, with streets and avenues operating together as one-way loops. This system should facilitate quick travel in and out of Midtown and between points in Midtown. These arteries should attract all movement of more than a few blocks so that a greater distance on arteries is quicker and preferable to a short one on local or distributor streets.
The wide streets 34th, 42nd, 57th and Central Park South, and the avenues which now have heavy traffic flows, First, Second, Tenth and Eleventh Avenues and Fifth and Eighth Avenues north of 57th Street and south of 42nd Street constitute a network of major streets and avenues which carry traffic in and out of Midtown, on and off the expressways. The speed and volume of traffic on these streets should be increased relative to all others in Midtown by various

means, such as long cycle progressive lighting and strict limitations on parking, delivery and supply. 34th, 42nd, 57th Streets are defined as crosstown arterials. Sidewalks should be widened on the right hand side of the traffic direction and traffic stops, delivery and supply prohibited on the left hand side. Delivery and supply should be prohibited during the peak hours.
Central Park South should be redesigned so that the present width is divided into a through road of three lanes with no stopping, and a service road of two lanes to provide for stopping of delivery and supply vehicles *(far left).*
First, Second, Tenth and Eleventh Avenues are designated as major north/south arterials. Stopping should be prohibited on the left side of these avenues and should be restricted on the right side during morning and evening peaks.

Minor arteries

A grid of smaller capacity streets is needed as the transition from fast traffic to building access streets. Whereas the major arteries run around the areas of concentration, the distributors must interlock with them and run through these areas to feed traffic onto the local streets. These streets therefore should be designed so that they are the logical turning streets for traffic travelling on the artery to within a few blocks of its final destination.
Some streets such as 58th, 59th and 60th are too narrow to be used as major arterials yet are necessary as crosstown or semi-crosstown routes.
58th Street and portions of 59th and 60th Streets are to act as complementary arterials in the reverse direction to 57th Street. Similar controls regarding progressive lighting must be implemented and stopping traffic strictly limited to one side of the street; delivery and supply also should be restricted to one side and then only certain times of the day.
Bridge and tunnel connections to the major arterial network are narrow streets which must have a minimum of two lanes clear at all times; stopping, delivery and supply must be restricted to one side of the street at certain times of day.
36th and 37th Streets are proposed as arterials of a special nature, namely crosstown streets connecting Lincoln and Queens Midtown tunnels, exclusive to trucks and commercial vehicles. Curbside parking will have to be regulated to maintain traffic flows, and in the long term may be eliminated by the provision of off-street truck loading bays.
In some areas of Midtown the mesh of the arterial

network is so large that traffic cannot be expected to make an arterial loop but will short cut through local streets. There is a need therefore for streets which can act both as local streets and yet carry through traffic for a few blocks. 46th Street running east and 51st running west can serve this purpose. With 48th and 49th Streets closed to delivery at some time of day, an extra load will be put on delivery facilities on 47th and 50th Streets, reducing their effectiveness as through streets. The minibuses operating on 48th and 49th Streets will loop on 45th and 52nd Streets and require a bus lane on each. The only streets remaining in a position roughly midway between 42nd and 57th Streets are 46th and 51st, which therefore have been designated as minor arterials.

Delivery and supply should be restricted to one side of these streets; the side will change on alternate days; stopping on the side not used for delivery should be prohibited during morning and evening peaks.

Local streets

These are the final destination and the origin of the traffic in Midtown. In a smoothly functioning system they are fed by and feed into the distributor/collector system. These streets are not designed to carry through traffic since this doubling of function would reduce their effectiveness as service streets.

The majority of Midtown streets should be reserved for local use — delivery and supply to properties adjoining the street and taxi and bus pick-up and drop-off.

Pedestrian streets

The pedestrian street assigns as much surface as possible to the pedestrian and provides an exclusive route for a minibus system and for emergency vehicles. Delivery and supply would be permitted at specific times and all other vehicles excluded at all times. These streets should be designed so that through movement of commercial vehicles is discouraged. Restricting access into a 'bus only' street to traffic turning off a crossing avenue could ensure that delivery vehicles remain on the street only for one block.

It is proposed that parts of some Midtown streets and avenues become pedestrian streets. These are 48th and 49th Streets, Broadway, Lexington, and Madison Avenues. Those sections designated as pedestrian streets are in the areas of high intensity use; they link the parks and the points of interest and concentration of population.

Parking

Street space in Midtown is too much in demand and too valuable for more essential uses than parking cars. Curb parking slows traffic flow, hampers delivery and supply, destroys the amenity of many streets and therefore should not be tolerated.

Analysis of the number of parking spaces in various zones within Midtown shows that they vary considerably in ratio to employment and in density. The ratio in the Grand Central-Rockefeller Center zone, for instance, is 11 spaces per thousand jobs while in an equivalent zone on the west side the ratio is 450 spaces per thousand jobs. This indicates that the use of cars is quite different from zone to zone and that the use of land for parking differs considerably from zone to zone. This differentiation can be exploited in the regulation of parking as new development takes place and in planning the location of public transit connections from distant parking to each zone. It is apparent that much of the west side is now used for parking the cars of people working in the central area. As the west side becomes intensively developed this will no longer be possible or desirable. The requirements for improved rapid transit and for construction of distant garages with transit connections to Midtown can be determined from analysis of these areas.

Off-street parking should be sufficient in capacity and design to accommodate essential automobile traffic only, not to react indiscriminately to demand. The method of regulation of the number of parking spaces in Midtown is critical. Four concepts of parking policy have been evaluated, each with different objectives and different method of regulation:

— Permit the construction of new private garages upon application and build municipal parking garages for short term parkers.
— Hold the number of parking spaces to a determined number or ratio based on either large areas (Community Planning Districts) or special small parking zones.
— Eliminate all parking within Midtown except specially rate-structured garages favouring short term parking.
— Build municipal parking garages outside of Midtown with good connections to Midtown, for long term parkers.

The results of the evaluation determined that no new municipal garages should be built in Midtown. Instead, the rate structures of existing garages should be modified to favour short term parking. The total number of

parking spaces in Midtown should be held to a determined ratio or number, resulting in a new reduction in relation to Midtown employment. Municipal garages should be built outside of Midtown with public transit connnections to places of employment.

Any new parking spaces that are provided will encourage the increased use of cars in Midtown and consequently increased congestion, pollution and interference with pedestrians and delivery and supply. Moreover, garage construction uses land which is essential to the growth of the core and in the case of municipal garages this is not easily returned to other uses.

Use of parking spaces in Midtown falls into four categories: residential spaces which can be related directly to the amount of housing; accessory spaces which are built along with hotels, department stores, large office buildings etc., and which should be regulated according to the requirements and impact of each individual project; long term spaces which are used by employees in the area to park their cars all day; and short term spaces which are used for one or two hour periods by shoppers, salesmen etc.

Provision of long term parking encourages commuting by car, creating congestion at peak hours not only in the vicinity of the garage but on all access roads, leading to demands for more roads, introduction of more cars and the vicious circle that every large city has experienced.

Provision of some short term spaces is necessary for trips that cannot be made by public transit. These trips generally occur at off-peak hours. The provision of short term parking spaces should however take place in the context of an overall stabilization or reduction in the number of spaces. This can be done by regulating rate structures to provide short term parking within existing garages.

The number of spaces can best be stabilized by a policy based on the particular development characteristics and planning objectives of small zones within Midtown. The zones around bridge and tunnel exits will have different parking requirements and availability of space than the zones of intense office development, or zones of high accessibility by rapid transit, or zones of residential development.

If limitations are made on the basis of small zones, then as construction occurs in the zone, land costs will rise and some of the garages will be priced out of the market. Limitations in other zones will prevent these spaces from being relocated. Thus a net decrease would result.

Conclusions

Vehicles travelling through Midtown should be separated from internal traffic by improving the peripheral routes. A new expressway should be built on the east side with no connections to Midtown; and the West Side Highway should be reconstructed as a Midtown bypass. These routes should carry the bulk of traffic between north and south Manhattan, freeing Midtown avenues for Midtown use *(right)*.

Internal traffic should be carried on an arterial network specifically designed and located for this purpose. 34th, 42nd and 57th Streets, Central Park South, Central Park West, and Eleventh Avenue should be made one way in order to increase capacity and eliminate turning problems. Traffic flow should be encouraged along these routes as well as First, Second and Tenth Avenues. The network formed by these streets and avenues would relieve internal streets and avenues for local uses.

48th and 49th Streets, Madison, Lexington and Broadway should be converted to pedestrian streets, closed to all traffic except for minibuses and limited delivery and supply. This will form a network connecting existing parks, subway stations, and major office, shopping and tourist areas. The same streets can be used for emergency vehicles.

Procedure

The close working relationship between consultant and client was of paramount importance to the execution of this study; that relationship was unique and contributed much to the success of the study. From the first meeting between Jacquelin Robertson, Director of the Office of Midtown Planning & Development (OMPD), and van Ginkel Associates there was consensus on the direction and strategy of the project. Both parties were convinced that Midtown Manhattan is an entity in which certain problems can be solved without necessarily engaging New York City as a whole. It also was agreed that any recommendations must be highly practical and capable of implementation at once – and that they should not involve major capital expenditures. This led to the conclusion that all recommendations should be formulated during the first phase, which should have a duration of five months. In order to achieve these goals, it was evident that frequent discussion within the management of other city agencies was imperative.

Apart from individual meetings between the consultants and the commissioners of various departments, a series of joint meetings were held. These were attend-

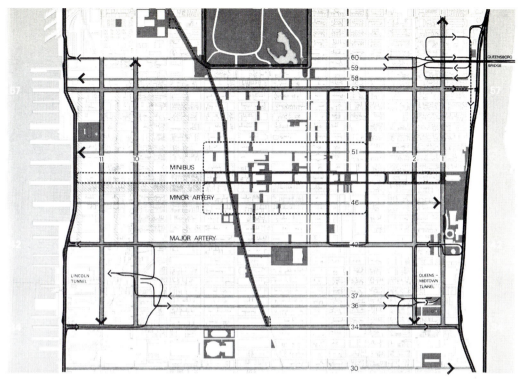

MOVEMENT IN MIDTOWN PROPOSED

ed by all the commissioners involved and their senior advisors, senior personnel of the Office of Midtown Planning and Development and van Ginkel Associates. At these meetings, over which Jacquelin Robertson presided superbly, the consultants indicated the direction that they were taking without making specific recommendations. Although there was a tendency to oppose any suggested change *a priori,* by the end of a full day closeted in a room without any interruptions, the 15 to 20 people usually achieved a surprising degree of consensus.

Owing to the exigencies of time and funds, the study did not start with the customary data collection. In any event, it was concluded that New York would offer too much data for immediate application. It was therefore decided that as soon as a problem was identified, specific data would be collected in order to resolve that

particular problem. Great quantities of information regarding traffic were readily available but proved to be unnecessary for problem identification as well as problem solving. Instead, theoretical maximum flows were calculated and distributed in ratios of these flows. However, a complete survey of existing parking facilities was made and checked against available data. The parking of trucks, both legal and illegal, was surveyed in detail along two avenues and two streets on two random days, on an hourly basis.

The good working relationship between OMPD and the consultants secured early dialogue with all parties involved and allowed the consultants to test their ideas on agencies of city government and in the private sector. Consequently, the work could proceed relatively easily, with minimum delay, and facilitated completion of a study of this scope in a short time.

The subway in New York City, Grand Central Station stop at 8.45 a.m.

RICHARD RIDLEY

[However good a design or a conclusion from years of research may be, it will have little avail if the message does not penetrate to those for whom this activity has been executed. When we talk of community participation, or even community control, we assume that the key figures in the decision-making on the side of the ordinary citizen are as well informed as their counterparts. Unfortunately reams of research documents are often useless as information for those who have neither time nor the formal education to withstand these verbal onslaughts.

As consultant to the District of Columbia Transit Development team, Mr Ridley studied the Ardmore and Glenmont lines from the point of view of environment, traffic and parking impacts, as well as the development opportunities for neighbourhoods around these lines. The technical studies, together with community proposals and other recommendations, have been used by the city council members who were participating on the Washington Metropolitan Area Transportation Authority. Several stations have been relocated or redesigned as a result of these studies.

The following contribution depicts the urban design of four transit stations and their surrounding areas on the Glenmont line of the Metro, working with the community to develop facilities that were needed in the neighbourhood. This work was under contract to the Community Renewal Program in the District of Columbia.]

METRO IMPACT STUDIES

CLIENT:

DISTRICT OF COLUMBIA COMMUNITY RENEWAL PROGRAM

JOB CAPTAIN

RICH RIDLEY

EARLY IN 1972, WE WERE ASKED TO ASSIST THE MAYOR'S OFFICE **WASHINGTON, D.C.** WITH MAKING DESIGN DECISIONS* IN TERMS OF RELATING **PROPOSED** Ⓜ **STATIONS** TO DIFFERENT NEIGHBORHOODS IN THE CITY

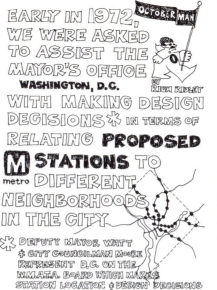
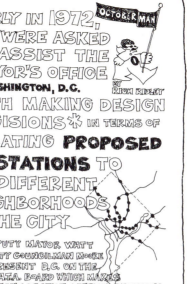

BY RICH RIDLEY

* DEPUTY MAYOR WATT & CITY COUNCILMAN MOORE REPRESENT D.C. ON THE W.M.A.T.A. BOARD WHICH MAKES STATION LOCATION & DESIGN DECISIONS

RESIDENTS HAD BEEN OBJECTING TO STATIONS, **LOCATION** AS WELL AS **DESIGN** *

metro?

PLANS ARE ALWAYS MADE DOWNTOWN

* THE TRANSIT DEVELOPMENT TEAM WAS CREATED BY THE DEPUTY MAYOR: STAFF ASSIGNED TO REVIEW & EVALUATE STATION PLANS BEFORE THEY REACHED THE BOARD — WE WERE RETAINED AS CONSULTANTS TO THE TEAM

WE PROVIDED TECHNICAL ASSISTANCE TO SEVERAL NEIGHBORHOODS:

1. ARTICULATING PEOPLE CONCERNS IN GRAPHIC TERMS
2. PROPOSING ALTERNATIVES WITHIN THE CONSTRAINTS OF Ⓜ PLANNING

OUR WORK **HELPED** MAKE CERTAIN CHANGES

HERE ARE 2 ILLUSTRATIONS:

---

1. DEANE AVE. STATION

THE PROPOSED PLAN HAD LOCATED THE STATION

BETWEEN A FREEWAY

& 2 R.R. LINES, OVER AN UNDERPASS

CONNECTING 2 NEIGHBORHOODS

WE TALKED TO RESIDENTS AS WELL AS PLANNERS IN THE AREA ≠ IDENTIFIED IMPORTANT ISSUES WHICH WOULD EFFECT OR BE EFFECTED BY THE NEW STATION

THE UNDERPASS FLOODS!

KIDS HAVE BEEN KILLED

CROSSING THE TRACKS IS THE ONLY WAY TO SCHOOL

TRAFFIC JAMS AT THE UNDERPASS

THE AREA NEEDS STORES

PUT STORES NEAR THE STATION

WE PROPOSED MOVING THE STATION TO A LOCATION NEAR AN EXISTING PEDESTRIAN BRIDGE OVER THE FREEWAY

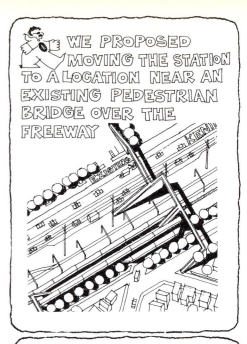

THE BIG ADVANTAGE

PEDESTRIANS WILL BE ABLE TO CROSS SAFELY

ALSO:

DEVELOPMENT CAN OCCUR NEAR THE STATION

BUS ≠ AUTO ACCESS WILL BE IMPROVED

WE ALSO DESCRIBED CRITERIA FOR THE ARCHITECTURAL DESIGN OF THE STATION

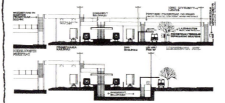

RESULT:

M metro HAS AGREED TO:

① RELOCATE THE STATION

② DEVELOP DETAILED DESIGNS FOR COMMUNITY REVIEW

2. RHODE ISLAND AVE. STATION

BASED ON THE SUCCESS OF DEANE AVE. STATION WE WERE NEXT ASKED TO LOOK @ SEVERAL STATIONS LOCATED ALONG 1 LINE ≠ PROPOSED TO RUN THROUGH SEVERAL NEIGHBORHOODS

GLENMONT LINE

 **HAD PROPOSED PARKING LOTS**

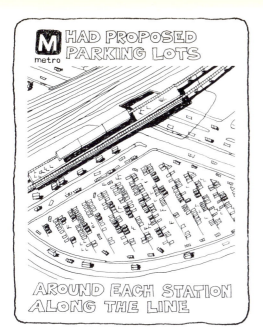

AROUND EACH STATION ALONG THE LINE

AGAIN, WE MET WITH SEVERAL COMMUNITY GROUPS

ONE ISSUE STOOD OUT,

PARKING AROUND IN·CITY STATIONS

RESIDENTS WERE CONCERNED ABOUT:

1. INCREASED TRAFFIC ON LOCAL STREETS
2. PARKING TAKING AWAY TAXABLE PROPERTY
3. ISOLATION OF THE STATION FROM THE COMMUNITY

THE CITY COUNCIL WAS ASKED TO HOLD HEARINGS ON THE ISSUE "PARKING"

WE PRESENTED ARGUMENTS FOR: **SEVERLY LIMITING SUBURBAN COMMUTER PARKING AROUND THE STATIONS**

1. THERE ARE **ALTERNATIVE MEANS OF ACCESS** TO THE STATIONS: JITNEYS, DIAL·A·RIDE, GROUP RIDE
2. THE POTENTIAL EXISTS FOR **NEW DEVELOPMENT RELATED TO THE STATION**

THIS WAS ILLUSTRATED SO EVERYONE COULD UNDERSTAND

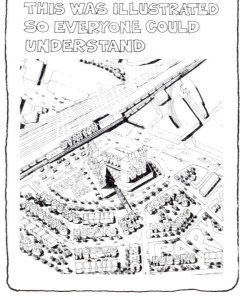

RESULT:

THE CITY COUNCIL ADOPTED A RESOLUTION CALLING FOR

3/4 REDUCTION IN PARKING / D.C. STATIONS

THE NEXT STEP:

 PREPARE DETAILED PLANS FOR:

1. A NEIGHBORHOOD TRANSIT SYSTEM
2. DEVELOPMENT AROUND THE STATION

72

This statement of council policy—abridged here—was issued in March 1973 since when there have been GLC elections which returned a new majority party.

In July 1972 the Council published a paper for public discussion entitled *Traffic and the Environment*. It described the increasing conflict between the pressure of traffic and the desire for a better environment. It asked Londoners to consider what should be done in the critical years before the major programmes to improve public transport and build new roads could take effect. The paper provoked wide public interest. As well as the many comments put forward in writing, there was discussion in the press, on the radio and on television, and the Council took account of all the views expressed.

The essence of the public reaction can be set down quite shortly.

There was strong agreement that —

Positive measures are needed to deal with the problem of the ever-increasing demand for the available road space.

Full recognition must be given to the relationship between traffic and the environment.

Restrictions on the car, though necessary, must be accompanied by improvements to public transport.

Better enforcement of traffic regulations is basic to the success of traffic restraint policies.

Heavy lorries are often the worst offenders against the environment particularly in shopping and residential streets.

There was less agreement on —

The priorities to be accorded to traffic in relation to the needs of the environment.

The priorities to be given to different types of traffic.

Whether existing methods of traffic control are adequate or new methods are needed.

Oxford Street. More pleasant for shopping and access made easier by excluding cars and lorries.

The Council accepts the first five views. For the rest it believes that new methods of control will be needed but that there is no simple answer to the question of priority between different types of traffic nor to the different economic and environmental needs of the community, one of which is the reasonable use of motor vehicles.

What is already being done successfully has also to be borne in mind. The completion of the first phase of the scheme to link a thousand sets of traffic signals to a central computer so as to speed up traffic flows, the installation of over 20 traffic lanes reserved for buses and the traffic scheme which now excludes virtually all cars and lorries during the day-time from part of Oxford Street are three examples from the present programme of action.

Changes in London Transport's services are part of the same total effort. They go hand in hand with traffic control. Among other things the Council is fostering the pre-purchase of tickets and experiments in bus services. The travelling public now pay less than 80 per cent of the cost of travel following the write-off of London Transport's capital debt, the increased grants won from the Government and the Council's own substantial contributions to London Transport's capital needs. There is now hard evidence of the surge of improvements — new rolling stock, station reconstruction and the new Fleet Line workings.

The time has come to take further bold steps forward. Some of the measures which are needed are either new or largely untried. Whilst therefore making firm recommendations for familiar and proven controls the Council also suggests new ventures. But where changes might risk serious damage to the environment or the economy of London there should first be an active programme of study and experiment.

Traffic restraint: the broad view

The Council has always said that restraint methods should be both fair and effective. They should be applied in such a way as to limit traffic which is of the least importance and the greatest nuisance and where the journeys can most easily be made by public transport.

To gauge the priority to be given to different types of traffic we set out four broad groups —

First, buses, taxis and other public vehicles — which should go wherever required.

Second, commercial vehicles and cars making business trips — which as far as possible should be allowed to make the journeys they wish but might have to be excluded from areas where they have no business.

Third, cars being used for shopping and leisure outside the busiest hours and the more congested areas — which should be kept away from sensitive areas where they have no business and should only be more generally restrained if they put too large a load on the roads they use.

Fourth, cars being used for journeys in the peak hours in congested areas, such as the journeys made by car commuters to work in central London — which should be the first to be limited.

But there are some people, such as the severely disabled, who should always be given special consideration when restrictions are proposed.

The broad grouping will present problems in practice: it will sometimes be difficult to say with certainty that a particular kind of journey falls into one, and only one, group. Nevertheless, the grouping does give an idea of priorities and a judgement of how effective individual traffic controls are.

The heaviest traffic and greatest congestion occurs in central London. But there is much congestion in the inner ring of London too. There, the traffic bound for the centre or en route across London is added to dense local traffic and the resulting pressures on environment are very great. Outer London is more spacious but even there, in terms of traffic, the main suburban centres are starting to seem very much like central London.

There are two principles which the Council believes should be generally followed. First, through-traffic should be directed away from the busiest centres and vulnerable residential areas wherever there are other routes which on balance are better able to take it. Second, the total amount of parking space in an area, on and off the street, must be related to the capacity of its roads to take the traffic generated.

Car parking

Car parking controls are already accepted as a way of preventing haphazard and untidy parking on the street and of limiting commuting by car. They will continue to provide the foundation for traffic restraint over the next few years. But there are difficulties and limitations.

In central London a quarter of all traffic passes through and is thus not susceptible to restraint by parking control. Another quarter consists of buses, taxis and lorries delivering or collecting loads in the area.

Proposed licensing area for public off-street car parks.

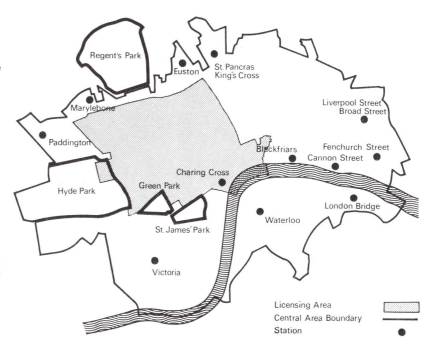

Cars make up the remaining 50 per cent and about three fifths of these park in public car parks, on and off the street, and two fifths in private car parks, some in people's homes but most in office car parks.

The use of public car parks can be controlled to some extent, either because they are owned or managed by local authorities or, in the case of privately-owned ones, by means of statutory regulations. The traffic using private car parks, like through traffic, is beyond present means of control.

Of course, as parking control spreads, a growing proportion of traffic through one locality would be affected by controls in other areas. But to resolve the problems by parking control alone would mean introducing comprehensive parking controls over hundreds of square miles; this is neither desirable nor practicable. That is why new ways of restraining traffic are needed. However, control by parking must continue; it is immediately available and will be a valuable complement to new ways of restraining traffic.

Public off-street parking

Public car parks are available to all comers and their use can be controlled by local authorities. For these

Licensing Area
Central Area Boundary
Station

reasons as much as possible of the off-street parking in town centres, beyond that required for essential access to individual buildings, should be provided in public car parks.

The pattern of charges should not favour those who leave their cars all day. The Council already has experience with the car parks on the South Bank of the reduction in commuters and the increase in the daily turnover of use resulting from the adoption of a standard hourly rate for all users. Some London boroughs have also adopted with success similar pricing policies but all should now seek to manage their car parks in a way which restrains traffic at key times.

The Council proposes, with the help of the City of Westminster and the London Borough of Camden, to introduce in 1974 as a first step a licensing scheme for part of the West End which will regulate how public car parks are operated. The area is shown overleaf and the intention is that within the area no-one shall operate a public car park except under licence from the borough council, the terms of which will ensure that a proper balance is kept between parking for short and long periods of the day.

In central London the construction of new public off-street car parks must be generally curtailed. The Council will allow them only on conversion of office car parks to public use or in districts where there is a severe shortage of public car parking at present.

In central and inner London, as the consents for temporary car parks on vacant sites expire, they should not be renewed except in areas of severe shortage. Where these sites cannot be redeveloped quickly they should be considered for temporary use as amenity open spaces. The Council will investigate with the boroughs what might be done to bring this about. At the moment these car parks provide space for 8,800 cars in central London alone and take up almost 50 acres of land there. Removal of these cars from the central London scene and the addition of, say, a score of green islands would be a significant improvement. There is however one category of public car parks which the Council intends to foster. It is the railway station car park. More traffic restraint in inner and central London means that fewer people will go there unless reasonable alternative means of travel can be provided. A car ride to the local station and the journey continued by train is for some a convenient alternative and therefore there should be more station car parks in outer London so as to encourage people to do this. The Council has set a target of an additional 25,000 station parking places. It has set aside £5 million over the next five years to help London Transport

and British Railways to achieve it and has asked the Government to provide an equal amount in grant. The boroughs' aid will be needed in planning the implementation of the programme.

Public on-street parking

In town centres and densely-populated areas uncontrolled on-street parking can choke the streets and make them dangerous and unsightly. Where this happens on-street controls should continue to be introduced in the future as they have been in the past. In addition, however, in inner London particularly, on-street restrictions will have to be introduced to deny free parking space at the kerb side to commuters. Table 1 shows the programme the Council wishes to be followed for the 40 square miles of the Inner London Parking Area (ILPA).

Table 1 — On-street parking control in the ILPA

	1961	1971	1981
Central area			
Number of meter spaces	10,500	21,000	20,000
Number of residents' spaces	—	7,000	9,000
Number of free spaces	53,000	2,000	—
Total	63,500	30,000	29,000
Remainder of ILPA			
Number of meter spaces	—	12,000	30,000
Number of residents' spaces	—	26,000	60,000
Number of free spaces	210,000	134,000	30,000
Total	210,000	172,000	120,000

The effectiveness of parking control, already limited by its inability to deal with through-traffic, is further reduced because, as the law stands at present, parking controls cannot be fully enforced. Many infringements of the parking rules cannot be brought home to the offender because he cannot be traced. The Council has been urging the Government to make owners of vehicles, rather than their drivers, liable for parking and similar offences which attract fixed penalties. The recent Government statement that legislation for this purpose will be introduced as soon as possible is welcomed.

Residential off-street parking

It is clearly safer and less intrusive if cars are not garaged on the street. That is why planning standards require generally that all new dwellings should have an off-street garage space. However, in central London and the denser parts of inner London heavy traffic restraint

and the close network of public transport will make some people prefer not to have a car there. The Council believes therefore that the requirement to provide a car space with each dwelling in those areas should be further examined.

Office car parks

There are about half a million parking spaces in London at private business premises, about one-tenth being in central London. They are usually located in the basements of office blocks, are frequently used for commuter parking and their use is outside public control. Table 2 shows how London's total parking stock is divided into the four categories of parking. It is clear that even if all 120,000 parking spaces in public off-street car parks were to come under control the potential gain would be limited by the existence of 523,000 uncontrolled private parking spaces. This is a particular problem in central London. Here, the 53,000 private parking spaces under office blocks are mainly used by car commuters who reach the centre by way of the congested streets of inner London.

For the future the Council has already said that the total stock of private parking must be limited and has set parking standards for new office and shop development intended to ensure that the size of the garages in these buildings should be very severely restricted. For the Greater London Development Plan, standards for different areas of London have been set in ranges so as to allow for differing conditions in particular areas. The evidence the Council now has suggests that the less restrictive end of each of these ranges may have been too generous and that borough councils, who in the main have to operate the standard controls, should adopt the more restrictive end of the scale.

The effect of this would be that the maximum provision for parking in new offices and shops would be

Central area of London — 1 space per 12,000 sq feet floor space

Inner ring — 1 space per 8,000 sq feet floor space More important

suburban centres — 1 space per 5,000 sq feet floor space

Remainder of outer London — 1 space per 2,000 sq feet floor space.

Moreover in designing new buildings the position and layout of this parking space should be convenient for its service use rather than for the all-day parking of private cars.

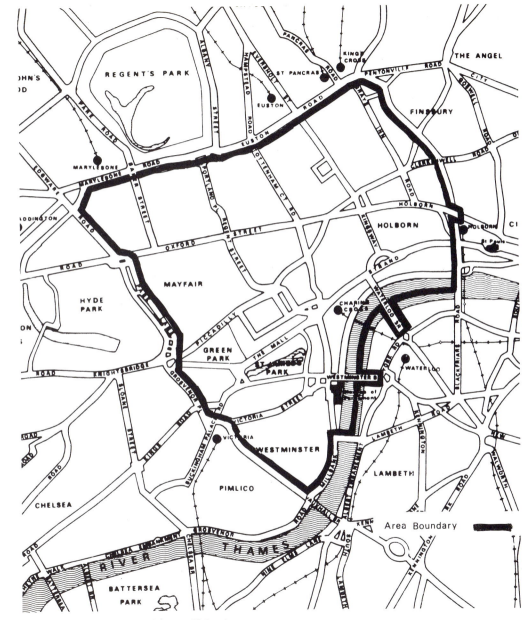

Area of proposed ban on lorries over 40 feet long.

75

Table 2 – Parking supply in Greater London 1971

Area	Off-street				On-street	Total
	Public	Private		Total		
		Residential	Non-residential			
Central	30,000	17,000	53,000	100,000	30,000	130,000
Inner ring	20,000	180,000	120,000	320,000	680,000	1,000,000
Outer	70,000	600,000	350,000	1,020,000	1,400,000	2,420,000
Total	120,000	797,000	523,000	1,440,000	2,110,000	3,550,000

Lorries

Heavy lorries can be a great nuisance in the streets of London. All of them are noisy and the largest of them negotiate narrow roads and sharp corners with difficulty; when parked in the wrong place they can be an eyesore and a danger. One cannot however wish them away entirely because nearly all London's supplies travel by road and there is little prospect of changing this. The Government and the motor industry are trying to develop quieter lorries. They should do more and do it quicker. Large buses with powerful but relatively quiet engines are already becoming available and given the will lorries could have the same treatment. Certainly the most universal advantage to Londoners and those who live in other towns and cities would come from tackling the noise at source.

But meanwhile some problems can be tackled by regulating where these noisy but important vehicles move and park. Sometimes restrictions will need to be matched by better facilities elsewhere. Certainly in the short term the absence of suitable alternative road routes and of lorry parks will limit what can be done. Many proposals when looked at in detail prove to be producing benefits for one area at the price of spoiling the environment in another.

The lorry parking problem is in two parts: first, the need to provide a limited number of strategic lorry parks with residential facilities nearby and second, the need for a greater number of smaller local parks. There is also need to limit lorry parking in quiet residential area.

The general question of strategic lorry parks outside London was investigated by a working party set up by the Department of the Environment which recommended standards for such developments. Sites are now being identified by regional study groups. A London working party, including representatives from the Department of the Environment, London borough councils and other interested bodies has been set up by the Council. This is considering urgently the question of strategic lorry parks in London and it seems there are likely to be a few suitable sites available. However the problem extends beyond the GLC boundary and the development of such parks outside London and convenient to the national motorways and the proposed orbital road is badly needed.

These problems cannot be solved by the local planning authorities alone; the road transport industry has a major part to play. If freight operators do not take initiatives in finding, acquiring and equipping suitable sites they may be faced with growing restrictions and no convenient alternative.

Heavy lorries have no business to be in city centres. The Council has decided as a beginning to ban through lorries over 40 feet long from an area in central London which is bounded by a reasonable route to take the diverted lorries. The area is shown in the map *(previous page)*. This will remove some of the most offensive and obstructive vehicles from the busiest area in London and will provide valuable experience on which the prospect for further lorry bans can be assessed. But the Council is in no doubt that with few alternative routes for the many vehicles which have business in Greater London they cannot be diverted from its streets entirely.

In some areas coach parking can also be a nuisance. Similar controls are needed to those put forward for lorries but tailored to the particular needs of the tourist industry.

Buses

Good bus services are an important counterpart to increasing car restraint. The Council has this year arrested the trend of declining service by asking London Transport not to cut the total bus mileage for any reason but staff shortage. Shortage of staff has in fact the greatest effect of any factor on the standard of services run.

But bus services would also benefit if they were better insulated from the delaying effects of traffic congestions. Much of the problem occurs at the approaches to busy junctions and allowing buses to avoid congestion at these places can provide major benefits.

The Council already has a large programme for installing bus lanes in the peak hours and this is being stepped up with the intention of having 120 approved by the end of 1974, of which about 70 should be in operation by the end of 1973. This will release buses from most of the worst effects of localised traffic con-

gestion. There will still be some places where buses suffer badly and where bus lanes are unlikely to be an effective solution. Other methods must be tried.

Oxford Street is an outstanding example of one of them. The restriction of car traffic and widened pavements have produced real benefits for buses and pedestrians. There are a score of places in central and inner London and others in outer London where the Oxford Street approach might be suitable.

There is also a series of minor but valuable steps which can be taken to help the bus on busy streets. Priority turns and traffic signal settings weighted to favour the bus have been introduced and proposals are in hand to ban parking at 2,000 of the busiest stops where buses are seriously obstructed at present.

But the bus stands to benefit also by general measures of car restraint and this increases the Council's determination to make these effective.

Pedestrians and cyclists

Most roads in London today have to cater for both pedestrians and traffic. Some of the risk and conflict this involves is built into the system and will not easily be changed. But there are opportunities for making journeys on foot safer and more pleasant. The Council is already active and intends to do more.

In residential areas the main task facing the Council and the London boroughs must be to keep out through-traffic wherever reasonably possible. Closing up the routes whereby traffic by-passes congested junctions at peak hours is one way of doing it. But the systematic creation of relatively traffic- free areas in which the only vehicles would be those with business there would be better.

In busy shopping streets where many of the problems lie there are no easy solutions. Studies of what has been done at home and abroad to keep traffic out of these areas all point to the need for adequate local by-passes. In the meantime in some of the minor street, like Carnaby Street, traffic can be banned. Elsewhere the opportunities are not so great, but there are still useful changes that might sometimes be made. A partial ban which restricts the types of vehicles or applies to a particular time of day, or the closing of some minor side streets can bring benefits which though hard won will be much appreciated. The Council is intent on following up the successful experiment in Oxford Street by further ventures elsewhere.

Crossing main roads is another problem for pedestrians. More refuges in the centre of the road are being

provided, a simple but effective help. Many of the crossings at signals and elsewhere have been made safe by the use of new skid-resistant road surfaces. New, clearer signals for pedestrians and the spread of the use of pelican crossings give a steady improvement.

Cyclists in London's busy and congested traffic face great difficulty. The busiest roads are not safe for them or ever likely to be and the densely built-up areas do not give ready opportunities for special cycleways. In less busy and more open areas the chances of improving conditions are better. The creation of relatively traffic-free areas will be a useful step forward. But only in rare circumstances, for example in the new and comprehensively planned area of Thamesmead, is the provision of cycleways likely.

More attention must be paid to reducing the clutter of road signs and to the opportunities for minor changes in landscaping. The Council intends that the high standards of maintenance of the actual road surface should be extended to maintaining and improving road verges, road-side trees and shrubs, footways and street furniture.

New methods of traffic restraint

In its simplest terms the basic problem of traffic in London is that with its present road system there is too much, particularly in central London, the inner ring, the suburban centres and residential areas. There is no scientific way of deciding by how much traffic levels should be reduced to produce a more pleasant environment but it is reasonable to assume that a reduction in traffic in central London by some 10 to 15 per cent would make both inner and central London better places to live and work in.

Restraint of traffic by parking control alone cannot achieve this. The shortcomings of parking control have been pointed out, the principal one being that it cannot stop through-traffic. Indeed even if parking control could reduce the amount of traffic in central London by 10 to 15 per cent, through-traffic would increase to take advantage of the less congested conditions and cancel out some of the advantage gained.

A method must be found which controls through-traffic. There are two possibilities for immediate consideration: restraint by physical means and restraint by fiscal means.

Restraint by physical means requires some roads to be made narrower by artifical means or even to be closed altogether. It makes congestion worse at the pinch point but it can prevent some traffic getting through.

King's Road Chelsea. Pedestrians fight it out with traffic. Should the Council treat this like Oxford Street?

A minibus takes advantage of a bus priority measure at the Swiss Cottage intersection.

There are however some circumstances when this form of restraint can be worthwhile, namely —

   where congestion is imposed on less important traffic to the advantage of more important traffic: bus lanes could help to achieve this on busy routes where environmental areas are protected from traffic

   where some characteristics of the road network means that restriction at one point avoids costly and critical traffic conditions beyond (an example of this is the metering of traffic on to a motorway to avoid massive congestion there).

The success of this form of restraint depends on how much these conditions apply and on traffic response. If most traffic continues to force its way through, the costs of the extra congestion will outweigh the benefits. If on the other hand many travellers transfer to public transport or travel at other times or to other places, this could be beneficial. Physical restraint is indiscriminate and restrains essential and less essential traffic alike. The uncertainies are such that this form of restraint should proceed only by careful experiment. The most likely form of traffic restraint by fiscal means in the near future is supplementary licensing. This is a system which would require the purchase of a special licence in order to use a vehicle at specified times in designated areas. The charge for the licence would be a significant addition to the cost of the annual road licence and sufficiently high to discourage the use of vehicles in the designated area. Supplementary licensing appears to offer the best and most immediate prospect of achieving the required traffic reduction in central London. But neither the Government nor the Council has yet sufficient understanding of the mechanics of such a scheme, how it would be enforced and its social and economic effects. An urgent study in depth of the implications and effectiveness of supplementary licensing is now required.

The way ahead

One of the criticisms made of *Traffic and the Environment* was that it concentrated on traffic problems but said little about environment. Perhaps the same comment will be made about this report. But a major problem of the environment of London *is* traffic and improvements to the environment go hand in hand with the essential task of taming traffic.

Commerce and industry and the public at large also have a part to play. A readiness to accept personal inconvenience and some incursion into freedom of choice which traffic restraint measures might bring can pay off handsomely if they help us all to live with traffic.

It is the borough councils, however, who are the GLC's principal partners in the business of creating a better environment. This paper is the outcome of a major dialogue with the borough councils, conducted in public and in private. The Council now puts forward this paper in the hope that borough councils can formulate their own urgent proposals within its framework.

Producing workable plans will involve many difficult compromises. It is all too easy to reject a firm plan of action because one or two of its aspects are unsatisfactory or even objectionable. This must be resisted and proposals assessed against the widespread and urgent need to live with traffic. The task is clear and the time is short.

MOBILE SHOPS IN CHANDIGARH

ADITYA PRAKASH

Initially people who come to cities require a job and a house. Then they require all the other amenities the city provides — variety, education, entertainment, etc. Once they have tasted these, they do not go back to the villages.

When there is development activity — whether extending a city or building a new one — who comes first? In India, apart from a few technicians, it is the building labour and the *rehri* (the mobile shop). When the development is over, both are driven out. Building labour moves to another developing site, so do the *rehriwallas* (the mobile shop merchants). But some tough guys stick on to reap the harvest of their labours. They consolidate somehow, against the law.

The law requires that people live in proper houses, shop at properly built shops, work in proper offices and move on good roads. But the labourers live in makeshift *kachcha* or thatched huts: the *rehris* station themselves on abandoned sites. Thus they have no place in the lawful scheme of things. It is held that they are denizens of slums: wherever they go they will create slums. They must not be part of the city. Everyone forgets that they provided daily needs when no one else dared step into the place for trade or work. However, it is fair to conclude that building labourers and the *rehriwallas* represent the economic standard of the country. This being so, it is important that we build from the bottom: any structure started midway is bound to fall.

The evidence shows that:

1   There are almost as many *rehris* in Chandigarh as there are other shops (regular lawful ones).
2   Wherever possible the *rehris* are located under shady trees, near the shopping sectors, on any vacant patch of land. The denser the population of the sector, the more the *rehris*.
3   Approximately 15% of the *rehris* cater for foodstuffs, perishable and non-perishable: foods made and served on the spot, fruits, vegetables, etc. But the *rehris* also sell general merchandise, clothing, footwear, crockery and toys, and provide such services as stove repairs, shoe repairs, carpentry, hair dressing, etc. In brief, except for some heavy items and luxury goods, almost all the daily needs can be had from the *rehris*.
4   There is a tendency for the *rehris* to turn into permanent establishments.
5   The investment on *rehris* is generally very small. Approximately £100 can establish a *rehri*, but in order to obtain legal protection many of them are hired by others who can provide such protection.
6   The busiest periods of the day for the *rehris* are the hour before the offices open in the morning (8 am in the winter, 10 am in the summer) and immediately after office closing time (5.30 pm and 8.30 pm respectively) until late after sunset.
7   For *rehriwallas* the day begins early when they buy the daily merchandise in the wholesale market, mainly fruit and vegetables, and prepare eatables (*golgappas, chaats,* etc.). It ends quite late in the evenings. The relaxation period is around lunch time, when business is slack.
8   The *rehriwallas* do a round of the residential streets after the menfolk have done to work, for about two hours, and again in the afternoon, providing foodstuffs for 'tea' when the menfolk return from work.
9   The average earnings of a *rehriwalla* in Chandigarh is about £150, and in the nearby city of Ambala £100 per month. This indicates that the city of Chandigarh has contributed to raising the income level of the common man.
10   Many of the *rehriwallas* are married and live in rented one- or two-roomed houses, or in garages. About 20%, mostly bachelors, spend their nights on the *rehri* sites. Thus the problem is not only of trade but of habitation for a substantial number of people.
11   Although only 20% of the *rehriwallas* spend the nights on the sites, 60% of the *rehris* remain there under the vigil of a guard whose expenses are shared by all.
12   The relaxation and recreation of the *rehriwallas* is fairly simple. During slack periods, they play cards. At night, taking some country liquor is common. They take one day off per month.

The various types of rehris in use in Chandigarh

The most common type of *rehri* is a wooden board platform, 66 x 39 in, mounted at a height of 34 in on a chassis of four bicycle wheels held together by steel rods and strip-framing. This *rehri* is variously used for selling vegetables, fruits, eggs or for general merchandise. Its chief advantages are: (a) it is reasonably light i.e. it can be pushed easily and lifted over obstacles (b) it can do business while mobile as well as while stationary (c) it is cheap.

The second type has a minor variation in the design of its wooden board platform. It has some small shelves on two sides on which plates can be placed. These shelves are used for eating the spicy foodstuffs served from the *rehri*.

The third type is in the form of a box mounted on a chassis with four bicycle wheels. One side of the box is hinged on top so that when it is opened it acts as a shade. Inside the box are narrow wooden shelves *(top right)*. The floor of the box is used by the owner for squatting upon, and from here he serves his customers from a counter, which is at a height of 34 in for the customers. This is a very sensible design for it provides protection for the merchandise and the owner as well as the customers. It is used for selling cigarettes, *pan*, tobacco and books, etc. It is not suitable for selling fruits and vegetables, nor is it very suitable for doing business while making the rounds of the streets.

The fourth type is essentially a delivery van *(below left)*. It is used for home delivery of milk in bottles, gas cylinders and other merchandise to and from shops But it also serves as a mobile shop for the sale of kerosene oil.

The cost of rehris

The others, who own their *rehri*, have either bought it readymade (for about £16-£28) or made it themselves (for £13-£16). This is the present-day cost of the basic *rehri* with only a wooden platform on the top. Particular *rehris* — like those selling *golguppas* and *chatwallas*, tea-stalls, *pan-bidi* and cigarettes have to get their *rehris* built-up for additional amounts and the cost goes up to anything from £60-£100. This includes the glass showcase with sliding shutters, a formica deck, and other attachments Some even have a large-size umbrella for protection from sun. The *rehris* are protected from the elements by tarpaulins during storms or rains.

The milk supply scheme and the rehris

The milk supply scheme of Chandigarh works as

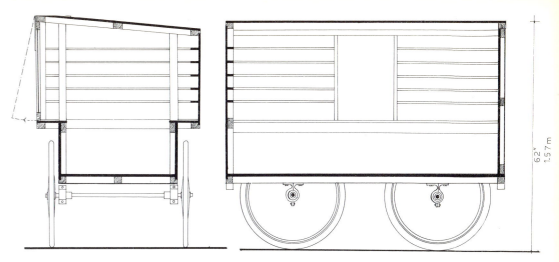

Above: An existing rehri, used for selling tobacco, cigarettes, books, etc.

Below: An existing rehri: a delivery van for gas cylinders, milk bottles, coal, kerosene, oil, etc.

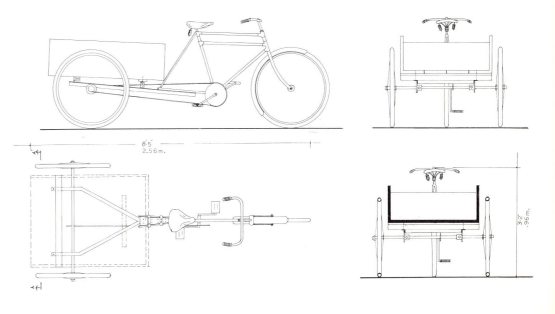

Top: An existing rehri, most common for selling fruit, vegetables and general merchandise.

Above: An existing rehri, for selling cooked foods and spicy delicacies.

follows. There is the central milk processing plant in the Industrial Area. Then there are milk distribution booths in nearly all sectors — suitably located. The milk van supplies milk bottles to these booths in the early morning and in the afternoon. To the booths people come to buy milk, morning and evening. It appears to be a satisfactory system. But consider the following:-

(a)   The milk booths remain unused most of the day. They open for about an hour in the morning and as much time in the afternoon.

(b)   People have to queue for milk early in the morning, which is very inconvenient for a large number of people. To those who can afford to send servants to collect milk, it seems all right, but the number of servants is dwindling rapidly — a sign of progress.

(c)   The milk distribution van stays idle for most of the time.

(d)   Staff have to be employed for short intervals to man the milk booths. Thus they cannot be regular employees. Such employment is always unsatisfactory.

(e)   If the milk van comes late, or the booth operator comes late, there is considerable confusion.

On account of some of these reasons, milk bars have been started by some enterprising shopkeepers, who buy a large number of milk bottles from the dairy, and sell them at some extra cost from their shop at all times of the day (while they sell other things also) and also run a home delivery service on cycle-driven *rehri*. This works very satisfactorily.

Now if the milk distribution scheme had been planned on the basis of cycle-*rehri* transportation and distribution system, how would this have worked, and would it have been an economic proposition?

It needs to be noted that, in India, newspapers are distributed by vendors, who collect them direct from the newspaper offices. No newpaper vans move round to distribute papers to vendors or news-agents. Another observation — no place in Chandigarh is more than about 5 km from any other point. Thus any place becomes easily accessible by bicycles. The required number of cycle-*rehri* vendors could be commissioned to collect milk bottles from the milk processing plant, and they could deliver the milk directly to the doorstep of each house. Each milk vendor could work out his own beat — like a newspaper vendor does. He could also undertake to vend such allied items as are normally handled by dairies e.g. butter, cheese, bread, etc. When not required to vend milk, the *rehri* vendor could deliver other articles of merchandise to people's homes from other shops, or he could run a mobile milk bar which could be also stationed at *rehri* sites.

Such a scheme would
(a) be more flexible
(b) provide employment to more people
(c) would cost the Indian economy less
(d) milk could be supplied cheaper and at the doorstep.

It may further be noted here, that the milk is often brought by villagers on bicycles to the milk collection centres and it is a profitable proposition for them.

The problems of the rehri

Most of the problems arise from the general illegality of the *rehri* business. Even if some *rehris* are issued licences to ply in the streets, no authority seems to accept them as desirable or healthy elements in a city. It is only the tough who can survive in such a situation.

The worst problem is that the *rehris* tend to become fixed on favoured spots. On some spots two or three *rehris* can be seen permanently fixed, their tyres deflated, their platforms joined together, and a large canvas or tarpaulin awning protecting them from the elements. In such a situation they are like ordinary ramshackle shops. They represent the peak of the illegal practice.

Other problems arising from the lack of acceptance of *rehris* as a proper institution are:

(a)   Unpaved sites full of dust and filth which become muddy when it rains;

(b)   Unsanitary conditions caused by lack of proper drainage and failure to collect litter and vegetable waste;

(c)   Lack of protection from rain and wind in inclement weather (though there is not much of this type of weather in Chandigarh) and from sun where there are no trees;

(d)   Lack of places of rest, recreation and social intercourse for the *rehriwallas*;

(e)   Lack of supply of tapped water and sanitary facilities;

(f)   Lack of adequate facilities for those who spend the nights on the site.

Desirability of rehris in the urban scene

1   *Economic.*   First priority should be given to the welfare of those who ply *rehris*. Those with regular shops can fend for themselves. They sell what the shopkeepers cannot afford to sell (e.g. ground-nuts, baked *dal, moth, channas, chaats, golgappas*), and provide services like stove repairs. The prices of the *rehriwallas* are low, because their investment is low. The investment of the government for providing proper *rehri* sites is bound to be much lower than regular shops. The *rehris* provide job opportunities for a larger number of people than the shops, because the latter tend to concentrate wealth in a few hands. What is more, the *rehris* can be mobile or stationary at will. They can be taken to any place, at any time, wherever there is activity and concentration of people. Thus, in Chandigarh, the *rehris* visit cinema halls, schools, hospitals and so on at appropriate times. During festivals, like *Dussera,* when a lot of people come to witness *Ram Lila,* the *rehriwallas* serve their needs. During important sports events, the *rehriwallas* are there. The state functions on Independence Day and Republic Day would be incomplete without *rehris.* Thus, they can serve you at your doorstep, or you can go to them on their sites. Since a large number of people ply *rehris,* there is keen competition between them. You can always be sure of reasonable value for your money. In fact all types of people throng to *rehri* markets and put up with the unsanitary conditions, because they find things cheaper there.

2   *Social.*   The *rehriwallas* are generally considered socially undesirable types. This largely arises from the illegal nature of their business, and their comparatively low economic standards. If their counterpart, the regular shopkeeper, does some illegal business, he can very easily hide it under the garb of his respectability, and, therefore, he remains a socially desirable person. Our observations in Chandigarh show that most *rehriwallas* are fairly well educated up to junior secondary standard. Whereas they may take some liquor, they do not form a group of drunkards. They are wise enough to realize that it is bad business to give any suggestion of being drunk during business hours. Most of them do a clean daily business. Most of them have families, and their children go to school. It may be that their counterparts in old cities like Ambala, where we made some observations, are not as well educated or as well behaved and that they suffer from a sense of inferiority. This is because they have always been nurtured in an environment of filth and ugliness so that they are unable to assert themselves. However, Chandigarh, though not accepting *rehris* as a regular urban institution, does provide a neat and serene environment which arouses a certain pride in the people who live there. That is why the *rehriwallas* there have a better economic and social status.

3 *Aesthetic.* This is one aspect about which everyone seems to feel strongly. There is dirt, there is filth, there is ugliness. Yet why does the place attract such crowds? Is it only that the things are cheaper there? This certainly is a very vital reason, but not the only reason. It has to be recognized that the place is full of vitality. Instead of closed door, quiet shopping, so many shops and so many things can be seen here at the same time. You flit from shop to shop, buy one thing here, another thing there. You bargain and you select, and you hear the full throated calls of the vendors extolling the virtues and low prices of their merchandise. You are attracted by the animated lively atmosphere. Is that not architecture? One of the considerations in aesthetics is the physical form. The normal shopping streets or squares can be said to have an architectural impact of their own. That is so, but that is not all. The apprehension about physical form arises from a lack of understanding of architecture in the urban scene. Too often architecture is misunderstood as the art of providing buildings. The fact of the matter is that architecture is the art of providing space which is attractive, full of character and animated by the human presence. In this sense, the space where *rehris* are located is a much more lively place than any shopping street. It is not beautiful because we do not design it, because we do not consider it worth our while to think about its potential for goodness and beauty. Beauty can be achieved with very little additional expense and some thoughtfulness for the human needs. The architect need not assert his ideas of elevational compositions, but he has to be an imaginative person. He has also to understand that his job is not merely to cater for rich clients. He has to serve the needs of man and of space.

Why not a motorized rehri?

Because
(a) It is against the economic standard of the people the *rehri* are catering for;
(b) The motor pollutes the atmosphere;
(c) The motorized vehicles have created the most difficult (almost insoluble) problems in our cities. It is not worthwhile adding to those by having motoriz-ed *rehris*;
(d) The energy utilization in a motorized vehicle is very low; it is very high in a modern pedalled vehicle (like a bicycle);
(e) Motorized vehicles are not suited to frequent halting as *rehris* often need to do.

The role of rehris in urbanization

The increase in per capita income is reason enough for the existence of *rehis,* but *rehris* also provide a better service in most articles of merchandise than the shops do. For this reason, they are an asset in the urban scene. How to make them beautiful and orderly is essentially the work of the architect.
At this stage it is worthwhile to review that happened in Chandigarh in the beginning of its development — when there were no markets and no shops. As we have seen, there was only building labour, a few engineers and architects and their staff. The labourers built their thatch roofed huts, and their needs were met by a wooden makeshift stall, just outside the city boundary. Some temporary shops were also built in sector 19 where the architects' and engineers' offices were situat-ed and an number of temporary houses had been built. These temporary shops met the daily needs of the people. The chief shoppers were the servants of the staff of the project. Servants were easily available then and salaries went a long way. At the very first oppor-tunity, shops were built by the government in Sector 22, where regular houses had been built, yet the temporary stalls remained, and gradually the *rehris* multiplied. They began to cater to the needs of the housewives who had now appeared on the scene. Very soon a regular *rehri* market established itself under the mango trees in Sector 23, next to Sector 22. It is still there. It was the first to be, more or less, officially recognized. Official recognition, however, did not mean provision of any facilities. It meant that the *rehris* were allowed to stay there. Recently some sites have been covered to provide shelter for the *rehris.* Recognition or no recognition, *rehris* have grown with the shops, and their numbers now seem to be equal.

Table showing rehri — shop ratio

Site:	No of Rehris:	No of Shops:
Sector 15	104	107
Sector 19	721	186
Sector 20	181	190
Sector 23	148	134

Thus, from the above table, we may note a very interesting factor — that in all but one of the cases, the number of *rehris* is approximately equal to the number of shops. There is no plausible reason for this fact which is very amazing indeed. The exception

is in the site in Sector 19, which happens to be right in the middle of a labour class colony and also has the reputation of being the oldest site in Chandigarh. It is only here that the ratio fails to hold, resulting in the conglomeration of more than 700 *rehris* on the site. The question that needs to be examined here is this. If the architects had thought of the *rehris* as a possible and desirable method of providing shopping facilities — and not as a tolerated temporary encumbrance — what would have happened? The answer is:

(a) The development cost would have been less;
(b) The design of *rehris* would have been taken with seriousness, and a variety of designs would have evolved;
(c) The sites for *rehri* markets would have been care-fully chosen and designed, the basic amenities pro-vided for;
(d) Employment would have been found for a larger number of people;
(e) As in many other fields, Chandigarh would have provided leadership in this field also.

The difficulty still remains of accommodating the families. The observations show that people with families earn enough from the *rehri* to be able to rent a small house. Even at the beginning, three to four *rehriwallas* combining together could acquire a house for their families assuming that both husbands and wives work during the day. This is by no means an ideal solution, but much better than people sleeping on the pavements and on verandahs and staircases. This could be proposed for the very beginning of a new town or the expansion of an existing town.

About the rehri sites

A good number of *rehris* are no longer mobile and have been turned into permanent booths, by stretching canvas cloth on top and raising a plinth. Generally grocers, *tandurs,* tea-stall holders and cloth merchants come in this category. There is another category of people who do not have any *rehris* at all. They come and spread their goods on the ground and carry them back home generally on their bicycles. They are poorest of the whole lot and their earning is between Rs 6-10 (30-50p) a day. This category covers a few crockery sellers, cloth merchants and *Datun* sellers. They con-stitute 7-10% of the whole lot.
The *rehri* sites are located in the densely populated areas of the town and by the side of the shopping streets. They are generally located on vacant grounds where old, thick and shady trees exist; and the name for a site, among the *rehriwallas*, is *Bagh* (garden).

Nearly 60% of the *rehris* are parked at the *rehri* sites, including grocers, general merchants and a few of the vegetable and fruit *rehris* whose owners bring their goods every day from the market in man-pulled or auto-rickshaws. All the general merchants and grocers who leave their *rehris* at the site, leave them fully covered with canvas cloth. There is generally one *chowkidar* at each site at night who is paid by the *rehriwallas*. Those who take their *rehris* home, park them either in garages (if they rent one) and in the court (in case of 10-15 marla houses) or by the side of streets adjoining their residences.

The maximum number of customers served by each *rehriwalla* at his peak time is:

Fruit, vegetable and *chaatwallas*   8-10 per hour
Tea stalls and *tandurs*   12-15

So the space needed by a fruit or vegetable *rehri* is about 8 x 10 ft and nearly twice this by the tea-stalls and *tandurs* (as *charpai* is the article of furniture used for sitting purposes). Some *tandurwallas* in Sector 20 have made their benches and dining tables out of an arrangement of concrete slabs, used by Public Works Department for making pavements.

Design criteria

To suggest general criteria for the design of *rehris* and *rehri* markets:

1   The *rehri* should be lightweight.
2   It should be provided with a cover of canvas or plastic to keep out sun and rain.
3   A design should also be evolved so that, instead being pushed, a *rehri* could be driven like a bicycle.
4   A design should provide facilities for a man to sleep if he has no house. Such a design should have the possibility of enclosing the *rehri* from all sides when required and of storing merchandise in a locked space.
5   The *rehri* markets should be developed in conjunction with the same sites on which regular shops are intended to be developed.
6   Even when the regular shops are built, sites should be earmarked for continuing *rehri* sites.
7   The *rehri* sites should be generously planted with shady trees.
8   The *rehri* site should be properly paved and well drained.
9   There should be provision of water taps at frequent intervals. These will not only supply the needs of water for the *rehriwallas*, but will also be used for washing the entire site at least once a day.
10   There should be an adequate system for collecting and disposal of garbage.

Site	Total No. of rehris	Permanent rehris	Foodstuff rehris		General merchandise	Various trades	Vacant	Peak hours
			Perishable	Non-perishable				
(1)	(2)	(3)	(4)		(5)	(6)	(7)	(8)
1 Outside P.G.I. Sector 14	16	4 (25%)	3 (18%)	12 (77%)	—	1 (5%)	—	Throughout evening
2 Neelam Theatre, Sector 17	18	0	6 (33%)	12 (67%)	—	—	—	5.30 pm to 8.00 pm
3 Jagat Theatre, Sector 17	21	0	6 (28%)	10 (48%)	—	5 (24%)	—	5.30 pm to 8.00 pm
4 S-E end of Sector 18 Market	17	5 (30%)	5 (30%)	7 (40%)	4 (25%)	—	1 (5%)	Evenings
5 Secretariat Sector 1	12	—	0	12 (100%)	—	—	—	11 am to 2.00 pm
6 Market Sector 8	20	4 (20%)	9 (45%)	6 (30%)	—	5 (25%)	—	Evenings
7 Market Sector 7	15	4 (27%)	8 (54%)	7 (46%)	—	—	—	Evenings
8 Lake Sector 5	28	—	10 (36%)	18 (64%)	—	—	—	Evenings
9 Vegetable and Grain Market	15	15	0	11 (76%)	—	2 (12%)	2 (12%)	6 am to 10 am
10 Sector 22 Near Sood Dharamsala	160	100 (63%)	40 (25%)	56 (35%)	54 (34%)	8 (5%)	2 (1%)	Mornings & Evenings
11 Sector 15	104	65 (63%)	45 (44%)	43 (42%)	1 (1%)	10 (9%)	5 (5%)	Evenings
12 Sector 23	148	40 (26%)	99 (66%)	21 (14%)	9 (6%)	14 (9%)	5 (3%)	Evenings
13 Shastri Market Sector 22	212	140 (66%)	58 (28%)	62 (29%)	71 (33%)	7 (3%)	14 (6%)	Mornings & Evenings
14 Kiran Theatre Sector 22	36	0	21 (61%)	14 (39%)	—	1	—	5.30 to 9.00 pm
15 Sector 20	181	110 (61%)	65 (36%)	66 (37%)	18 (10%)	24 (13%)	8 (5%)	Evenings
16 Sector 20 Market	49	15 (30%)	11 (22%)	28 (56%)	25 (10%)	3 (6%)	2 (6%)	Evenings
17 Sector 19	721	430 (60%)	214 (30%)	136 (19%)	247 (35%)	89 (11%)	35 (5%)	Evenings
Total	1773	932	600	521	409	169	74	
Percentage		53%	34%	29%	23%	9%	4%	

63%
Maximum number of rehris are of foodstuffs

11 Sites which have more than fifty *rehris* should be provided with community facilities, such as toilets and a common place for sitting together for relaxation and gossip. This should consist of a small room and a shady open space.

12 Sites should be earmarked for *rehris* near places for public entertainment, or where large numbers of people are expected to gather. Such sites need be no more than a paved area for about ten *rehris*.

13 Housing for *rehriwallas* should be provided near the sites which are likely to have more than fifty *rehris*. These would normally be near the shopping centres of the higher density sectors or neighbourhood units.

14 The organization of *rehri* sites should be kept flexible. Thus it is not necessary to develop and pave a whole *rehri* site from the beginning. The development can take place gradually as the number of *rehris* visiting a site increases. In a competitive market, fluctuations are always likely to take place.

15 It should be ensured that the site is cleared of all *rehriwallas* for a certain period of the day. Thus each *rehriwalla* must go on his rounds during that period and the time should be utilized for cleaning up the whole site.

The proposed designs

As a system, the existing designs of *rehris* serve their function very well. There is no objection to their continuing as such. But the two designs prepared are intended to incorporate the following features:-

Design No 1 (above right)

This design is primarily intended to cater for a cover which can be of canvas or plastic material, obviously providing protection against the sun where no shady site is available. Secondly, it may also serve as a place for sleeping for a single person. Up till now this has often been done, bearing in mind the fact that a large number of people emigrate to cities in search of employment. Vending is one of the quick methods of earning a livelihood in the cities. But these emigrants generally have no houses and, therefore, settle in some shacks wherever they can find them.

I do not see anything wrong in their converting the *rehri* into a sleeping place at night till such time as they are able to afford and/or rent a reasonable house. To this end three things have been done in the design:- (a) The size of the platform has been made 72 in long. (b) A storage box has been provided under the platform in which merchandise can be stored so that the platform can be cleared for sleeping. (c)

Roller curtains have been provided on all sides; they can be rolled down in cooler weather and can also be used during the day in hot weather. It is, however, assumed that toilet and other facilities are made available on the *rehri* site by the community.

Design No. 2 (above)

This design envisages a possibility of faster movement on a tricycle device, so that the merchandise for which *rehris* are most commonly used i.e. fruits and vegetables, can be vended from house to house with greater speed and less fatigue. No *rehris* of this type exist. But this can certainly be an advancement on the common *rehri*. It is intended for the more well-to-do *rehriwalla* — the one who lives in a proper house, and seeks to do a little more business at the same time. This type of *rehri* can also work in conjunction with a shop, in that it can return to replenish merchandise after short intervals. It does not have the disadvantage which the delivery

type of existing *rehri* has, as its platform is at the work top height — convenient for doing business.

Location of rehri sites in Chandigarh

It is by no means our intention that the shops should be replaced by *rehris*. The shops have got to be there. But they need not be in as large numbers as they are today.

Let us imagine the urban scene of Chandigarh, particularly its neighbourhood units or sectors. At present, each is crossed by one street of shops at the middle of its longer (1200 metre) side. The maximum distance to reach the farthest shop of the sector is about 500 metres. That is not excessive. But for the items for which a housewife has to shop daily, or sometimes twice a day, this is not very convenient. Such items are milk, bread, vegetables, meat, fish, etc.

If we imagine the shopping street of a sector with a well defined site for the *rehris*, we shall not vitiate the urban scene; in fact we shall enliven it. At present the line of shops is interrupted at the place where the open space of the sector (running SW-NE) crosses it. It is at this place that a very suitable *rehri* market can be developed. Since no physical volume is built, it will not interrupt the flow of open space. Further, in the pedestrian movement along the open spaces, the *rehri* markets will provide suitable landmarks. Then, morning and evening, there would be jostling crowds, bargaining, shouting, teasing, with all enjoying the pleasures of selling and buying.

The open spaces of the sectors are expected to contain community facilities like community centres and health centres. Such complexes could also contain the basic amenities for the *rehri* markets. These need only be toilets and a room for sitting together. It will be in conformity with the Chandigarh Plan that these areas are well provided with trees, so useful for open air markets.

Conclusion

The conclusions to be drawn from this study are the following:

(1) *Rehris* create a lively marketing scene in Indian urban situation.

(2) By very little expenditure it is possible to create good *rehri* sites, and good *rehri* designs which will make a *rehri* market hygienic, and even beautiful.

(3) For most of the items of merchandise, the *rehris* render a superior service to the consumers.

(4) In any development activity, or new town building activity, priority should be given for the provision of *rehris* and *rehri* sites.

THE 'STREET' AND 'HIROBA' OF JAPAN

SHUN KANDA

Human activities and needs find expression in forms and patterns which reflect and shape our lives. The built environment is the ultimate public statement of the human condition. Yet this man-made environment on the whole is insufficiently studied for information about the underlying infrastructure of human activity systems. The extant environment can be perceived, identified, studied for analysis; and it can be designed and altered.
The purpose of this investigation will be to demonstrate the interaction of spatial and physical expression with the non-physical forces at work within a cultural setting, and in the process to evaluate and develop a measure and understanding of the quality of the built-environment in meeting human purposes. The investigation may be addressed not so much to the Japanese mind, but more in order to stimulate those who live outside its cultural and societal orientation. In studying the characteristic Japanese sense of space and its expression, it is hope that a better insight will be gained concerning public spatial expression in the realm of environmental design.

Historical perspective: the 'street' and 'hiroba'

To the west, the terms 'town square' or 'public square', are familiar. Cities in history, from those of the Greek civilizations up to the present day, had their expressions of community life in the square. Be it the 'agora' of ancient Greece, the 'piazza' of medieval Italy, the Baroque 'place' of France, the square purported to be the gathering place of the people, humanizing them by mutual contact — a three-dimensional physical public place, symbolizing the social, economic, cultural, political, and religious life of the community at large.
In Japan, no squares are to be found: that is, they are non-existent. To understand the particular absence

of this public spatial form, it is helpful to have an insight into the historical development of Japan. The socio-political pattern of ancient Japan, in fact of feudal Japan up to very recent times, could not be said to have fostered an egalitarian form of society.

The highly stratified social structure of Japanese society, whether it be the emperor and the royalty at the apex or the feudal *daimyo* residing at its helm, signified the basic determinants of the people's life and course of events. This is unmistakably reflected in the physical form and in the content of the community.

Ancient Kyoto, or Heiankyo as it was called, with its extremely geometric and ordered gridiron layout illustrates this case *(next page)* : the city design concept of Heiankyo consisted of its boulevards and smaller streets. There is not a single identifiable public space in the plan. The only definition, other than the perpendicular streets at regular intervals, is the single main thoroughfare running across the centre, dead-ending at the Palace gate. The only exceptions to the regular block system are the several temples spottily located within the grid system. The temple complex and other public facilities are not centrally situated but simply exist off the street, scattered within the city. There is no square.
The Heiankyo plan represented the dominant socio-political image of that society. Every element was part of a total hierarchy. The palace, that enclave of the royal ruling clan, dominated everything else. This physical entity was central. It sufficed to contain one focal domain, and that certainly did not reside in the public.
A not too dissimilar pattern is reflected in the medieval feudal system of the castle-town where the public life of the populace was carried on outside its walls. Here the blacksmiths, the carpenters, the goldsmiths, the shoemakers, the weavers, the traders and merchants went about their busy daily tasks, reconciled to their position and place in society. There was no special need for public gatherings, no need to act en masse, when the patterns of their lives were largely predetermined. Their routine life was highlighted only by the occasional festivals and public ceremonies, either religious or political.
Religion in the ordinary life of a Japanese was a very private affair (and still is, today) and the temples and shrines in many ways were distinct from their daily activities. People worshipped within their humble homes, while the ecclesiastics enjoyed

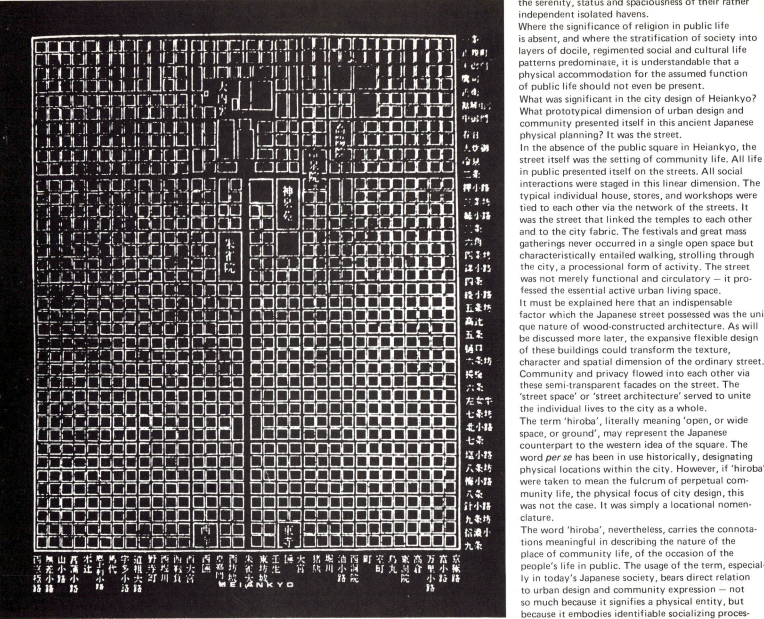

the serenity, status and spaciousness of their rather independent isolated havens.

Where the significance of religion in public life is absent, and where the stratification of society into layers of docile, regimented social and cultural life patterns predominate, it is understandable that a physical accommodation for the assumed function of public life should not even be present.

What was significant in the city design of Heiankyo? What prototypical dimension of urban design and community presented itself in this ancient Japanese physical planning? It was the street.

In the absence of the public square in Heiankyo, the street itself was the setting of community life. All life in public presented itself on the streets. All social interactions were staged in this linear dimension. The typical individual house, stores, and workshops were tied to each other via the network of the streets. It was the street that linked the temples to each other and to the city fabric. The festivals and great mass gatherings never occurred in a single open space but characteristically entailed walking, strolling through the city, a processional form of activity. The street was not merely functional and circulatory — it professed the essential active urban living space.

It must be explained here that an indispensable factor which the Japanese street possessed was the unique nature of wood-constructed architecture. As will be discussed more later, the expansive flexible design of these buildings could transform the texture, character and spatial dimension of the ordinary street. Community and privacy flowed into each other via these semi-transparent facades on the street. The 'street space' or 'street architecture' served to unite the individual lives to the city as a whole.

The term 'hiroba', literally meaning 'open, or wide space, or ground', may represent the Japanese counterpart to the western idea of the square. The word *per se* has been in use historically, designating physical locations within the city. However, if 'hiroba' were taken to mean the fulcrum of perpetual community life, the physical focus of city design, this was not the case. It was simply a locational nomenclature.

The word 'hiroba', nevertheless, carries the connotations meaningful in describing the nature of the place of community life, of the occasion of the people's life in public. The usage of the term, especially in today's Japanese society, bears direct relation to urban design and community expression — not so much because it signifies a physical entity, but because it embodies identifiable socializing proces-

ses within the life of the city. 'Hiroba' is defined by human activity — in viable urban space and time. These activities can be characterized basically by certain contextual qualities which may distinguish the unique sense of the Japanese 'hiroba'.

It will become apparent that the 'hiroba' is not necessarily perceived as a fixed physical expression but rather as an expression of a spatial consciousness — of a dynamic, spontaneous, coexistent and symbolic nature.

In the absence of the square, it could be said that in the cities of Japan, architectural space opens out to the street, that life flows between architecture and the street, that life and street, architecture and the city 'coexist'. The chief characteristics of Japanese festivals and public events is that the setting is out in the street. The form of much of the traditional festival activity and ritual entails winding through the wide thoroughfares as well as through meandering narrow alleys of the community. There is very little static form of activity, it is basically kinaesthetic and continuously changing.

As has been cited earlier, traditional Japanese architecture with its paper, wood, or bamboo screen walls and the hung wooden lattice facades lent itself uniquely to the phenomenal interiorizing of the street — the street space freely filtered through beyond the facade. The typical physical street is extended and an altogether different spatial entity can be perceived. A community space emerges. In this coexistence of the private and public space-time, the 'hiroba' manifestly acquires form and meaning.

Physical staging of community activity seldom occupied a singular locational permanence. In the absence of the square, such activity process had to be temporal in nature. All supportive facilities, dispositions, forms and details for the event were portable, flexible, multi-use, instantaneous, improvisational and provisional. The resulting space-time was 'provisional' in nature.

In the city of Takayama, a community renowned for its festivals, this provisional phenomenon can best be observed. One visitor to this town on a typical day and another at the occasion of a festival will be struck by the difference: the atmosphere, texture, fabric — in fact, the whole sensate environment will have been transformed. The wooden lattice at the front of the houses lining the street are taken down completely, allowing exposure into these usually private spaces; festive paper lanterns are hung at every entryway; colours, textures, proportions, scale and volume are altered. The street literally erodes, revealing a 'hiroba'. A community space unveils itself.

A place produced by activity is restricted in terms of time. The Gion Festival of Kyoto, held annually on July 17, gives new value to the streets for a specified limited duration. This temporary activity-space is in motion; rather than a physical space, it is a sort of linear 'happening'. The processional happening sustains a sense of place; but then the moment ends, the spell is broken.

This type of temporary design and spontaneous sense of place can also be evidenced at some temples and shrines. Although religious in nature, these seasonal occasions held within the temple precinct are extremely popular and serve as exciting highlights of a community. By introducing special decorative elements and symbols, by the use of portable and non-permanent facilities, such as outdoor podiums, platforms, drinking and eating booths, canvas-sheltered display stands and shows, a 'hiroba' is achieved. The religious architecture remains merely a backdrop. The visual association with surrounding nature, the stone pavement, the stone lanterns, the special symbolic non-city aura of the environment, all contribute to the makings of a 'hiroba' — for those moments.

In the absence of a real square, the case has always been that the community life process had its occurrences in open areas (never designated 'hiroba'). Alleys, streets, street corners, religious precincts, vacant city lots, river-banks, frontage grounds at transportation nodes, etc., comprised these substitutive areas. They occur in the city fabric marked by specific functional labels. Interestingly enough, it is only when these assigned functions and uses are diverted that 'hiroba' life comes into being.

This nature of 'substitution' originates out of different circumstances and demands, as for example, climatic conditions. Because the summer sun is extremely brilliant and Japan lies in the monsoon

INTERIORIZING OF THE STREET

zone with abundant rainfall through much of the year, outdoor activity there often encounters inconvenience and impracticality. Thus, 'hiroba' occurrences at temple enclaves may be attributed to the shade and solace offered by its rich foliage. When we consider once more those factors that underlie the Japanese form of a 'hiroba': the coexistive nature of the events, the duality of street architecture, the transient and evanescent characteristic of public activities, or the provisional quality of supportive physical elements, the concept of 'substitution' appears to be more than an accident.

Japanese public spatial expression

At the root of community life process lies a 'need' for mutual contact and information exchange with fellow men. In maintaining 'hiroba' as an expression of this fundamental process, certain activity-elements may be seen to be present. The 'sense of hiroba' should sustain the following:

(a) The motivation for coming together, generated by the pattern of daily community life process, such as the purchasing of food and clothing; obtaining and transmitting information of the community, etc.
(b) The purpose of recreation, relaxation and amusement.
(c) The scope for social pleasantries, such as neighbourliness, friendliness, spontaneous associations and encounter with members of the community.
(d) The feeling for 'togetherness' as in all types of community activities , including festivals and religious rituals.
(e) The need to profess or appeal, such as public oratory, political demonstration and mass riots.

The presence of these factors or a mixture of these forces constitute the variable inputs; however, the indispensable determinant relies on the fact that every individual be allowed free and unrestricted access, entry, and participation.

When we study Japan's city-planning and civic legislature, the lack of any references to this expression of community consciousness is noticed. 'Hiroba' as a city-design concept is missing. Streets, city parks and rivers have their appropriate 'ordinances', but there exists no comparable clause pertaining to 'hiroba'. If no form of ordinance is found, it can be inferred that neither the awareness, interest, nor financial appropriations be expected. Some potential and certainly unintended public open spaces have prevailed — but in the recent history of urbanizing expansion and density, they have disappeared.

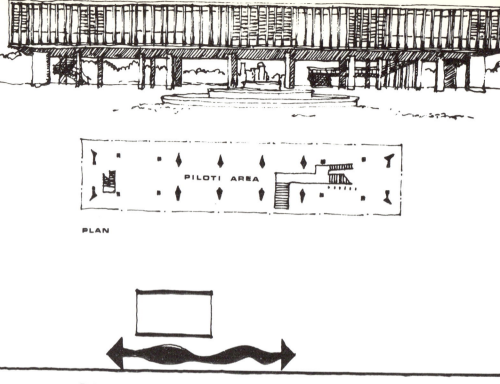

PLAN

PUBLIC SCALE

Tokyo's urban structure is patterned out on the criteria of 'ward organization' — that is, the city as a whole is put together piecemeal. (There are twenty-three wards, or sectors in Tokyo.) As a result, left-over gaps, especially where the parts come together, can be discerned in this type of planning. These breaks in the city fabric could have become relevant public open spaces, but they were quickly assigned specific functional uses or have totally disappeared.

We have noted that these areas sometimes demonstrated the advent of 'hiroba' by over-riding the intended use, inherently vulnerable in its vague 'boundary' or 'edge' delineation and in its invisible proprietorship.

The post-war years in Japan engendered efforts by many architects to recognize and restate socially cohesive architectural projects. It could be said that architecture turned toward urban design. Foremost among the architects who took this matter up is Kenzo Tange, with his Peace Memorial Centre at Hiroshima; his achievement here was marked by a careful treatment of all adjacent streets and parks as a totally planned unity; by his comprehension of the urban structure with the added advantage of a well located site; and by the opportunities inherent in a memorial dedicated to the 'peace movement' at a place to be the receptacle of world-wide communication and interaction. In the hands of Tange the use of 'piloti' at once spatially connected the architecture and the city. The public domain and architecture filtered into each other at the ground level and the result established a scale of the 'masses' as opposed to that of isolated individuals.

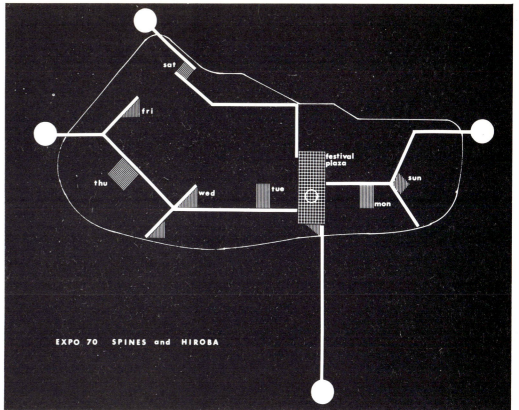

EXPO 70 SPINES and HIROBA

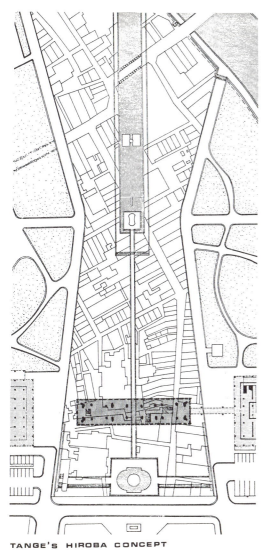

TANGE'S HIROBA CONCEPT

The 1951 CIAM (Conference International d'Architecture Moderne) conference had as its theme 'The City Core'. In Japan, under a new postwar Constitution and active rebuilding of the devastated city centres, architects were ever cognizant of community consciousness and social responsibility. With many of the city halls and other civic centres being rebuilt across the country, they envisioned vital 'community hiroba' at every feasible design opportunity. The CIAM theme had a uniquely significant influence on Japan. Despite such exertion of efforts, these designs often did not materialize. This was significantly due to the fact that the populace at large did not identify civic buildings as being part of their meaningful symbols of daily living. Feelings of affinity with these seats of government were hardly harboured in the citizens' hearts, especially for those who recalled the taste of the country's political machinery in pre-war Japan. City halls were hardly the catalytic force for socializing. A 'hiroba' was doubtless unlikely here. Other limitations handicapped the architects: the governmental planning policy and attitude, for example. No urban blueprint existed, no city-design plan. Hence there was no framework enabling a designer to conceptualize a public centre within a total organizing fabric. In most cases, the architect was forced to take the problems independently including that of understanding and analysing, presumptuously interpreting the city structure, and thereby arbitrarily drawing up the grand plan.

In trying to understand the factors underlying Japanese public spatial expression, I would like to dwell on several pieces of evidence from the existing Japanese consciousness and milieu.

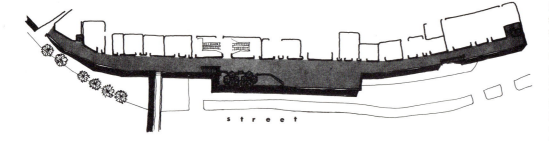

AKASAKA TOKYU PLAZA PLAN

The most glaring physical example of recent creation comes to mind — that of EXPO '70 at Osaka. To its planners, architects and designers, EXPO '70 posed an opportune, exciting and serious experiment in contemporary urban scale and content, including that of the sense and form of public open spaces. We note that practically for the first time in Japan, the term 'hiroba' was employed integrally incorporated in the original concept and over-all physical design. But if these 'hiroba' were to be a new spatial expression of the public environment, if they were to emulate the Western concept of the square, they did not materialize. The 'Festival Hiroba' under the huge space-framed canopy at a central location within EXPO, and the necklace-chain 'Monday' through 'Sunday Hiroba' cannot be credited as such. Both were strictly based on functional nomenclatures; the former for programmed exhibitions of various festival performances, and the latter identified monorail

stops. The former was essentially an amphitheatre, normally closed off to the public and admitting a capacity number spectator participation only at designated show times. The latter was an elaborate version of our existing railroad station frontage, a traffic node focusing its void on the station gates.

By careful observation, however, it becomes obvious that indeed there was a concerted form of activity in public, a continuous social interface, and above all, a 'place' for these occurrences — but that was to be found in the streets of the EXPO site.

What we learn from this experiment is that on the one hand, the planners and designers have yet to understand the nature of their own Japanese spatial orientation in public life, but on the other hand that there is a significant reawakening to physical planning of the total fabric of public environments. In this endeavour, however, priority must rest in understanding not its counterpart forms in western society,

but in appreciating the dynamic, kinaesthetic and symbolic expression indigenous to the Japanese behaviour in public.

Another significant parallel is seen in the recent hotel commercial concourse, 'Akasaka Tokyu Plaza' — here again, the term 'plaza' being used intentionally and assumedly designed as such. As may be studied from the illustrations, the 'plaza' physically is one linear promenade deck disconnected from vehicular traffic. The main activity is in shopping and browsing, inherent in this strictly functional linear dimension. It is not a gathering place and any social interaction is at a minimum. It is a street: safe from traffic and congestion, extremely inviting and pleasant. Needless to say, the public did not create it — it originated as a private commercial venture. 'Akasaka Tokyu Plaza' is a misnomer.

Much of Japanese public life takes place in semi-open spaces, often replacing its original and intended uses, such as at temple precincts, shopping arcades and transportation terminals. Shinjuku Terminal's West Concourse is such an example. An extensive underground circulation-spine blossoms open at the busy pedestrian intersection node of the West Concourse. The substitutive nature of space-time 'hiroba' manifests itself here: a spontaneous and candid intercourse born from among whoever happens to be present. Ironically, though, this particular area has very recently come under the scrutiny of the transportation authorities, who, of course, administer the premises. It has been pointed out that the mass of youth frequently coming together here for an impromptu event of singing *en masse* constitutes a violation of the traffic safety laws. The matter is now being deliberated in the judicial courts. It is unlikely that we will in the future see a sign proclaiming 'This is a hiroba' at this location.

Tokyo is a city of streets, narrow, twisting, wandering lanes that serve as the lifelines and playgrounds of the city's vibrant existence. Few streets have sidewalks, except in major shopping and business areas. Because homes and shops are so cramped, much of life is forced into the street, where children play, neighbours meet, vendors pass by, and shop-keepers carry on their day's work. The inescapable fact of life in Tokyo is life itself, for it is all around and ever-present. The resident of the city is never out of sight or hearing, not of one human being, but of tens and hundreds of fellow men. Yet the city's alleyways within a typical block, shielded from vehicular exposure and diverting suddenly from the main current of street flow, have often led to the establishment of an entirely intact, micro-scale en-

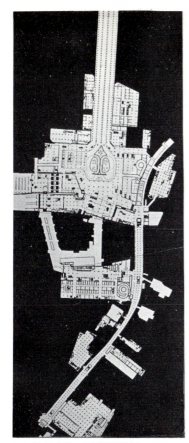

SHINJUKU TERMINAL

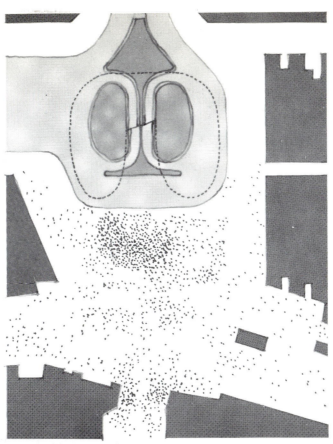

WEST CONCOURSE

intersection sometimes has a different identification. 'Sukiyabashi', 'Yurakucho' and 'Sony Building Corner' are such examples. 'Sukiyabashi Park' is essentially an extension of the street, deriving its definition from the intersection. It exists as a legible physical form, announcing perhaps too humbly its sense of community gathering-place. Within the assumed city fabric of Tokyo, this place emerges as a totally unexpected discovery, an altogether unprecedented and foreign entity in public spatial expression. The meaning of 'hiroba' is quite unintended here, for it was planned by the metropolitan park bureau as a mini-public park — they did not employ the term 'hiroba'. Existing because of the park ordinances (as explained earlier, there is no 'hiroba' ordinance), it found its way into the heart of this city.

As a compromise forced by the climate and societal limitations, the phenomenal Japanese 'hiroba' has evolved its way indoors. Perhaps the most interesting and ultimate substitute for an outdoor public gathering-place in the city environment today is the 'kissa-ten', or tea-drinking parlours. It is indeed so ubiquitous and unexceptionally familiar to everyone that its significance and relevance to contemporary urban reality is taken for granted.

Factors listed below have generated this public 'living room':

(a) The absence or lack of public free space in the city environment.
(b) Domestic life existing separately from social life in the typical household so that socializing process must take place elsewhere.
(c) The highly uncomfortable condition of the city — congested traffic, crowding, noise, and polluted air.
(d) The climatic inclemency discouraging social activities outdoors throughout much of the year.
(e) The difficulty posed by an overcrowded city to shelter an oasis of quiet and semi-privacy.
(f) The carry-over from the traditional habits of tea-drinking as a relaxing, social interaction catalyst.
(g) An air of non-discriminatory and anonymous participation.
(h) The reinforcement appropriate to the social and cultural *mores* and behaviour of the Japanese.
(i) Sheer convenience.

Thus, the 'kissa-ten' as a visible form and appropriate meaning contribute to the making of a place in the community, a sense of 'hiroba'.

Public spatial expression is influenced by ethnic cultural patterns. In Japan, the concept of 'uchi' and 'soto' (literally, 'inner', and 'outer', respectively) have

vironment. A linear oasis at day and at night for those who recognize its existence and who seek a particularly intimate relish of city life.

During the feudal ages, the governing edict discouraged the location of shops in the main streets. The odour from the fish-stores, for example, would not be considered a favourable amenity. Thus, merchants and vendors set up their business in the back-streets of these castle-towns. Some were permanently erected stores, while often stalls and temporary concessions under one roof along the alleys assumed the form of a linear market. The post-World War II phenomenon, as found in Shinjuku, typically represent eating and drinking concerns catering to the daily appetite of the masses. Unlike the modern restaurants behind

glass walls in slick buildings, the unique character of these back-street diners breathe not so much with efficient business transactions and service, but carry on a direct, face-to-face communion between the customer and the proprietor, and among those present. In the anonymous fabric of the city, sensitive scale and meaningful activity have created an invaluable form of public spatial expression. The city needs only to be discovered!

In this intense urban living space, a 'hiroba' does exist: ironically enough again, not designated by name as such. One instance of such a place is 'Sukiyabashi Park' in central Tokyo.

The Japanese name intersections, rather than the streets leading into them. In fact, each separate corner of one

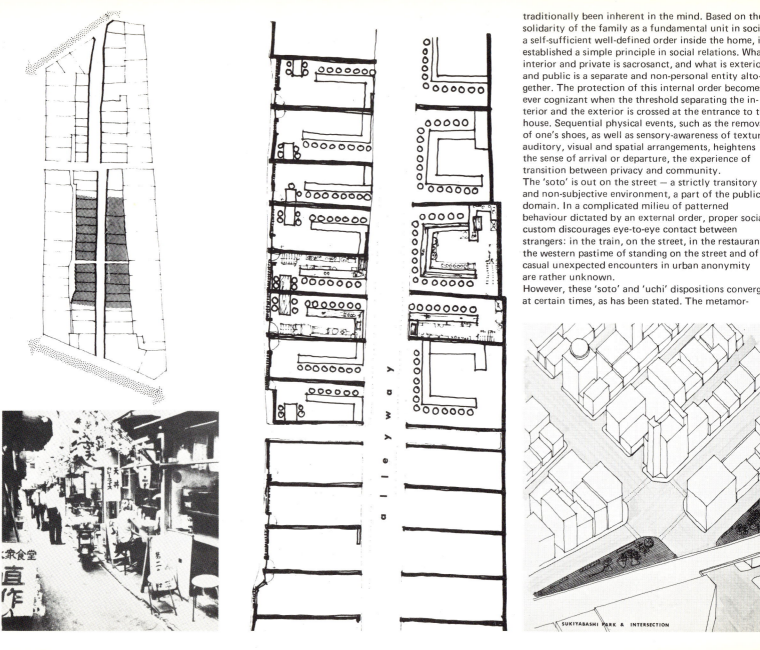

alleyway

traditionally been inherent in the mind. Based on the solidarity of the family as a fundamental unit in societ a self-sufficient well-defined order inside the home, it established a simple principle in social relations. What interior and private is sacrosanct, and what is exterior and public is a separate and non-personal entity alto-gether. The protection of this internal order becomes ever cognizant when the threshold separating the in-terior and the exterior is crossed at the entrance to the house. Sequential physical events, such as the removal of one's shoes, as well as sensory-awareness of textural, auditory, visual and spatial arrangements, heightens the sense of arrival or departure, the experience of transition between privacy and community.

The 'soto' is out on the street — a strictly transitory and non-subjective environment, a part of the public domain. In a complicated milieu of patterned behaviour dictated by an external order, proper social custom discourages eye-to-eye contact between strangers: in the train, on the street, in the restaurants; the western pastime of standing on the street and of casual unexpected encounters in urban anonymity are rather unknown.

However, these 'soto' and 'uchi' dispositions converge at certain times, as has been stated. The metamor-

SUKIYABASHI PARK & INTERSECTION

phosis of the street at festivals occasions this fusion —
the 'soto' and 'uchi' are literally indistinguishable.
Only because of this peculiar architectural relationship between the street and the Japanese life could
this threshold be crossed; for if, hypothetically, we
were to substitute a town centre for the festival
setting, 'soto' and 'uchi' may well persist.

The significance in looking at Japanese spatial expression lies in the recognition of its remarkable dis-
similarity from the traditional western idea of space.
To illustrate, it must be stated here that etymologically, 'space' as a term is non-existent; and 'space'
as a physical entity practically does not exist. The
Japanese sense of space does not describe a physical
embodiment but rather an 'experiential' place. It
involves a connotation of time in that an event may
serve to define a place and that it is of a subjective
nature, whether they be tangible forms and visibly
defined spaces or those created by movement and
happenings.

In this respect, it can be seen that Japanese architecture was the art of creating a particular 'place'
in physical form. Just as 'hiroba' signified an
'experiential place', the Japanese concept of a town
is not in the visible form of a physical entity. A town
involves a sense of place; it is experienced as a synthesis of scattered and apparently unrelated symbols,
usually in the form of its architectural content, but
including other modes of expression. To the outsider,
the town appears foreign, not simply because of the
unfamiliar physical statements, but in his failure to
grasp the indigenous sense of place.

The development of this thesis has been to propound
that what I have been referring to as 'public spatial
expression' constitutes the vital infrastructure — the
matrix of life — in the structure of our modern communities. It is this human infrastructure that sets the
tone of the cities, which establishes life styles, which
is where the life of cities goes on, which, in fact, is
important in founding the quality of our built
environment.

It has been shown that the efforts in understanding
and supporting this infrastructure have been largely
ignored in contemporary life. That, in fact, much
of the confusion in searching for an external order in
our environment and in knowing how to prevent
the city from degenerating into stagnation and in-
humanity must be overcome by a serious and sensitive
analysis of its underlying micro-structure.

That public spatial expression is indeed the occasion
of public participation in creating the living environment — and this we desperately need today.

Bibliography:

Dober, Richard P, *Environmental Design*. New York,
1969.
Dubos, Rene, *Man Adapting*. New Haven and London,
1965.
Gans, Herbert J., *People and Plans*. New York, 1968.
Giedion, Sigfried, *Space, Time and Architecture*.
Cambridge, 1954.
'Space and the Elements of the Renaissance', *Magazine
of Art,* Vol. XLV, 1952.
Goffman, Erving, *Behavior in Public Places: Notes on
the Social Organization of Gatherings*. New York,
1963.
Interaction Ritual: *Essays in Face-to-Face Behavior*.
Chicago, 1967.
Goldfinger, Erno, 'Urbanism and Spatial Order,'
Architectural Review, Vol. XC, 1941.
Hall, Edward T., *The Hidden Dimension*. New York,
1966.
The Silent Language. New York, 1959.
Halloran, Richard, *Japan, Images and Realities*. Tokyo,
1969.
Itoh, Teiji, *Minka wa Ikite kita*. Tokyo, Bijyutsu
Sjuppan-sha, 1963.
Kikutake, Kiyonori, *Ningen no Kenchiku*. Tokyo,
1970.
Lynch, Kevin, *The Image of the City*. Cambridge, 1960.
Site Planning, Cambridge, 1971.
Matsumoto, Y. S., *Contemporary Japan: The individ-
ual and the Group*. Philadelphia, 1960.
Morse, Edward S., *Japanese Homes and Their
Surroundings*. New York, 1961.
Nitschke, Gunter, 'The Japanese Sense of Place',
in *Architectural Design,* March, 1966.
Paine, Robert T., *The Art and Architecture of Japan*.
Baltimore, 1955.
Perin, Constance, *With Man in Mind*. An Interdisciplin-
ary Prospectus for Environmental Design. Cambridge,
1970.
Sommer, Robert, *Personal Space:* The Behavioral Basis
of Design. Englewood Cliffs, 1969.
Stanislawski, Dan, 'The Origin and Spread of the Grid-
Pattern Town' in *Geographical Review,* Vol. XXXVI,
1946.
Thompson, Homer A. 'The Agora at Athens and the
Green Market Place', in *Journal of the Society of
Architectural Historians,* Vol. XIII, No. 4, 1954.
Tunnard, Christopher, *The City of Man*. New York,
1953.
Zuckner, Paul, *Town and Square, From the Agora to
the Village Green*. New York, 1959.

93

'SENSE OF PLACE' IN GREEK ANONYMOUS ARCHITECTURE

S G THAKURDESAI

94

Man's attitude towards life and social and cultural structures influences his perception of space. This study is an attempt to understand the significance of the process of creating and using an outdoor environment as a result of Greek attitudes to life and social and cultural structures.

The unique qualities of climate, sea and earth play a very important role in shaping the behavioural patterns of Greeks. More than nine months of the year they associate with outdoor life very intimately. Even domestic activities (such as cooking) are often performed in the open courtyard rather than in an enclosed room. Hence it is frustrating for Greeks to stay indoors during the winter. As a result of this, indoor spaces have remained comparatively undesigned — particularly on the islands. However, in the mountain villages on Pelion or up in the north of Greece indoor spaces have developed much more than on island architecture, mainly due to climatic conditions.

'The Greek man could and did spend most of his leisure hours out of doors. That in itself meant that he had more leisure; he did not need to work in order to buy settees and coal. After all, the reason why we English have invented 'le confort anglais' is that we cannot be comfortable and warm except indoors.'[1]

A similar attitude of making interior spaces comfortable and colourful is expressed through various furniture designs and interesting lighting by Scandinavian people. They make 'places' inside to suit their moods and temperament. Architecture in the desert — especially in India (12th century AD) — is an example of another extreme of climatic influence. Since the outside was unbearably hot and dry, Indians made the interiors romantic by creating built-in spaces in stone and by controlled lighting; inside became their world of intimate associations.

But for Greeks their world was and is outside the house. 'House is the place where Greeks did not go.'[2]

To some extent, interior spaces of Greek domestic architecture are like workshops or stores, or are only accommodation. Sometimes they display ceramics and cloth pieces to decorate walls, but that is just an attempt to exhibit their material possessions or to hide the damp surface of the wall. A piece of furniture like a straight-back, sturdy, wooden chair, the design of which has remained unchanged for centuries, shows a static and passive interest in making indoor spaces into a 'place '.

Greeks exchanged ideas, thoughts and developed wits and manners by communicating with others. As talk was always essential to them, they became very social. Socrates could be pointed out as an extreme example of this kind. He preached his doctrine by talking in the street. Greeks lived in streets, in the places of assembly, gymnasia, markets, colonnades and theatres. The major part of a Greek's life was spent outdoors.

Some scholars maintain that Greek democracy and drama could still have developed if roofs and walls had been necessary. The scale of the public assemblies and theatres explains the interests of the people. Since most of these places were open to the sky, it was open to all. Greek culture was not the product

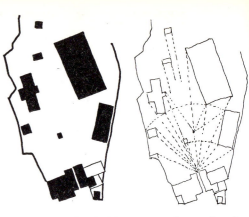

The centres of Greek cities are a conglomeration of sculptural elements which can be seen at rhythmically related intervals when seen from the 'Propylon'.

of climate alone, nevertheless, it would not have developed as it did otherwise.

This explains a unique association of Greeks to outdoor life and spaces. The space in the image of man is 'place'.[3] But it seems that the concept of 'place' is unique in every cultural, social, and climatic setting.

Western consciousness of a space is related to the comprehension of science and mathematics current at that particular time. In order to understand concept of place in the east one needs to know religious philosophy as well as metaphysical thought. The symbolism of the *mandala* explains that for the east, space was an imaginary quality perceived by disposition of symbols.

Even in the architecture of ancient Greece, the sense of space was nowhere similar to the eastern or western concept. Greek architecture is mainly associated with the temple and is most celebrated for its refinement of classical form. At the same time it is known that the temples were not normally intended to shelter men but to house the image of a god, immortal and separated from men. The gods themselves were an image in the landscape. Though sacred architecture, in itself, can explain how Greeks explored and praised the character of a god and specific places, it is a one-sided picture which only explains his thoughts of 'place' for a god, rather than his own sense of place. Moreover, the Greek temple is a sculpture, and Greek cities are a conglomeration of sculptural elements.

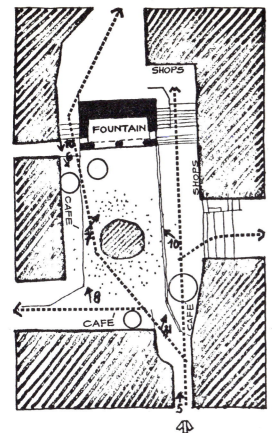

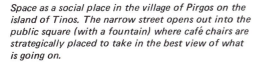

Space as a social place in the village of Pirgos on the island of Tinos. The narrow street opens out into the public square (with a fountain) where café chairs are strategically placed to take in the best view of what is going on.

'The Aristotelian system consisted of continuous matter without void. Here we have the explanation of why Greek cities were creations of individual elements rather than the result of coherent integrated spatial conceptions.'[4]
According to the theory of C. A. Doxiadis,[5] the arrangement of buildings was based on Greek concept of a circular universe and of human vision which extended across a 180° arc of that circle, when viewed from one place. That place was called 'Propylon', and then buildings and solids were set within the arc so that all the buildings could be seen from one place at rhythmically related intervals.

It seems from the above discussion that the development of democracy, drama and even education took place outdoors and in open spaces where people met and gathered, which means basically that Greeks related to outdoor life in a community where some human activity took place. In other words, active, dynamic space of everyday life was part of the culture, for the 'Agora' — a gathering place — is the most influential creation of the Greeks. Greek image of space is based on 'social place' or sociability of place. Even today, Greek anonymous architecture shows a continuity of this concept of sense of place, which grows from a space associated with human activity. In a broad sense, man was the measure of all things. In the environment of Greek anonymous architecture 'places' are developed slowly, gradually, and are moulded and shaped by the behavioural pattern of the people. Looking at the 'places' closely it becomes obvious that people strongly identify themselves as observer of and participant in the places which generate activity.

The *plateia* (public square) in the remote village of Pirgos on the island of Tinos is a case in point. One enters the village and follows a winding narrow street, until it meets and opens out in the plateia, which apparently is the heart of the village. Streets from other directions also meet in the plateia. The main street that cuts through diagonally and continues on the other side of the plateia becomes in a true sense the intersection of streets. It is an almost rectangular open space with a huge old tree that offers shadow all over the plateia. As one enters this charming open space, one sees the fountain as a most inseparable feature of the plateia along one of its sides. The remaining three sides are occupied by grocery shops, cafés, barber's shops and the local administration office centre. All these put together constitute the main centre of action. Since the main street cuts through the plateia, there is always someone passing by. All these elements make for colourful action, but in order not only to observe the passing scene, but also to be able to participate in it, people select a place to sit that will offer maximum opportunity to communicate with each other. In this case two corners facing each other diagonally become places of interest. To the Greek, a sense of place is not just an open plateia but those specific corners, which serve their purpose as an indicator of where to sit. For example, no-one sits directly under the tree in the Pirgos plateia because from there they cannot grasp the action fully. Note that the café positions are basically at the beginning or the end of the main axis in the plateia, one covering the view of the main entry, the other facing the most important architectural feature — the fountain. The tree blocks the view partially and thus moderates a stare to a mere casual observance of the newcomer.

Sometimes the church is the centre of attraction of a plateia. The centre of the fortified village of Olympos, on the island of Chios, is occupied by a large tower surrounded by a relatively wide space. A church faces onto the wide area, which has become the plateia — with barber's shop, cafés, administrative office and some other shops. From the bottleneck of the entry street, as one approaches the barber's shop, it is possible to overview the whole of the plateia and all movement across it. Accordingly people first occupy

both sides of this narrow street even though this leaves very little space for other people to pass through. Yet they do not find it uncomfortable because it is the best place from where to observe action and participate in it if necessary. So the need of participation becomes clear by the selection of the place and the way in which it is occupied.

A side wall of the church also faces the plateia. The bottleneck here is just not the right place for Greeks to select to sit just as the rest of the space around the tower has been disregarded. It is obvious that though the other side of the tower has almost an equally wide open space, no-one makes that a 'place' mainly because it is not a major through-way and the elements which generate action — the fountain, administrative office, café, etc. — are missing. Consciousness of place is not related to a perception of space as physical form nor to a metaphysical concept. The Greek sense of place seems to be determined by sociability, by the kind of space that is generated by movement and maximizes human contacts.

Looking back at ancient Greeks and the places they created, one begins to see how in its true nature, the character is unchanged through the ages. Agora', which means assembly and is derived from the verb 'to gather', is a particular characteristic of the Greeks. Agora was also a heart of the city, where daily events of social-interaction, politics and business took place. The economic function of the agora was not its original function; in fact, it was regarded as a degradation of the original idea. The agora, situated at the meeting point of a number of streets, assimilated in its general form and in the arrangement of its buildings to the irregularity of the winding and tortuous streets. Even today, the plateias show a significant similarity in their character, which in turn is the result of a specific attitude of a particular people to life.

An open-air meeting hall was the indispensable attribute of the political and social union which was the essence of Greek synoicism. It was a social and political unification, which required as its functional instrument a 'place' where this unification could become a reality. This social and political unification is being achieved in the plateias of today.

An administration centre, a barber's shop, a church

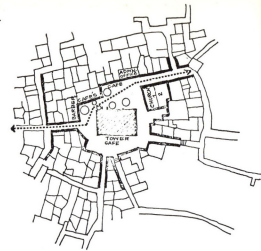

The church square as the centre of interest in Olympos on the island of Chios. Chairs are clustered alongside the major through-way although there is plenty of space on other sides of the church.

96

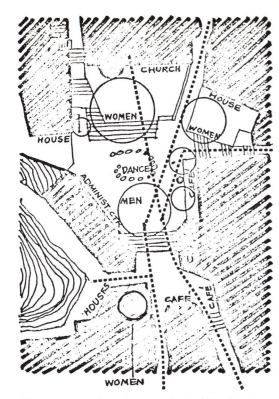

Women congregate on the upper level of the plateia for the Easter festival in Olympos on the island of Karpathos. Normally they do not encroach on the men's social life on the plateia at all.

and cafés become real potential for social and political interactions among people. Like ancient Greeks, the central concern of the people is to be able to talk with each other. The agora later became a market place so that no clear line could be drawn between the civic centre (or assembly) and the market place, (though sometimes they were different). The most important thing is that these functions and elements helped Greeks to come together and associate themselves with the 'places' that had maximum potential of interaction. Two corners in the plateia at Tinos and the bottleneck part of the plateia at Olympos are illustrations of that kind. Ancient cities like Priene and Miletus, planned by the Greek city planner, are the best examples of the basis of social

order, and its special emphasis on the composition of the agora in relation to the whole city. The temple was never positioned facing the agora but was either placed sideways or on higher ground, somewhat out of the way and reached by steps leading from the agora. The 'public place' was the sphere of Man; even women had no equal rights nor could they interfere in politics or public speaking.

Separation of the sexes

Even today on the islands, women have no real place in the plateia or agora. In some places, they cannot even talk with young men in the plateia. In Olymbos, on the island of Karpathos, this social trait is strongly reflected in the use of the plateia. During the Easter festival it becomes more distinct and interesting. This plateia is situated on the highest level of the village, along with the church. The church is approached by a few long steps with an open platform which, in fact, is a part of the plateia. The plateia is also approached by a number of steps but it still is a wide landing of a continuous street. Cafés are located just before the steps start. As one comes up into the plateia, there is a café and an administration centre. The main side in front is lined with the church which is placed sideways. Along its sides narrow roads continue further. During the Easter festival, women and men group separately; women stand on the steps in front of the church and the men stand on the opposite side, outside the café. There is no intermingling of the sexes. The reason why women stand on the higher level of the plateia is that they want to show off their costumes, wealth and beauty. It also gives them a sense of security. Some women will withdraw from the plateia altogether, but will take up a vantage point on a roof terrace to view the proceedings from a distance.

For the women, social structure is a great obstacle in developing any association with the plateia. This structure which society imposes on its members is again visible in the plateia at Anogia on the island of Crete. Cafés are lined up along the two opposite sides. On the right-hand side of this wide open space stands a church that can only be entered by going off the plateia. Here again the plateia is not a place for women. Around the café men sit facing the movement towards the church. Old men who are no longer very active sit along the wall of the church. On festival days women congregate near the entrance to the church which is in a side street off the main plateia. Women's associations seldom extend far beyond the

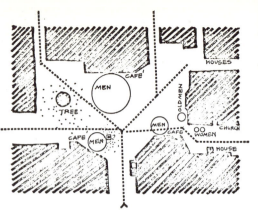

outside of their own house. The women generally sit and gossip just outside their own front door. They usually sit sideways to the street, which enables them to communicate with passers-by without appearing to involve themselves too directly in the activity along the street. Basically the woman's place is restricted to her interior domain — her interior courtyard. Very rarely do people have any private space between their house and the street. However, the public space — the street — is usually cared for by the people who live along it. The women whitewash the outsides of their houses at frequent intervals, and also paint around the edges of steps and around the joints of the paving stones. This makes them more visible at night in areas without street lamps. Each woman develops her own way of doing this. Sometimes they even paint over adjacent rock protuberances, claiming them as part of their territory, fulfilling their 'sense of place'.

'Places' and Activities

'Places' are created at or along the line of activities. This can be better understood by observing the emphasis given in the plateia at Pirgos on the island of Chios. Here, the plateia is surrounded by streets. Along the three sides are all kinds of shops and cafés, local administration offices and on the remaining side is a church which could only be entered by a side street off the plateia. Though all sides have shops and activities, the major road is easily perceptible since people sit along the road opposite the main entrance of the church, along the south side of the square to the end of the plateia and further into the roads leading to the residential areas. All the cafés are along this side of the plateia from where the men can see the women going to and from the church as well as observe the main movement through the plateia. They seldom sit in the open centre. It is important to notice here that the other side of the plateia has little action and is therefore virtually deserted. Sometimes, if life cannot be observed sufficiently intensively, the plateia is abandoned and people seek out other 'places'. On the island of Kea, in the main village of the same name, a steeply rising street curves into the well-kept plateia with a statue in the centre, many trees, and stone paving carefully painted along the

The segregation of men and women's social activities in Anogia on the island of Crete. Women usually sit outside their own front door, sideways to the street. Whitewash defines their own territory.

98

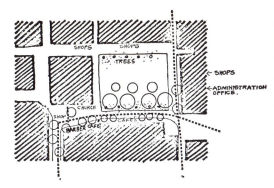

joints. One side offers a very good view of the valley
and fortress. The administration centre and café
face each other, giving an excellent sense of enclosure.
However, this apparently beautiful plateia is left
empty of people. Instead, they congregate around
the corner of the approach street where some steps
lead to the other side of the village. Some sit on the
steps and some on chairs facing the street. From
here they can see people approaching and talk with

*The men of Pirgos on the island of Chios (like those
of Olympos) sit alongside the major through-way
watching the women going to church and other activities and seldom use the centre of the square or the
other sides.*

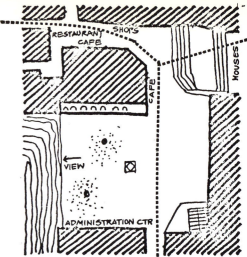

them as they pass. They do not sit directly outside the café, because this would not give them as good a view of people coming and going. They are not interested in the wide view available from the veranda of the café on the plateia. They are only interested in watching and talking to people.

The same phenomenon is apparent in Skyros, the

In the main village of the island of Kea the fine square (which has a very good view) is deserted as a place to sit, in favour of the steps by which people approach the other side of the village.

principal town of the island of Skyros. Its main plateia is raised about 6 feet above the road. It contains a small church, two rows of trees, the administrative offices and a café and has a fine view of the valley. But it is only used during the summer holidays, when many of the young men and girls return to the island from their work in Athens. For the rest of the year the men sit in the right-angle corners that occur along the main street. In the busy port of Chios, however, the men sit facing outward, watching the movement of people and boats coming in and out of the harbour. But in the evening, when there is little harbour activity, they

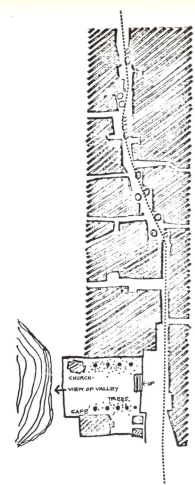

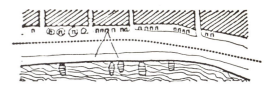

turn half the seats to face inward, forming two sides of a pedestrian parade.

People can talk to each other by sitting side by side, without facing each other. This is one of the cultural characteristics of the Greeks. So people can sit in a line or in a number of rows, but all facing action. In Chios, it's like a fashion parade. People watch what happens in between two opposite rows of seats. This attitude is similar to the audience—spectator relationship in a theatre. But what differentiates these people from the audience in a theatre is that each spectator is also an actor. And this attitude can be traced back to the ancient history of the Greeks with their creation of the first theatres. Significantly enough, theatres began on threshing floors which have an interesting structure with a natural slope on one side from where to watch. Before the Romans changed the essential nature of the form of the Greek theatre, they had natural settings and a natural form, that is to say, plays were not performed on the built-up stage, but on the open space surrounded on three sides by the audience. It was the built-up stage that began to draw a distinction between the audience and the actors. That happened very late in the history of the Greek theatre and yet differed significantly from the Roman conception of form. Even at that time the spectator was able to participate in the play because the form of the theatre still made it possible.

This attitude of watching and participating in action in a more or less natural setting still prevails among the Greeks. (Contrary to the Roman practice, incidentally, they cannot and do not draw distinction by changing levels between observer and object.) They want to see and to be seen. This direct and joint participation together results in the 'special places' in the general realm of gathering places. Even along the major street of a town or village like Koropi and Markopolo in Attica, people sit on the very narrow footpath, next to vehicular traffic. Even in that situation, 'place' to them involves participation with the people walking by. They don't necessarily need a wall behind them, and that is clearly illustrated in the plateia at Pirgi.

If the café is set back 15 to 20 feet off the street people often sit along the edge of the street rather than along the wall; the same thing happens on the port of Tinos where people tend to come close to action.

Left: Again in the main town of Skyros the pleasant plateia is only used during the holidays. Normally chairs are bunched in the right angles of the narrow street.

Above: In the port of Chios people sit side by side rather than face to face, so that they are free to look out as well as chat. The chairs which face the busy harbour during the day are turned back in the evening so that the parade of pedestrians along the street can be watched.

Greeks sit as close to the action as possible, whether by a road full of traffic or a harbour. They make themselves comfortable on the pairs of chairs placed on each side of the table, and so create a 'place' out of doors for themselves.

The chairs themselves contribute to the sense of place. Almost always these are the traditional straight-back chairs which are not very comfortable. However, as Greeks tend to sit for a long time, they have found that it is much more practical, convenient and comfortable to use more than one chair at a time, employing the additional chairs for resting their arms or legs. This means they can very easily change the position of the chairs and thus the position of their body. It is partly in response to this habit that chairs are invariably placed in pairs on either side of the café tables.

In summary, these observations indicate that for the Greeks a 'sense of place' involves an outdoor area potentially rich for the maximum social contacts.

In Greek anonymous architecture, the people create and shape outdoor 'places', not buildings, since their 'sense of place' does not involve interior space.

References:

1 HDF Kitto, *The Greeks,* London, 1959.
2 Finley Hooper, *Greek Realities,* London, 1968.
3 Aldo van Eyck in Alison Smithson, *Team Ten Primer,* London, 1968.
4 CA Doxiadis, *Architecture in Transition,* London, 1963.
5 Gutkind, *Urban Development — Southern Europe — Greece, Italy.*
6 see drawings in RE Wycherley, *How the Greeks Built Cities.*

A PUBLIC INFORMATION SYSTEM FOR ADAMS-MORGAN STREETS

JOHN WIEBENSON

The place

To outsiders, Washington DC's name usually conjures up images of tree-lined streets giving grand vistas of City Beautiful settings, peopled by dignitaries and documents. These are all here, but so are people: 800,000 in the District, and about 3,000,000 in the metropolitan area. They live in what has become a late-twentieth-century American city, complete with freeways and smog, flight to the suburbs, fear and hope, dope and debutantes. This is no longer a Georgian capital city; it is now the southern end of the BosNyWash megalopolis.

Yet, deep within, L'Enfant's Mall can still be found, leafy and green, and usually empty. Wrapped around this are the agencies and departments of the Federal Government. Next, there is a layer made up of the central business district, Georgetown's sedate houses, and a number of other inner neighbourhoods of lesser prestige. At about 20 blocks north of the White House, Adams-Morgan is one of these inner neighbourhoods.

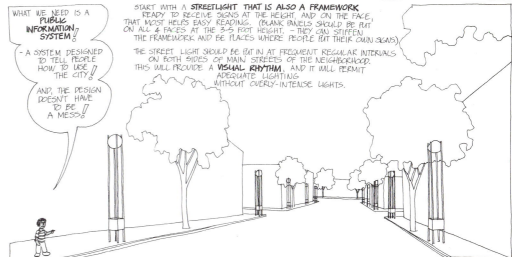

Left: Typical signs now found along Adams-Morgan's streets, standing in typical disarray and giving little information.

Adams-Morgan has about 30,000 residents (±5,000, depending on the boundaries used). Most of them are black people, although substantial numbers of Spanish-speaking people and whites also live here. Incomes vary from poverty to luxury, with most of low to moderate. All age groups are here, too: the young and single, the elderly, and people with school-age children. This neighbourhood has houses, apartment buildings, schools, churches, small factories, stores and services. Most are in three- or four-story buildings more than forty years old. These are generally in good shape, or could be put in good shape. New building projects, designed to replace delapidated structures or to fill in empty spaces, are announced from time to time: but usually nothing happens.

There are quiet streets here and streets busy with shoppers, and with commuters rushing through. A major District recreation area is next door, bringing other people near-by and restaurants and specialty stores bring a few more all the way into Adams-Morgan, but this is basically an area cut off from the use and attention of the rest of the city.

All this makes Adams-Morgan fairly representative of inner-city neighbourhoods, with most of their problems and possibilities.

The study

One of the most critical of these problems-and-possibilities is *information,* particularly information about public services for the poor.

Even though this country, acting through its various governments and through private groups, has been

Left: Existing this-way-to sign for Washington's tourists — hard to read, but it helps.

ADD ON **STREET NAME SIGNS** TO AT LEAST 2 STREET LIGHTS AT EACH INTERSECTION.

- MAKE THEM OF TRANSLUCENT FIBERGLASS SO THAT, AT NIGHT, THEY WILL BE BACK-LIT AND READABLE.

THEN, TO HELP PEOPLE FIND **IMPORTANT PLACES**, PUT THIS-WAY-TO SIGNS AT CORNERS OF MAIN STREETS WHERE PEOPLE WOULD TURN OFF TO THOSE PLACES.

COLUMBIA NW ROAD 1900 →

19TH NW STREET ← 2100

ADAMS SCHOOL

HAPPY HOLLOW PLAYGROUND

ADAMS MORGAN COMMUNITY CENTER

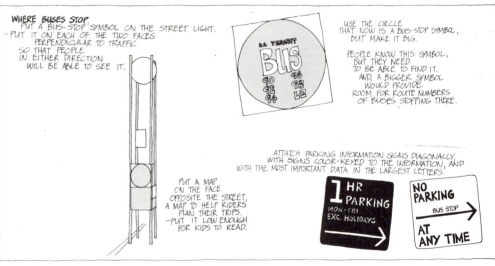

WHERE BUSES STOP
PUT A BUS-STOP SYMBOL ON THE STREET LIGHT.
- PUT IT ON EACH OF THE TWO FACES PERPENDICULAR TO TRAFFIC SO THAT PEOPLE IN EITHER DIRECTION WILL BE ABLE TO SEE IT.

A.1 TRANSIT BUS 90 96 92 98 94 L2

USE THE CIRCLE THAT NOW IS A BUS-STOP SYMBOL, BUT MAKE IT BIG.

PEOPLE KNOW THIS SYMBOL, BUT THEY NEED TO BE ABLE TO FIND IT. AND, A BIGGER SYMBOL WOULD PROVIDE ROOM FOR ROUTE NUMBERS OF BUSES STOPPING THERE.

PUT A MAP ON THE FACE OPPOSITE THE STREET, A MAP TO HELP RIDERS PLAN THEIR TRIPS.
- PUT IT LOW ENOUGH FOR KIDS TO READ.

ATTACH PARKING INFORMATION SIGNS DIAGONALLY, WITH SIGNS COLOR-KEYED TO THE INFORMATION, AND WITH THE MOST IMPORTANT DATA IN THE LARGEST LETTERS.

1 HR PARKING MON-FRI EXC. HOLIDAYS →

NO PARKING BUS STOP → AT ANY TIME

gradually increasing the availability of services for poor people, in all too many cases those for whom the services have been designed have not heard of them. Therefore, an indigent old man can still be starved into senility, because he knows nothing about a hot-meal scheme, or even about food stamps. Or, an expectant mother will miss pre-natal care, and later her child will miss pre-kindergarten, because she has not heard of these services. The list of available services for the poor now includes legal help, consumer advice, special learning opportunities, help with community planning, and many others. The list of services known to the poor is much shorter.

Television or newspaper stories will sometimes tell a little about a service, helping to spread the idea a bit, but most information about public services is based on word-of-mouth and on small notices taped to the services' front doors. There have been recent changes to this picture, however. Some of the services themselves are recognizing the problem, and are cataloguing other services their 'clients' need to find. And some of the more socially oriented small newspapers, such as Washington's *DC Gazette,* are publishing whole directories of services.

Last year, funding for working on this problem was found by two people from Adams-Morgan: Topper Carew (whose New Thing Art & Architecture Center provides services and classes here) and Tunney Lee (whose architecture and planning office was here). They proposed to exploit the information-giving possibilities of the neighbourhood's *streets,* reasoning that these were the one public facility used by every resident daily. In addition, they felt that this would provide a strong handle for seriously amending the

105

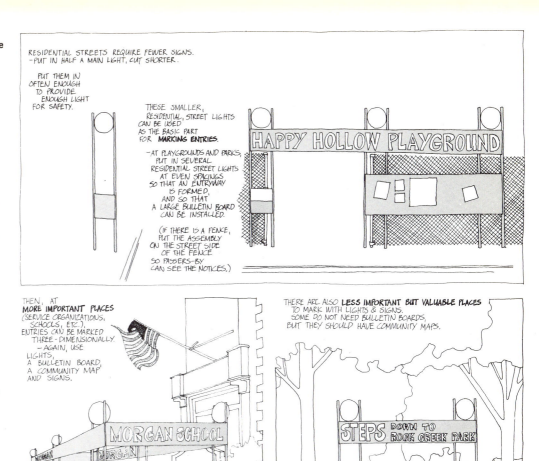

RESIDENTIAL STREETS REQUIRE FEWER SIGNS.
-PUT IN HALF A MAIN LIGHT, CUT SHORTER.

PUT THEM IN OFTEN ENOUGH TO PROVIDE ENOUGH LIGHT FOR SAFETY.

THESE SMALLER, RESIDENTIAL, STREET LIGHTS CAN BE USED AS THE BASIC PART FOR **MARKING ENTRIES**.

-AT PLAYGROUNDS AND PARKS, PUT IN SEVERAL RESIDENTIAL STREET LIGHTS AT EVEN SPACINGS SO THAT AN ENTRYWAY IS FORMED, AND SO THAT A LARGE BULLETIN BOARD CAN BE INSTALLED.

(IF THERE IS A FENCE, PUT THE ASSEMBLY ON THE STREET SIDE OF THE FENCE SO PASSERS-BY CAN SEE THE NOTICES.)

HAPPY HOLLOW PLAYGROUND

THEN, AT **MORE IMPORTANT PLACES** (SERVICE ORGANIZATIONS, SCHOOLS, ETC.), ENTRIES CAN BE MARKED THREE-DIMENSIONALLY. -AGAIN, USE LIGHTS, A BULLETIN BOARD, A COMMUNITY MAP AND SIGNS.

MORGAN SCHOOL

THERE ARE ALSO **LESS IMPORTANT BUT VALUABLE PLACES** TO MARK WITH LIGHTS & SIGNS. SOME DO NOT NEED BULLETIN BOARDS, BUT THEY SHOULD HAVE COMMUNITY MAPS.

STEPS DOWN TO ROCK CREEK PARK

Left: Meagre sign telling who owns the park rather than who might use it, or how to use it.

neighbourhood's image of its streets. New street signs and symbols, and new *goals* for those signs and symbols, could be a powerful means for helping residents to see their neighbourhood with a new awareness of their own community.

Workers who developed the study included some members of New Thing, some young children from the neighbourhood, and myself. As the work progressed, goals were refined until they became:

(a) *Announcement* of available services and their locations. (Recreation and play, ranging from museums to kite-flying places, were included as services, partly because of their being important too, and partly because announcing them can suggest that the city is also a place to enjoy.)

(b) *Reinforcement* of neighbourhood awareness, identity and pride.

The means to these goals became:

(1) *Public signs* (including street signs, bus-stop signs, parking information signs, etc., and especially *important place* signs and *this-way-to* signs), all designed as a system.

(2) A *neighbourhood walking tour,* passing all important places.

(3) Monumental *landmarks* in the neighbourhood, as there are in the rest of the District.

(4) An Adams-Morgan *services map* (for handing out and as fixtures at bus-stops, schools and other key public places).

The future:

Street information systems for other neighbourhoods do not need to be duplicates of Adams-Morgan's.

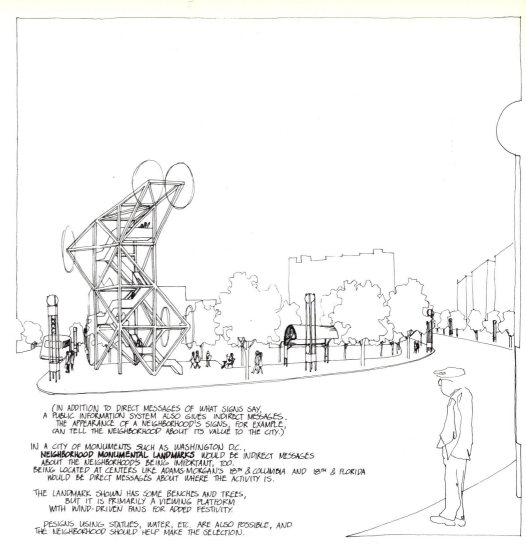

(IN ADDITION TO DIRECT MESSAGES OF WHAT SIGNS SAY, A PUBLIC INFORMATION SYSTEM ALSO GIVES INDIRECT MESSAGES. THE APPEARANCE OF A NEIGHBORHOOD'S SIGNS, FOR EXAMPLE, CAN TELL THE NEIGHBORHOOD ABOUT ITS VALUE TO THE CITY.)

IN A CITY OF MONUMENTS SUCH AS WASHINGTON D.C., **NEIGHBORHOOD MONUMENTAL LANDMARKS** WOULD BE INDIRECT MESSAGES ABOUT THE NEIGHBORHOOD'S BEING IMPORTANT, TOO. BEING LOCATED AT CENTERS LIKE ADAMS-MORGAN'S 18TH & COLUMBIA AND 18TH & FLORIDA WOULD BE DIRECT MESSAGES ABOUT WHERE THE ACTIVITY IS.

THE LANDMARK SHOWN HAS SOME BENCHES AND TREES, BUT IT IS PRIMARILY A VIEWING PLATFORM WITH WIND-DRIVEN FANS FOR ADDED FESTIVITY.

DESIGNS USING STATUES, WATER, ETC. ARE ALSO POSSIBLE, AND THE NEIGHBORHOOD SHOULD HELP MAKE THE SELECTION.

Left: Two of Washington's larger monuments which help make this a city of monuments.

106

Indeed, if neighbourhoods are to be fully reinforced, each system should have its own design. There are endless possible modifications, with the only considerations being: location of signs for easy viewing; legibility of words; lighting where it is needed; a design framework; and identification of local assets of main streets, public services, and play possibilities.

Some streets (such as Washington DC's Pennsylvania Avenue) and some parks and rivers, etc. do not belong to any one neighbourhood, but to the entire city. These should be given a city-wide identity, therefore. But other streets and facilities should have the identity of the neighbourhoods they serve.

There is a chance that the Nation's Bicentennial (1976) will generate forces that will build Adams-Morgan's public information system as a demonstration project, but no other support is likely to appear. Among the study's proposals, only the map is certain to be realized, because it is so cheap to produce.

Local financing for the system is not likely, owing to the substantial investment in new glare-producing, freeway-type street lights for the neighbourhood, and in its old, bent bus-stop signs, no-parking signs, etc. In addition, the District's signs are under the jurisdiction of so many diverse bodies that no early collaboration can easily occur. But, if the entire system could be built, it would not be a radical departure for the District. Existing *this-way-to* signs for tourists, rhythmically placed glare-free lights on more prestigious streets, bold entry signs and symbols at the Corcoran Art Gallery, etc., all suggest that this proposal is only concerned with bringing Adams-Morgan's public information up to standards of other parts of the city, but with the coherence necessary to reinforce neighbourhood identity. And, of course, with concern for helping poor people to find the services provided for them.

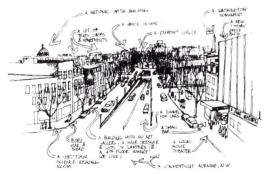

A SCENIC PATH CAN BE ANOTHER INFORMAL MESSAGE - ONE THAT TELLS A NEIGHBORHOOD THAT ITS SPECIAL PLACES (SCHOOLS, PARKS, ETC.) ARE IMPORTANT. IT WOULD DO THIS SIMPLY BY GOING PAST THEM.

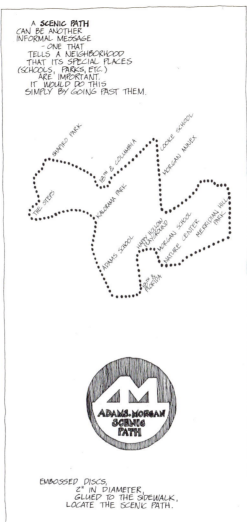

EMBOSSED DISCS, 2" IN DIAMETER, GLUED TO THE SIDEWALK, LOCATE THE SCENIC PATH.

A PUBLIC INFORMATION SYSTEM ALSO REQUIRES A MAP OF PUBLIC SERVICES.

(A PIECE OF SUCH A MAP FOR ADAMS-MORGAN IS SHOWN HERE. IT IS IN 3-D FORM FOR CLARITY, AND IT POINTS OUT SERVICES & BUS STOPS. IT GOES BEYOND NEIGHBORHOOD BOUNDARIES, WHEREVER NECESSARY, TO SHOW OTHER SERVICES THAT MIGHT ALSO BE IMPORTANT TO RESIDENTS. THE SERVICES ALL APPEAR AGAIN, AT THE EDGES, LISTED UNDER PROBLEM AREAS SUCH AS "LEGAL HELP", "HEALTH", ETC. THE LISTS ARE ALSO IN SPANISH, BECAUSE SO MANY SPANISH-SPEAKING PEOPLE LIVE IN THE NEIGHBORHOOD.)

THE MAPS SHOULD BE AVAILABLE IN A FOLDED, POCKET-SIZED FORM, AND THEY SHOULD BE DISPLAYED AT SUCH PUBLIC PLACES AS SCHOOLS, BUS-STOPS, PARKS, AND SERVICE ORGANIZATIONS.

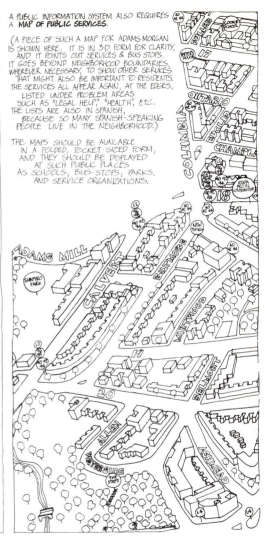

Left: Washington, DC, seen from Connecticut Avenue, NW.

THE NEIGHBOURHOOD MUSEUM AND THE INNER CITY

JOHN R KINARD

Where I come from, a small community in Washington, DC, called Anacostia, the world's first intermediary museum was established as an extension of the Smithsonian Institution. As everyone knows, the Smithsonian is a giant in the museum world. Less well known is the fact that it is a long-established giant willing to take a risk. The timing was right and the dedication needed to foster change was present. This renowned institution willingly moved into a completely unexplored area, without expertise and without overwhelming endorsement, but firmly resolved to accomplish its purpose.

The Smithsonian Institution's pioneer effort could be among the most significant advances in the museum world. Its effect, not only on museums in the USA but also the world over, is yet to be estimated. How did it begin?

The Anacostia Neighbourhood Museum began in an abandoned movie theatre located across the river about a mile and a half from the Smithsonian on the Mall, but light years away as far as visitors from Anacostia were concerned. When the Smithsonian announced its interest in taking museums to the people and its plans to open such a museum, requests came in from a number of low-income communities in Washington. Smithsonian representatives held informal but constructive and exploratory discussions with a number of these groups. Although small in area, Anacostia was selected because it represented all of the urban ills prevalent in modern cities of America. In cities around the world the specific problems might be different, but there are needs wherever people live together.

An advisory council made up of all segments of the Anacostia community (civic and youth groups, tenant councils, schools, the police, the clergy, and others) was formed. These people met with Smithsonian staff during the winter and spring of 1967. The Museum opened the following September.

Some of these same men and women are now on the Museum's Neighbourhood Advisory Committee which provides the impetus behind the entire idea of community participation.

We must realize that the Smithsonian could not have been successful had it not been for those community leaders in Anacostia who seized the moment, saw a golden opportunity for a new lease of life in their area, and who, through their persistent efforts, were able to show good reason why the world's first neighbourhood museum should be established in Anacostia.

The neighbourhood museum exists to serve the people of the area of which it is a part. At the same time that it is dependent on the sponsoring agent for its needs, it is independent in its operation. It determines its own priorities in regard to personnel policies, exhibits, educational programmes, and all other activities. As a free agent, it invites its neighbours to serve on an advisory committee.

People who have no decent place to live or lack educational skills have no interest in air pollution or Graeco-Roman civilization or even African culture. They are forced to concentrate on the struggle to survive, to house and clothe and educate their families.

So we must begin with where the people are in the circumstances in which we find them. The urban industrial centres have their own history. In Anacostia it is one of crime, drugs, unemployment, inadequate housing, sanitation, rats, to mention but a few of its problems.

The neighbourhood museum concerns itself with an analysis of the community and its history. It poses such questions as where did we come from, who are our heroes, what is our heritage, who are we as a people? What have we done to better ourselves and the community in which we live? What are our social, economic, political, and educational assets and liabilities?

With this approach we see the neighbourhood museum as a mechanism for enfranchising and recognizing people who don't normally visit a museum. In contrast, it is all too apparent that the current trends followed by the traditional museums, as they address themselves to modern man in a highly sophisticated and technical age, are inadequate for a great number of people. The traditional museum presents life as it once was and not as it is now. The times demand that the museum presents life as it really is and people as they really are. When we set up a museum to portray people only as we wish to see them, we are building monuments that are a credit to our ignorance. The old ways of doing things are no longer useful.

The museum need not be a sombre place where a select few come for quiet study of the relics of the past; nor need it be an ivory tower where aesthetes may isolate themselves from the real world. In contrast, the neighbourhood museum, by its very presence, stimulates the minds of the unconcerned and uninitiated. It offers them new experiences, a new concept of themselves and, thereby, a greater sense of self-esteem and a greater awareness of their role in the community. A museum comes alive through the interaction of individuals with each other and with the people of yesterday, yesteryear, or a thousand years ago. Through this interaction, individuals gain a greater sense of appreciation, not only of others, but of themselves.

The museum must be an outgrowth of felt community needs and pressures. It exists to re-present those needs whatever they may be and to take firm action toward creative solutions. All programmes and exhibitions should be an expression of community interests.

Visitors to the Museum's exhibition 'Black Patriots of the American Revolution'.

The traditional museums serve a totally different purpose. Their sense of community has been limited; their function has been object-oriented rather than people-oriented. Such institutions were not designed to serve the poor, the uneducated, or the minority groups of a nation. There has been very little in the traditional museum that touches on the lives of these people or their history, very little they can relate to or identify with.

Life for the neglected minorities must begin where they are now at this moment in time. The individual must understand where he is if he is to understand the past more fully. He must construct a new world for himself so that he can take pride in the past. It is the museum's function to trace how earlier cultures dealt with problems much like those we face today, so that the past may be made relevant to the present. Through such comparisons the museum visitor is able to see, not only himself, but mankind struggling to master situations that affect the quality of his life. The various media of the exhibits convey the alternatives to these problems and stimulate the museum visitor to use what he has seen in determining his own solutions. This is the

philosophy that underlies our efforts — a generous concern for the enhancement of every area of man's life.

To insure its involvement and strength, the neighbourhood museum must attract a significant number of neighbourhood people on all levels. In so far as it is possible, the staff should live in the area. They must be sensitive to the community's needs and aware of its heritage. They need to get to know the established leaders of the community and the dynamics which motivate them.

A search should be made for those leaders whom the community has produced — the known and the unknown, the titled and untitled. These people should be included on the advisory board of the museum where they will have a voice in the decision making. Through such opportunities, local people are able to express their ideas and their interests.

To comprehend the workings of any community, we must examine its constituent parts. No other educational institution is better equipped than the museum to do this in a creative, innovative fashion with a wide variety of media — dioramas, maps, models, photographs, artifacts, films, and slides.

The museum allows for experimentation within a variety of activities — new learning techniques in the presentation of exhibits, training programmes, research on urban problems, and creative expression through drama, dance, and arts and crafts. In preference to an exhibit of the works of a Michelangelo or Raphael, the logical starting point for projects in the arts is the creative potential of the neighbourhood residents and what they are able to achieve.

Instead of individuals telephoning the museum to ask if the staff would like to have this object or that, we must go one step further and encourage people in the community to seek out these things — to get to know their neighbours, discover what their interests are, accumulate objects for the museum, publicize our programme and plans, talk about what's going on to everyone they meet, lay a foundation for future fund-raising efforts — these are but a few of the many ways to involve the community.

The neighbourhood museum can be a rewarding undertaking for the sponsoring museum: not by way of an apology for past omissions but as a challenging opportunity to become involved in a new, creative way. Museums will need to decide, either individually or collectively, whether to broaden their interests, expand their functions, and redefine their reason for being. In the USA we have made a humble beginning. It is our hope that museum intermediaries will make a significant contribution in the service of man — today and tomorrow.

Left: Visitors to the Museum's exhibition' · · · Toward Freedom', which related the story of the Civil Rights movement.

Below: Visitors to the Museum's exhibition 'Rat: Man's Invited Affliction'.

Right: Children visiting their special room in the Museum.

111

BRITISH INNER-CITY PLANNING
A PERSONAL VIEW

MIKE FRANKS

In the last thirty years Britain has seen an unprecedented amount of legislative energy devoted to the problems of 'planning'. Yet there is now more anxiety about social deterioration in our cities than ever before. What happened to all those hopes of a better society that politicians invariably attached to post-war planning schemes? It would seem that Britain's reputation for 'good planning' is based on the presence of a mass of legislation, some grand comprehensive schemes and on our so-called success in New Town development. Sadly, in all these cases, if there has been any success at all, only the middle mass of society has benefited. Both the urban and the rural poor continue to pay a high price to maintain these 'beneficial' changes. Numerous forms of social pathology are mushrooming in the inner city, and the pale monocultures of our New Towns (or 'super-villages' as Reyner Banham more accurately describes them) contradict the reputation which some planners still think is deserved. Delinquency, violence, bad housing, community friction and educational failure can all be found concentrated in the inner areas of all British cities. British town planners have always been concerned with palliatives, not cures. The profession has its roots in the response to the problems of the nineteenth-century growth of industrial cities. Its attempts to deal with the developments of a post-industrial society are rather like those of a man trying to stave off an avalanche with an umbrella.

Although the greatest concentration of poverty and stress are to be found in the centre, it would be a mistake to see the city solely in terms of a series of physical zones, each containing a set of definable characteristics. In fact, many of its problems are not separately confined within geographical areas. Areas of bad housing and run-down back-street industry exist outside the inner city; areas of high-class housing exist inside it. Many social, ethnic and cultural groups living in transition areas have more in common with similar groups several miles further out from the city centre than they have with their neighbours a mile on either side of them. Yet urban planning is area-based, and its emphasis is on locality rather than characteristics. A myth about the need to plan the city as a series of contiguous areas thus overshadows attempts to develop policies to alleviate poverty and stress on an integrated non-area basis and then apply an integrated set of policies to any given area. In time, we will come to a more considered balance between subject and area-based policies, but at present our planning energy is often lost to those in greatest need.

Planning consideration is needed for the problems of today as much as those of tomorrow.

Furthermore, the aspirations written into inner city plans are usually far grander than can actually be achieved given the limited context within which the plan has to be drawn up and implemented. In any case, the present emphasis on medium- and long-term planning in Britain is often brutally unconcerned with conditions here and now. These facts alone would be enough to call for a reassessment of such processes, but when one sees plans exacerbating the very situation they seek to solve the need for a new approach becomes imperative.

The changing emphasis away from physical and towards social planning in recent years is a reflection of technological and social change throughout society. All the evidence suggests that the disorientation which this change produces is widespread and rapid and that planners, no less than any other section of society, are being affected by it. Recently, Alvin Toffler, in his disturbing but convincing book, *Future Shock,* has said. '. . . we are — without plan, without serious philosophical consideration, without even elementary caution — creating a new society, and blindly superimposing it on the old'. Urban planners, among others, have helped to promote the belief in the past that it was possible to accommodate the rate of change by good comprehensive planning. Now, we are beginning to admit that it may be impossible, given the present level of understanding and the machinery for implementation. In recent years, much of the firm ground of conviction has given way to a quicksand of contradictions which is giving rise to professional self-questioning. This of course is a healthy sign, but at a certain point it becomes destructive unless answers begin to be provided. The old patterns of planning activity are too deep-rooted and inflexible to adapt quickly, and the realisation of this has caused frustration and may have sapped the will to try to make bureaucracy work.

This essay seeks to show that, despite the numerous anomalies and misconceptions that attach to British town planning, the opportunity still exists, especially in the inner city, for the urban planner to play an effective and constructive part in helping to counteract anti-social trends. He can still become involved in the formulation of policies and the establishment of frameworks that would allow for the greatest amount of personal fulfilment and individual dignity for every member of that society. Furthermore, there is scope for this role both inside and outside the orthodoxy of a planning office and inside and outside the so-called orthodoxy of political non-involvement.

I have worked as an urban planner since 1964. The four examples chosen to illustrate the text are the ones within my experience which cover the widest range of planning roles over the two basic types of inner city work (transitional zone and central areas). Liverpool is one of the best examples of a local authority that has constantly tried to improve its planning techniques in the face of a deteriorating inner urban situation. The fact that it is failing to tackle the problem adequately is more a reflection on inner city urban planning as a whole than on Liverpool's City Planning Department. One could criticise many individual aspects of the way the work is being done, but the major influences on Liverpool's future lie outside its administrative boundaries — some of the solutions could even lie with the regional policy makers of the European Economic Community.
In Liverpool, I worked for the City Planning Department on inner city residential areas. In Chiswick, near central London, I am working in my own time on a voluntary basis, again on transitional zone housing. The other two examples I have taken are central area schemes of considerable complexity. In Covent Garden I take my perspective from inside the Greater London Council (GLC) — probably the largest bureaucracy of its type in the world; in Piccadilly I act as an adviser to the Save Piccadilly Campaign (see Ed Berman's article) and am an advocate for possible ways to tackle the planning problems involved.
In each case the intention has been to examine and learn from the way in which public and private sector interests combine to produce urban development. By coming to understand the way in which various forces interplay in urban change, I hoped also to understand the range of possible roles the professional urban planner can assume in such change. His intervention can be either direct or indirect; he can work either for those seeking to propagate change or for those unwittingly caught up in it. Or, in some cases, he should be able to represent the views of one whilst being employed by the other. The work I have done has been action-orientated because it was important to demonstrate through personal example rather than academic debate that in any given situation a planner has something to offer, even if his role was of only limited importance compared with that of other individuals and groups. This experience,

when added to that gained as a local authority planner, is providing me with a far more rounded view than I would otherwise have of what people think a planner does, what powers the mass media and the public ascribe to him and what actually results from planning.

The planner and his client

75% of Britain's professional planners are directly employed by some form of national or local government body, and almost all the rest rely in part on government contracts as consultants or specialist researchers. The planner's professional institute is thus so dominated by public servants that it is unlikely to bite the hand that feeds it by being over-critical. The manoeuvring that goes on in bureaucracies is not understood by those outside it. Because of their internalised objectives one group or department of officers may find themselves in conflict with another (planners and traffic engineers are a good example), and even when the differences have been resolved officers and their politicians are often still trying to out-manoeuvre one another in their attempts to decide what happens. Nor do the politicians themselves agree. What the public sees when a statement or a plan comes out of a town hall is the tip of the iceberg: the submerged portion is never seen and rarely discussed. In the present situation, planners are often, without realising it, in danger of being agents of control rather than instruments of acceptable change. The planner's work lends him to being used to promote policies which secure power for those who already have it; his role, like that of many of his fellow professionals, may be important to government partly in so far as it helps to maintain the established order. If individual planners are thus denied the scope to express their professional opinions because this would be unacceptable to their political masters, then it becomes necessary for planners as a profession to promote an increase in the range of client groups. If the percentage of planners working as public servants could be reduced from 75 to 50%, and a wider range of client groups were able to pay for a professional service, a far healthier situation would arise. However, it would require government initiative in the form of financial assistance to allow low-income communities to commission professionals.

Working in some situations directly to the 'client', instead of through a hierarchy of chief officers and a committee of politicians, I have learned at first hand what ordinary people think of planners and of

large public corporations. Government, with all its compartmentalised divisions and its predominantly autocratic and elitist approach, is a total mystery to them and planning as a subject leaves them bewildered and often annoyed. At the same time, working inside local government, I have felt annoyed or frustrated because the public can not or will not recognise the complex problems planners have to face. It has been an edifying experience to be one of 'them' and one of 'us' at the same time. But, as R D Laing points out in *The Politics of Experience*, ' . . . the peculiar thing about them is that they are created by each of us, repudiating his own identity . . . . just as I am one of them to him, he is one of them to me'. One of the keys to a more effective planning process must be free public access to information and the availability of people to interpret it. An aware public and a receptive and open government would go a long way towards enabling the professional planner to 'de-mystify' his role and to allowing him to enter into a much closer relationship with the real client. If it was also recognised that professional roles could not be separated from personal values, planners could hire their labour to those clients they most wished to advise. Their skills should be just as much, if not more, at the disposal of those least able to compete in society as they are at the disposal of those who can afford to buy advice whenever they need it.
When he is working in local government or its equivalent, the urban planner is caught in the triangle formed by truth, policy and expediency. His professionalism can be undermined by his political masters because his professional 'union' does not back him up enough. Only by being able to choose to serve any of a number of different client groups can planners say they are providing a professional service and only by acting as planners independent of government sanction will there be radical assessment of their role. This is why an increasing number of planners have chosen to involve themselves directly in the life of inner city communities — not always with the desired effect.
There is an undeniable argument for a planning role that seeks to reconcile conflicting interests (as far as is technically possible) to a point where those holding conflicting views can clearly understand what are the basic options and can therefore decide what measures they wish to adopt to secure their own interests. This would represent a new role for the bureaucratic planner and would have to be complemented by other planners using their skills to help any of the various outside interest groups to make their own case. One is useless without the other. The bureaucrat can only

say what could be, someone else must say what should be and they will need professional advice to do it. Within the next five years there are bound to be a number of experiments by local planning authorities along the lines of those tried in Liverpool and elsewhere to examine the potential of a reconciliatory role for the bureaucratic planner, because there is no doubt that some form of 'social' as opposed to physical planning is in the process of being accepted, albeit in a diluted and inadequate form. Social planning in this context is taken to mean the total effort by all agencies working in concert to achieve satisfactory environmental change (which includes the economic and social structure that exists within that environment). To this generally accepted definition I would add the need to deal with issues that have been identified as a result of widespread public debate. This form of plan making and implementation would stand in sharp contrast to the present compartmentalised approach developed over the past hundred years whereby numerous different public interests work separately towards their own goals, which may often have been internally derived without any reference to the public at large.

LIVERPOOL

Liverpool's planning history deserves far more space than it can be given here. The growth of the sanitary reform movement in the nineteenth century, together with important developments in municipalisation, gave way to inter-war suburbanisation and, latterly, to post-war planning. Now Liverpool is once again in the forefront of change with the development of social planning and community politics. Curiously, the reasons for Liverpool's fame are not easily defined. Perhaps its unique flavour is a blend of its strong mercantile tradition, which fostered an outward-looking view; its geographical isolation from the mainstream of English life, stuck way across the marshes and miles below the lowest bridging-point of the estuary; its exponential demographic and economic growth following the Industrial Revolution, and, not least, its multiracial community. The large numbers of Irish and Welsh immigrants, especially, have made a strong impact on the city since they began to move there in the mid-nineteenth century. Chinese, West Indians and Jews have made their own individual contribution to the city's character, and a further complexity has been the contrasting and often conflicting outlooks of the strong Catholic and Protestant communities. Liverpool has such an individuality that, although many of its most favoured sons leave the city, they con-

Everton Heights — post-war slab blocks of the early 60s gradually replace the slums. A decade later they are slums. themselves.

tinue to talk obsessively about it with a mixture of irony, irreverence and pride.

A pioneering spirit still exists in Liverpool. It can be found in planning no less than in other spheres, and in planning often arises out of the need to take desperate, and sometimes avant-garde measures to cope with desperate situations. This situation arises, as in other cities, out of the conflict between the spirit of economic enterprise striving for new horizons on the one hand, and, on the other hand, the dismal housing conditions of the urban poor, who threaten to disrupt the whole working of the economy, either by being a drain on the city's finances or by taking strike action against the city bosses.

In post-war Liverpool comprehensive redevelopment was as fashionable as in other cities. The 1947 Town and Country Planning Act gave local authorities massive powers to clear slums and redevelop large areas in their entirety. Indeed, one of the Act's specific intentions was to stop piecemeal change. Scores of high-rise blocks built in the 1950s and 60s showed Liverpool's determination to tackle the problem of bad housing. 50% of the populations was moved out to overspill residential areas on the edge of the city as a result of redevelopment. These dormitory areas have proved to be quite as problematical as the inner areas they were built to relieve, because they, too, were designed as physical and not as social entities. No enough thought was given to the new land-use plans. Capital expenditure programmes inevitably altered over time and many essential local services, such as shops, meeting halls and recreational facilities, were never built. No employment opportunities were created within the residential areas and the transport services were very limited. The working-class extended families of the inner areas were forced to become the nuclear families of the overspill suburbs. The closely populated over spill areas in Kirby, Aintree and Speke, all built as pale versions of the Garden-City ideal miles from the centre, now show evidence of social malaise similar to inner city areas such as Everton, Vauxhall and Granby, which have been depopulated in a most depressing way.

Indignation through hindsight is all too easy, but it is hard to look back at what has happened to Liverpool's inner areas without being disturbed by the brash and autocratic manner in which politicians decided they knew what the people wanted and by the physically-oriented way architects and planners put forward their solutions. By the early 60s the visual evidence of a massive housing programme and very little else was starting to disturb the City Fathers.

Planning in Liverpool at that time was being done by the City Architect's and the Housing Departments which were responsible for the comprehensive housing schemes of the 50s and 60s. The Council was prevailed upon to create a separate Planning Department in 1963, at a time when such an innovation represented a considerable breakthrough. This innovation provided a new and exciting tool with which to combat both the long-standing and the newly-created environmental and social problems besetting the city.

Many architects, some Liverpool born like myself and fresh out of university, went to work in the Urban Design section which together with the Development Control and Policy and Research Divisions constituted the Planning Department. We were not planners and we had no concept of urban change. Our naive enthusiasm and preoccupation with architectural form must have been a headache for the inner-city residents we met. We talked about how the area was going to be well-designed in the future; they talked about the lack of jobs and the bloody-mindedness of Town Hall officials. We were miles apart and we could not even see it.

In 1965 a target of 33,000 homes in the Inner Areas were scheduled by the Medical Officer of Health for clearance by 1972. (The intention was to clear 78,000 houses in the whole of Liverpool by the late 1980s.) In retrospect, it seems unbelievably brutal. Politicians stood for election on how many slums they had cleared and how many new homes they were going to build. The tragic results of this aggressive brave new world approach can be seen today, not only in Liverpool but in every inner city area in Britain. The Housing Numbers Game only deals with tomorrow; it forgets about today.

Liverpool's clearance target was accepted by the Planning Department and became the basis of its redevelop-

ment programme. In the Urban Design section, we were all disturbed by the quality of the housing that was being produced, yet our attachment to the slums and the dignity of the poor was more romanticism than clear perception. Nevertheless, we were making some effort to understand the whole process and we had moved a considerable distance from the old form of physical planning. Not very much of benefit to local residents was being achieved in the inner areas of Liverpool in 1965, but it is clear, looking back, that the Department was starting to develop interdisciplinary techniques which are now becoming common practice. Head of the Department, Walter Bor, was one of the members of the Planning Advisory Group set up to consider improvements or possible revisions to the 1947 Act. The ideas generated by the Group were put into practice in the Department's everyday work and were finally embodied in a major new Planning Act in 1968. In addition to this, the hesitant steps we and a number of other planning departments in the country were taking in discussing plans with the public became the subject of a major study, headed by the late Arthur Skeffington MP in 1969 on public participation in planning.

Liverpool's intelligent attempts to adjust their planning machinery to deal with the City's multiple deprivation problems were recognised by the fact that first Walter Bor and then his successor Francis Amos became Presidents of the Royal Town Planning Institute. Both men were in the forefront of planning thinking and many of their ideas were put into practice in Liverpool. We were trying to implement Skeffington even before I left, but the Liverpudlians' inbuilt apathy towards government made it difficult.

Looking back one could see why community politics has taken such a strong hold in the City. Despite the serious attempts to coordinate the activities of other departments, the Planning Department's role was merely advisory. For the residents in the inner city little seemed to have changed after the new department was set up and again with the advantage of hindsight I can see many areas where we went wrong, particularly in phasing and trying to ensure that any benefit resulting from a plan came out of the first actions and did not have to wait until all actions were well underway. Our enthusiasm to achieve something made us too confident and in urban planning, such an approach is highly suspect because of the sheer complexity of the problems.

In recent years there has been introduced into inner city deprived areas what are known as Intervention Programmes — experimental programmes designed

to harness together administrators, professionals and researchers in the cause of social reform. Planners and other specialist disciplines, including sociologists, welfare economists, political scientists, social administrators and a range of field-work activists have found themselves working at the interface between traditional land-use/transportation planning and social policy. In Liverpool amongst several other cities there have been a number of experiments in positive discrimination designed to redress a

Liverpool clearance areas — many of these will have to be grassed over because the money for redevelopment has run out.

societal imbalance. Although these experiments have not yet proved outstandingly successful, they have begun to reveal the complex interrelationships between cause and effect that exist in the range of government actions designed ostensibly to deal with poverty. Since I left Liverpool the innovatory experiments in the inner areas have continued. A series of government sponsored reports gave rise to an Urban Programme with a capital expenditure of about £3 million annually since 1968. Urban Aid has been granted to projects concerned with areas of educational priority, immigrant problems, special social needs, children's play, advice centres and other projects mainly centred on the inner city. But in 1972-3 the annual budget only represented about 0.5% of all government expenditure in this field and only 1% of the expenditure on the social services. Little wonder that field work activists and many politicians concerned to see government concepts of order and stability replaced by serious attempts to redistribute power and opportunity are concerned that the underlying political motive of the Intervention Programmes appears to be different from that expressed by government politicians. Critics like Socialist Member of Parliament, Michael Meacher, claim that such experiments are crisis expedients aimed at easing political pressures and represent a 'shop window display of concern at minimum cost . . . in a way that cannot fundamentally alter society'.

Several experiments were set up in Liverpool following a series of national studies begun in the early 1960s. These were the 1967 Plowden Report on the Needs of New Communities, the Seebohm Report, 1968, on Local Authorities and Allied Personal Social Services and the Skeffington Report, 1969, on Public Participation in Planning. An Educational Priority Area (EPA) covered a large part of the inner area with a population of over 100,000. 30 schools were given special attention by a team of three people.

A Community Development Project (CDP) was started in 1969 but incredibly it was not in the same area as the EPA *(see plan)*. CDPs have tried to comprehend through the co-ordination of all agencies in the social welfare field — together with the local residents — what the social problems were in an area and one of their prime aims is to develop community awareness. The problems of coordination for those working in the CDP in the Vauxhall area of Liverpool have been immense and once more there have only been limited gains. In 1969, Shelter, the national campaign for the homeless, chose an area of stress housing called Granby within Liverpool's EPA to run an experiment similar to a CDP but closer to the housing and planning field. They called it the Shelter Neighbourhood Action Project (SNAP), and their work together with the report in 1972, *A New Chance for Cities,* and the evidence of the limited success of the EPA and CDP studies must have influenced a subsequent announcement that Central Government were to sponsor six total approach studies which, it was said, would examine all the interrelated aspects of inner city deprived area need that EPAs, CDPs, SNAP and other Urban Aid Projects had thrown up. Liverpool once again was chosen for one study but since they were announced in July 1972 this comprehensive approach has been cut down to deal with environmental issues only, and even in the limited field there has been

Positive intervention programmes in Liverpool's Inner Areas.

116

considerable technical difficulty for the study teams. Social planning in some form is being developed and some worthwhile precedents are being established but so far have failed to make any impact on inner city problems. (There were a number of serious fights in Liverpool 8 — part of the EPA — in the summer of 1972 between groups of coloured and white youths.) In April 1973 the results of the local government elections came as a profound shock to established local politicians. Community affairs and lack of faith in Town Hall politics played such a strong part that the Liberal Party who had been a very minor influence in local authority affairs swept to power by stressing their concern for intensely local issues. Party politics in Town Halls may be a thing of the past. Whatever the explanation, the growth of inner city community newspapers (Liverpool has one of the highest number of such newspapers in the country) and community action generally, both of which stress the anti-bureaucratic approach, are making the achievement of adequate machinery to tackle the problem very hard indeed. As John Dykman (now Professor of Planning at the University of California) once pointed out, the problem is not 'bureaucracy or grass roots' but 'what bureaucracy'. Turning away from bureaucracy usually ends up with the establishment of an alternative bureaucracy.

CHISWICK

Chiswick is a predominantly middle-class area on the western fringes of inner London and at the extreme eastern end of the London Borough of Hounslow, into which it was protestingly incorporated in the London Government Act of 1963. It differs in character from the rest of the borough and it is physically remote from Hounslow Town Hall, so that there is little rapport between the local people and a council elected primarily to represent working-class and lower middle-class suburban areas in outer London. This has encouraged the growth of numerous protest groups, amenity societies and other voluntary bodies, although the catalyst for these groups was the threat posed to the area by the road proposals explicit or implicit in the Greater London Development Plan of 1969. (These involved no less than three six-lane motorways forming a triangle as they met and crossed through Chiswick.) There is in any case a massive traffic problem in the area and middle-class protests aimed at the statutory bodies responsible for transport policies have tended to dominate other planning issues.

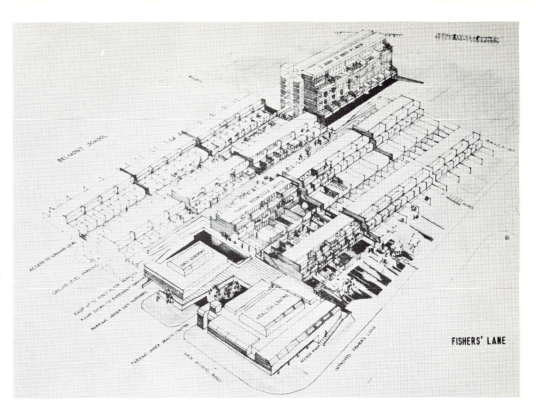

Architecturally Fishers Lane is a good scheme — but why allow 200 houses to run down to replace them with 200 more?

This preoccupation with transport partly explains the absence of protest, or even of much public debate, about the running-down of a 7-acre area immediately behind Chiswick High Road (a shopping centre with an annual turnover of £5,000,000). There were once 200 terraced houses, of a type now very fashionable in London, contained in five streets in what is now known as the Fishers Lane Redevelopment Area. With a park to the north and all the facilities and accessibility associated with a town centre to the south, the residents — many of whom had lived there for fifty years or more — were very well served, and would have been very happy to remain had they been given the choice. (An identical but unblighted area a quarter of a mile away has been the subject of considerable im-

provement investment.) However, for reasons now obscured by time, the Fishers Lane area has been scheduled for redevelopment for more than fifteen years. One or two houses owned by the council have been empty and boarded up for almost this length of time; several have been empty for five to ten years and others have been boarded up more recently. Council valuation officers have been purchasing houses by agreement for a similar period.

By 1972 the majority of people were being moved out and some sections of the terraces had been demolished. What little debate there was on Fishers Lane centred more on the future proposals for an underground car park with housing on a deck above than on the deteriorating living conditions of the existing residents. However, by early 1973, conditions in Fishers Lane had become so bad that a group of residents went and asked for help at a meeting of the Brentford and Chiswick Public Relations Council (an association of about

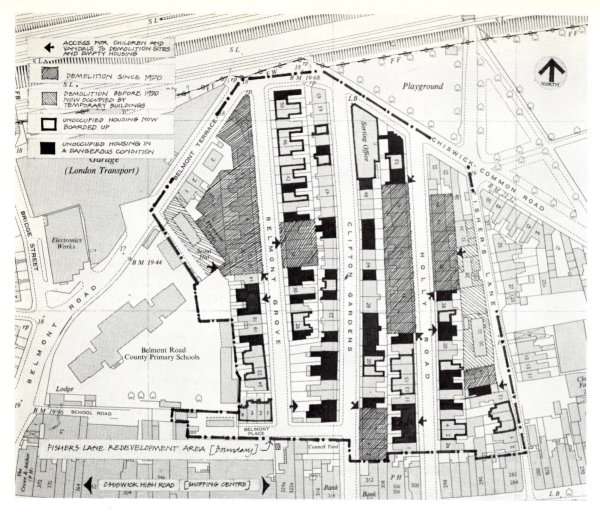

Above: Results of FLAC survey (March 1973)

Top right: Fishers Lane area — good housing being allowed to deteriorate while elderly people are still living next door.

Right: Demolition before rehousing in areas like Fishers Lane creates far more problems than it solves.

thirty voluntary bodies in the area to which I was informally involved). I was asked to speak at a public meeting of the residents at which, somewhat surprisingly, more than 80 of the remaining 170 tenants turned up. The Fishers Lane Action Committee (FLAC) was set up, and I was voted in as their technical adviser. An executive committee was set up, more to do the work than to act as representatives, and we surveyed the area during the following week. The results of the survey were appalling *(see plan)*.

There could be no excuse for leaving people caught up unwittingly in the redevelopment process to exist in such degrading and unsanitary conditions. The map shows the haphazard and unthinking way in which closure and demolition have occurred. From the survey it was possible to see the frightening number of dangerous structures, the leaking roofs, the rising damp, and houses and demolition sites supposedly boarded up yet still accessible to children and vagrants. It revealed the extent of the public health hazard from overcrowding, vermin and poor sanitary arrangements. Over the years, the residents had asked council officers and local politicians for assistance, but little help had been forthcoming. No-one at a technical or political level in Hounslow Council was prepared to tell the residents of their rights or explain how future proposals would affect them. Local people were afraid that if they protested the process of rehousing them would slow down. So they had lapsed into apathy and tried to close their eyes to their conditions.

I find it a point of acute concern to realise that Fishers Lane may well be an inevitable product of the type of planning that has become standard local authority practice in inner city situations in Britain. I may have played an unwitting part in the creation of similar situations in Liverpool and elsewhere, and it is this realisation that has made me, and many other similarly-placed professionals, extremely circumspect about the benefits of large-scale redevelopment schemes in housing areas where improvement to existing property is possible. The condition of many of the houses in the Fishers Lane area after years of neglect by landlords indicates that the machinery for dealing with urban change is either inadequate or inefficient. In Fishers Lane, as elsewhere, the fault cannot be laid at any one door. It was not planners who were responsible for maintaining an up-to-date record of public health conditions in the area, and acting on that information; that was the responsibility of the Public Health Inspector. It was not the planners' job to know how many people in the area were suffering from nervous strain because of uncertainty about their future; that was the direct concern of the Director of Social Services. It was not the planners' fault that the Information Officer did not go out and inform the residents about future plans or that local politicians chose only to deal with isolated cases of hardship, and then only when they were asked. But the escape for an indifferent bureaucrat has always been to believe that outside a strictly limited area, somebody else can be seen to be responsible. In this vast and complex arrangement of departmental responsibilities few planners learn enough about the relationship between different departments, and the role of the politicians responsible for each. They are even less aware of public reaction to their plans, or of the way in which people might suffer because of the existence of those plans.

The extent to which the statutory obligations of a local authority were not being fulfilled on behalf of the residents of Fishers Lane was staggering. It is hard to understand how this neglect could be so widespread and sad to reflect that it took such a serious state of affairs to bring the residents together to take action. A campaign was mounted to draw attention to the situation in the area and on all occasions we were careful not to exaggerate. Conditions spoke for themselves and all that was necessary was to show that the residents were aware of their rights, that they intended to

follow all matters up and that they expected special treatment to compensate for past injustices. Chiswick's two widely-read and socially-aware local newspapers helped to spread the debate and punch home the message with good reporting and dramatic photographs. Conditions in the area even received national press coverage. The aims of the Committee, as agreed at the first meeting, were: *'Immediate rehousing for everyone — or make the area fit to live in NOW'*. The Council was acutely embarrassed at finding itself in a cleft stick. In law, especially under the Public Health Act 1936 and the Housing Act 1957, it was obliged to ensure that housing conditions in any part of the borough did not fall below a carefully defined standard. It had failed to do this, yet it could not rehouse all the remaining residents because it had insufficient dwellings to provide the reasonable choice required by Section 87 of the 1957 Act.

Having prepared its ground by seeking to be reasonable at all times and by allowing people to judge for themselves what the conditions were, the Committee then met with the local councillors in whose ward the Fishers Lane area lies. They were sympathetic to the residents' needs and made concerned noises about how they would speak to this or that official — as if they should not have done this much earlier. It was only when they were told that the Committee had been advised that they were entitled to start legal proceedings against the Council under Section 99 of the Public Health Act 1936 that they promised to arrange an urgent meeting with the Leader of the Council to see what could be done. This was arranged within the week, and it was probably the most high-powered local authority meeting I as a planner have ever attended.

The Fishers Lane Committee explained what they wanted and the Leader of the Council revealed that he had just set up a special working party of all the relevant departments, co-ordinated by the Chief Administrative Officer, to deal with all problems in the Fishers Lane area. All this in one week and so little in fifteen years! How ironic that the machinery to co-ordinate Council action on a deprived area should have to be forced on politicians at a stage when it could only deal with the tail-end of the problem. Had this 'corporate management' occurred at the start of the project the problems would probably not have arisen.

In the short period that FLAC has been in operation some real gains have been secured. The rate of rehousing has increased dramatically and the housing offered to the residents has been more suited to their needs than previously. There have been considerable

improvements in general living conditions for those still there. The residents are no longer the 'forgotten people of Chiswick', as one FLAC committee member described them, and for an all too brief period there was a revival of the old community spirit.

In acting as an enabler, helping the residents to acquire some of their basic rights, it has been possible to be involved in the kind of social planning that I believe to be necessary in the inner city. Methods were used that were designed to make the residents less invisible but there was no deception or distortion of fact. The planning role in Fishers Lane has been far more directive than advisory, and in some situations has almost been that of an advocate. But it did produce a reaction to the orthodox machinery which has promoted a policy of self-help amongst the remaining residents. They have become aware of their rights, and the council has become aware of their existence. The role for an adviser in the remaining short period before everyone is rehoused can be far closer to the non-directive professional one it should be.

And after everyone has been rehoused and those once attractive houses have been bulldozed, the latent controversy about the proposed underground car park and the deck housing will start up. Perhaps the lessons learned in the area already will allow this to be a reasoned dialogue between the council and the people of Chiswick — in other words, the planners and the planned-for.

COVENT GARDEN AND PICCADILLY

Covent Garden and Piccadilly Circus lie half a mile apart in the heart of London. History and patterns of activity make each unique; both areas owe much of their character to the informality and lack of pomposity associated with the interaction of a variety of activities. And both, of course, are the subject of major speculative interest by property developers. The area covered by the Piccadilly Circus Redevelopment Scheme is much smaller than that of the Covent Garden Comprehensive Development Area: 7.5 acres compared with 100. However, planning studies in Piccadilly might reasonably have covered a much larger area since the Circus is simply the focal point where several sectors of London's West End come together, the centre of the whirlpool. It is the combination of the activities in the surrounding sectors which gives the area of Piccadilly its particular character. If it had been planned in its broader context, the scheme might have covered perhaps 30 acres and included parts of Soho, the Chinatown area that

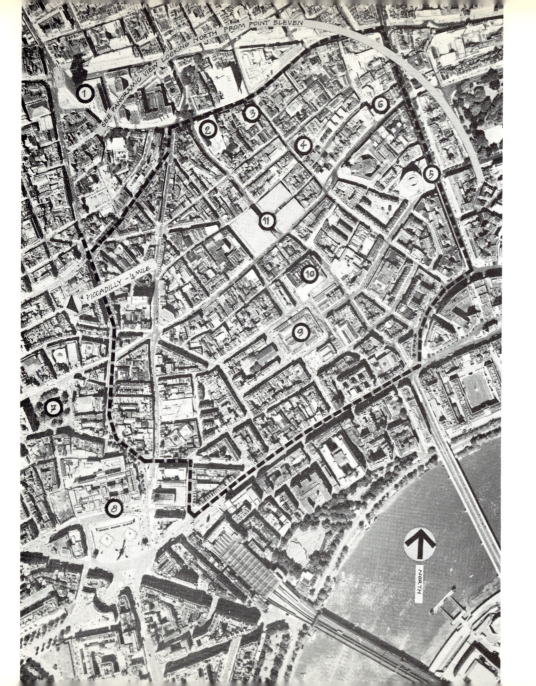

120

Panorama showing piecemeal redevelopment on the northern boundary of Covent Garden (plan left)

1 — Centre Point
1, 2, 5, 6 — 1950s-60s piecemeal redevelopment
3, 4 — Early 1970s piecemeal redevelopment
7 — Leicester Square
8 — Trafalgar Square
9 — Central Market Building
10 — Royal Opera House
11 — Demolition for speculative development of ¼ million sq ft of offices

divides Piccadilly Circus from Covent Garden, the theatre and cinema area of Shaftesbury Avenue and Leicester Square, the gentlemen's clubs of St James and the high-class shopping streets of Piccadilly and Regent's Street. Instead, Westminster City Council, whose responsibility Piccadilly is, chose to include in their scheme only the hub of the area, the Circus itself, simply because this was where the developers were concentrating their attention. Thus, the Piccadilly scheme deals in essence with a major traffic intersection, a large underground public transport concourse, and four principal sites which lie between the roads radiating from the Circus.

The areas of activity and land-use in Covent Garden are less confined into sectors but are spread around a large but well defined area bounded by main central London traffic routes rather than being intersected by them. Piccadilly is one of the several important nodal points in Central London whereas Covent Garden is one of its uniquely historic areas. Whereas, within the defined study area, Piccadilly has scarcely more than 150 residents, Covent Garden has almost 2,500. In addition to the places of entertainment which both areas contain, Covent Garden has a wide mixture of

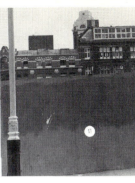

service industries, especially theatre-support industries such as costumiers and theatre wokshops. The area is the centre of the publishing industry (or was until some firms sold their holdings to **property** specu-lators) as well as various types of design studios. And intermingled throughout these activities is the Covent Garden Market, London's largest wholesale vegetable, fruit and flower market, which has exercised a **unique** influence on the whole character of the 100 acres. It was the decision taken almost 20 years ago by central government to move this market to a new site south of the river that led ultimately to the designation of a Comprehensive Development Area (CDA) in Covent Garden. It was recognised that the removal of the market in 1974 would leave 15 acres of land wholly associated with market uses to be replanned. In addition, land owners in adjacent areas had for some time been tailoring leases so that they fell in at the time when the market was moving. Consequently, a whole range of other uses in the area were likely to come to an end at the same time as the market. Plan-ning applications for extensive new users and large new buildings were inevitable; developers had been active for several years assembling parcels of land in expecta-tion of an extensive process of redevelopment. An analysis of these redevelopment intentions in 1967 showed that possibly 60% of the area was likely to be altered by 1980.

The Covent Garden area lies across the boundaries of two of the new Inner London Boroughs created by the London Government Act of 1963, and provision was made in the Act for a Consortium of the two Boroughs, Westminster and Camden, together with the GLC, to work on a scheme for the area. Planning in Covent Garden from the outset was thus the re-sponsibility of a special planning team whose offices were located within their study area and away from

the main GLC buildings across the river. Since its inception the team was an interdisciplinary one which included sociologists, estate surveyors, economists and urban designers.

It is interesting to speculate whether a similar team might have been set up for Piccadilly had it straddled two boroughs as Covent Garden did. Instead, it was the sole responsibility of Westminster, whose traditionally compartmentalised local government structure and civic design planning approach did not allow for the establish-ment of a special team working from within the study area. Here, as elsewhere, Westminster chose to plan on an *ad hoc* basis, seeing its role as one of containment rather than initiation. It was the developers who took the initiative; Westminster sought simply to see that their schemes conformed with civic design standards, and that they met land-use and traffic requirements. When Westminster sought for some planning gain, it was often by offering the developer extra profit-making uses as an inducement, such as office space. The gains were usually for traffic or visual amenity (never for social benefit) and in many cases the results were unsatisfactory. A perfect example of this, not far from Piccadilly but in the Camden area, is the notorious 'Centre Point' office block which was given planning permission in exchange for the public sector benefit of a small traffic island around the base of the block which, like the block itself, has never been used. In the 1968 Piccadilly scheme, public ownership of the London Pavilion site was to be surrendered in return for a mas-sive £8 million new underground concourse to be built jointly by the developers. In Covent Garden this method of acquiring planning gains has never been used because of the decision to plan on a 'comprehen-sive' basis using more wide-ranging powers of land and property acquisition available under CDA legislation. Westminster could, of course, have chosen to make

Piccadilly a CDA, if they had wanted to broaden its physical context and to invest it with more planning energy. Instead, there was a lack of enthusiasm to treat it as an integrated study because this would have cut across departmental boundaries and Westminster is a very hidebound bureaucracy. Yet, despite their very different planning bases, the schemes pro-duced for both Piccadilly and Covent Garden have aroused violent opposition since the early seventies. Before then, opposition was largely confined to the visual impact of certain buildings; in the 1968 Piccadilly scheme, objections focused on a very tall block on the Criterion site which was considered by the Royal Fine Arts Commission to be too **high**. There were no substantial objections to the 1968 Draft Plan for Covent Garden; it was received favour-ably in the press, though its complexity meant that very few were able to grasp its full implications. By 1970, however, public debate in the planning field had widened its scope and sharpened its attack. This was partly the result of *exposés* in the late sixties of the huge fortunes made by property de-velopers who had exploited planning situations and loopholes in the law, whilst at the same time pro-ducing very ugly buildings. Resentment against this was coupled with an awareness of the general inability to control the rate of change, which was often seen as destroying the familiar and the loved and dis-placing people at the same time. The whole conser-vation movement in the inner city owes its start to this mood; and it came to a head at the time when the proposals for the Covent Garden CDA were be-ing submitted to the Minister for the Environment, and when a new set of developers' proposals for Piccadilly were on public exhibition. (And it says a great deal about the failure of urban planning in Britain that when the resentment came into the open

as an attack on all aspects of bureaucracy's approach to the inner city, it could carry so much weight.)
In both areas a strong radical opposition group arose whose sole purpose was to defeat the plan. Both the Save Piccadilly Campaign and the Covent Garden Community Association were umbrella organisations which include a wide variety of interest groups. Ed Berman describes the Save Piccadilly Campaign elsewhere; the Covent Garden Community Association included local residents, architectural and other students, community workers, young professionals from a variety of disciplines, local small business interests and local churchmen. Other protesters included groups formed to protect the theatres, and individual journalists who took up Covent Garden as a crusade. Additional support came from such old timers of the planning protest lobby as the Civic Trust and their numerous offshoots. Finally the mass media jumped on the band-wagon with reporting that was often notably biased.

In Covent Garden the planning team knew that one of the most effective arguments which the public might have put up against the plan was that, while it might have been a good plan in its own terms, those terms were wrong, particularly the directive for the Ministry that public sector development had to be financed from GLC Covent Garden revenue alone. Instead, opposition centred on the intensity and scale of redevelopment allowed for in the plan, the height of the buildings, and what was seen as the 'hounding-out' of small-scale activities and the loss of cheap rented accomodation. The advocates for the opposition and the numerous journalists who wrote *ad nauseam* on the subject encouraged such beliefs as:

1   The 'planners' had chosen to redevelop the whole areas.
2   They could, had they wanted to, have chosen a number of more acceptable options.
3   They had specifically opted for high-density comprehensive redevelopment.
4   They were unconcerned about the plight of poorer people because both residents and small businesses were being pushed out of the area.
5   They had not chosen to consult with anyone during the production of the plan.
6   There had been a brutal disregard for buildings and areas of historic and architectural interest.

In the face of this anti-planning barrage — which would have been more to the point in Piccadilly — GLC politi-

cians chose to go limp. They did not respond publicly to the mass media, with their endless misinterpretations and their cavalier approach to accuracy, on the grounds that the arguments should take place at the forthcoming public inquiry. The opposition in Covent Garden thus synthesised in the objections to the plan put before the Inquiry, which began in mid-71 and lasted 42 days, the longest of its kind ever held. The objections were essentially political; the plan was hardly opposed on technical grounds. Yet the Ministry-appointed Inspector's role was to assess the technical merit of the plan. Technically, the Covent Garden Plan is one of the best of its generation and the Inspector was only able to fault one or two minor points of detail. Otherwise, in his report to the Minister, he accepted it in its entirety. The plan itself was vindicated; it had been developed at the end of an era of so-called comprehensive planning and, but, unlike most of its predecessors, it had been well researched and its studies were broadly based. It contained the essential ingredients that would have allowed it to adapt to changes in public attitude over its 15-year life-span. But its critics had dismissed it as anti-social, responding in an understandable way to something the Team was powerless to alter — the way the pressure of market forces made rapid and widespread changes inevitable. But without the availability of Government subsidy or changes in the law to slow the process down this is all any plan can do.

The Inspector's assessment may have been on technical grounds, but the Minister's response was wholly political. He waited 20 months before reaching a decision, whilst he gauged the mood of public opinion. (The Greater London Development Plan Inquiry was going on during this time, and what was being said there was a fair indication of the way public opinion was shaping.) His published response, when it came, increased emphasis on public participation as well as conservation, and looked for less emphasis on large-scale redevelopment and provision for the motor car. He asked for an 'informal' plan to be drawn up with 'full public participation'; and in the new spirit of conservation he designated 250 buildings as having architectural and/or historic merit, which effectively meant that they could not be demolished without special permission. (These buildings were indiscriminately scattered about the area and many of them were of doubtful architectural merit.) The Plan already contained a Conservation Area of 25 acres and a large number of carefully considered preserved buildings.
But the decision to designate the extra buildings was a natural outcome of the drive begun by the 1967 Civic Amenities Act, which placed an overwhelming

emphasis on the conservation of building fabric. These powers to preserve buildings and conserve whole areas which have been written into statute in recent years are amongst the most autocratic controls ever given to planning authorities. The Minister has subsequently admitted that he knew the new listings were of doubtful value in themselves but he used them to slow down the plan. Yet in Covent Garden, as elsewhere, the powers do nothing to preserve the uses to which the buildings are put, and the small businesses on whose behalf many objections were put forward may still find themselves ousted, even though they may now find themselves in a designated building. If a property owner cannot demolish because his building is to be conserved, he improves it instead and puts up the rent. Thus an ironmonger who has been in Drury Lane for decades has still to close down, because his rent has gone up 400%, and there is almost nothing the planner can do to help him.

When the team had analysed the Minister's proposals they found that the whole plan had been rendered unworkable. Yet when the GLC announced that they had decided to scrap the plan and start again, the Department of Environment was shocked. The Minister had simply wanted to slow the progress of redevelopment, but he had thrown the baby out with the bathwater.

This is the situation as it stands now. The market will move in 1974, leaving 15 acres of empty land. Huge areas of Covent Garden are in the hands of private developers; they are desperate to recoup as much money as possible on their land and, without a plan, there is no firm basis on which to withstand their pressures. However, politicians and planners are now involved in a wide-ranging debate with the public about future terms of reference; all proposals for change will be subject to *ad hoc* decisions taken with full public participation. This will be the case until an acceptable new plan has been formulated as a result of public participation, not consultation. At least this is the goal. Fortunately, the team is a large one and works in the heart of its study area, and there are encouraging signs that a rapport is developing with the public.

The Covent Garden Information Centre set up in 1971 adjacent to the team's offices is being expanded, and officers are available to explain the extremely complex set of legal and procedural parameters within which the plan must be drawn up: they spend up to 20% of their time doing so. Many of these parameters are very hard for the public to grasp. It is difficult, for instance, for laymen to understand that old and run-down property, with its multitude of picturesque

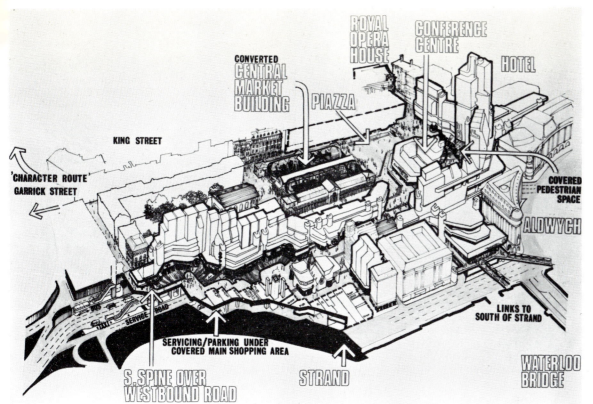

CONVERTED **CENTRAL MARKET BUILDING**
ROYAL OPERA HOUSE
CONFERENCE CENTRE
HOTEL
PIAZZA
KING STREET
'CHARACTER ROUTE' GARRICK STREET
COVERED PEDESTRIAN SPACE
ALDWYCH
TAXI SERVICE ROAD
LINKS TO SOUTH OF STRAND
SERVICING/PARKING UNDER COVERED MAIN SHOPPING AREA
S. SPINE OVER WESTBOUND ROAD
STRAND
WATERLOO BRIDGE

Part of a feasibility study for the 1968 Covent Garden Plan — architecturally over-ambitious but backed by some carefully thought out planning.

low-rental activities, is simply an outward sign of the end of an economic cycle that is about to be renewed; or that the numerous derelict sites in the area are not empty because no-one is interested in them: many have outstanding planning permissions granted during the office boom of the fifties and sixties and consequently a potential purchaser might have to pay anything up to £5 million an acre for them. The team has always tried to explain to the public at every possible opportunity the implications of the existing rights regarding property and planning law and the limitations of the power to stop demolition. We point out examples of the unfortunate results of piece-

meal development (which many members of the public advocate) by pointing to the many office blocks built around the area in the fifties and sixties. A notable example of the problem we face is a site in the heart of Covent Garden which has an outstanding planning permission for around ¼ million square feet of offices dating back to the fifties. If the GLC were to use its powers of compulsory purchase, the ratepayers of London could foot a bill for anything between £14 and £20 million in compensation. Many people would prefer to see such money being spent, for instance, on buying out bad landlords in twilight housing areas, or on subsidising inadequate public transport facilities. In such situations, the planners have been forced to negotiate with the developers; yet our opponents have always seen this as assisting developers to make money, not surprisingly when past examples of negotiations on major developments in Central London have been so

unsuccessful, and speculators have made vast profits at the public's expense. It is extremely difficult to explain to people that, because this country operates on a mixed economy principle, the public sector still relies heavily on the private sector taking risks in investment; in the inner city, where land prices are so high, the developer and financier are expected to do most of the developments. Even so, the abandoned Covent Garden Plan had proposed the compulsory purchase of 35 acres of land in the area over a period of 15 years. The use rights on the acquired land could then have been redistributed in a planned way and additional public sector uses such as a 100% increase in housing plus the associated provision of schools and open space could have been built out of the profit accruing to the public and not the private purse.

Another source of local resentment in areas such as Covent Garden is the process of 'gentrification'. This is generally taken to mean the replacement of run-down, low-income uses by improved facilities catering for higher-income demands. This process is attractive to planning authorities for a number of reasons. But if there is too much emphasis on 'tidying up' it becomes very hard to accommodate the needs of smaller less powerful interest groups, who may well be paying the price for the general gain to the community at large. On the other hand, there are very few ways in which a planning authority can 'blight' an area in order to keep the low-income users there. Statutory blight — that is, the inhibiting effect of local authority plans on the basic rights of a land owner to invest in his property — if proved, involves the payment of compensation at full market value. Both the Save Piccadilly Campaign and the Covent Garden Community Association have been forced to use blight as a weapon. The aim was to stop a plan that they considered would 'gentrify' an area, or worse still, would create 'concrete jungles' which would simply be monuments to profit. Although this 'blight' may slow the process of change down and possibly defer the date at which a low rental user has to leave, it only helps in the short term.

One of the fundamental problems in the public attitude to the Covent Garden Plan was that, because it was 'comprehensive', too much was ascribed to its power to control change. Indeed, Covent Garden is likely to be the last CDA in this country; the CDAs of the 1947 Act, allowing for the use of planning powers over a whole area, will now be superseded by the 1972 Planning Act, which designates Action Areas instead. These are much closer to the concept of adaptive planning strategies and is the way in which Covent Garden is operated. In the GLDP, Piccadilly is designated an Action Area, but has never been planned as one and still remains an exercise in environmental cosmetics.

Covent Garden is now an important arena for the evolution of new planning techniques, not least in the increasing involvement of the public in planning processes. There have to date been three major public meetings in Covent Garden, plus a large number of informal discussions with various interest groups about the most suitable machinery to develop a new plan in which the maximum number of people can participate. In other words, the people of Covent Garden now have a chance to discuss the terms of reference for any future plan.

There are signs that the campaigners are modifying their initial approach, which was to pursue a campaign of opposition to all established authority, indiscriminately grouping professional and political levels together as 'them' without trying to understand the individual roles of each. (Though a number of planners, architects and journalists claiming to speak for the community in Covent Garden even now advocate that the Development Team be sacked because they are wedded to an old plan; few if any of this fraternity have come to the team's offices to find out at first hand who we are and what we do.) The scope and activity of the Information Centre is now being expanded even further to help service whatever participatory machinery is set up. In Covent Garden, we may yet see an aware public discuss the future in a positive way with a receptive bureaucracy. It will be as much the public's fault as the government's if loopholes are still left for the developers.

I have played the role of an enabler in both Covent Garden and Piccadilly; in the former as a planner working for the local authority, in the latter as an informal adviser to the 'opposition'. (This role has proved to be quite useful to the Save Piccadilly Campaign, and another architect and myself have subsequently been co-opted as non-voting members on to the executive committee.) There is no contradiction in working for established authority in one area and for those who oppose that authority in an adjacent area. From an ethical point of view, I have no professional responsibility to my employers with regard to Piccadilly. I have no privileged information relating to it, and my chief officers know of my interest in it; I have established that I am free to work in my own time for whomsoever I choose, within the bounds of discretion. Technically, there is no conflict between the roles, since in most of the situations that have arisen in Piccadilly I like to believe that I and other technical advisers to the Campaign have given the

There is still no fixed idea for the use of the Central Market Building but the building itself will remain, whatever use is finally chosen.

same advice as we would have given as local government officers, only without having to penetrate a smokescreen of procedural 'red tape'.
The primary difference between working in Covent Garden and working in Piccadilly is that in the former one chooses a technical role with little political power except that of clarifying where political options lie, and in the latter one chooses a political role with less power to influence the technical thinking applied to the subject. If Westminster were to be as open about their planning process as we have tried to be in Covent Garden, the role of a professional planner could be of value in giving greater insight into ways of dealing with a complex technical situation. In Covent Garden professionals working within the community are taking the first hesitant steps towards working with the team to clarify problems and options. Local people should benefit from their change of emphasis from community advocates to community advisers. It will mean that if the public are not satisfied with what a GLC planner tells them, they can ask for a second opinion from an outside adviser who will be able to use the same data. People are beginning to understand that there is very little of our data that cannot be released to them because of its confidential nature.
In Piccadilly we are able to talk to Westminster's politicians simply because we hold a considerable initiative at the moment. But we are not encouraged to discuss technical matters with professional officers and we certainly do not have access to the data with which those officers work. Until we do there is likely to be a stalemate situation in Piccadilly, with successful blanket opposition to all development. Thus, the

people who are now losing most from bad political handling and an inadequate technical approach in Piccadilly are Westminster City Council and the developers. The council and its planners continue to remain isolated from the everyday affairs of Piccadilly. They have passed up the opportunity to set up an information centre, like ours in Covent Garden, in the heart of the area, and so have left the 'opposition' in full possession of the field. The short-term situation in Covent Garden is much more promising, and in the long-term it is likely that planning processes evolving there in the next year or so may set a valuable precedent for future developments in British inner-city planning.

Conclusion

If the reader senses a certain ambiguity, and even hints of schizophrenia, in the various parts of this essay, there is no apology. Inner city planning is a complex and politically ambiguous activity. To claim to have linked all the disparate parts together would be absurd.
Yet of all the periods to be working in planning, I believe this one to be the most challenging. Now is not the time for acrimonious charges that planners working within the system have 'sold out', or that voluntary activists working outside it have 'dropped out'. A constructive approach is required in both areas and, for those who wish to be part of a radical reappraisal rather than to help to dismantle the entire system, it will require energy from inside *and* out to create anything of value.
The notion that planning could be about the redistribution of scarce resources may have increasing support among the new generation of planners, but in reality there is still a wide gap between the thought and the deed. The essential need at this moment is to move the whole subject into a much broader political arena. If we believe that everyone should have some say in decisions that can affect their future lives, then our present form of government must be modified. Ours has often been described as a democracy founded on apathy, and that apathy makes a mockery of any enthusiastic planner's talk about participation. The examples I have taken may have helped to show that there is not yet either the public will or the political intention to do anything more than allow society to stagger from one problem to the next, while planning is used primarily as an economic optimisation technique lodged firmly in the hands of established authority. The avoidance of conflict in-

herent in this bureaucratically dominated approach produces mediocrity. Conversely, many deprived groups in society can only secure their needs, and perhaps even their basic civil rights, by creating conflict. Far from producing instability in society, therefore, the encouragement of differences and the development of various ways to allow all interests to share the benefits of urban change would be far healthier than trying to decide everything simply on the basis of the greatest good to the greatest number.

In the present situation a variety of approaches may be needed to achieve real gains. David Donnison, Director of the Centre for Environmental Studies, in his paper *Micropolitics of the Inner City*, details the range of potential tactics when he writes: 'advocacy and the aggressive use of legal rights and processes, petitions, demonstrations, strikes, civil disobedience and guerilla tactics have each had their successes'. But, as he says (and this is the reason why I would wish to continue working in local government), 'micropolitical groups succeed by gaining the support of larger populations and higher levels of government . . . . . The success of those who fail to win this support is short-lived at best'. Whatever the route taken, the pressures 'must eventually lead to action through conventional administrative machinery'.

Meanwhile, however, much of urban planning is still preoccupied with fabric rather than people; with the conservation of buildings rather than with the fostering of desirable change. The *ad hoc* and often contradictory nature of public sector activity in the face of serious urban need is so far short of being effective that much of it could usefully be abandoned tomorrow. But this would be as negative a response to our inner-city problems as that of many of the big guns in the anti-planning lobby, who would prefer to scrap those things they do not like whilst holding onto those they do, instead of offering realistic alternatives.

We must admit to ourselves that, as planners, we are not able to plan comprehensively. Nor are we a privileged group set apart from the rest of society; our role should be far more as advisers working with communities than as advocates standing apart from them. We must be prepared to recognise that real planning is still in its infancy. It would be misguided to defend the present techniques just because they are attacked by the public and because, as planners, we feel our honour is at stake. There is a constructive drive towards adapting what exists rather than destroying it, and if this results in a lesser role for traditional planners, so be it. Resistance to this

adaptive process must be seen for what it is: more guided by self-interest than by rational argument. Perhaps the evolving corporate management strategies of social planning will not produce answers in the inner city as fast as the speed of change throws up problems. But social planning must be given a chance to work, as long as it is tied to widespread public accountability (otherwise we will simply be promoting an even more remote elite of urban managers). The present hierarchical nature of government structures must be changed so that the structure becomes more lateral. If planners — and, indeed, all public servants — could be made more directly accountable to the public, instead of hiding behind their politicians' skirts, there would be far fewer Fishers Lane situations. (Equally, politicians should not be able to use their planners as scapegoats. Neither situation would arise if the public more clearly understood the role of each group in the planning process.)

Whatever the answers to the weaknesses of current planning, it is certain, as David Eversley, one-time Chief Strategic Planner of the GLC, has said, that 'solutions will not be invented overnight, and they will probably emerge from a long drawn-out dialogue between the planners and the planned-for and within the planning profession in its widest sense'. Compartmentalised and sectarian thinking has always led to inadequate answers. Solutions cannot be looked for solely from academics who may not like getting their hands dirty; nor from action-oriented professionals who may not want to stand back from their work to see where they are going, nor, again, from administrators who may wonder what all the fuss is about, when to them it is simply a matter of getting things done. At the moment it is apparent that these three groups do not adequately communicate with one another, let alone come together to advise the public on what could be achieved and to implement proposals once that stage has been reached.

The painful transition period from a land use/transportation orientation to one in which socio-economic and policitcal considerations play the dominant part is far from over and a successful conclusion to the changeover is by no means guaranteed. The energy and resources devoted to intervention programmes and community development generally are minute compared to government enthusiasm for an increased growth-rate. This cruel realisation makes it hard for planners who can see many of the urgent problems but are not able to provide the answers to remain within orthodox planning frameworks. Many have ceased trying to make their work relevent to need and have become detached

bureaucrats. Others have chosen to leave the constraining influences of local government to work for deprived communities on a much more personal basis, thus making planning departments even less able to adapt to new requirements. Whilst government institutions continue to keep the public in the dark about what they are thinking right up to the last moment there will continue to be a negative and destructive response to plans. This atmosphere of mistrust and non-comprehension is hardly conducive to the sort of radical change that is desperately needed. But a start has been made; innovations in the production of adaptive planning strategies, experiments in participatory democracy and the development of public awareness about the need for new machinery to deal with its needs are setting valuable precedents. Planners both in local authorities and in community groups are opening up the debate and helping to prove that planning in its widest sense could provide a service to deprived inner city groups at least as much as to central area profit seekers.

THE SAVE PICCADILLY CAMPAIGN

AN ANNOTATED DOSSIER OF CAMPAIGN PUBLICATIONS

ED BERMAN

126

On 1 May, 1972, a new Piccadilly plan was unveiled for public view. The Westminster City Council put forward the scheme which had been developed by the architects of the three property developers who control virtually all the land in the designated action area. By making this announcement, the Westminster Council inadvertently made themselves seem to the public as proposers, if not proponents, of the comprehensive redevelopment. This was a critical error of tactics and the success of the opponents to the scheme can be largely pinned to this error.

As the planning authority, Westminster has the responsibility to appear neutral, else even the exhibition which set forward the plans and the concomitant survey would have been a mockery.

The history of the Council's capitulation to the public outcry against the high-rise office form of comprehensive redevelopment is largely the history of the Council's attempts to appear fair.

On 14 December, exactly seven months to the day after the formation of the Save Piccadilly Campaign, the Westminster Council (referred to by some during the Campaign as 'the WC') announced the effective rejection of the developers' plans, and laid out a stringent new 'low-rise' brief for any new plans.

This is how the process went. In late May, the Campaign issued an attractive two-colour handbill with a picture of Eros and the Piccadilly skyline as the background *(far right)*.

The original meeting for the Campaign had been held at Inter-Action's Almost Free Theatre, a 100-seat off-Broadway type theatre within the Trocadero site. Nearly 100 local interested parties had attended a Sunday meeting. They were willing to put in some finance. In response to the handbill about £40 ($100) per week was guaranteed, just sufficient to run an office (loaned by International Language Centre and Inter-Action) but precious little else.

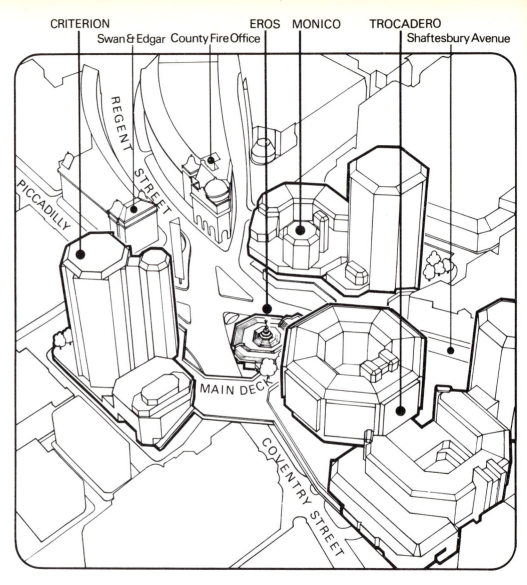

May 1972 Rejected Scheme

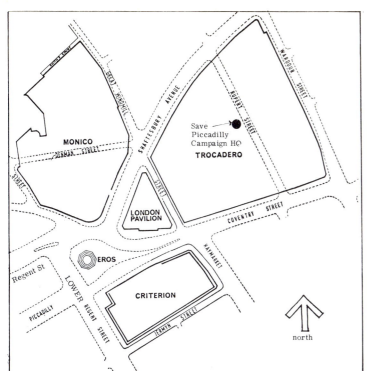

PICCADILLY CIRCUS
UNDERGROUND CONCOURSE
Owned by London Transport

MONICO SITE
Owned by Land Securities Investment
Trust - chairman Lord Samuel.
Frontage on to Shaftesbury Avenue
owned by Greater London Council.

LONDON PAVILION SITE
Owned by the GLC.

TROCADERO SITE
Owned by Stock Conversion &
Investment Trust (J Levy & R Clark).
Some freeholds owned by Electricity
Supply Pension Fund.

CRITERION SITE
Owned by Crown Estates leased
to Trust Houses Forte - chairman
Sir Charles Forte.

Site bounded by Haymarket /Coventry
Street /Shavers Place
Owned by the GLC.

WESTMINSTER CITY COUNCIL
ACTION AREA - bounded by Wardour
Street /Coventry Street /Shavers Place
/Jermyn Street /Lower Regent Street /
Glasshouse Street /Smith's Court /
Great Windmill Street /Shaftesbury
Avenue. Approximately 7 acres.

The Campaign had few experienced activists in it.
We opted to fight a rational battle using research,
quiet lunches, and intensive lobbying rather than
verbal pyrotechnics. The first paper issued set the
tone for the Campaign:

Information Brief 1A   5th July 1972

Can a Stable Political Policy Support Comprehensive Redevelopment?

Opportunism has never been the basis for social
change or development. No group entrusted with the
responsibility of serving the various and often conflicting public interests would ever consciously
fly in the face of all public groups united in outcry.
Ironically the Westminster City Council and Planners
now seem to find themselves in this unenviable,
difficult, and wholly unexpected position.
The extraordinary universal public opposition to the
recently unveiled proposals for comprehensive redevelopment of Piccadilly Circus must be more than
mere emotion-pumped-up journalism. Earlier plans
were proposed and rejected without this added element of well-informed non-partisan opposition.
It is clear that the public is now aware that they must
express themselves in community organisation. As
important, planning disasters both in London and
abroad are well known and serve as constant warn-
ings for those who might repent such errors without
learning the lessons. The easy answer of comprehensive
redevelopment which was logical and necessary in
blitzed areas in the past becomes unnecessary and
illogical when you have to inflict a blitz on your own
community first. But comprehensive redevelopment
has become a reflex action to those who have been
involved in planning since 1945.
When blitzing the live centres of cities, planners
upset balances more subtle and delicate than any
able to be reconstructed. Previously only wars
involuntarily occasioned such widespread destruction.
Is the need so great for comprehensive redevelopment?
Will it serve the interests of the community at large?
Much public criticism comes from the unfortunate
way in which the Westminster City Council have been
forced to deal with the idea of a new Piccadilly without seeming to answer these questions. Behind closed
doors with no public participation or surveying until
after the unveiling, the planners accommodated the
prospective developers' demands but not the needs or
even the demands of the general public or their representatives.

Only new regulations requiring developments to take place for the greater benefit of the environment and the public can ensure that Piccadilly will not become a memorial to the new urban dinosaur. The saving of Piccadilly is not an emotional issue but a critical environmental issue with crucial social, political, and economic ramifications.

The argument is not simply one of democratic process but one of need and utility. The following points seem to lead one to the general conclusion that a plan calling for the comprehensive redevelopment of Piccadilly would be totally unwarranted. Revitalisation of the fabric of existing buildings seems called for, with well integrated in-fill development wherever necessary.

Points for Consideration in Opposing any Comprehensive Redevelopment of Piccadilly

1. The public reaction to the relatively inaccessible Westminster exhibition of the new plan at New Zealand House found only 35% in favour of this comprehensive redevelopment.
A recent Liberal Party poll in London of 3,291 people found 92.9% opposed to the new plans.
2. Much is made of providing new hotels for tourists but in doing this in Piccadilly the developers will be removing a major living tourist attraction. Further, the need is not for luxury hotels for tourists but low-priced hotels which will be impossible on this site.
3. The argument for offices is much the same. There is a need for offices in London to maintain its competitive position in the new Europe. But the worst place to put ½ million square feet of office space is in this centre.
4. Any comprehensive development scheme will destroy this alive centre of London for the better part of a decade. If and when it were completed, it would never revitalise itself. The examples of Euston Towers and Elephant and Castle are there as evidence.
5. A spokesman for the Metropolitan Police has stated that arcades, a major feature in the proposals, are totally dead at night out of fear of bodily and property damage.

6. The Chairman of Westminster City Council and midwife of the proposed scheme has argued his case in emotive terms describing it as a 'slum', attempting to bring lurid pictures into the minds of people unfamiliar with the area. The designated area is by no means a slum nor is it commercially similar to its neighbour, Soho.
Furthermore, any dilapidation of the existing fabric of the buildings has been deliberately caused by the landlords. Any and every tenant is there only with the full approval of these landlords. These landlords, derelict in their maintenance responsibilities, are, of course, none other than the self-styled property 'developers'. If your landlord broke your windows and then told you to move because he had to re-build your house completely, you might find grounds to complain.
7. The latest proposed plan includes a 10% increase in traffic capacity. This fact alone should convince any person in control of the facts to abandon any support for comprehensive redevelopment. One of the original major arguments in support of comprehensive redevelopment in 1962 was the putative need for a 50% increase in traffic capacity. If we now need only 10%, why do we still need comprehensive blitzing?
8. The vertical separation of traffic and pedestrians is opposed by London Transport and by the evidence of its unpopularity wherever else it has been attempted. Such a provision not only kills the life of a shopping area but presents enormous problems to public transport at a time when it needs all the support it can find.
9. Any comprehensive redevelopment scheme will increase peak hour traffic and decrease off-peak users of public transport. This is a disastrous situation for an already beleaguered system.
10. The plan involves the destruction of listed buildings. The fact that the Criterion Theatre will be saved should be carefully analysed. Are architectural reasons the only valid ones for preservation? An environment should be preserved for its scale, sense of life, and usefulness as much as for its historic or beautiful buildings. Saving one building as a token memorial in a cemetery of high-rise tombstones will make it a mausoleum. The totality of Piccadilly must be considered perhaps as a Conservation Area.

11. Even in areas of major public concern, the Planning Acts give developers a pre-emptive hand. The developers could tear down their buildings before a public enquiry. Some regulation is needed in order to prevent the democratic process in this area from becoming a farce.
12. Allowing a comprehensive development will radically change the entire centre of London with untold and unknown effects. The proposed plan only includes less than 4% of the same type users at present! A 96% change is a form of magic act which is beyond the rational projection of people seriously concerned with the environment and the community.
13. Thus there is a re-zoning of the designated area for different uses which counters the great weight of the Greater London Development Plan as well as London Transport and a host of amenity societies.
14. The economic impact so patently the prime consideration in justifying the content of the new plan will have a spin-off effect similar to a nuclear reaction. For example, the West End Theatre will never recover without massive Government subsidy. What theatre owner would resist the astronomically higher return of development of his acreage when compared to the travails of the greatest cultural asset of this nation, the Theatre?
Eight theatres only are being saved from this fate. The Minister of the Environment has moved quickly to prevent this nuclear reaction. But if the argument is true for eight theatres, is it not true for the life of the entire area?
Sometimes one hears that something — anything — must be done now since the matter has dragged on for so long. In such a mood, irreparable mistakes are often made out of frustration. The only logical course which will solve the few existing problems in the designated area without creating a mass of new ones is revitalisation of the existing fabric of buildings plus in-fill development wherever necessary.
The plans as proposed are a public embarrassment. They are an insult to the Council Representatives of the ratepayers of Westminster, who will be blamed for something done in their name without consultation or any appreciation of the new mood and new evidence against comprehensive redevelopment.

With the issuing of the first paper the Campaign attracted widespread support from conservative, liberal and left-wing quarters. Two issues were going to be fought:
1. The question of comprehensive redevelopment itself.
2. The question of public participation in planning.

The Campaign never allowed itself to be seen as the negative antagonist. Rather, we simply claimed for ourselves the role of watchdog and focusing agent for the massive unorganized public opposition to the developers' high-rise profit dreamscheme.
The next paper issued focused on the critical need for reform in planning:

Paper No. 2   5th July 1972

Proposals for Planning Reform and Participation

Introduction

There is widespread dissatisfaction with the activities of property developers, particularly in central London. Each new redevelopment scheme is greeted by a hostile press, action groups have been formed all over London, public opinion where tested is shown to be overwhelmingly against such schemes as the Piccadilly Circus redevelopment, and a debate in Parliament found opposition on both sides of the house.

The problems in central London are probably the most acute. High land prices and the increasing appetite of the developers to replace existing buildings with comprehensive redevelopments will drive out small businesses and the residential accommodation that remains; greater plot ratios will impose strains on communications and other services in the inner city; and there are aesthetic and environmental problems in the scale and design of the new architecture.

In outer areas, competition for land is making it uneconomic to provide low cost housing and the large number of road improvements that are proposed will put even greater pressure on resources. London is facing a period of major redevelopment. The Greater London Development Plan lists 58 Action Areas, 46 Comprehensive Redevelopment Areas and 28 Areas of Opportunity. In addition, there is likely to be substantial piecemeal redevelopment elsewhere and the road building and improvement programme will increase further the need for redevelopment.

In this situation, the current dissatisfaction with the process of property development is understandable and requires a channel of expression.

The developers are operating in a situation of restricted supply, in a period when land prices have been spiralling upwards. They have a near monopolistic control of the situation, operating on such a large scale that they can dictate rent and type of lease, leaving sites undeveloped or premises unoccupied without materially affecting their profitability, running whole areas down with the intention to redevelop before consent is granted.

The developments that are put up take little account of the needs of the people who are displaced in the process, and local authorities have no real control over their activities except through refusing planning permission.

In Piccadilly Circus, which is proposed as an Action Area in the GLDP, the choice lies between accepting the proposals of the developers with only marginal alterations or leaving the area to become even more blighted if planning permission is not granted. There is another alternative, that of revitalisation, but only with the co-operation of (unlikely) or legal coercive power against the property developers.

Planning legislation has not responded to the new situation. The present provisions cannot exert sufficient control. The Government have already realised that problems exist. They have acted to save theatres by listing them and have indicated that they will ensure that empty office buildings are soon let. More is needed if we are to be able to plan London to meet the needs of all its citizens.

Save Piccadilly Campaign proposes that local groups co-operate to press for a wide ranging programme of law reform and public participatory policy review.

Some Practical Suggestions

I   Law Reform

There are areas of planning and landlord and tenant law which could be strengthened to protect tenants and give local authorities more effective control in their planning.

(a) Demolition should be strictly controlled. At the moment only listed buildings are protected. Any other building can be demolished without planning approval. No building should be demolished before planning consent for its replacement has been obtained.

(b) More effective provisions should be introduced for the protection of conservation areas, which might allow local authorities to compulsorily purchase property not kept in a fit state of repair at a valuation based on existing usage and physical condition.

(c) The conservation area principle could be extended to include areas of cultural and national interest.

(d) Planning consent should be non-transferable to avoid speculation and reduce the level of unlet buildings. It should also relate to a specific commencement date and construction time-table and be valid for as short a time as possible, perhaps for a period of one year. Outstanding planning consents could be cancelled if not put into effect within the same period and without compensation.

(e) Granting of planning consent confers substantial added value to the site, and often large sums in compensation have to be paid for cancelling permission. This is a one-sided situation which might be resolved by imposing a development levy based on the additional floor space and type of accommodation that is proposed.

(f) Landlords with unoccupied property that is in a fit state of repair should be subject to harsh penalties, rising with the length of time that the property remains unoccupied.

(g) Punitive penalties ranging from severe stress to government management and compulsory purchase powers could be legislated in reference to any vacant or unrepaired building.

(h) Protection of tenants of long standing, both residential and business, through being given the right to equivalent premises at prices equivalent to those that they were paying prior to being displaced. Statutory provision for different modes of public participation in the planning process.

II   Public Review

In view of the present situation, the Department of the Environment should be asked to review publicly and urgently:

(a) The future of central London in the light of the substantial pressure for redevelopment.

(b) The land-price spiral in city centres; its likely impact on the function and character of the inner city, the environmental and social problems that might arise and what steps might be taken to reverse present trends.

(c) The role of local authorities in their dealings with the private sector in redevelopment schemes.

(d) The importance and proportion of social amenities that should be provided together with recommendations as to how they should be financed.

(e) The level of outstanding planning consents in London.

(f) The available resources in terms of unused land and unoccupied buildings in London in both the public and private sectors.

(g) Policies with regards to office dispersal from central London, together with recommendations on the function and the operation of the Location of Offices Bureau. This might include research on why companies choose to remain in central London.

(h) Policies relating to land ownership. The possibilities of greater owner occupancy through the extension of the leasehold reform act and of increased public ownership of land in city centres might also be examined.

III   Moratorium

The Department of the Environment should be asked to impose a moratorium on demolition and redevelopment schemes in central London pending the reports and conclusions of the public reviews suggested above.

IV   Transport

(a) The GLC (Greater London Council) should be asked to produce alternative plans for central London giving greater priority to pedestrians, with participation of the public and interested groups.

(b) The GLC should be asked to speed up research on new modes of public transport and review policy on existing public transport to include suggestions for alternative methods of financing and making it a public service.

V   Public Participation

In the light of the stated aims to increase public participation in the planning process, the Government, the GLC and local councils should be asked to work out ways in which this might happen and to implement these as soon as possible.

Proposals for Implementing a Programme of Action

In order to develop and implement these and other suggestions, Save Piccadilly Campaign proposes that an independent working party of interested people from community groups and organisations concerned with planning be set up. Such a group might have a brief to include:

Examination of proposals for legislative reform and pressing for their implementation.

Making recommendations to the Department of the Environment and the GLC on areas of policy that should be reviewed publicly.

Examination of proposals for legislative reform and making recommendations to the GLC and local councils.

Setting up an information service for use both by local groups and planning departments of the GLC and local councils.

Carrying on research into aspects of the planning situation where more information is needed.

Having set up an independent working party on the question of participation, the Campaign turned to setting an example with a participatory planning week-end (16-17 September, 1972). The article *(opposite)* from *New Society* summarizes this experiment.

A number of papers were researched and issued on different proposals of the Campaign and various effects of comprehensive redevelopment.

A Programme to Fight the Piccadilly Development
Paper 1: Some Notes Towards a New Position
Paper 1A: Can a Stable Political Policy Support Comprehensive Redevelopment?
Paper 2: Proposals for Planning Reform and Participation
Proposals for the Pedestrianisation of Rupert Street
Proposals for the Revitalisation of the Piccadilly Circus Underground Concourse
'Good-bye Piccadilly' Newsletter No 1
'Goodbye Piccadilly' Newsletter No 2
Survey of Restaurants in Soho
Survey of Food Stores in Soho
Survey of Residents in Redevelopment Area
Survey of Shops That Supply the Theatrical Trade
Architects' Brief (Alternative Brief/Brief for Developers/Map/Letter)
Save Piccadilly Campaign's Participatory Planning Weekend
Results of the Participatory Planning Weekend
Results of the Participatory Planning Sessions

Not all the work was serious. A play for pubs, *Comedy of Eros,* attacked the developers in lighter tones. Surprisingly, this near-scurrilous piece of political theatre appealed to the venerated critic of the *Sunday Times (page 134)*.

Badges, buttons, bags, posters, stickers — all of the standard paraphernalia of campaigns were used as well. The Campaign went to great lengths to attract attention to its viewpoint. An improvised play, *The Bonkers (Property Development Corp),* with high-rise people attacking pedestrians for cutting into their profits caused a stir. The trip to the USA (26 November) to establish a 'Friends of Piccadilly' group in the USA focused more and more publicity and pressure on the planning authorities whilst attracting significant support.

A great deal of the work of the Campaign cannot be abstracted or reproduced in reports. These hundreds of hours of lobbying, of creating a dialogue in an atmosphere of trust, cannot be put on paper. Curiously, a lot of the Campaign's time was spent

Stick
to the
Piccadilly
we love

Save Piccadilly Campaign

New Society 14 December 1972

Piccadilly participation

Paul Harrison

Where *is* Piccadilly? Westminster city council, whose fourth set of plans for the area were published as a "green paper" last week, does not seem to have looked at this key question. Should the public's *perception* of what makes up a meaningful whole for them to be taken into account *before* redevelopment plans are drawn up?

The Save Piccadilly Campaign in September asked people on the streets *where* they thought Piccadilly was, and it has just analysed their results. People were shown 38 photographs taken in the West End, and asked which were in Piccadilly. Only 27 per cent saw Piccadilly as the immediate Circus area; 29 per cent saw it as the wider West End, and 44 per cent saw it as the "bright lights" area extending to Leicester Square. When asked to shade in Piccadilly on a map of the West End, 43 per cent marked the whole area between Coventry Street, Shaftesbury Avenue and Charing Cross Road; 37 per cent shaded the Circus itself.

The survey results are not simply a measure of public ignorance (for example, 8 per cent thought Selfridge's was in Piccadilly, another 13 per cent thought Carnaby Street was). They are a fascinating study in a neglected aspect of planning. The point, says Michael Norton, the campaign organiser, is this: should planners not plan within the frameworks in which the public think and perceive?

And *what* is Piccadilly? The survey found that the people the campaign questioned (and it has no scientific pretensions for its sample) saw it as the centre of London, crowds, people; secondly, tourists, cinemas, young people, neon lights; and so on. Fewer mentioned the unpleasant characteristics: drug addicts, dirty bookshops, criminals, empty buildings. Their main dislikes were too much traffic and that the area was too dirty. What they liked most was people, atmosphere, lights and variety.

But this is only one aspect of the continuing saga of Piccadilly, which shows every sign of becoming a classic test case of what is meant by participation in planning. The Town and Country Planning Act, 1971, says only that the proposed alternatives should be publicised, that interested parties should be given adequate opportunity to make representations, and that the local authority shall consider these. It does not say *who* should be consulted, how, or what weight should be given to their views. Westminster's *Public Consultation Paper*, which sets out four alternatives, including a preferred option, is only the first stage in the Skeffingtonisation of Piccadilly planning. Today there will be a question and answer session. More promising, the Piccadilly subcommittee is actively considering the idea of a consultative conference of interested parties, and has enlisted the advice of the Save Piccadilly Campaign in deciding on the format this will take.

Save Piccadilly (address 9 Rupert Street, wc2) is one of the most experienced agencies working in this field. In September they held a "participation planning weekend" which could serve as a model for other such ventures. As well as the surveys mentioned above, it staged street theatre, film shows

Draw in 6 proposals & help Save Piccadilly

and a "Paint Piccadilly" mural into which people could project their ideal landscapes. Spectators and passers-by were handed maps of the area and asked to cross-hatch the streets they would like to see pedestrianised, put Eros where they would like to see him, mark the height of buildings they would like to see on the Criterion block, and propose uses for empty floors above the Gaming House (see map).

After the film shows, spectators were involved in discussions on the future of the area, and encouraged to make suggestions. Some that emerged could usefully be considered by Westminster council: clean up the buildings; provide play facilities for children; facilities for sitting down; make Leicester Square traffic free; encourage buskers; nationalise the area; run a Grand Prix through Central London to draw attention to the traffic hazards; make illegal the six-month break clauses on leases for many properties in the area. Some have already been taken up: ban heavy lorries from central London; have a consultative conference.

The Save Piccadilly survey showed the main lines of at any rate some people's desires for the area. Some 80 per cent wanted no comprehensive redevelopment at all; 87 per cent said there should be no offices, 60 per cent no hotels (these two factors were predominant in the previous plan); 80 per cent wanted more room for pedestrians, only 1 per cent more room for cars. And 72 per cent even of motorists said it should be made more difficult for the motorist to get in to central London.

Westminster council has itself produced an exercise in analysis of public desires, as expressed in comments following its exhibition of plans in May of this year. Only 30 per cent of comments were favourable, against 65 per cent which were opposed to all or part of the scheme. Of those objecting, 30 per cent were against the proposed 50 per cent increase in traffic capacity, 16 per cent against the quantity of offices, 12 per cent to the bulk and scale of the proposed buildings, 17 per cent to the loss of the Criterion block.

The Save Piccadilly Participatory Planning Weekend 1972. 'We want to make Piccadilly Circus a place fit to bring your children' (Alderman Herbert Sandford).

in convincing the other side (the WC) that they were not on the other side — that the real enemy was unbridled greed and not the social needs that were being used as the prime justification for the cleaning up of Piccadilly. It was clear that the developers were greedy and it was unlikely that the Councillors would deny social need as an essential element in their brief.

Some seven months after the Campaign started, a formal 'Green Paper' policy statement was issued by Westminster Council.

The paper was circulated with a questionnaire to

2000 people who commented on the May 1972 exhibition held at New Zealand House (¼ mile from Piccadilly Circus)
400 people who wrote to Westiminster Council after the May 1972 proposals were announced
500 copies to premises within the redevelopment area and 100 feet from it
1000 people randomly selected from Westminster Council's ratepayers
200 copies to Westminster Chamber of Commerce
500 copies to press, TV and radio

In addition to this, the WC announced on 14 December, 1972:

We have designed a special questionnaire to be completed by the public which will give us the most comprehensive breakdown of public reaction to the 4 options. This questionnaire has been especially designed for computer processing. We shall not ignore written comments sent into us by members of the public and **all public comment will be taken into account.**

But the content of the questionnaire was carefully designed to secure votes for the preferred option, as were all the consultation procedures. Well-known market researchers were asked their views of the questionnaire and they agreed that it was highly biased. The special sub-committee of WC councillors (set up in summer 1972) drew up a list of six broad principles. These principles were that:

(a) Some improvement in traffic capacity — perhaps in the region of 10% — should be provided.
(b) There should be no pedestrian deck.
(c) It would be essential to provide attractive pedestrian facilities at ground and subway level including an extended underground shopping concourse.
(d) The height and bulk of new buildings should be restricted to match existing structures.
(e) Office floor space should be increased by 10%. Any residential accommodation demolished should be replaced.
(f) The front part of the Criterion building (218-223 Piccadilly) and the whole of the Lillywhite building should be retained. Rupert Court should also be retained and 26, 28 Rupert Street, and 27, 29 and 31 Wardour Street should be preserved.

Sadly the principles were not based on any thorough-going analysis although the Campaign had made repeated requests for such work to be done.
The options presented by Westminster were as follows:

Option 1:
Maximum rehabilitation and improvement of the area, with development allowed on the Monico site between Denman Street and Shaftesbury Avenue and in Jermyn Street behind the Criterion Theatre.

Option 2:
Re-routing southbound traffic down Shaftesbury Avenue behind the London Pavilion down a rebuilt Lower Great Windmill Street. Redevelopment as for Option 1, but also the whole of the south side of Shaftesbury Avenue between Wardour Street and Great Windmill Street, Great Windmill Street and the north end of Rupert Street and Wardour Street

in the redevelopment area. 35 Haymarket and the shops below would be redeveloped.

Option 3:
(Westminster made a point of stressing that this was the option they preferred.) Comprehensive redevelopment within the six principles. Rupert Street and the south of Wardour Street should be preserved. Eros would be placed in a piazza and the London Pavilion would be rebuilt next to Eros. There would also be an extended underground concourse.

Option 4:
As for Option 3 but without replacing the London Pavilion.

Only Options 3 and 4 contained a 10% increase in traffic capacity although many of the elements of each option were interchangeable.
The Campaign's views as expressed in its publications can be summarized as:

(a) The planned traffic increase of 10% is both unnecessary and unwanted.
(b) The plan deals only with shapes of buildings and traffic flows, and not with the real needs of people who live, work or use the area. There are a great number of facilities which could be provided and which are needed. Any plan should incorporate these.
(c) All but Option 1 involve a large measure of redevelopment and Options 3 and 4 are plans for comprehensive redevelopment which will kill the life, character and atmosphere of the area.
(d) Options 2, 3 and 4 will involve the eventual demolition of the whole of the south side of Shaftesbury Avenue. This is not stated anywhere in the Green Paper and is anyway unnecessary.
(e) The needs of pedestrians are considered only after the needs of cars. It will become more difficult to cross the road at road level and the underground subway provisions have already earned the scheme the nickname 'Mole Circus'.
(f) There is no mention of public transport in the Green Paper despite the crucial importance of this to London's traffic.

These criticisms were largely regarded which appeared as a major victory for the Campaign and all the media and members of the public who pressured the Council. But is it really?
90% of Piccadilly can still be blitzed under the WC's preferred scheme. Even architects know that new buildings will not replace traditional familiarity. Any large-scale rebuilding will sterilize the area.

Architects will be given budgets for maximizing profit, not for creating warmth or free public congregating areas. The new rents on new buildings will be up to 500% of the old without adequate compensation to the present users. No-one but the largest commercial organizations will be able to afford the new rents. In such a situation no campaign of any kind will ever rise again. The managers of the few multiples now in the area were the only ones not to join the Save Piccadilly Campaign. They had no no personal or vested interest. They were the blank faces representing the faceless distant holding companies.
The only answer for Piccadilly and other inner city areas like it is renewal based on a consideration of the social and economic needs of the city as a whole. Clearly, one of the levels of government (local Council, metropolitan Council, or national government) must take over the job of the rebuilding or development of such strategic areas. Perhaps the inner city has to be treated like the building of a new town or city with a rigidly controlled, government appointed Development Corporation in the driver's seat. Even this will require new concepts and possibilities of public participation.
Ultimately the inner city must be revitalized in response to social need — not economic need.

Postscript
On 15 March 1973, Westminster Council held a press conference announcing the end of the voting part of consultation. They also announced that Option 3 had won, thus maximizing the amount of redevelopment possible for the developers.
We issued the following statement:

Concerning the Future of Piccadilly Circus Putting the Con into Consultation
    'Westminster Council's attitude towards public consultation over Piccadilly Circus has made a mockery of the concept of a public voice in planning matters. They have acted without integrity.
    The Council have deliberately misled the public in the following ways:
1. By arbitrarily and without previous notice stopping the voting on the Green Paper. In doing this they have made public consultation a public 'con' [confidence trick].
2. By stopping the voting at a time when ballots were flowing in at an increasing rate for Option 1, the option the Council opposed. This is equivalent to one political party stopping the

counting of ballots after their safe wards had been counted.

The integrity of the Council must seriously be called into question. How could a public authority establish a public consultation without naming a closing date?

Furthermore, on 12 March, Alderman Sandford, Chairman of the Piccadilly Sub-Committee, instructed the Chief Information Officer of Westminster Council to make the following statement:

'Therefore you will see that it is not our wish to veto public discussion by applying a deadline to processes which cannot be easily regulated by a time schedule.'

Two days later, these words have been totally contradicted.

There must be a public enquiry over the manner in which Westminster Council has conducted this so-called public consultation.

Westminster Council have used the votes of under 700 people to give Piccadilly away to the developers. It is a derisory number of people to have contacted in three months.'

Journalists writing about the situation almost unanimously agreed on the inadequacy of the consultation process. Des Wilson, in his *Observer* column (25 March, 1973), commented:

'Opponents of Westminster City Council's plans for Piccadilly Circus have been shaken by the abrupt ending of public consultation on the scheme. They claim the council's questionnaire had no closing date (true), that analysis of the response was cut off without warning after only 1,200 replies (true), and that the closure came when public reaction was swinging away from the council's plan (possible).

'Frankly, the council deserve the criticism — not because the consultation activities were handled, or suddenly halted, with any skulduggery, but they were indisputably clumsy and underline the need, at a time when many major redevelopment schemes are arising in our cities, for councils to get expert help and advice on how to consult the public effectively.'

The Council were supposed to publish the final brief (based on Option 3) by the beginning of April 1973. By August 1st 1973, the brief had still not been prepared. Several important events happened in this four-month period between April and August. The most important of all was the election of a Labour-

controlled Greater London Council on April 13. The Labour Party had campaigned on promises of dropping the Ringway developments and curtailing 'property spivs'. With this new Greater London Council, all unreasonable redevelopment schemes had a fair chance to be knocked out of commission. The Campaign's diary from this point on reads like that of a moral dentist trying to extract results from promises.

16 April: Letter to Westminster Council requesting up-to-date figures on the Green Paper balloting, and reminding the Piccadilly sub-committee chairman that he had made an assurance at the 15 March press conference that all votes received in the future would be taken into consideration.

18 April: Save Piccadilly Campaign submits to Westminster City Council 2400 applications for Piccadilly Circus to be made a Conservation Area under the Town and Country Planning Act 1971.

28 April: Letter to Sir Reginald Goodwin, the new leader of the GLC, pointing out the significance of the London Pavilion to the redevelopment plans and pressing the GLC to retain this building; requesting that Piccadilly Circus be redesignated as a Conservation Area; and pressing the GLC to drop the requirement for widening Shaftesbury Avenue.

31 May: Sir Reginald replies to the above assuring the Campaign that he appreciates the importance of the London Pavilion site to the future of the Circus, and also that he will review the question of traffic capacity at Piccadilly Circus and in particular the questionable need for widening Shaftesbury Avenue in the light of the GLC's general objective of putting pedestrians and residents before traffic.

21 June: Second letter to Westminster Council asking for a reply on the Green Paper voting.

22 June: A press release issued attacking Westminster Council for not keeping its promise to announce the new brief.

22 June: Reception at Hayward Gallery for the 'How to Play the Environment Game' Exhibition, attended by Greater London Councillors, Westminster and Camden Councillors and Geoffrey Rippon, Minister of State for the Environment. Rippon promises in an Inter-Action video interview that Piccadilly will not be comprehensively redeveloped.

2 July: Westminster Council finally replies to our letter of 21 June. They do not agree that they undertook that votes received after the

March press conference would be taken into consideration; the draft brief is to be considered by the Piccadilly sub-committee later in July (three months later than promised) following which the public will have a further opportunity to comment upon it.

9 July: The Westminster Council Town Clerk replies to 18 April Conservation Area applications: in the light of the redevelopment and rehabilitation plans for the area, and also because the listed buildings in the area are adequately protected, the City Council does not consider that it would be appropriate at this stage to designate the Circus as a Conservation Area.

Next, the following letter was sent to the Minister of the Environment, reminding him of his promises and requesting these be requited by declaring Piccadilly a conservation area.

28 July 1973

Dear Mr Rippon,

Thank you very much for attending our reception for 'How to Play the Environment Game' at the Hayward Gallery last Monday. You were kind enough to do an 'on the record' video-tape with me which has encouraged a number of people involved in our campaign. During the course of our discussion you spoke of your intention to conserve a significant part of the environment, not only in Covent Garden, but in Piccadilly and elsewhere and I hope that you can aid us in our attempt to have the Piccadilly Designated Area declared a conservation area.

We applied to Westminster Council on 18 April 1973 for Piccadilly Circus to be declared a Conservation Area under the Civic Amenities Act 1967. The Council have subsequently refused on what we consider to be inadequate grounds.

We recognise that to have collected 2400 signatures in one afternoon does not constitute a statutory fulfilment of the criteria for a Conservation Area, but we do believe that it reflects the emotive feeling towards buildings in Piccadilly Circus that are known and loved.

We understand that in the Covent Garden situation there are regular meetings of an Advisory Committee consisting of members of the public and that this committee has recommended that the whole of the Covent Garden be designated a Conservation Area. We further understand that officers from your

Ministry are giving this proposal favourable consideration.

If this situation in Covent Garden is seen together with the recent designation of 250 buildings of architectural and historic importance it seems obvious to us that you are now taking a far broader approach to the concept of conservation.

Many of the buildings which are at present unlisted in Piccadilly Circus are in our opinion of greater merit than many of those on your recent Covent Garden list.

We would urge you to give serious consideration to an additional list for the Piccadilly Circus area and to ask Westminster Council, as a matter of some urgency, to reconsider their refusal to designate the Conservation Area.

Thank you for your consideration.

Yours sincerely,

Campaign Chairman

When the new brief is finally published by the Council, the developers will have to decide whether or not to redevelop within the criteria laid out. If the developers decide that it is more profitable to redevelop than to renovate, they will presumably submit new plans within a few months. We would then expect a Public Enquiry to be called by the Minister of the Environment. A critical aspect for justifying this enquiry and sinking the new plans will have to be the Council's arbitrary and misguided abuse of the consultation process. On the other hand, the low-rise overall brief, which even Option 3 falls subject to, may make renovation with in-fill development the most viable financial course for the developers. In this case Save Piccadilly will have achieved its objectives — to preserve the character and uses of the area whilst cleaning it up and allowing for natural regeneration. The issue of the role of the 'public' in shaping and determining the plans for its own future remains ambiguous.

*Above: High-rise people attacking pedestrians for cutting into their profits, from the improvised play **The Bonkers** (Property Development Corp.).*

GOODBYE PICCADILLY

ORDER IN OUR THINKING: THE NEED FOR A TOTAL APPROACH TO THE ANTHROPOCOSMOS

C A DOXIADIS

Our confusion

One of the main reasons why man in the City is suffering today is because, unable to understand what is happening around him, he reacts to the most pressing symptoms but does not deal with main causes. In other words, because we do not understand the situation, we have not been able to formulate goals that can respond to it.

The confusion in our understanding can be illustrated by looking at how ideas of the city have changed over the last two generations. Forty years ago, when I was a student, discussions of the city referred only to monumental buildings and slums, to expansive avenues and narrow, romantic alleys. Later, when I was a young professional, cities were described in terms of their traffic problems and the solutions were technologically impressive highways. In the 'fifties, it was the social aspects of city problems that were considered paramount. In recent years the emphasis has shifted to problems related to the natural environment. Thus in forty years, the public image of the city of the high-income countries has shifted from buildings, to transportation, to society, and now to nature. This means we have continued to be sidetracked into concentrating upon certain symptoms of the problem of urban disease. But these fashionable, isolated approaches to some extent blind us to the substance of the problem as a whole.

We tend to forget that the City of Man represents the summit of Man's pyramid of action, the area of the minimum influence of Nature and the maximum activity of Society, expressed through Man's Shells (constructions) and Networks (mobility).

The city cannot be understood by a single element but only by all five elements considered together.

I recently attended an international meeting of influential people who are very much concerned about the 'environment,' and the need to preserve it.

Most of the speakers concentrated on pollution by chemical. Their statements were careful and diplomatic. During coffee breaks, people spoke to me about their personal views, which ranged from indifference because the discussion was not dealing with social or cultural problems, to anger because no mention was being made of the need to save historical monuments. Each person had his own point of view, each view was perfectly valid, but the total image was missing, and the result was again confusion and chaos. We have not formulated our goals, and therefore we can neither evaluate the present situation nor define the road that we should follow.

The reason for this confusion is that Man is now in the midst of an explosion which has upset the balances that have been created in various parts of the earth as a result of long centuries of effort by different cultures.

Our real subject: the anthropocosmos

We will solve none of today's problems if we concentrate on isolated relations, such as between Man and Nature, Man and Buildings, Man and Networks or Man and Society. All our mistakes can be attributed to just such isolations of relationships. To take a single example: the motorways that were supposed to solve the traffic problems of cities created many new problems for Society, for Nature and for Man's cultural values.

We live in Nature. Our real frame is not just the earth, for if the sun were to lose its energy or the planets of the solar system disappear, our life would be totally disoriented. But we are no longer at the primitive stage of utter dependence on the forces of Nature. We have learned how to come to terms with it. History shows that Man has always fought Nature in order to survive: killing animals, or burning forests to start cultivation. His goal was to create his own system of life by achieving a balance between the existing system and its laws and his own interests. Thus, even at the start we must consider not just Man and Nature, but Man and his human settlement, which combines Nature and Society and which, in its first stages, could be called a 'biosphere'; later to be replaced by a system totally constructed by Man (expressed in his Shells and Networks) which may be called a 'technosphere'.

Our task is to define the system of our life expressed by human settlements so clearly that it can contain every part, aspect, expression or opinion, known or unknown, foreseen or unforeseen. Once defined, our task is then to learn to control this sytem wisely for the sake of all mankind.

Success will depend on our ability to create new balances corresponding to new developments. This means discovering what we dislike and can change, what we love and can keep, and what we love but must change. The first is easy from the conceptual point of view, but the last is very difficult. However, we shall be forced to change situations that we love. We need houses for those who have none, and these may cover fields that are beautiful in the spring. The question is which fields to choose, how many and where, and how to create parks and gardens that will result in a better balance between Man and Nature than before.

The whole system of our life must be both our subject and our goal. Our subject, because if we leave out any part of it the system becomes disrupted. Our goal, because if we cannot constantly maintain a balance within it we shall be destroyed. This system of life is Anthropocosmos — the World of Man. It contains everything that we can imagine and it has only one aim: to satisfy Man. Man's aim cannot be to satisfy Nature — either for the sake of the mosquito or the dinosaur: other forces eliminated the latter, with only the dinosaurs protesting.

Our only road: order instead of chaos

To achieve a balanced Anthropocosmos (World of Man) we must approach all problems in a systematic way, avoiding partial views of particular elements or special goals. Our only road is constantly to create order out of the chaos around us. This is no easy task. We have been trying for years at the Athens Centre of Ekistics to handle a number of research projects[1] in a strictly systematic way *(above right)*. We follow a precise method of classification of the subject matter of the articles in the EKISTICS journal (see over for this method; the *fig. opposite;* shows how this article would be classified). We use the same general system in our annual seminars[2], and in university lectures, teaching courses and conferences concerned with or interested in ekistics.

Our experience tends to show that we are on the right track, but there is still a long way to go. The subject is so vast, it contains so many elements and so many different viewpoints that people become overwhelmed by the amount of information. We can take heart from the fact that Man has managed to extricate himself from periods of confusion in the past. However,

137

<table>
<tr><td colspan="2">COMMUNITY SCALE</td><td>i</td><td>ii</td><td>iii</td><td>I</td><td>II</td><td>III</td><td>IV</td><td>V</td><td>VI</td><td>VII</td><td>VIII</td><td>IX</td><td>X</td><td>XI</td><td>XII</td></tr>
<tr><td colspan="2"></td><td>1</td><td>2</td><td>3</td><td>4</td><td>5</td><td>6</td><td>7</td><td>8</td><td>9</td><td>10</td><td>11</td><td>12</td><td>13</td><td>14</td><td>15</td></tr>
<tr><td colspan="2">EKISTIC UNITS</td><td>MAN</td><td>ROOM</td><td>DWELLING</td><td>DWELLING GROUP</td><td>SMALL NEIGHBORHOOD</td><td>NEIGHBORHOOD</td><td>SMALL TOWN</td><td>TOWN</td><td>LARGE CITY</td><td>METROPOLIS</td><td>CONURBATION</td><td>MEGALOPOLIS</td><td>URBAN REGION</td><td>URBANIZED CONTINENT</td><td>ECUMENOPOLIS</td></tr>
<tr><td rowspan="5">ELEMENTS</td><td>NATURE</td><td></td><td></td><td></td><td></td><td></td><td></td><td></td><td></td><td></td><td>•</td><td>•</td><td>●</td><td>●</td><td>•</td><td>●</td></tr>
<tr><td>MAN</td><td></td><td></td><td></td><td></td><td></td><td>•</td><td>●</td><td></td><td></td><td></td><td></td><td></td><td></td><td></td><td></td></tr>
<tr><td>SOCIETY</td><td></td><td></td><td></td><td></td><td></td><td>•</td><td>●</td><td></td><td></td><td></td><td></td><td>●</td><td>●</td><td>•</td><td>●</td></tr>
<tr><td>SHELLS</td><td></td><td></td><td></td><td></td><td></td><td>•</td><td>•</td><td></td><td></td><td>•</td><td>•</td><td>●</td><td>●</td><td></td><td></td></tr>
<tr><td>NETWORKS</td><td></td><td></td><td></td><td></td><td></td><td>•</td><td>●</td><td></td><td></td><td>•</td><td>•</td><td>●</td><td>●</td><td></td><td></td></tr>
<tr><td colspan="2">SYNTHESIS: HUMAN SETTLEMENTS</td><td></td><td></td><td></td><td></td><td></td><td></td><td>•</td><td></td><td></td><td></td><td></td><td>•</td><td></td><td></td><td></td></tr>
</table>

<table>
<tr><td colspan="2">COMMUNITY SCALE</td><td>i</td><td>ii</td><td>iii</td><td>I</td><td>II</td><td>III</td><td>IV</td><td>V</td><td>VI</td><td>VII</td><td>VIII</td><td>IX</td><td>X</td><td>XI</td><td>XII</td></tr>
<tr><td colspan="2"></td><td>1</td><td>2</td><td>3</td><td>4</td><td>5</td><td>6</td><td>7</td><td>8</td><td>9</td><td>10</td><td>11</td><td>12</td><td>13</td><td>14</td><td>15</td></tr>
<tr><td colspan="2">EKISTIC UNITS</td><td>MAN</td><td>ROOM</td><td>DWELLING</td><td>DWELLING GROUP</td><td>SMALL NEIGHBORHOOD</td><td>NEIGHBORHOOD</td><td>SMALL TOWN</td><td>TOWN</td><td>LARGE CITY</td><td>METROPOLIS</td><td>CONURBATION</td><td>MEGALOPOLIS</td><td>URBAN REGION</td><td>URBANIZED CONTINENT</td><td>ECUMENOPOLIS</td></tr>
<tr><td rowspan="5">ELEMENTS</td><td>NATURE</td><td>●</td><td></td><td>●</td><td colspan="11">———————————————→</td><td>●</td></tr>
<tr><td>MAN</td><td>●</td><td></td><td>●</td><td colspan="11">———————————————→</td><td>●</td></tr>
<tr><td>SOCIETY</td><td></td><td></td><td></td><td></td><td></td><td></td><td></td><td></td><td></td><td></td><td></td><td></td><td></td><td></td><td></td></tr>
<tr><td>SHELLS</td><td></td><td></td><td></td><td></td><td></td><td></td><td></td><td></td><td></td><td></td><td></td><td></td><td></td><td></td><td></td></tr>
<tr><td>NETWORKS</td><td>●</td><td></td><td>●</td><td colspan="11">———————————————→</td><td>●</td></tr>
<tr><td colspan="2">SYNTHESIS: HUMAN SETTLEMENTS</td><td></td><td></td><td></td><td></td><td></td><td></td><td></td><td></td><td></td><td></td><td></td><td></td><td></td><td></td><td></td></tr>
</table>

Top: Scope of the research projects conducted at the Athens Center of Ekistics.

Bottom: Classification of the subject matter of this article.

until recently the dimensions of city problems were at the human scale in terms of walking distances, seeing, etc. After thousands of years of experience of these dimensions, it was not too difficult for Man to understand the totality of his system of life. He could discover the causes of his problems and invent reasonable solutions. Huge increases in the dimensions of space and energy and decreasing time make it extremely difficult for Man to discern his system of life — his position in his cosmos. We have to turn from sentimental to objective approaches: instead of seeking to follow psychological or political lines of thought, we must try to hold to scientific methods to seek out the truth. This requires that we create an orderly system to confront our present chaos. The only way to do this, that I can see, is:

1. Define our total system of life — the anthropocosmos — in such a way that any part of it can be clearly located.
2. Define all relationships (casual and non-casual) that may exist between any parts of the system so that we can understand its operation and its changes.
3. Define a method for the evaluation and measurement of all parts of the system and its interrelationships (including those that cannot be scientifically measured), so that we can recognize the relative importance of each problem.

The anthropocosmos model

The system of our life consists of five elements in the following order of creation: Nature, Man the individual (the forgotten element); Society (more important in some political systems than the individual); Shells; Networks.

Nature consists of air, land, water, flora and fauna. Each part has many different aspects. Climate, an aspect of the air, is related to temperature and humidity, rains and winds, etc. In total, Nature can probably be well represented by 32 components.

Man varies from individual to individual, but he can be examined systematically in terms of 12 phases of his life.[3] Man also consists of his body, his five senses, his mind and his soul, meaning he can be seen in 8 different ways. Thus Man, throughout his life, can be represented by 96 components. What a baby sees, what an adolescent hears and what an old man needs in order to move around in space are very different.

Society can be regarded in two basic ways: in terms of size and in terms of development. A Society is very different if we are dealing with a small neighbourhood of a few hundred people or a metropolis of

THE EKISTIC GRID

COMMUNITY SCALE	i	ii	iii	I	II	III	IV	V	VI	VII	VIII	IX	X	XI	XII
	1	2	3	4	5	6	7	8	9	10	11	12	13	14	15
EKISTIC UNITS	MAN	ROOM	DWELLING	DWELLING GROUP	SMALL NEIGHBOURHOOD	NEIGHBOURHOOD	SMALL TOWN	TOWN	LARGE CITY	METROPOLIS	CONURBATION	MEGALOPOLIS	URBAN REGION	URBANIZED CONTINENT	ECUMENOPOLIS
ELEMENTS — NATURE															
ELEMENTS — MAN															
ELEMENTS — SOCIETY															
ELEMENTS — SHELLS															
ELEMENTS — NETWORKS															
SYNTHESIS: HUMAN SETTLEMENTS															
POPULATION	1	2	4	40	250	1.5$_T$	9$_T$	50$_T$	300$_T$	2$_M$	14$_M$	100$_M$	700$_M$	5.000$_M$	30.000$_M$

$_T$ (Thousands)
$_M$ (Millions)

Ekistic Logarithmic Scale

The contents of each article appearing in EKISTICS is classified within a small ekistic grid, appearing on each title page. Coverage of the total issue is classified in the grid appearing with the foreword. The method of this classification is as follows:

1. The scale of the settlement(s) with which the article deals is selected from among the fifteen ekistic units listed along the abscissa of the grid. These range from Man to Ecumenopolis, in order of population size, following a logarithmic scale.
2. The subjects dealt with in the article are then selected from among the sub-heads to the five ekistic elements

that form the ordinate. If the article arrives at a synthesis of these elements — either theoretical or in the form of a physical plan — this is also noted.

Each ekistic element has been divided into four sub-heads that are listed below.

The position of a dot in any square of the grid indicates which of the four sub-heads is being referred to: a dot in the top left-hand corner indicates the first sub-head; a dot in the lower left-hand corner, the fourth sub-head.

Note: The nomenclature of the sub-heads of the five ekistic elements is subject to revision.

Ekistic Elements (Revised December, 1972)

NATURE
1. Environmental analysis
2. Resource utilization
3. Land use, landscape
4. Recreation areas

MAN
1. Physiological needs
2. Safety, security
3. Affection, belonging, esteem
4. Self-realization, knowledge, aesthetics

SOCIETY
1. Public administration, participation and law
2. Social relations, population trends, cultural patterns
3. Urban systems and urban change
4. Economics

Key to Individual Grids

SHELL
1. Housing
2. Service facilities: hospitals, fire stations, etc.
3. Shops, offices, factories
4. Cultural and educational units

NETWORKS
1. Public utility systems: water, power, sewerage
2. Transportation systems: road, rail, air
3. Personal and mass communication systems
4. Computer and information technology

SYNTHESIS: HUMAN SETTLEMENTS
1. Physical planning
2. Ekistic theory

several millions. To evaluate this aspect of Society we can use the classification of the 15 ekistic units that range from a single individual to the total population of ecumenopolis.[4] As for Man, we have also to differentiate between primitive and more advanced societies. For this, we can use 6 developmental phases, thus arriving at 90 components (15 social units in 6 phases).

Shells represent all types of building construction, and can be classified in various groups: indispensible buildings, such as houses; symbolic structures, such as temples; technological structures, such as power stations. Experience shows that these can usefully be classified in about 20 categories.

Networks include all land, sea and air routes as well as utility systems (water supplies, sewerage systems, gas and electricity conduits) and all telecommunications networks. The totality of these can be classified in about 20 categories.

In sum we now have 258 important components derived from the five basic elements that form our anthropocosmos. However, these 258 elements can only be understood in terms of the relations between them: such as how the invasion of babies in a road changes its character; how the advent of a factory can change a local microclimate (by raising the air temperature or emitting fumes, etc.). This means it is necessary to multiply the 258 components by 258, resulting in about 66,600 relationships, some of which may be causal, like the ones mentioned above, and some non-causal. For instance, it may be difficult to judge the effect of a certain type of planting upon a specific building, other than its aesthetic appeal. However, in the light of my own experience, I will enumerate certain ways in which we can review these components and their relationships that can, I believe, help to lead us out of the present chaos.

First we must differentiate between the units of space. The impact of a factory upon a small town is very different from its impact upon a continent. Any phenomenon can only be understood if we examine it in its appropriate unit of space, from the smallest unit of Man himself (with his body, his clothing, his furniture) to the next unit, the room, then the house and the neighbourhood, up to the city and, finally, the whole earth.

Next comes the time scale, divided into 10 units, from one second to a thousand years. Any evaluation of the components and their relationships must be regarded in terms of time. Some noises may bother us only for a second; some ocean pollution may

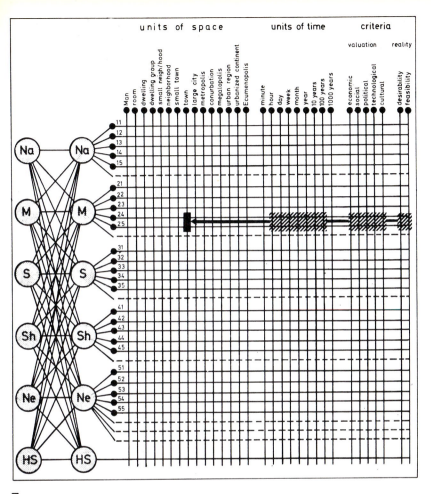
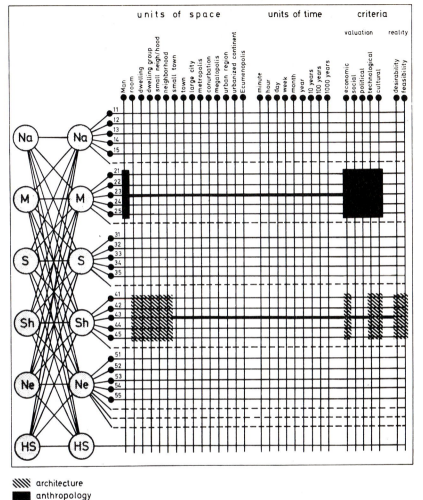

■ part of the total model given in detail in figure 2

▨ architecture
■ anthropology

Above: The anthropocosmos model.

Right: The anthropocosmos model and the sciences covering parts of it.

affect the situation for eternity. One's actions tomorrow may have little effect upon a metropolis, but they can seriously affect one's own home. This means we have also to deal with 150 units of space-time.

The third criterion is an evaluation of their quality. To arrive at any understanding of the meaning of the components of the five elements and their relationships with Man and his values, we have to examine them in the light of Man's basic concerns: economic, social, political (or administrative), technological (or functional), and cultural (or aesthetic).

Fourth comes what I call the reality: the criterion of desirability and feasibility. We may dream of an ideal city in a wonderful garden, but we have to recognize that it is not feasible today, and may never be so.

town or ekistic unit 8

time scale		one day					one week					one month					one year					ten years					one hundred years				
		E	S	P	T	C	E	S	P	T	C	E	S	P	T	C	E	S	P	T	C	E	S	P	T	C	E	S	P	T	C
		DF	DF	DF	DF	DF	DF	DF	DF	DF	DF	DF	DF	DF	DF	DF	DF	DF	DF	DF	DF	DF	DF	DF	DF	DF	DF	DF	DF	DF	DF
fourth phase: toddler	body																														
	eyes																														
	ears																														
	nose																														
	skin																														
	taste																														
	mind																														
	soul																														
fifth phase: preschool age	body																														
	eyes																														
	ears																														
	nose																														
	skin																														
	taste																														
	mind																														
	soul																														

E economic
S social
P political
T technological
C cultural

D desirability
F feasibility

Part of the anthropocosmos model.

The result is that we have 10 criteria of evaluation (5, each seen in 2 ways) and 1500 units of time-space. By means of them we can evaluate what is happening, or what may happen, to any element or relationship. We can perceive its structure and follow its development, and recognize whether or not it is healthy. If it is not, we can see how it can be enabled to move from observation and diagnosis to therapy.

In this way we can begin to establish an order out of the present chaotic and confused situation. We have 258 basic components of the system of our life — our anthropocosmos — and these have 66,600 relationships between them, which can be understood and evaluated by means of a system of 1500 units. Our total conceptual model, which can illuminate all aspects of the anthropocosmos as a developing system, has 100 million parts. This is a frightening figure, but it helps if we look at a simplified graphic model *(page 139, left)* on which we can record, in an organized way, everything that exists or is happening in the system as a whole, or in any particular part of it. On this model we can pinpoint our subject, be it town or metropolis, natural environment or society, children or industry *(left)*. At another scale, we can then see what role each of the disciplines play in this context *(page 139, right)*. If we make the effort to place our specific problems in this model, we can see where we stand, where we can go, and where and how we can join forces with others to cover the complex system of the anthropocosmos.

I have personally used this model in many ways, and have gradually reached the point of publishing it[5] and presenting it to clients and scientific groups. It has always proved helpful. I have never received any meaningful negative comments and I have found that it can be used both for very simple empirical problems and for heuristic and — in part — for deterministic ones. I am therefore convinced that its wider use can help to bring order into our thinking about the complex problems of today.

References:

1 see EKISTICS 199, June 1972 for a summary
2 see EKISTICS 197, April 1972 for a summary
3 C A Doxiadis, *City for Human Development,* ACE Monographs: Research Report No. 12, 1972.
4 C A Doxiadis, *Ekistics: An Introduction to the Science of Human Settlements,* London, 1968.
5 see EKISTICS 193, December 1971.

A COLLECTION OF PATTERNS WHICH GENERATE MULTI-SERVICE CENTRES*

CHRISTOPHER ALEXANDER
SARA ISHIKAWA
MURRAY SILVERSTEIN

A multi-service centre is a community facility, which provides a variety of special services to citizens. It is intended especially to help solve some of the problems of low-income communities. Experimental multi-service centres have been started in many cities throughout the United States. However, there is not yet any general agreement about the form which multi-service centres should take — either in their human organization, or in their spatial organization.

Our report deals chiefly with the spatial organization; but since human and spatial organization cannot properly be separated, many of the specifications given in this report, go deeply into questions of human organization as well.

We have not designed a prototype in quite the conventional sense, and must begin with a word of explanation about the nature and purpose of prototype buildings.

A prototype design is a generic scheme. It has no special site, no real client, no climate, no particular size. It is a kind of imaginary building, which is meant to convey certain essential ideas to designers of similar buildings. It is usually presented by means of loosely drawn schematic drawings, so that designers who are designing a building of this type, can mould it to fit whatever specific local conditions they are confronted with. It is meant to convey some essential, generic ideas, which can be applied many times over to special cases. It defines a family of buildings; and it is meant to define this family of buildings in such a way that anyone who understands the prototype will be able to design specific members of this family.

The ultimate purpose of a prototype design, then, is to provide guidelines which will generate a large number of specific buildings.

Under close scrutiny, this idea does not stand up very well. The range of variation, which will be required by the different members of any family of buildings, lies well outside the range which can be accurately conveyed by any single drawing — no matter how 'prototypical' it is. This is true for the family of buildings called 'multi-service centres'. Some will be large, some small. Some will have many services, others will have fewer services. Some will be on main streets, others on side streets. Some will be in very dense neighbourhoods, others in neighbourhoods of lower density. Some will be multi-story, other will be single story. Some will be in warm climates, others in cold climates. No one prototype design can do justice to this range of variation. A prototype would tend to standardize the buildings, where standardization is inappropriate; it would tend to overlook the uniqueness of each special case.

Our approach to prototypes is intended to overcome this difficulty. *We have tried to reconcile the uniqueness of each community with the fact that certain organizational principles are valid from one community to another.*

What we have devised then, is a system of generating principles, which can be richly transformed according to local circumstances but which never fail to convey their essentials. This is rather like a grammar. English grammar is a set of generating principles which generate all the possible sentences of English. It would be preposterous to suppose that one could convey the full richness of the English language by means of a few well chosen 'prototypical' sentences. Our system, then, is more in the spirit of a grammar than the conventional prototype permits. We call our system of generating principles a *pattern language for multi-service centres*. It is a system of patterns — with rules for combining them — which generates multi-service centre buildings.

This version has five parts:

In part I, for the sake of concreteness, we present one-sentence summaries of the 64 patterns in the pattern language.

In part II we discuss the nature of the individual patterns.

In part III 23 patterns are shown in full.

In part IV, we show how these patterns may be combined to form multi-service centres. We give six examples of multi-service centres designed for different communities — all of them generated by the pattern language.

*Note on the title

At the time we wrote this report five years ago, we were struggling to find a 'language' with the properties that are described in the text. As the reader of the full report will discover for himself, the patterns work, but the so-called 'language' does not: this part has therefore been eliminated in this edited version. We have now finally solved the problem of creating a language which does work, and does allow people to design buildings of all kinds, for themselves. This work will be published by the Oxford University Press at the end of 1973 in three volumes. The volumes will be called:

The Timeless Way of Building
The Pattern Language
Without Plans

We are continuing to publish this report, (with the original title *A Pattern Language Which Generates Multi-Service Centers*) both for the patterns and designs which it contains, and for its theoretical interest, and are delighted to see this shortened version of it in the *Architects Year Book*.

I: Summaries of 64 patterns

19 of the 64 patterns given in this summary are presented in full in Part III. So that the reader can scan the patterns, and get a general sense of their content, we present a one-sentence summary of each of the 64 patterns. In reading these summaries it is important to remember the following points:

Each pattern prescribes some feature of a multi-service centre building. It describes a relationship which is required to solve a problem which will occur in that building. The summary does not describe this problem; it describes only the pattern.

1.* *Small target areas:* The multi-service centre serves a target area with population of 34,000 ± 20%.

2.* *Location:* Service centres are located within two blocks of a major intersection.

3.* *Size based on population:* The total size of an MSC, which services a target area of population N, is .9N square feet.

4.* *Community territory:* The service centre is divided into two zones, services and community territory; community territory includes space for community projects and a public arena.

 5.* *Small services without red tape:* No one service has a staff size greater than 12; each service is physically cohesive and autonomous; the services are loosely organized with respect to each other.

 6. *Expansion:* The number of services can grow and the size of any one service can grow; but the relationship of all services to community territory does not change.

 7. *Entrance locations:* The building's main entrances are immediately visible to a person approaching, on foot or by car, from any direction.

 8. *Parking:* Either parking is provided for everyone [this will require .5N square feet for a target population N], or there is emergency parking only; staff-only parking is never provided.

 9.* *Arena thoroughfare:* There is a natural pedestrian shortcut through the MSC's community territory.

 10. *Open to street:* Major community projects, services and arena activities are plainly visible to passers-by, in the street.

 11. *Arena enclosure:* The public arena is as open as possible to the world around it, while still maintaining the required Effective Temperature inside.

 12. *Locked and unlocked zones:* The building is zoned according to three different time schedules: with one door closing each zone off from the next: 9am-5pm, 9am-11pm, and 'always open'.

 13.* *All services off arena:* All services open off the public arena; their frontages are roughly equal.

 14.* *Free waiting:* All services share a common waiting area, which contains a variety of activities; this waiting area is part of the public arena.

 15.* *Overview of services:* All the services housed in the MSC are instantly visible to a person entering the centre.

 16.* *Necklace of community projects:* Small, store-front type stalls, organized and run by members of the community, ring the multi-service centre.

 17. *Community projects two-sided:* Like store fronts, each community project opens onto the street; wherever possible it opens onto the public arena as well.

 18.* *Windows overlooking life:* Windows near places where people spend more than a minute or two, all look out on areas of 'life'.

 19. *Core service adjacencies:* Personnel in core services are placed according to frequency of interaction; this will typically lead to formation of three cohesive units: administration, community organization and programme-evaluation.

20.* *Activity pockets:* The entire edge of the arena is scalloped with pockets of activity, alternating with points of access.

 21.* *Self-service:* The waiting area contains a self-service facility, where job listings, welfare rights information and other do-it-yourself services are open, without restriction, to the public.

 22.* *Pedestrian density in public places:* If the estimated mean number of people in the arena at any given moment is P, the size of the arena is 150P to 300P square feet.

 23.* *Entrance shape:* Major entrances are either deeply recessed or they stick out from the face of the building, for visibility.

 24. *Subcommittee watchdogs:* Subcommittees of community residents have offices in the multi-service centre; they are empowered to represent the community's interests in the centre, and are set up to receive complaints and suggestions.

 25.* *Building stepped back from arena:* Buildings around public courts should be raked back at an angle less than 40 degrees.

 26. *Vertical circulation in services:* Services requiring space beyond that allocated to them round the arena, are directly connected to upper stories by interior stairs.

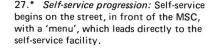 27.* *Self-service progression:* Self-service begins on the street, in front of the MSC, with a 'menu', which leads directly to the self-service facility.

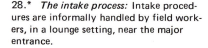 28.* *The intake process:* Intake procedures are informally handled by field workers, in a lounge setting, near the major entrance.

143

29. *Outdoor seats:* Outdoor benches are arranged overlooking activity, in the sun, and protected from wind; and especially suited for old people.

30.* *Ceiling heights:* Ceiling heights of all rooms and spaces are established according to the diameters of the 'social bubbles' appropriate for those spaces.

31.* *Short corridors:* Straight corridors are never longer than 40 or 50 feet.

32. *Child care position:* The child care station is visible along the path from the entrance to the services.

33. *Service layout:* Clients go directly from waiting areas to interview and other service spaces; they do not pass through the secretarial pools that back up the interview staff.

34.* *Street niches:* There are niches along the face of the building and at the entrances, where people can linger and 'window-shop'.

35. *Information-conversation:* There is an information station in the service centre, dispensing coffee and talk.

36.* *Dish-shaped arena:* The arena floor is dished at a slope of 7%.

37. *Director's overview:* The MSC director's office is situated so as to have an inconspicuous overview of the public life of the centre.

38.* *Community wall:* Associated with the MSC there is a section of wall that is given over to the community; it may be used for registering complaints, posting petitions, painting murals, etc.

39. *Arena diameter:* To enhance social cohesion the maximum diameter of the arena is 70-80 feet.

40.* *Office flexibility:* Office space in the service area is a continuous sheet of interconnecting rooms; the rooms are between 8' x 10' and 16' x 20'.

41.* *Town Meeting:* The MSC contains a tiered wrap-around meeting room, which is to be a hub for local political meetings.

42.* *Sleeping OK:* There is a section of the arena set aside, where people can rest and eventually doze off; if the demand exists, this section of the centre may be left open all night.

43. *Waiting diversions:* A number of activities like TV, checkers, pool, are part of the arena life, and they are woven through the waiting areas.

44. *Elevator-ramp:* There is a ramp and/or elevator connecting every change of level between public areas in the MSC.

45.* *Blockworker layout:* There is a handfull of open, informal booths near the entrance of the MSC where field workers meet their clients when they come to the centre; behind these booths each field worker has a small private work station.

46. *Radio/TV station:* There is a local TV (or radio) station broadcasting out of a community project space just off the public arena; some part of each broadcasting day is spent transmitting 'services' into people's homes (in-home job training, for example).

47. *Meeting rooms clustered:* Meeting rooms and classrooms are clustered near a kitchen, in that part of the building which remains open in the evenings.

48. *Barbershop politics:* There is at least one place where people naturally collect to talk politics and gossip, like a barbershop or a lunch-counter or a small grocery store or a laundromat, immediately adjacent to the multi-service centre.

49. *Staff lounge:* There is a lounge, near a kitchen, where staff members can take breaks and have their lunch; the lounge is wide open to a heavily travelled staff circulation route.

50.* *Interview booths:* Each interviewer has a private booth, much like the ones found in certain restaurants; the interviewer meets his clients in this booth on a less formal basis than the typical office permits.

51. *Stair seats:* Wherever stairs spill into the arena, they are wide enough for people to use them as seats.

52. *Window signs:* Provision is made for posting signs and leaflets along the windows that front on the street, so that people who stop to read them can look in, beyond the sign, and get a glimpse of MSC life.

53. *Form-filling tables:* There are tables and chairs in the waiting areas where people can sit down to fill out agency forms.

54. *Accessible WCs/cloakrooms:* There is at least one set of cloakrooms off the arena and accessible to the public.

55. *Secretary's workspace:* Each secretary has her own work station, surrounded on three sides by low partitions.

56. *Informal reception:* The receptionist for each service sits on a dais at a combination counter-desk; she meets the client, approaching the reception counter, at his eye level.

57. *Child-care contents:* The MSC child-care station emphasizes those kinds of play experiences that are most missing from the surrounding community; e.g. plants, sand and water, climbing, 'caves'.

58. *Seats outside meeting rooms:* There are small sitting alcoves outside the centre's meeting rooms, so that people can linger after a meeting and turn over their thoughts.

59.* *Square seminar rooms:* This is the best shape for seminars, where full and mutual participation is desired.

60. *Self-service contents:* The self-service facility contains a library, job listings, welfare rights information, research findings on the illegal practices of local landlords, language labs, teaching machines, etc.

61. *Arena storage:* There are storage spaces off the arena, where arena furniture and equipment can be locked away; the storage area is 7% of the arena size.

144

62. *Window heights in meeting rooms:* Are 40″ or higher; this means that people's faces are never silhouetted against windows.

63.* *Pools of light:* Lighting is not uniform throughout the multi-service centre; rather, it is in pools, each pool covering a special and delimited 'social bubble'.

64.* *Warm colours:* The primary sources of illumination throughout the service centre, in combination with the colours of floors, walls, ceilings and furnishings, should be chosen to give warm light.

We wish to draw the reader's attention to three minor peculiarities in the patterns.

First: Some patterns have a wider context than a 'multi-service centre' — community buildings, any building, etc. This is likely to confuse a reader, if he does not realize that the 64 patterns given here are *part of a much larger language.* It would be arbitrary to restrict the context statements of all the patterns to multi-service centre.

Such patterns as 'short corridors' — Pattern 31 — are very important, and need to be mentioned in this report — they have a reasonable influence on the shape of the multi-service centre — but we cannot pretend, for the sake of this report, that these patterns apply only to MSC's.

Second: Although we believe that the more important patterns for multi-service centres are all here, when it comes to details we have given no more than a sprinkling. Thus, we have stated a pattern which describes the proper window height in meeting rooms (Pattern 62) — but we have not given the number of windows such a room requires; nor have we given the window height for other kinds of rooms; nor have we given a thousand other details.

The reasons for this, again, centre on the fact that the fragment of language presented here is no more than part of a much larger language, and that many of the patterns in this larger language have very general context statements. It would be impossible to state all these patterns in a report which deals with multi-service centres.

Further, many of the patterns, and especially these smaller, rather general ones, are widely known by practising architects — and there is no need to state them.

However, there is no hard and fast line between large, innovative, multi-service centre-only patterns and these other small, familiar, general patterns. One or two patterns, (like 63, Pools of light; and 64, Warm colours) apply to almost any context: but they are very important, and not widely known, so we have included them. We have therefore drawn the line more or less where we wanted to. Most of the patterns deal specifically with multi-service centres, and are of large scale importance: but a few of them dwindle off into matters of great generality, a few into relatively unimportant details.

Third: We have defined 64 patterns. But we are by no means satisfied with all the patterns. Some are highly unreliable, and inelegantly argued; they have been included only for the sake of completeness. In one sense this doesn't matter. *They are all open to criticism* — and it is worth stating them, even if they are wrong or banal, so that they get improved by criticism. We ask that the reader accept the 64 patterns in this spirit.

But since some readers may use this report as a way of understanding the concept of a pattern, not as a source of patterns for multi-service centres, we have marked those patterns which we like best, and which best convey the concept of a pattern, with an asterisk in the preceding summaries.

The asterisked patterns are: 1, 2, 3, 4, 5, 9, 13, 14, 15, 16, 18, 20, 21, 22, 23, 25, 27, 28, 30, 31, 34, 36, 38, 40, 41, 42, 45, 50, 59, 63, 64. Twenty of the above patterns are given in detail in Part III of this article. For a complete understanding of all the patterns we refer to the original report available from: The Center for Environmental Structure, 2701 Shasta Rd, Berkeley, California, USA.

II: The idea of a pattern

If we examine the patterns as they are presented in the following pages we shall see that each pattern has two parts: the PATTERN statement itself, and a PROBLEM statement. The PATTERN statement is itself broken down into two further parts, an IF part, and a THEN part. In full the statement of each pattern reads like this:

IF : X   THEN : Z / PROBLEM : Y

X defines a set of conditions. Y defines some problem which is always liable to occur under the conditions X. Z defines some abstract spatial relation which needs to be present under the conditions X, in order to solve the problem Y.

In short, IF the conditions X occur, THEN we should do Z, in order to solve the Problem Y.

No one of the patterns is, in any sense, an absolute statement. Any one of the patterns may be wrong; all of them can be improved. Specifically, there are two ways in which the pattern statement might be wrong. First of all, the problem may not in fact occur as stated under the conditions X, or it may not be as serious as it is claimed to be, or it may only occur under special circumstances, which are far less general than those defined by X. Second, it may not be true that the relationships defined by Z solve the problem Y. We expect both these kinds of criticism to be levelled at the patterns; indeed, it is essential for the life of the patterns that these criticisms be raised.

The system of patterns is meant to define a prototype building. Obviously no one will accept this prototype, or the individual patterns, if he is not free to make up his own mind about the validity of the patterns. To make up his mind, he must be free to criticize the patterns.

We expect the patterns to grow and change under the impact of such criticism. In this sense the prototype which we defined is merely temporary; if we are successful, we hope that it will evolve, as criticisms and improvements accumulate, so that the patterns which define multi-service centres ten years from now, will look very different from the ones which are stated here.

The format of the patterns is designed to make criticism easy. As far as possible, all the tendencies and needs and difficulties in the problem statement are supported by empirical evidence. This evidence makes it easier to challenge the validity of the patterns. Often the form of the evidence which supports a conjecture, itself helps to define the kind of evidence which would be needed to refute the conjecture. Where we have not been able to find any relevant published evidence, and where we have been unable (for want of time or money) to make experiments or observations ourselves, we have tried to state our conjectures as openly and clearly as possible — so that even in these doubtful cases, empirical discussion and observation can begin.

III. The Patterns

Small target areas (1)

Pattern
___

If:
An urban area is to be served by multi-service centres

Then:
All the multi-service centres should be small and the target areas correspondingly small.

The target areas should contain 34,000 persons, ±20% (i.e. 27,000 − 41,000). The corresponding floor areas, as given by Pattern 3, are 25,000 − 37,000 square feet, with a modal figure of 31,000.

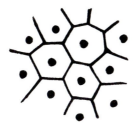

Problem
___

The task of determining the best size and distribution for mult-service centres is very difficult. There are strong reasons for large centres, and there are strong reasons for small centres.

To examine these reasons, we shall compare three broadly distinct patterns of size and distribution:

A. Large centres, serving large target areas.
B. Large centres, serving large target areas, supplemented by a series of smaller subcentres, equally spaced throughout the same target area.
C. Small centres, each serving small target areas.

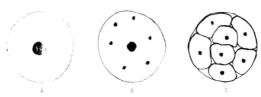

The major needs which influence the size of centres are these:

1. The need for 'multi-service'. Clients do not want to be referred from one agency in one part of town, to another agency in another part of town. Even more important, experience has shown that many clients' problems, when correctly diagnosed, turn out to require some kind of service different from the service which the client sought (i.e., a client comes in asking for help in housing; after analysis, it turns out that he needs legal aid in fighting his landlord).

This is essential to the whole concept of multi-service

centres. (See for instance: 'Criteria for Review of Pilot Neighbourhood Centers', Federal Agency Groups, April 1967; Alfred J Kahn, Grossman et al., *Neighbourhood Information Centers*, Columbia School of Social Work, New York, 1966, pp. 92-95; U.S. Congress, Senate, 89th Congress, 2d Session, S. 3443, *A Bill to Offer Means for Coordinating State Health and Welfare Services at the Community Level by Providing Common Facilities and Encouraging their Administration as Elements of a Comprehensive Whole.*)

2. The need to reach the hard-core poor. So far the service centres have a shocking record; althought they have reached certain parts of the poor community, they have not succeeded in reaching the very poor. For example, when the four Oakland centres had been in existence nearly two years (1966) only 7% of the poor (income below $4,000) in the four target areas had visited a centre for any purpose. In the North and West Oakland target areas, only 4% and 3% of the poor had visited a centre. ('Poverty and Poverty Programs in Oakland', Survey Research Center, University of California, Berkeley, 1967, pp. 122-126.)

These two needs are in conflict. The idea of multi-service requires that each service centre have a full complement of services. Each centre must therefore have a large enough target area to support various specialists, and must therefore be large.

On the other hand, the problem of reaching the poor requires that the centres be small, and closely spaced. It requires that they be small for two reasons.

First, we know that many poor people, and especially the hard-core poor, have very limited access to the city. We may describe this by saying that each person has an *orbit* — where orbit is defined as the parts of the city which a person visits at least once a week. A person's orbit usually consists of certain paths, connecting his home with a few special destinations. In the case of a person who is poor or old or unemployed, this orbit may be no more than four or five blocks in diameter. Evidence for this phenomenon can be found in the Kirschner Report (Kirschner Associates, *A Description and Evaluation of Neighborhood Centers*, 530 Jefferson Street, N.E., Albuquerque, New Mexico, 1966, p. 30).

It is fair to say that such a person will not visit any dubious enterprise, like a multi-service centre, unless it lies directly within his orbit.

Second, we know that people, and especially poor people, are not well served by rule-bound bureaucratic institutions. The functional issues are partly discussed in Pattern 5, where we show that the size of individual services should be small. There are also indications,

145

that the overall size of the centre as a whole can have a similar effect, and should be kept as small as possible. (See: Kirschner, *op. cit.,* pp. 26, 31, 57; also Kahn, Grossman, et al, *op. cit.,* pp. 92-93.)

We may sum up these remarks: As the scale of the operation grows, more and more of the agency's functions are translated into administrative jobs which can be performed by administrators. The result is that the community member is being handled mainly by clerks, rather than by professionals. The symbolic and realistic feeling of harassment resulting from a direct confrontation of the community member with an alienating and impersonal bureaucracy is detrimental to the success of the service centre. Many individuals, especially from poverty areas, are not equipped to handle these impersonal confrontations and would rather not obtain any service than have to place themselves in such an uncomfortable situation.

Before trying to estimate the size implications of these facts, we list a number of minor factors which also have bearing on the size: (Numbers continue from 1 and 2 above.)

3. Scale economies. A large centre may be able to support services which a smaller centre cannot support at all.

4. Scale economies within a single service. If a service serves a large target area, and is therefore itself relatively large, the aggregation of personnel within the service may give rise to increased efficiency through the division of labour among these personnel. Simple tasks, such as typing, mailing, communications, and administrative chores, can be taken away from interviewers and professionals, thus giving them time to operate more intensively in their own special field.

5. The need for growth potential within the centre. The centre is intended to provide a setting in which the community can create new services easily. To create new services, the centre clearly requires as large a base population as possible. For example, it might be easy for a large centre to start a photographic club, but hard for a small centre to do the same.

6. The need for political power. The centre will be unable to initiate new programmes, unless it has political power. A large centre wields more political influence than a small centre.

7. The need for simple comprehensive record keeping. This is another facet of the referral problem. If clients are referred from service to service, it is impossible to keep track of their records,

with the result that they are asked the same stupid questions over and over again.

8. Equilibrium over time. The structure and function of community services does not remain constant over time. Changes in the demand structure for services introduce changes over time into the service system. It may be that in the long run smaller centres of a more modest scale will develop to compete with the larger centre. If more than one centre develops in the community there will be a tendency among these two centres to specialize in particular services. The construction of a large single structure may then prove to have been too large to begin with. A system designed with an eye to the uncertain future should not provide for too large a service centre as a beginning venture. The possibility that the service system will reach a locational equilibrium with more than one facility places a limit on the size of the first facility, even if it is to be a single structure housing all service personnel, in view of the uncertainty of future developments.

9. The need to minimize capital costs, maintenance costs, and salary costs.

We now have 9 factors which influence the size and spatial distribution of multi-service centres, the first two major, and the other 7 relatively minor. Let us now compare the three possible patterns, A, B, C, on the basis of these factors. (9 does not appear in the table, since current data gives no indication about the relative costs of A, B, and C.)

	Satisfies	Doesn't Satisfy
A	1 3 4 5 6 7	2 8
B	3 4 5 6 8	1 2 7
C	2 7 8	1 3 4 5 6

This table leaves it unclear which is the best solution. At first sight, A would seem to be the best. A solves more problems than either B or C. B is next best, and C is worst.

However, if we take into account our assumption that items 1 and 2 are of prime importance, and that items 3-9 are of less importance, then B, which solves neither 1 nor 2, is clearly unsatisfactory, while A and C might be equally good.

Since the difference between A and C is merely one of size, we may then ask: what size best resolves the conflict between the positive and negative aspects of size? We incline towards the small centres on the following

grounds. It is fairly easy to modify the organization of a small centre in such a way as to satisfy 1 (i.e. to take advantage of the idea of multi-service); on the other hand, it is extremely difficult to modify the organization of a large centre in such a way as to satisfy 2 (i.e. to be friendly, unbureaucratic, and so distributed that there is at least one in every 'orbit').

Let us ask, then, what is the smallest multi-service centre which can fully satisfy the demands of '*multi-service*':

As the basic measure of size for a multi-service centre, we use the number of interviewers and client-contact personnel in the Centre.

Many services may have no more than 1 interviewer. We know from Pattern 5 that no service should have more than 12 staff in all, hence 4 interviewers. We know, also, that the services tend to be unequally distributed in size. There are usually many small services, and a few large ones (job-counselling, welfare).

Let us now try to set concrete limits on the size. We begin by assessing the range of problems that a multi-service centre must be equipped to deal with.

From Robert Perlman and David Jones, *Neighborhood Service Centers,* U.S. Department of Health, Education and Welfare, Washington, D.C., 1967, pp. 26-27:
The most extensive study of client problems has been done by ABCD and the Roxbury Center, where a client's statements of his difficulty was recorded as nearly as possible in his own words in order to ascertain the problem or problems to which he gave the highest priority. ABCD's report on the Roxbury Multi-Service Center notes that clients varied greatly in their problem statement, some mentioned two or three problems. If the primary problems are categorized, the percentage distribution is as follows:

Problems Cited by Clients at Roxbury Center

Problem Category	Percent
Employment	25
Family	21
Housing	16
Financial	14
Legal	12
Education	5
Health	4
Seeking Information	3
	100

We can discount Seeking Information for our purposes since it is not a 'service'. That leaves seven broad problem categories. We have found that these seven categories cover the spectrum of problems in poverty areas fairly well. Thus, in Hunts Point for instance, the problems were identified as:

Health
Housing
Education
Legal Services
Social Service (family, financial)
Manpower (employment)
Addiction (health)
Early Childhood (family, education)
Economic Development (employment, financial)

It stands to reason then, that every MSC should provide some service in each of these seven categories. If we assume that 1 interviewer is required for the categories of service which are least in demand — i.e. education and health — we may use the Roxbury percentages to estimate the number of interviewers required in the other categories. Thus:

Employment	4
Family	4
Housing	3
Financial	2
Legal	2
Education	1
Health	1
	17

This suggests that in order to provide 'multi-service' an MSC must have about 17 interviewers, and a large enough target area to support them.

The arguments in Pattern 3 tell us that a population of N persons require a total of .0005N service interviewers. To support 17 interviewers, a centre must therefore serve 34,000 people. Since it will be impossible to give every target area exactly 34,000 persons, we arbitrarily set upper and lower limits of ±20%.

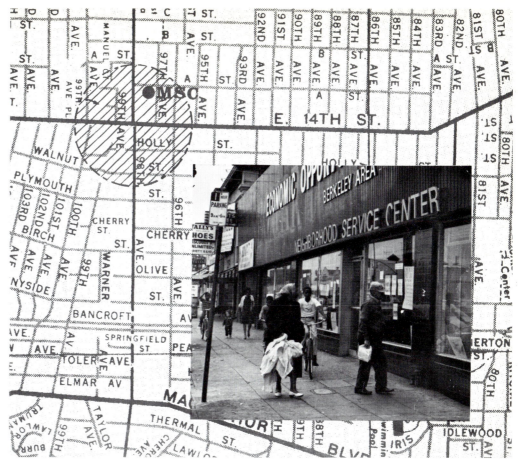

Location (2)

Pattern

If:
A service centre is to be located in an urban community,
Then:
The site should be within two blocks of a major intersection, with at least twenty stores and major pedestrian activity.

Problem

One of the key problems which multi-service centres face is the problem of reaching people in the target area.
Many people do not know that multi-service centres exist, or what they do. Even when they do know, they do not always come in and use the services. (Kirschner Associates, *op. cit.*, pp. 24, 27 and 42.)
The physical location and design of the multi-service centre can aggravate the problem of outreach. If the centre is hidden, no one gets to know about it by seeing it; and people are not reminded of its existence. If the centre is out of the way, off the beaten track, then even people who have heard of the centre, and have half made up their minds to go there, do not go, because it is too hard to get there, or too hard to find.
In positive terms: The location and design of the centre can help out-reach in two ways. If the centre is conveniently placed it will help to encourage people who have already heard of the centre, but who are still half-hearted about going to use the services. If the centre is prominently placed, it will remind people of its existence, and perhaps even advertise itself to

people who haven't otherwise heard of it.

There is strong evidence for the fact that location and openness do play a major part in reaching clients. The Berkeley Multi-service Centre moved its location in the autumn of 1967. Before the move, the Centre was located in a house, standing 100 feet back from the street — a quiet residential street, half a block from a non-commercial, vehicular artery.

After the move the Centre was located on a major commercial artery, San Pablo, half a block from the main intersection of University and San Pablo, one of the two main commercial areas in the heart of the poor community.

In its first location, the entrance to the Centre was set back from the street, about 100 feet, the door was not visible from the street, and the windows were so placed that you could not see into the building from the street.

In its second location, the Centre occupied a one-time furniture showroom; the whole 90 foot long front of the building was glass, immediately adjacent to the sidewalk; the door was easily visible, in the centre of the facade; there were few partitions inside, so that the inside of the Centre was almost totally visible from the sidewalk.

Here are the figures for client business before and after the move:

	Number of people dropping in, per day	Number of people with appointments, per day
Before the move	1-2	15-20
Two months after the move	15-20	about 50
Six months after the move	about 40	about 50

During this period there were no major increases in outreach, and no major changes of programme. It is therefore unlikely that the increases are due to any other factors besides the change in location.

Size based on population (3)

Pattern

If:

There is a multi-service centre serving a population of N persons,

Then:

The multi-service centre contains .3N square feet of service space, .15N square feet of space for core services, and .45N square feet devoted to meeting rooms, circulation, self-service, arena, and other ancillary spaces. The total floor area of the multi-service centre is .9N square feet. All figures to be taken ±20%.

Problem

To establish these figures we take the following computational steps:

1. Compute the number of people who might visit the service centre per day.

2. Compute the number of service interviewers who will be required to handle this load.

3. Compute the total backup staff required to help these interviewers.

4. Compute the total square feet of service space required to accommodate this staff.

5. Compute the square footage of ancillary facilities.

It must be made clear from the outset, that the computations are all approximate. We shall therefore round all numbers to the first significant decimal place.

1. To compute the percentage of N people visiting the centre, we must first recognize that the number of people who visit the centre depends on the number of people in the target area who *know* that the centre exists, and that it offers services. In most existing target areas this number is far below N, in many cases as low as 0.2N.

This problem is well known. Many steps are being taken in the newest centres to overcome it by means of advertising, extended outreach programmes, and more effective house-to-house contact work.

For the purpose of this pattern, we shall make the very strong assumption, that the outreach programme has been completely successful, and that everyone in the target area knows about the centre. *We therefore assume that 100% of the population, i.e. N persons, know about the centre, know where it is, and what it does.*

We may now ask what percentage of these N people will come to visit the centre.

In Oakland 28% of the households who knew about their local centres, visited them during a one year period. (In more detail, 24% of the households with incomes above $4000/year, and 33% of the households with incomes below $4000/year — but these differences are small compared with the level of accuracy in this discussion. 'Poverty and Poverty Programs in Oakland', Survey Research Center, University of California Berkeley, 1967, Table 38, p. 121.)

The mean household size in the four Oakland target areas is 2.75 (computed from figures given in 'Profile of Target Areas for Economic Opportunity Program', Department of Human Resources, City of Oakland, Table 1*, 1964).

We may therefore estimate that .28/2.75 or about 10% of the people who know about the centre, will visit it during a given year.

On the basis of our earlier assumption, we may therefore expect that the centre will have 0.1N clients per year, or 0.008N clients/month.

2. We now try to estimate the number of interviewers require to handle this client load.

The following computation concerns only service interviewers who are working directly with clients, in the service programmes. It does not include field workers, community organizers, administrators of the multi-service centre, or any other members of the core service programme. They will be discussed later as 'ancillary facilities'.

The following table (adapted from Perlman and Jones, *op. cit.*, Appendix A, pp. 81-82) shows the numbers of service interview stall (excluding field workers and core service personnel) and the number of clients they served in a number of East Coast centres.

This table, averaged out, suggests that one service interviewer can take care of about 16 clients per month. (The figure must be interpreted with care.) It is important to recognize that some of the clients came back many times (figures given by Perlman and Jones, for the Roxbury multi-service centre, *op. cit.*, p. 39, suggest that the mean number of visits, per client, is 4.8). This means that each interviewer is in fact dealing with 75 client *visits* per month, an average of about 4 per day. The rest of his time is taken up by paper work, telephoning, and meetings undertaken on behalf of his clients.

The service centre therefore needs one service interviewer for every 16 clients/month who come in for help. On the basis of the previous assumptions, we may say then, that a centre serving a population of

	MFY	CFO	CPI	Rox	JFK	Shawmut
Service interview staff	12	12	81	10	9	3
Client intake/month	111	359	301	194	173	35
Clients/interviewer/month	9.3	30.0	3.8	19.4	19.2	11.7

N, needs 1/16 (0.008N) = 0.0005N service interviewers.
This estimate is supported by figures obtained from existing multi-service centres. The following table

(adapted from Perlman and Jones, *op. cit.,* Table 1, p. 11) shows the target area populations and the number of professionals serving them for a variety of centres.

	MFY	CFO	CIP	ABCD
Target population per centre: N	54,000	12,000	13,000	26,000
Number of professional workers/centre	24	7	17	14
Population/professional worker	2,250	1,760	776	1,880

The average of the four figures in the last row is 1670. These centres have .006N professionals to serve populations of N. Since about half of these professionals are field workers, this gives a figure of about .003N in-house service interviewers. The figure is lower than ours; but it applies to a situation where outreach was far from perfect. If outreach were better, the figure would have to be raised. We must remember, also, that the number of professionals available influences the number of persons in the community who can get help; thus the CPI centres, with .013N professionals, have a higher relative rate of intake than the others (*op. cit.,* p. 81).
3. Rough estimates suggest that each interviewer requires two backup staff to help him (assistants, typist, researchers, receptionists, PBX operator, etc.). Thus in East Oakland legal aid, 1-1/2 full-time interviewers require 4 full-time backup; in West Oakland family counselling, 2-1/2 interviewers require 4 full-time backup; in West Oakland legal aid 2 interviewers require 4 full-time backup.
On this basis, we estimate that a centre serving a target population of N persons, will require a total staff of 0.0015N persons.
4. Various sources suggest that general purpose office space, requires approximately 200 square feet per person (including all circulation and extras).
For instance, one source gives 150 square feet per person as net figure, with another 65% for all circulation and extras — making a total of 250 square feet per person. However, this figure applies to whole buildings — the percentage of circulation within a service unit would probably be rather less. (M V Facey

and G B Smith, 'Offices in a Regional Centre', Research Paper No. Two, Location of Offices Bureau, London, January 1968, p. 27.)
The best estimate for gross square footage per person seems to be 210 square feet, (though this is still liable to vary according to detailed conditions). (See Ottomar Gottschalk, *Flexible Verwaltungsbauten,* Quickborn bei Hamburg, 1963, pp. 33-35.)
On this basis we may estimate that the multi-service centre will require a total of .3N square feet of service space.
5. Finally, we estimate the square footage required by core services and ancillary facilities. Core services includes all community organizers or block workers, all centre administration, all subcommittees and evaluation personnel. Ancillary facilities includes all community project space, meeting rooms, classrooms, circulation, self-service, arena, child-care, storage, cloakrooms.
Our experience shows that core services require about .15N square feet of space, and that major circulation, arena, meeting rooms, classrooms, child-care and other ancillary spaces require about .45N square feet. We cannot yet support these figures with any detailed item by item account.

Community territory (4)

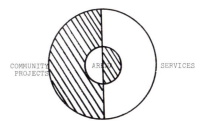

Pattern

If:
There is any multi-service centre

Then:
1. The building should contain a major area which is established as *community territory.*
2. Community territory is distinct from the area devoted to services, but is interlocking with it.
3. Community territory contains two main components: an *arena,* and an area given over to *community projects.*

The *arena* is a public area, open to passers-by (whether or not they are visiting the service centre), shaped in such a way as to encourage public discussions (both formal and informal), equipped with walls for day-to-day notices and posters, microphones, and loudspeakers.
Community project space is defined according to three functions:
(a) It provides space where any community group can set up an office or workshop oriented towards a specific community problem. (Examples of such projects include a group fighting slumlords, a group concerned with school reform, a couple of women who decide to run a child care centre, typing classes, local tenants seeking action on rat control, a police complaints committee, and so on.) Office equipment and duplicating machinery will be provided in this zone for each community project, as well as for the community at large. Community project spaces will be owned by the community and as free as possible from any administrative strings concerning keys, janitors, permission, etc (See Pattern 17.)
(b) Community projects also include offices for local political bodies, and for the subcommittees which have control over the service programmes and to whom

clients can make suggestions, and complain about services.

(c) The community project zone also contains small shops, run by local businessmen, perhaps with the help of SBA grants. Examples are coffee shops, barbers, book stores, laundromats, tobacconists, flea markets. These shops should be rent controlled.

Problem

The functional failures of existing multi-service centres. This pattern is the most important of the 64 patterns. In it, we try to revise the overall concept of a multi-service centre, in a way that is radical enough to over-come the massive failures of the present centres. *For, in blunt terms, the multi-service programme has, so far, been a massive failure.* Less than 10% of the poor go to multi-service centres (see Pattern 2). The centres do not help the hard-core rock-bottom poor at all.

To some extent the failure has been caused by inade-quacies in the services themselves. The shape of the building will make little difference to that. But to a large extent, the failure has been caused by the *nature* of the existing centres, by the way they have been conceived: In spite of new names and new ideals, multi-service centres do not meet the real needs of the poor; they perpetuate the indignity of 'welfare handouts'. The key to this failure is the syndrome of 'powerless-ness'. It has been demonstrated again and again that the poor are effectively trapped in a subculture of poverty, that this trap is a self-perpetuating, vicious circle, and that it precludes effective participation in society's major institutions. Because people are poor, they can get no jobs; because they have no jobs they have neither the money nor the opportunity to move about and use the city; because they cannot travel about the city, they are not well versed in the processes which govern the rest of society, and they are not able to participate in its processes and institutions; because they are effectively shut off from the rest of society, they have no power in the political arena; and they have few local leaders; because they have no power and no voice their needs and complaints and the details of their situation are not widely known to other members of society — certainly they are not represented. Because they have no voice, no power, no process by which they can communicate with centres of action, no jobs and no participation, they do not have the most central freedom that any free man has — the freedom to call their own shots and to determine their own future. And so poor people stay demoralized, and isolated. And above all they stay poor.

In short, poverty is a syndrome which hinges principal-ly on various facets of powerlessness.

(The syndrome of poverty and powerlessness has been well documented in the past few years. See, for instance, Lewis' technical discussion of the 'culture of poverty', Oscar Lewis, *La Vida,* pp. xlii-liii, New York; Michael Harrington, *The Other America,* Baltimore, 1963; Moynihan's infamous report describing the self-per-petuating, identity-killing nature of the conditions under which poor poeple live, in Lee Rainwater and William L Yancey, *The Moynihan Report and the Politics of Controversy,* MIT Press, 1967; Abram Kardiner and Lionel Ovesey, *The Mark of Oppression — Explorations in the Personality of the American Negro,* Cleveland, 1951.)

Like all syndromes, this syndrome can only be broken if it is attacked on all fronts simultaneously. During the last few years, this has been happening to a *limited* extent:

1. A little more money and much more attention is being given to the poor and their situation.

2. Many forceful and articulate leaders of the poor have gained national stature; many more have emerged as local spokesmen.

3. More and more, poor people are speaking and acting out against the system that is keeping them down (e.g. Poor People's Campaign, various ghetto rebellions).

4. More and more poor people are finding that intense organization and confrontation are the route to political power.

5. More and more young people in poor communities are finding their voice: they are making concrete de-mands on society and they are finding strong identity in the process (e.g. Black Panther Party, 'Ten Demands', published in newspapers and leaflets around the San Francisco-Oakland Bay Area).

6. People with professional training and technical skills are beginning to put themselves at the disposal of the poor (e.g. Architects' Renewal Committee in Harlem, Medical Committee for Human Rights, Lawyers' Guild).

All these steps are, in some sense, reactions to the central feature of the poverty syndrome: powerless-ness. Each one of them attacks some aspects of power-lessness. Where all of these things happen simultaneous-ly, there is some real hope that the poverty syndrome can be broken down.

The multi-service programme is intended by policy makers to play a part in breaking the poverty-powerlessness syndrome. Yet, in fact, as they are presently conceived, multi-service centres do little to counteract the manifestations of powerlessness, and indeed, they often help to perpetuate them.

For example:

1. It is known that the rules of the welfare system force people to tell lies, in order to get their money — thus demeaning them yet again. The message which comes through consistently is that the recipient is, in one sense or another, not what he should be.

(See for instance, the following verbatim quotes, from statements by Alameda County welfare recipient, taken from William L Nicholls II, Esther S Hochsheim and Sheila Babbie, *The Castlemont Survey, A Hand-book of Survey Tables,* Survey Research Center, University of California, Berkeley, 1966:

Therefore, it was better for me not to work . . . I could make it otherwise. They seem to do everything they ca to discourage you from having any ambitions at all.
I went to apply for help when I needed it years ago and they tried to push me off — discourage me. I don't like their attitude. They look down their nose at you.
You have no private life. They want you to go out and look for a father for your children and when you do, they act like something is going on.
It took a great deal of pride swallowing to go to them in the first place and they didn't try very hard to help and they're still not doing anything.
They don't have any respect.

4. Even in those cases where service centres try to initiate community 'action' this idea remains in the heads of the centre staff — it does not communicate it-self effectively to the members of the community. Thu Kirschner (*op. cit.,* Appendix III), reports that only 20 of all service center clients recognize the community ac tion function of the service centre, while 80% of the agency staff recognize it.

5. Even when the centre is run by an elected local boar the board members often feel that they are not really in control — they feel that the real decisions are being ma by staff members.
There seems to be a great deal of frustration associated with board membership, especially as compared with being a paid staff member . . . Council members feel that their views are not respected, that they have no control over the centre and/or that they are inadequate to cope with the complexity of affairs confronting them. There are exceptions to this generalization, but they are rare. (Kirschner Associates, op. cit., *p. 46.)*

6. In at least one case on record, centre administra-tors have refused to allow controversial community meetings to take place in the centre — thus driving community organizers out, to hold their meetings some-where else, and reinforcing the suspicion, already rife in the community, that the centre represents govern-

150

ment interests, and is not really theirs. (Personal communication from Gene Bernardi.)

7. The established services tend to 'take over' the centre — thus making it foreign territory to the community. It becomes a favour to be there, not a right, for community residents. Interviews with 200 multi-service centre clients showed that in answer to the question: 'Who runs the centre and decides what is to be done?', only 8% said neighbourhood people. The remaining 92% mentioned the centre director, centre staff, social workers, federal government and other assorted agency personnel. (Kirschner Associates, *op. cit.*, Appendix V.)

Now the question arises, what should a multi-service centre be like, if it is to be effective in fighting poverty and powerlessness.

The limited though real success of the various measures now being taken against powerlessness (i.e. black power tactics, community organization, welfare rights groups, rent strikes, the mission rebels, ARCH, the emergence of many articulate leaders, etc.) makes it clear that a successful multi-service centre, must, likewise, concentrate on the problem of giving power and self determination to the poor.

They fool around and by the time they investigate if you come down there real nice, you won't get anywhere. If you raise hell with them they'll give you what they think you should have.
When we were getting aid they had my husband and me picked up at my home at 2 a.m. and threw us into jail saying we had received money we weren't entitled to . . . We could have lied in the beginning and said the boys didn't help us at all and gotten full aid, but we tried to be honest and this is what they did to us.

2. In the same vein, the whole idea of coming in to receive 'service' perpetuates acceptance of the fact that people in the community are being told what to do, and are not able to call their own shots.

Thus, one can say of the target population that most have not yet been reached in a meaningful way at all; that some have become clients for services and perceive the centers as givers of services and themselves as recipients of services; and that a still smaller number regard themselves as active members of society with the right and ability to influence it.
(Kirschner Associates, op. cit.)

More concretely, Scott Briar and others ('Mexican-American Recipients Orientations Towards and Mode of Adaptation to the Welfare System', School of Social Welfare, University of California,

Berkeley, dittoed, June 1966), found that only 33% of Negro recipients, 28% of Mexican-American, and 20% of the white recipients disagreed with the statement 'It's best to do anything they tell you to do'.

3. Although many multi-service programmes have made special efforts to hire staff from the local community, it has been shown that within a few months these staff members lose their ability to perceive issues as the members of the community see them — their perceptions tend to become like the perceptions of other staff members. (Burt Waldrich, 'Indigenous Worker as an Agent to Social Change', Ph.D. Thesis, Department of Social Welfare, University of California, Berkeley, 1968, measured the ability of community workers hired by services to retain their affinity with the clients, by asking community service aides to try to predict client responses to a series of questions. He found that '. . . length of time on the job is strongly and inversely related to ability to predict clients' responses (Table XI). Aides who have been in the programme less than one month are considerably more accurate than the professionals'.) Apparently there is something about the present organization of multi-service centres that tends to replace the client's point of view, by the staff member's point of view, and that tends, therefore, to prevent the real needs of the poor from coming into sharp focus.

The poor can and will articulate their needs, *if given the proper setting and means.* It cannot be left only to the hiring of indigenous members of the community in programmes and services (although that may help). Board members, if they are to represent the community, must be given the incentive and prestige which should be associated with their positions; everyone must feel that he has control over his own destiny; that he can call his own shots; that he has some power.
None of this is possible without community organization. *If the multi-service centre is meant to help the poor, it must help the process of community organization.* This means, essentially, that the multi-service centre should have two features: *First, the whole centre must be built around the process of community organization. Second, the centre must be clearly recognizable as community territory.*
In more detail:

1. The community cannot organize itself without professional organizers, acting in concert with the entire community; but the entire community should be encouraged to participate. It must be easy for any member of the community to organize the community

around a given issue. This process requires a physical nerve centre. The multi-service centre should be the nerve centre for ongoing community organization.

2. The service centre cannot be a hub of community organization, unless it is clearly recognized by every member of the community, as community territory. Yet administrators of existing service centres have not succeeded in making places which belong to the community — they are still thought of as 'foreign' territory. The service centre must be clearly recognizable as community territory — a place where everyone has the right to be, day or night; a natural place to go at any time, especially in time of need. When we translate the idea of community organization and community territory into *physical* terms, they yield two components: the arena, and the community projects zone.

1. The most immediate instrument people have for solving a community problem is to rally around the issue at hand and to get other people interested enough to support their point.
Thus the community needs a public forum, equipped with sound system, benches, walls to put up notices, etc., where people are free to gather; a place which belongs to the community where people would naturally come whenever they think something should be done about something. We call this public forum the arena.

2. Once a group is ready to move, it takes typewriters, duplicating machines, telephones, etc., to carry through with a project and develop broad-based community support — whether it involves setting up typing classes, volunteer child care service, writing to central government, or the board of education, demonstrating against the county health service, conducting an investigation into police brutality, building a third party, and so on. (Gene Bernardi interviewed Benny Parrish, Community Organizer, formerly with the California Council of Community Development, and Art Schroeder, Neighborhood Organization Director of the East Oakland Service Center. Both men said that the most common and effective action-oriented projects were those using group appeal, negotiations and demonstrations'. . . an office and equipment, telephones, mimeo machines and paper for leaflets, newsletters and press releases, are all essential for these projects . . . There was hardly ever a demonstration without a leaflet.')
The community needs a place where people can have access to storefronts, work space, meeting rooms, office equipment, etc. The place would inevitably become known as community territory and would serve as an inspiration for the exercise of community

initiative. We call this space the *community projects zone.*

The community projects zone and the arena, together, form a base for community organization. And together they establish in a clear-cut way, the fact that the service centre is community territory. (See also patterns 16.)

A multi-service centre with these physical features, and parallel social innovations, has some chance of breaking down the syndrome of poverty and powerlessness.

Small services without red tape (5)

Pattern

If:

Any community centre in a poor community offers services,

Then:

The services may include any of the following, and any others which the members of the community develop:

Individual rehabilitation for the chronically unemployed	Family counselling
	Welfare counselling
Child welfare	Parole assistance and liaison
Health advice	Apprenticeship and on the job-training programme
Fair employment practices	
Psychiatric services	Consumer advice
Neighbourhood Youth Corps	Veterans' affairs
	Building and housing
Motor vehicles assistance	Group homes for teenage student mothers
Legal Aid	Probation rights
Vision care	Credit union
Welfare rights	Headstart
Small businesses	Parent child centre
Police complaints	Planned parenthood
Recreation programmes	Soup kitchen
Cancer society aid	Chest x-ray and vaccinations
Nursery	
Travellers aid	Civil Service test preparation
Farm labour office	
Real estate counselling	Jury service
Relocation agency	Services for the ageing
Emergency financial aid	Emergency housing
	Tenant rights
Income tax service	Emergency housing repair
Drug addiction	
Job-skills training and placement	

The services should have the following characteristics:
1. No one service should have more than 12 staff members, total.
2. Each service should be autonomous as far as possible: it should be housed in an identifiable, physical autonomous unit, with direct access to a public thoroughfare.
3. The services should be arranged in a loose informal way: so that there is no hard and fast distinction between services provided by agencies, and services which are initiated and run by members of the community.

Problem

Bureaucracy is one of the greatest enemies of effective service programmes in low-income communities. Its essential feature is 'red tape', a middle-class invention. The poor do not know how to deal with red tape; they are overwhelmed by it, and antagonized by it. To overcome red tape, individual service programmes within a community centre must be *small* (12 persons maximum) and *autonomous;* and further, they must be *loosely arranged,* so that new services, created by members of the community, can immediately be housed alongside existing programmes. (Gideon Sjoberg, Richard Brymer, and Buford Farris, 'Bureaucracy and the Lower Class', *Sociology and Social Research, 50,* April, 1966, pp. 325-337.)

Two main features of the red tape syndrome can be identified:
1. Lack of personal relationships, size of organization, and frameworks of rigid rules.
2. Feelings of impotence on the part of the client.

These suggest that red tape can be overcome in two ways. First, it can be overcome by making each service programme small and autonomous. A great deal of evidence shows that 'red tape' occurs largely as a result of impersonal relationships in large institutions. When people can no longer communicate on a face to face basis, they need formal regulations — and in the lower echelons of the organization, these formal regulations are followed blindly, and narrowly.

Second, red tape can be overcome by changing the passive nature of the clients' relation to the service programmes. There is considerable evidence to show that when clients have an active relationship with a social institution, this institution then loses its power to intimidate them.

We conclude, therefore:
1. No service should have more than 12 persons (all staff, including clerks). We base this figure on the fact that 12 is the largest number that can sit down in a

face-to-face discussion. It seems likely that even smaller staff size will work better still.
2. Each service should be autonomous — not subject to regulations from parent organizations outside the centre. This should be emphasized by physical autonomy. In order to be physically autonomous, each service should have an area which is entirely under its own jurisdiction; including access to some public thoroughfare, and complete physical separation from other services.
3. The centre must encourage the community to formulate new service programmes on its own initiative. (The fact that this will require extensive community organization is dealt with in Pattern 4.) To give these new services full support, they must be able to take their place, along with the existing services. This requires a very loose and flexible arrangement of service areas.

These conclusions are reinforced by the very great variety of possible service programmes. As we see from the list given in the pattern statement (above) a centre could theoretically provide as many as twenty or thirty different services. The more of these services the multi-service centre can provide (consistent with the constraints of Pattern 1), the better for its clients. All the services listed above have been proposed, or implemented, in some real multi-service centre, somewhere in the country.

Arena thoroughfare (9)

Pattern

If:

There is any area in a public building where people are meant to feel free to loiter without a 'reason' (like the arena in Pattern 1)

Then:

1. There is a natural pedestrian path through the area (if possible a shortcut, with respect to the bounding sidewalk).
2. There are no steps along this path.
3. The path has the same surface material as the sidewalk it touches: the two are continuous.
4. Entrances along this path (where the path meets the bounding sidewalk) are open, if climate permits it, and at least 15 feet wide.
5. The path is lined with opportunities for involvement like displays, notices, etc.

Problem

When a building is to have a fairly open public area

within it, the following conflict develops:

1. People will not come in and use the public space if they feel they are committing themselves to use the building in some formal or regulated way.
2. People seek public spaces where they feel it is all right to be, without a specific reason.
3. If people are asked to move along or to state their reason for being in a place they will no longer use it freely.
4. Having to enter a public space through doors, corridors, changes of level, and so on, tends to keep away people who are not entering with a specific goal in mind.

The following passage from Erving Goffman, *Behavior in Public Places,* New York, 1963, pp. 56-59, describes the problem perfectly.

. . . Being present in a public place without an orientation to apparent goals outside the situation is sometimes called lolling, when position is fixed, and loitering, when some movement is entailed. Either can be deemed sufficiently improper to merit legal action. On many of our city streets, especially at certain hours, the police will question anyone who appears to be doing nothing and ask him to 'move along'. (In London, a recent court ruling established that an individual has a right to walk on the street but no legal right merely to stand on it.) In Chicago, an individual in the uniform of a hobo can loll on 'the stem', but once off this preserve he is required to look as if he were intent on getting to some business destination. Similarly, some mental patients owe their commitment to the fact that the police found them wandering on the streets at off hours without any apparent destination or purpose in mind. Lolling and loitering are often, but not always, prohibited. In societies in which cafe life is institutionalized, much permitted lolling seems to exist. Even in our own society, some toleration is given to 'lolling groups', in which participants open themselves up to any passing momentary focus of attention and decline to maintain a running conversation unless disposed to do so. These clusters of persons passing the time of day may be found on slum corners, outside small-town stores and barber shops, on the streets during clement weather, in some metropolitan wholesale clothing districts, and, paradoxically, on the courthouse lawns of some small towns.

Here it is useful to reintroduce a consideration of subordinate involvements such as reading newspapers and looking in shop windows. Because these involvements in our society represent legitimate momentary diversions from the legitimate object of going about one's

business, they tend to be employed as covers when one's objective is not legitimate, as the arts of 'tailing' suspects have made famous. When Sam Spade affects to be examining a suit in a store window, his deeper purpose is not to try to suggest that he is interested in suits but that he has the same set of purposes as a person in a public street who diverts himself for a

moment in going about his business to gaze in a window. Similarly, as an ex-bum tells us, when one's appearance and real purpose put one outside of the current behaviour setting, then a pointedly correct subordinate involvement is of the kind that is associated with these subordinate involvements.

One idiosyncrasy that he [a friend] has discovered but cannot account for is the attitude of station policemen toward book readers. After seven-thirty in the evening, in order to read a book in Grand Central or Penn Station, a person either has to wear horn-rimmed glasses or look exceptionally prosperous. Anyone else is apt to come under surveillance. On the other hand, newspaper readers never seem to attract attention and even the seediest vagrant can sit in Grand Central all night without being molested if he continues to read a paper.

In order to provide an opportunity for 'lolling', the area which is to be public must be a direct continuation of the public sidewalk. There must be no breaks in continuity which might suggest that this space is

private, regulated territory. Hence, specifically: The surface must be continuous with the sidewalk, made of the same material. There must be no steps from the public sidewalk into this space. If there is any change in level, it should be a continuous ramp. There must be no doors between the public sidewalk and the space. If climate control is essential, this should be provided by air-curtains. The openings must be large enough to create a 'public' space — hence at least 15 feet across.

Further, if the space is a dead end, people may feel inhibited from exploring it, since a venture into it marks them clearly as 'interested persons'. To overcome this difficulty, the space must have at least two openings, one at each end, so that it can be used as a through passage by people who are curious. It will then give them the opportunity to explore it, while seeming to take a walk for some other purpose.

This effect will be enhanced if the area is so placed that it provides people with a natural shortcut. They will then go through it for pure convenience, and will need no excuse whatever for being there.

Finally, the path must be lined with excuses for involvement. (See the last two paragraphs of the Goffman passage.)

All services off arena (13)

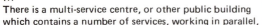

Pattern

If:

There is a multi-service centre, or other public building which contains a number of services, working in parallel,

Then:

1. There is a floor clearly identified as the *main floor*.
2. Each service has all its interview space on the main floor (even though back-up personnel may be working on other floors).
3. On the main floor, all the services open off a common waiting area (the arena, if Pattern 4 holds).
4. Each service has approximately equal frontage on this waiting arena, typically 10-20 feet.
5. If the service has a receptionist, she must be directly visible and accessible from the arena.

Problem

This pattern is based on the following demands:

1. The members of the community regard the services themselves as the most important part of the multi-service centre.
2. Since the services are intended to operate in parallel, no one service or group of services should dominate the others.
3. In order to make the referral process successful, it must be very easy to get from one service to another.
4. The success of multi-service requires that people be aware of *all* the services available in the building.
5. Multi-service is improved when the interviewers of one service are in touch with interviewers of other services.

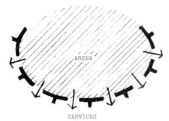

ARENA

SERVICES

In more detail:

1. Since the members of the community regard the services themselves as the most important part of the service centre, they are not willing to let these services fade into the background.

This sentiment was clearly expressed by members of the Hunts Point community in subcommittee meetings during 1967-68.

The services must therefore occupy the main floor of the centre.

2. The problem of one or several services dominating the others is based on the following observations:

(a) People using the public building tend to associate it with the kinds of activity they see as they enter.

(b) Those activities taking up the most space on the ground floor tend to catch a user's eye first.

Once one service dominates others, the principle of multi-service becomes diluted; the centre appears more like a two-service or three-service centre; weak services get shuffled to the back, and they become weaker.

These observations suggest that, each service should be on the main floor, and that no one service should have more public frontage than another.

3. The whole idea of multi-service hinges on the possibility of referrals from one service to another. This is simple in theory. In practice, unfortunately, many clients who are referred from one service to another, do not follow through on the referral.

In a follow-up study of referrals in Oakland, Gene Bernardi found that 55.6% of all persons referred did not go to the place they were referred to. (Gene Bernardi, 'Preliminary Evaluation of Neighborhood Organization Programs — Individual Contact and Referral Activity', Department of Human Resources, City of Oakland, California, 1967, Table V.)

This probably happens because it seems like too much trouble, the service is far away, hard to reach, the client does not want to go through the whole thing over again, etc. He will be much more likely to follow through on the referral if the service in question is right there, on the same floor; the person referring him can point directly at it, or take him over and introduce him.

Again, that part of the services where the interviewers work, should be on the main floor; and all the services should be visible from any one of the services.

4. The concept of multi-service must come to have meaning in the mind's eye of the client. There is some evidence to indicate that this rarely happens in service centres today. Gene Bernardi interviewed clients waiting for service at the East Oakland MSC.

Four of the five persons interviewed could not name any services the centre offered other than the one they were waiting for; the fifth person was a 'veteran' at the centre, having been there many times, and could name all the services offered. (The East Oakland Centre offers four services, none of which are clearly marked and visible to the client as he enters and as he waits.)

(The Kirschner study, *op. cit.,* pp. 25 and 45, also illustrates this point.) To help solve this problem there should be a common waiting room for all services; all service programmes should open off this waiting area; and the essential activities of information giving, reception, interviewing, etc., for each service, should be immediately visible. There is then some hope that clients will get to know the other services.

5. Inter-service communication between staff interviewers must be fluid. Clients get better help with their problems when staff members from various agencies are able to coordinate their efforts, and deal with the problem on a 'case' basis. In theory this is obvious, but in practice it has been a very difficult relationship to achieve. (Kirschner *op. cit.,* p. 34. p. 44 and Perlman and Jones, *op. cit.,* p. 34.)

Good integration of services thus seems to depend to some extent on open and informal lines of communication among staff interviewers throughout the centre.

It is hard to know why this kind of communication has been so difficult to achieve in practice, and how physical organization might help. It seems clear that convenient places for informal contact among staff members would help. But here we are looking more for sources of on-the-job coordination. Intuition tells us that a staff member is most likely to be in touch with other staff members who work near him, and on the same floor.

Thus all interviewers should be located on one floor off a common space. (The earlier part of this pattern says this floor should be the ground floor and that the common space is the waiting area.) If any service needs more space than it can have on the main floor, the clerical staff should move onto another floor, with some convenient vertical connection between them and their ground floor counterpart.

This pattern enhances inter-service communication among interviewers, at the expense of intra-service communication between interviewers and clerical staff. It is true that this is an unusual step, and that the individual services may try to resist it. In defence, we must point out that the communication between services is, *from the point of view of multi-service,* more important functionally than the communication between interviewers and clerical staff within a given service.

Free waiting (14)

Pattern

If:

There is any large institution where clients have to wait for appointments and interviews (this includes hospitals, medical centres, multi-purpose centres, offices of various types, government agencies, the faculty areas of university departments, etc.).

Then:

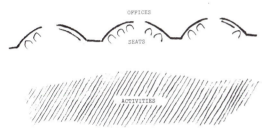

Designate each of the rooms where an interview is to take place, as an 'office'.
We require the following:
1. Immediately outside every office, within sight of its door, there are seats. The exact number of seats depends on the average number of people waiting at any one time, plus a safety factor. The safety factor must reflect the idiosyncrasies of waiting fluctuation for the particular institution.
2. Within view of these seats, there are exhibits of material relevant to the subjects which are most usually discussed in the office interviews.
3. The exhibit and seating areas are directly connected to a larger open area called the waiting activities area. The activities in this area will vary from institution to institution. In a multi-service centre they might include a public discussion arena, and pool tables. In a medical centre they might include a swimming pool, a coffee counter, and exercising equipment. This area is not exclusively for use of people waiting for appointments. *Though its use may be restricted, it is also open to people not waiting for appointments.*

4. The waiting activities areas are equipped with a public address system, so that a person waiting can be paged when the interviewer is ready.
5. Each interviewer can speak directly into the public address system through his own telephone.

Problem

All large institutions with busy professionals subject their clients to endless waiting. The client is usually forced to sit in some waiting room, reading old copies of *Reader's Digest* and *Life*. From the client's point of view this waiting is almost always unpleasant. This problem arises in the following way:
The interviewers have to squeeze as many interviews as possible into a busy schedule, and cannot afford to be kept waiting between interviews. For this reason interviews are always scheduled very tightly.
At the same time, some interviews take longer than others, and the exact length of any one interview is unpredictable.
This means that clients will inevitably be kept waiting. There is no way of making appointments which can overcome this difficulty.
Further, since people never know exactly when their turn will come, but must be on hand at the very second the previous interview is finished, they cannot even take a stroll or sit outside. They are forced to sit in the narrow confine of the waiting room, waiting their turn.
Yet, people get bored and tense sitting and waiting with nothing to do. If they are nervous about the problem to be discussed in the interview, the longer they wait, the more nervous they are apt to become. Psychologically, waiting is also demoralizing. Nobody wants to wait at somebody else's beck and call.
Evidence for the deadening effect of waiting comes from Scott Briar's study, 'Welfare From Below': Recipients' Views of the Public Welfare System', in Jacobus Tenbroek, (Ed.), *The Law and the Poor*, p. 52, San Francisco, 1966. We all know that time seems to pass more slowly when we are bored or anxious or restless. Briar found that people waiting in welfare agencies always thought they had been waiting for longer than they really had. Some of them overestimated their waiting time as much as four times. Although 'applicants rarely have to wait more than thirty to forty-five minutes to see the intake social worker', they perceived the wait to have been anywhere from forty-five minutes to two hours. For most people the best possible antidote for the waiting feeling is to get involved in something interesting which has nothing to do with waiting. *For this reason, there must be waiting areas within*

which various activities are available. The activities will vary from institution to institution. In a multi-service centre, the public arena, the child care centre, the pool tables, the TV and checkers lounge, are all examples of activities which qualify as waiting area activities. *Displays relevant to the subject of the forthcoming interview also provide clients with something to do while they are waiting.*
People feel less bored waiting, when they are able to watch other people doing things. They spend hours watching a skating rink, watching people going by on a busy street, watching children playing, watching a construction site. Even if the people waiting do not participate in the activities described above, these activities will still provide them with something to watch.
In order to boost the number of people taking part in these activities, the activity area should be open to other people, besides those who are waiting.
It is clear from the above, that the activity area will be useless unless people feel free to go there without worrying about the possibility of missing their turn or losing their place in line. *There must therefore be a public address system in the activity area.* Since the activity area will be fairly noisy, the public address will not disturb its atmosphere.
The interviewer cannot afford to waste time finding clients who are not waiting at his door. Each interviewer must therefore have direct access to the PA system (preferably through his own phone).
There will always be some clients who are especially anxious about missing their turn or being forgotten. These clients usually want to keep watch over the door of the interviewer, both so that they can see when he is ready, and also to make sure that they are seen by him. *There must therefore be seats immediately outside each interviewer's door, each seat visible from the door.* For these clients, the problem of boredom and confinement cannot be solved by going out into the activity area. *However, since watching people helps, each seat must command a view of the activity area.* Above all, the seats must not be enclosed in 'blind' areas typical of waiting rooms today.
In summary then, people who are waiting must be free to do what they want. If they want to sit outside the interviewer's door, they can. If they want to get up and take a stroll, or play a game of pool, or have a cup of coffee, or watch other people, without having to fear that they are losing their place in line, they can.

155

Overview of services (15)

Pattern

If:

There is any public building with various departments which service the public

Then:

1. All departments open off a common space, and all entrances into this common space have sight lines to each of the departments.
2. Each department should have its name written near its entrance in large letters.
3. The departments should be located below the level of the building entrances, so that the sight lines from the eye of a person entering to the signs carrying the names of the departments, are ten degrees below the horizontal.

Problem

A public building deals to a large extent with people who do not know the exact relative locations and internal contents of its various departments. *It must be very easy for each person coming into the building to become immediately oriented in it.*

Further, the person who is coming to the building may not know the way in which the departments are categorized, or even if he knew what service he needed, he may not know the name given to the service in this particular building. (Thus, what is called 'Job Counselling' in one multi-service centre, may be called 'Urban League' in another, and 'Manpower' in yet another.) *It must be easy for someone to find what he needs, even if he doesn't know the exact name.*

Sometimes, a person is unaware of the existence of a certain service — a service that would be useful to him if he knew about it. Further, even though he will not usually want to use all the available services, he should know them all so that he is confident he is not missing anything he might need. *It must be clear to people what all the services available in the building are.*

It is possible that these problems might be solved by a directory of the kind found in the lobby of many public buildings and office buildings. However, directories often leave unclear what each service is, and just where in the building it is, even after it has been clearly identified.

In order to solve these problems properly, the person who comes into the building, must immediately be confronted by all the departments — this means actually seeing the entrances to all the services, together with a clear and simple sign identifying them.
This makes it clear that the services should be fanned out in such a way that all of them are directly visible from the main entrances.

This specifies the arrangement in plan. To guarantee effective visibility, the arrangement in section also needs to be carefully specified.

It is well known, informally, that we see an array of buildings better if we approach them slightly from above. People get a better view of something when looking down at it, than when they are looking at it on the level or looking up at it. There are two reasons.
1. The normal line of sight for a person standing on a horizontal plane, is 10 degrees below the horizontal. (Henry Dreyfuss, *The Measure of Man,* Chart F, New York, 1959.) It is also known that looking *up* at things is tiring. This has been measured only in the extreme case (Kinzey and Sharp state that looking up at an angle greater than 20° above the horizontal is tiring, *Environmental Technologies in Architecture,* p.354, New York, 1963.), but it seems likely that any deviation from the line 10 degrees below the horizontal is relatively uncomfortable according to its magnitude.
2. When a person looks straight ahead, fixating on the horizontal, his field of vision extends about twice as

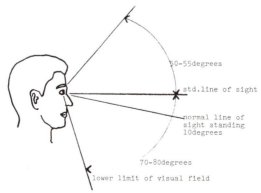

50-55degrees

std.line of sight

normal line of sight standing 10degrees

70-80degrees

lower limit of visual field

far *below* the horizontal as it does *above* the horizontal. This supplements the first effect. It is shown on the diagram below. (The source again is Dreyfuss, Chart F.)

Both these effects make it clear that a person entering a building, will be able to see the various services and their signs most easily, *if they are more than 10 degrees below the horizon for him.* Of course the person has to see over the heads of others, so that the signs must be at least 6 feet from the floor in front of it.

Necklace of community projects (16)

Pattern

If:

A multi-service centre has any street frontage which is not either entrance space, public open space, or transparent glass showing interior public space

Then:

1. With the exceptions stated, the building should be surrounded, at ground level, by a necklace of community projects.
2. These community projects should be individually built, and built after the superstructure of the multi-service centre itself.
3. The ground floor frontage zone committed to these projects, should be given a roof, a floor slab, and conduit boxes in the rear wall, at the time the superstructure of the multi-service centre is built; so that when the time comes to build the individual community projects, they can make use of these elements.

Problem

The physical outside of an MSC makes a strong impression in the community.

If it is recognizable as standard office space, it will convey the message of administration and red tape.
Various experiences lead us to believe that any office building which looks like an office building (i.e. equally spaced standard windows; concrete, steel, and glass exterior, etc.) placed among residential buildings in a community creates the impression of disrespect for the community. (See, for instance, recent statements by Harlem inhabitants, as reported in Blyden Jackson, 'Building Harlem Down', *The Guardian,* March, 1968), and many committee members of the Hunts Point Multiservice Centre made similar comments. On the positive side: Art Schroeder, Neighborhood Organization Director in the East Oakland Service Center says:

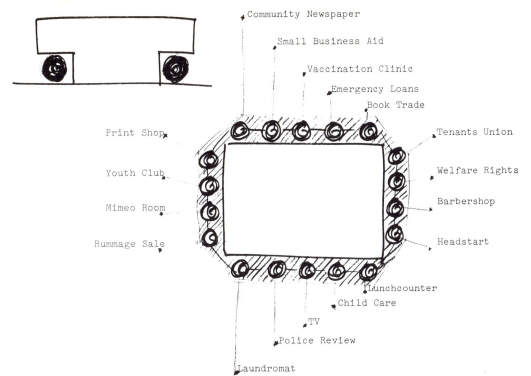

Community Newspaper

Small Business Aid

Vaccination Clinic

Emergency Loans

Book Trade

Print Shop

Tenants Union

Youth Club

Welfare Rights

Mimeo Room

Barbershop

Rummage Sale

Headstart

Lunchcounter

Child Care

TV

Police Review

Laundromat

It is especially important that they be privately built; if they are not, they will seem standardized, and impersonal. But this is clearly difficult. The individuals and groups in the community who try to build community projects will be very short of funds. In order to make it as easy as possible for them to build space, the most expensive elements should be provided in advance. These are foundation, floor, roof and services. It therefore makes sense to create an overhang, with roof and floor slab complete, and with electric conduit boxes in the wall.

Self-service (21)

Pattern

If:
There is any multi-service centre

THE MISSION REBELS

Then

1. The multi-service centre contains a *self-service area.*
2. The self-service area contains all the basic information required by people who need help. It includes information about currently available jobs, information about the legality of eviction, the procedures to be followed in divorce cases, the location of currently available apartments, citizen rights under welfare law, schedules for training classes, teaching machines for skills like typing and shorthand, etc. This information may be in the form of card catalogues, books, pamphlets, displays, etc., according to its nature.
3. Where the centre is used by people from two language groups, as at Hunts Point, all information is in both languages.
4. The self-service area is at the centre of gravity of the waiting area, and transparent so that its inside is visible from all points in the waiting area.
5. The self-service area is continuous with at least

In order to attract people who might be potential community organization members, the Center should be spacious, with outdoor waiting space, with trees, garden, grass, and a proper combination of sunning and shade places.

Benny Parrish, Community Organizer, formerly with the California Committee for Community Development, says:

Our office was like a house — the thing I liked — it was like a living room.

The Kirschner Report (*op. cit.,* p. 31) says:

The casual, informal atmosphere of small neighbourhood centres can be disarming and hence appealing to poor people who are uncomfortable in formally organized settings. This is why large, bureaucratically organized centres tend to be self-defeating in terms of outreach. The forbidding appearance of such centres makes them little different from the central offices of traditional service agencies.

How can the building be made less bureaucratic, less oppressive, less disrespectful to the community? To begin with, the internal operations of the centre must, itself, have these qualities. If not, any such appearance would be fake. Assuming that the internal operations of the multi-service centre *is* in fact personal, respectful of the community, non-bureaucratic, and non-oppressive, then how can the building be organized so that these qualities are visible from the outside. One clue may be this: Red tape is seen as the opposite of *small informal* organization, *private* ownership, *simple direct* relationships. (Alvin W Gouldner, 'Red Tape as a Social Problem' in Robert K Merton's *Reader in Bureaucracy,* pp. 410-418, 1952.) In order to make it clear to people outside the building that the multi-service centre is not subject to red tape nonsense, the outside of the building, at ground floor, should be entirely made of community owned projects, which are small in scale, *privately* built, *individually* accessed, *not* under the aegis of *formal* receptionists.

part of the service area.

6. There are no receptionists or intake workers located at the entrance to the self-service area. A person can enter the self-service area and browse there for as long as he wants, without having to explain himself to any receptionist or intake worker.

7. Within the self-service area, there is an advice area. This advice area contains at least one easily accessible assistant, visible from the self-service area, and obviously on hand to help people find the information they want, or to answer questions about it.

Problem

Most service programmes today effectively perpetuate the structural asymmetry of the dole — the great bureaucratic hand reaching down and dropping a few crumbs into the pockets of the poor. If service programmes ever hope to break the chains of poverty, this structural asymmetry, with all its psychological implications, must be destroyed. ('The welfare system . . . imposes restrictions that encourage continued dependency on welfare and undermine self-respect . . . Drastic reforms are required if it is to help people free themselves from poverty.' Report of the *National Advisory Commission on Civil Disorders,* p. 457, 1968.)

One way to help break down the traditional service posture is to offer as much service as is practically possible on a *self*-service basis, with the centre seen as a resource to aid people making their way through the self-service process. Consider the following analogy: In a supermarket we walk around and select the goods we need, and if we have any questions we ask the grocer; it would be offensive for a grocer to say to a man entering the market, 'Sit down, tell me a bit about yourself and your family, and I'll make out your grocery list.'

Of course this analogy does not hold completely. Many services require technical insights that only trained personnel can be expected to master. But more often than not the service process is made more complicated than in truth it needs to be. We are all familiar with the way large bureaucracies tend to overhandle information, shuffling endless papers, filing endless forms.

This red tape process must be limited to its barest essentials; the key image of the service centre must be as a community self-service institution. Insistence on the self-service ideal means that the actual services that agency renders be made perfectly clear to the community; what an agency can and cannot do, and under what conditions, must become perfectly explicit.

Much of the information relevant to problems — phone numbers about jobs, time and place of job training classes, legal questions concerning eviction, location of apartment rentals — can quite easily be made available to the public in the form of written information and signs. When an agency worker holds this information, it contributes to the illusion that the client is a lowly person not capable of understanding the world, while the agency worker is a superior person who knows what is best for the client. This is precisely the kind of experience a poor person needs least; rather, he is looking for the kind of experience that tells him that initiative, when forcefully exercised, *pays off.* This experience, and not the bureaucratic dole, must be available at every chance, throughout the centre.

When the centre opens it is likely that only a few services will be able to adopt the self-service format. However, it must be made clear that a major responsibility for the staff will be to put ever more services into the self-service format; this thought must be expressed and encouraged by the organization of the building.

What evidence is there that a self-service programme can help solve the problem of the bureaucratic dole? Some people argue that even the most enlightened self-service programme will fail when it is offered to the poor; these people argue that the poor have been on the bottom for so long, their initiative so often unrewarded, that a self-service programme could never really get started, it is an unworkable ideal. And it follows quite logically from this position that the job of the staff, no matter how liberal, is to take the poor by the hand and lead them through the service centre paces — like the grocer presuming to write up a shopping list for each of his customers. No matter that this attitude begins as good faith; it always ends with the petty bureaucrat who believes that the function of poverty is to test his generosity. Sartre has expressed this mentality perfectly: 'They are the uncomplaining poor; they hug the walls. I spring forward, I slip a small coin into their hand, and, most important, I present them with a fine egalitarian smile.'

There is some evidence to suggest that in fact the best way to extend service to the poor is simply to make the service openly available, in a setting where people can discuss their needs and the usefulness of certain services with members of their community; and then ask questions and guidance from a resource group of competent technocrats:

A. *The Mission Rebels,* a group organized to support

the needs and solve the problems of young people in San Francisco's poverty-striken Mission District, is notoriously successful; it is based completely on the self-service principle; the Rebels have turned down help which had the flavour of the bureaucratic dole associated with it; they demand that help be given on their own terms, when and where they need it; their motto is, 'We can do it ourselves'. ('Kids say it isn't as important to come here every night as to know something is here — that it isn't an agency but that Mission Rebels is *theirs,'* Rev. James contends.)

B. In his definitive paper, 'The Power of the Poor', Warren C Haggstrom, shows that it is the *lack* of self-service type programmes, with their associated attitudes and institutional structures, that keep the poor psychologically powerless, their needs consistently unmet. (See Ferman, Kornbluh, and Hober, [Eds.], *Poverty in America,* p. 315, Michigan, 1965.)

C. In 1964, Students for a Democratic Society began a number of projects aimed at organizing low-income people. Two kinds of project philosophy emerged: There were those who assumed they knew exactly what the poor needed, and tried to organize around these assumed needs — such a project was JOIN, Jobs Or Income Now; secondly, there were those who assumed that the process of defining a community's needs and the programmes required to solve them could only come from a community-instigated process of self-service — this was the philosophy of NCUP, Newark Community Union Project. Of the two approaches the NCUP approach was by far the most successful; and it turned out that the kinds of services that the community selected were quite different from what the organizers had expected. NCUP and similar projects have become institutions in a handful of poor communities across the United States; the JOIN approach has never established itself so strongly. (See Tod Gitlin, 'The Radical Potential of the Poor', *International Socialist Journal,* pp. 861-886, December 1967.)

Also, the fact that NCUP has, in recent months, outlived its usefulness is a tribute to its success. It put people into the mood of doing things for themselves, and once this mood found its indigenous expression there was no need for the NCUP staff to hang around.

D. The 'Kerner Report' on civil disorder calls for a thorough overhaul of service programmes. As a basic strategy the report calls for the elimination of 'features that cause dependency'. If taken seriously, this would mean the dissolution of special service programmes altogether, replaced by pure self-service operations, like the income supplementation plan. (See Report of the *National Advisory Commission on Civil Disorder, op. cit.,* p. 462.)

One piece of evidence comes from a statement written by two doctors; it refers to the Peckham Health Centre, a community health centre which they ran for many years:

The 'self-service' aimed at throughout the buildings is a primary need of the biologist. A healthy individual does not like to be waited on; he prefers the freedom of independent action which accompanies circumstances so arranged that he can do for himself what he wants to do as and when he wants to do it. The popularity in tube stations of the moving-staircase compared with the lifts attests to this. It is not merely speed, but the possibility the moving-staircase gives for independent individual action as opposed to collective action dependent upon an attendant, that is significant. Servants tend to bind and circumscribe action, for their presence makes inevitable the establishment of a routine that only too often rebounds upon their employers.

Self-service has the merit of engendering responsibility and of enhancing awareness as well as of increasing freedom of action. As unhampered in the Centre as in their own houses, the members are free to improvise to suit all occasions as they arise. As the embryo newly lodged in the womb begins to build its cells into the substance of the uterine wall, so each new family emboldened to strike out for itself in this living social medium can add its own quota of 'organization' to the Centre — the outstanding characteristic of which is the abiding fluidity of its constitution, permitting continuous growth and the functional evolution of its society from day to day and from year to year.

So in the Centre there are no attendants, no waitresses. This means that where possible all equipment has had to be designed to be handled by the members themselves. In the main the furnishings are light stackable tables and chairs which can be moved from place to place as occasion demands; the cafeteria utensils also are stackable and devised to be taken and replaced by the members. These are seeming trifles, but they have their far-reaching significance in the type of social organization that is growing up in the building. (Innes H Pearse and Lucy H Crocker, The Peckham Experiment, *pp. 74-75, New Haven, 1946.)*

Having established a functional case for the self-service concept, we now argue that the self-service facility should be part of the waiting area, and continuous with some part of the service area.

1. People will not come to the centre expecting to use the self-service facility; it is a new concept in service centre programmes and people will not be familiar with it.

2. When people have to wait for an appointment they usually try to find something to do to pass time. (See Pattern 14.)

3. People waiting will not leave the waiting area for more than a minute or two for fear that they will miss their call.

Taken together, these three facts suggest that self-service should be a part of waiting. In the beginning, people will come to the centre primarily to use the agencies; inevitably they will have to wait for their appointments. If the self-service facility is in the waiting area and recognizably open to casual use, people will use it to pass time, and hence become familiar with the self-service system.

Finally, the success of self-service is unpredictable. If it is highly successful, one would hope that the whole centre might become more and more oriented towards self-service. If this happens the service will need to expand.

If self-service doesn't work, or if it turns out that people in self-service need more help and advice from staff members — then the self-service area will need to be more nearly a part of other services.

In both cases, it should be continuous with at least one service area.

Pedestrian density in public places (22)

Pattern

If:
There is a public place which is intended to be 'full of life', and the estimated mean number of people in the place at any given moment is P,

Then:
The area of this place should be between 150P and 300P square feet.

Problem

Many of the public places built by architects and planners in recent years, though intended as lively piazzas, are in fact deserted and dead.

Of course one cannot say categorically, that the number of people per square foot *controls* the apparent liveliness of the place — other factors, including the nature of the land use round the edge, contribute to it.

Another issue is the grouping of the people and what they are doing. Moving people, especially if they are making noise adds to the liveliness. A small group, attracted to a couple of folk singers in a plaza at the University of California, gave much more life to the plaza than a similar number, sunning on the grass. However, the number of square feet per person does give a reasonably crude estimate of the liveliness.

Informal observation shows the following figures for various public places in and around San Francisco:

Golden Gate Plaza, noon:	>1000	Dead
Fresno Mall:	100	Alive
Sproul Plaza, daytime:	150	Alive
Sproul Plaza, evening:	2000	Dead
Union Square, central part:	600	Half-dead

One observer's subjective estimates of the liveliness of these places, are given in the right hand column. Although the subjective estimates are clearly open to question, they suggest the following rule of thumb: if there are more than 300 square feet per person, the area begins to be dead. If there are 150 square feet per person, the area is very lively.

Appendix:
Since this pattern applies to multi-service centre arenas, we now give the upper limit on the arena size, as a function of N, the total population in the target area served by the multi-service centre. We know from the arguments presented in Pattern 3, that a centre serving a population of N persons, will require about .0005N service interviewers. Since each interviewer sees about 4 people per day, and a typical interview lasts about 30 minutes, the number of people being interviewed at any given moment is about .00012N, and the number of people waiting for interviews will be about the same. Besides the services, other MSC activities draw people into the arena. They include people coming to classes and meetings; people using self-service; people coming in to see the director and community organizers; people being interviewed for jobs in the multi-service centre; people using community projects; people using recreational facilities, etc. In fact people coming in for these ancillary activities most likely equal those coming into the MSC for services. We guess that the people in the arena at any given moment may be twice the number of people waiting, thus P = .00025N. This gives an arena size of 300P or .07N square feet.

Entrance shape (23)

Pattern
___

If:
There is any main entrance to a public building

Then:
Either, the entrance projects strongly beyond the building front. *Or,* the entrance is set into a deep, flared, recess. *Or,* some combination of the above. Although the heart of the pattern lies in these relation-

ships there are many important refinements which are, for the moment, too hard to pin down. The relative colour of the entrance, the light and shade immediately around it, the presence of mouldings and ornaments, may all play a part. Above all, it is important that the entrance be strongly differentiated from its immediate surroundings.

Problem
___
A person approaching the building must be able to see the entrance clearly. Yet, many of the people approaching the building are walking along the front of the building, and parallel to it. Their angle of approach is acute. From this angle, many entrances are hardly visible.
An entrance will be visible from an acute angled approach if:
1. The entrance sticks out beyond the building line.
2. The entrance is so deeply recessed, that the void is visible from this angle. In this case, it will help further, if the recess if flared, so that the far side of the recess shows up as a source of differentiation.
3. The building front flares back gently, and the entrance sticks out into the recess so created. This will be useful, if the building is built all the way forward to the building line.

Building stepped back from arena (25)

Pattern
___

If:
There is a public courtyard where people congregate,

Then:
The buildings around the courtyard are raked back at angles of less than 40 degrees:

Problem
___
If the buildings around an open court are too close around it, then people do not feel comfortable in the middle of the space; they will not stop there, sitting or standing, but will move to the edge instead. This makes the space useless as a meeting place — no one will use it.
This much corresponds to common experience and intuition. But in order to solve the problem, we must be able precisely to specify under *which* circumstances people feel oppressed by buildings around them and under *which* circumstances they do not, and to do this, we must know *why* people feel oppressed.
We conjecture that people feel uneasy when high buildings surround them, essentially because, consciously or unconsciously, they are afraid things will fall on them or be thrown down, afraid because they are threatened by the possibility of something hovering above them, and self-conscious about people looking down on them.
If this conjecture were true, we should expect that the feeling that a building is threatening should come into play most forcibly when there are parts of the building too high to be seen clearly, but placed so that their 'presence' is felt, towering above. This will happen if the building rises above the field of clear vision.
It is known that a man normally fixates about 10° below the horizon, and that his visual field extends about 50° above his line of sight. (Henry Dreyfuss, *op. cit.,* Chart F.) His clear vision therefore extends

about 40° above the horizontal. Anything more than 40° above the horizontal, from where he stands, will be out of view — but 'felt'. It therefore seems reasonable to expect that buildings become oppressive if they subtend more than 40° to the horizontal, in an open court.

There is a second argument which suggests that a stepped-back court may help to solve the problem, irrespective of its angle.

If the conjecture stated is correct, then the feeling of oppression and threat is probably caused, at least in part, by the fact that things can fall down out of windows and off roofs. (This might explain why a deep canyon in the mountains, though sombre, is not nearly as threatening as a deep well-like court in the heart of a building, lined with windows.) If the building is stepped back, then things cannot fall out of windows or off the roof, and people who lean out of windows will not be able to look down *onto* the people below. The threatening feeling should vanish almost entirely.

Since so little is known about the phenomenon, we shall for the time being assume that our conjecture is correct. The pattern is based on the conclusions which follow from the conjecture. *It must be emphasized, though, that there are no sound theoretical or empirical grounds for the conjecture.* It may well turn out that the phenomenon of oppression is caused in some entirely different manner.

Short corridors (31)

Pattern

If:
There is any building with rooms opening off corridors

Then:
No straight stretch or corridor has more than 5 or 6 doors opening off it along one side, and its length is no more than about 5 times its width.
For most buildings this means, in effect, no straight stretch of corridor more than about 50 feet long.

Problem

This problem is based on the following conflict:
1. In buildings where a number of rooms are to share a circulation path, it is common practice to string the rooms along a straight corridor. This is deemed the technically efficient solution, since it minimizes circulation space and reduces the construction costs of 'turning corners'.
2. However, the intuition persists that, from a human point of view, long corridors with many rooms off them are dys-functional. People dislike them; they represent bureaucracy and monotony. Let us try to make this intuition more specific. What evidence is there that long corridors contribute to human uneasiness?

We refer first to a questionnaire distributed by Murray Silverstein in 1965. The sample was small (12) and limited to college graduates, so the results are, at best, provocative. The questionnaire asked people to describe those elements in buildings that contributed most to impersonal and institutional feelings. Subjects reported experiences with many different building types: army barracks, dormitories, office buildings, government agencies, and so forth. The most recurring theme in their remarks was the unpleasantness associated with long corridors. One person wrote, '. . . long corridors set the scene for everything bad about modern architecture.' (This material is unpublished. For a more detailed discussion see Sim Van der Ryn and Murray Silverstein, *Dorms at Berkeley: An Environmental Analysis,* Centre for Planning and Development Research, Berkeley, 1967, pp. 23-24, 62-63.)

Similarly, Russell Barton asserts that the long corridor condition contributes to 'institutional neurosis' — a condition wherein building inhabitants become less lively, unmotivated, and their concentration span limited. (Russell Barton, *Institutional Neurosis,* New York, 1959.)

Finally, we refer to a study by M Spivack on the non-conscious effects of long hospital corridors on perception, communication and behaviour:

Four examples of long mental-hospital corridors are examined . . . It is concluded that such spaces interfere with normal verbal communication due to their characteristic acoustical properties. Optical phenomena common to these passageways obscure the perception of the human figure and face, and distort distance perception. Paradoxical visual cues produced by one tunnel created interrelated, cross-sensory illusions involving room size, distance, walking

161

speed and time. Observations of patient behaviour suggest the effect of narrow corridors upon anxiety is via the penetration of the personal space envelope. (M Spivack, 'Sensory Distortion in Tunnels and Corridors', Hospital and Community Psychiatry, 18, No. 1, January, 1967.)

All of this evidence is speculative; none of it proves the intuition. However, it is extremely suggestive. If we assume the intuition is correct, then the question arises: *how can we establish an upper limit on corridor length?* Evidence suggests that there is a definite cognitive breakpoint between things seen as 'reasonable' circulation spaces, and things seen as 'long corridors'. We shall try to define the point where this change in perception occurs.

The following two results are highly suggestive: It is known that when a person sees four or five regularly spaced objects of the same kind, he perceives them as a *unit.* He can judge their number without counting them. When the number of objects goes above these numbers, he no longer sees them as forming a unit. He now sees them as a *collection.* If he wants to estimate their number, he has to count them, one by one, in sequence. At this stage, it seems likely that the feeling of monotony and repetition sets in. In its most extreme form, we might say that the perceiver, faced with a 'collection', sees the objects as digits. If the objects were offices along a corridor, then the perceiver would begin to see the offices, and their inhabitants, as digits. (G Miller, 'The Magical Number Seven, Plus or Minus Two: Some Limits on Our Capacity for Processing Information', in D Beardslee, and M Wertheimer [Eds.], *Readings in Perception,* p. 103, New York, 1958; also E L Kaufman, M W Lord, T W Reese and J Volkmann, 'The Discrimination of Visual Number', *American Journal of Psychology,* 62, pp. 498-525, 1949.)

Another experiment, done by the authors, is also relevant. It was found that, in the perception of rectangles, there is a definite cognitive break between that class of rectangles with ratio 5 : 1 or less, and that class of rectangles with ratio greater than 5 : 1. Rectangles from the first class are seen *as rectangles* with a specific proportion. Rectangles from the second class are seen merely as 'long thin things'. The first of these results suggest that there may be a clear cognitive distinction between corridors which have five or less equally spaced doors, and those which have more than five.

The second result suggests that there may be a clear cognitive distinction between rectangles (and hence, perhaps, corridors) which have a ratio of less

than 5 : 1, and those which have a ratio greater than 5 : 1.
(As it happens, both of these breakpoints coincide approximately: given standard corridor widths, and standard office sizes, they both make a distinction between corridors less than 40-50 feet long and those more than 40-50 feet long.) Since common sense indicates that a corridor becomes unpleasant when it has five or more equally spaced doors down one side, and when it is more than five times as long as its width, it is very likely that this breakpoint is the one we are looking for.

The assertions upon which this pattern rests await experimental investigation. However, we wish to note here that even if research corroborates the assertions, the original conflict still remains unsolved. Part of the reason that buildings are now built with long corridors, is because it is cheaper. Even if we can establish the unpleasantness of long corridors on a sound empirical basis, it still remains to find a cheap way of making buildings with short corridors.

Street niches (34)

Pattern

If:
There is any building, open to the public along a pedestrian path, where it is hoped people will stop, linger and become familiar with the building's services, before they actually enter,

Then:
Along the building's frontage, where it meets the pedestrian path, should be a series of niches with the following characteristics:
1. The niches are set just off the sidewalk; in effect they are extensions of the sidewalk.
2. The niches display the service that the building offers; they contain display windows and/or panels for posting displays.
3. The niches provide relief from the pedestrian path: thus they may have seats, radiant heat, a different surface texture; anything that seems appropriate to the immediate neighbourhood.
4. The niches are at least 5 feet deep.
The exact number and size of the niches will vary according to the amount and nature of the building's display needs.

Problem

A public building has a curious relationship to the land around it, quite different from the relationship

between a private building and the land which surrounds it. A private building is distinct and separate from the land around it; the building is private and the land is public. But a public building is public; it belongs to the community, just as the land around it also belongs to the community. The wall which connects it to the land outside, instead of being a barrier, should be more like a seam; its form should unite the two, so that they become clearly visible as interlocking parts of a single extended community domain.

Though there is almost certainly psychological truth in this idea, it is not in itself a sufficient basis for a pattern. We now present a rather more detailed analysis, based on the insight just stated, yet expressed in detailed functional terms.

We know that people like to 'window shop' as they walk along the street. When given the chance, *people will spend a long time exploring a building's merchandise before they decide whether or not to enter.* But as long as it is done from the sidewalk, window shopping is rarely more than a short glance: *There is a countervailing tendency for people not to linger while they are moving along a city path.*

The conflict between these two tendencies may be resolved by deep niches, set into the building, along the pedestrian path. Because they are both inside the building, and outside it, people feel freer to linger in them.

The picture shows a deep display niche off a San Francisco sidewalk. This kind of form truly gives people a chance to get out of the stream of movement, and look over merchandise. It was informally observed by the authors that people who enter this niche spend on the average one minute and ten seconds exploring the display before either going in or returning to the sidewalk. On the same block, where display cases front immediately on the sidewalk, people spend on the average fifteen seconds window shopping. That is, given the opportunity created by the niche, people spent almost five times more time window shopping.

There is also some evidence to show that such forms actually do help people become familiar with merchandise before they enter a building. A men's clothing shop across from Union Square in San Francisco has a T-shaped niche, like the one in the picture. This niche lets people step off the sidewalk, into a carpeted foyer, and inspect the clothing before they enter the front door. A salesman in this store compared his experience there with his experience at another store, with a more conventional display case (one facing directly onto the sidewalk). He said the difference was dramatic: merchandise put into the T-niche display was usually sold out in a week, compared with much longer time periods for similar goods displayed at the other store.

Dish-shaped arena (36)

Pattern

If:
There is any large public space used for informal social gatherings as well as public meetings

Then:
The space should be a shallow half dish with a slope of about 7%.

Problem

Public gathering places function better if people are able to see each other across the crowd. It is difficult to achieve this in an area completely flat; but a very slight slope helps tremendously. The main square in Sienna provides a classic example:
In a dense crowd of people who are all the same height, the required slope to see what is going on in front of the crowd is about 14%. This figure is arrived at by assuming that a person's eye is roughly 5 in below the top of his head, and that people in a dense crowd are close packed, 3 feet apart, thus:

However, such tight crowds are unlikely. Usually people place themselves in ways that are more random and unregimented.
We guess that a person of average height will usually be able to place himself at least 6 feet from the next person of similar height. This means that the more common instance would be:

It gives a lower limit of 7% on the slopes.
Since other needs (i.e. everyday comfort, the possibility

of bazaars or dances) require that the arena be as near to level as possible, the slope should certainly be no greater than 7%.
In conclusion, we show that the 7% figure is well below the limits of safety and convenience.
1. At what slope does a surface become uncomfortable to walk on, and dangerous for a crowd? Preferred slopes for crowded ramps given by various sources are as follows:
Henry Dreyfuss, *Measure of Man,* Whitney Library of Design, New York: 10%.
Time Saver Standards, p. 1289: 12.5%
California Building School Code: 12%
National Safety Council: 10% for wheelchairs
David Arbegast ('Steps, Ramps and Inclines', Master's Thesis, Department of Landscape Architecture, University of California, Berkeley, 1951) states that the comfort of slopes depends on the ramp's length. He measured 12 ramps of various lengths and slopes for comfort. His findings are shown on the following graph:

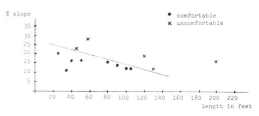

From the above graph, we see that for 100 feet lengths (the maximum likely dimension of the arena), the maximum comfortable slope is 15%.
However, David Arbegast further states (*Ibid.,* p. 51.):

Through the survey it was found that ramps give a greater sense of security if partially enclosed or contained, by walls, plant materials, etc.

Since the arena is a wide space surrounded by more space, its slope should be well below the 15%.
2. At what slope does it become uncomfortable to

stand, or sit in an ordinary chair, for long periods? Informal experiments on streets of various slopes, suggest that the upper limit for comfort is about 10%. Thus, both figures are greater than the 7% we specify.

Community wall (38)

Pattern
___

If:

There is any community space functioning as a centre or rallying point for the community

Then:

Along a major path within this community space, there is a Community Wall; this wall is characterized as follows:

1. It can be seen by the public, walking or driving through the public space.
2. It is at least the size of a standard billboard and may be as large as the entire side of one block.
3. It is surfaced with concrete or wood panels; or any other material that can take periodic repainting.
4. Parts of it are within reach of pedestrians; these parts are available for ever-changing community messages and information.

Problem
___

One of the most characteristic things about the bureaucratic society, is the fact that no man feels his complaints are legitimate concerns of society, except in those rare cases where they can be expressed in terms of law infractions.

This is especially true of poor people. Since no one listens to their complaints, they don't bother to express them, and nothing happens.

The civil rights movement has recently made it clear that when a determined, massive effort is made, to express dissatisfaction, this dissatisfaction gets results. The simplest way of stating this fact is this: pure information about dissatisfaction is a first step toward getting action. It is therefore crucially important that complaints be made public, be put on the public record. If the facts show that thousands of people are dissatisfied because some need is not being met, and these facts can be made public and self-evident, the public officials cannot *ignore* the problem for long. (See for example, 'The Roles of Intelligence Systems in Urban Systems Planning', *Journal of American Institute of Planners, 31,* No. 4, pp. 289-296, November 1965.)

But information alone will not bring action. It must be coupled with constant pressure by the public, on the institution in question.

This of course is a political task; it is a job for a staff of community organizers. The question here, however, is whether or not the physical surroundings can help this process.

In low income communities there is no device for making the volume of felt complaints public and visible, other than demonstrations by the people themselves. It is suggested here that a central and highly visible community complaint wall would help keep the mass of complaints visible; and would help the people who are struggling to rectify these conditions to maintain solidarity.

However, it seems clear that a complaint wall would have a very difficult time getting off the ground and becoming a rallying point in this country. The idea of using public buildings and billboards as 'walls' on which to state grievances is not generally acceptable: the walls are usually private property and

people write on them at risk of jail sentences. Thus, if we want a community wall to take hold, we will have to find a legitimate way of getting it off the ground.

The Wall of Respect in Chicago is one such project that has already proven itself; and we shall look to it for clues.

The Wall is the side of a typical slum building; it was turned into a mural, communicating black dignity, by local artists. The establishment and maintenance of the Wall became a source of neighbourhood solidarity. Two facts about this situation seem to be important. First, the Wall was commissioned: a small group took the initiative to begin it and see it through. Second, the complaints on the Wall were woven into a more general, artistic message.

Thus, it seems essential that, if a community wall is to become a focus for complaints and a community rallying spot, it must be initiated and maintained,

in the beginning, by a small group, and be part of a more dramatic community mural.

This suggests that the community wall be central and highly visible to the community; that it be of a material that allows constant re-painting; and that it be large enough (at least the size of a billboard) to weave notices and complaints across a 'commissioned' mural.

Pools of light (63)

Pattern
___

If:
___

There is any area which requires artificial illumination, and in which people are to be stationary — i.e., sitting, working, talking, resting — and where the average diameter of social group in the space is D feet

Then:
___

The light level should vary in such a way that there are discernible 'pools' of light.

These pools should have the following characteristics:
1. The perceived diameter of any given pool should be of the order of D feet.
2. The pools should be spaced at distances at least equal to the diameter of the pools.
3. The brightness ratio of pools/background should not exceed 40 : 1.

There is an unfortunate, but for the moment necessary, vagueness in these definitions. We do not know what stimulus properties correspond to the perceived 'boundary' of a pool of light. It must depend both on absolute brightness, and on the brightness gradient. Until this is determined, the definitions cannot help being vague.

Problem
___

Evenly distributed light fails to support the characteristics of a space as 'social' space.

In any given space, at a given moment, there are social groups of well established dimension and definite social activity. These groups may involve 1, 2, 3, 5, 10, or 100 persons — according to the occasion. We conjecture the following:
1. If such a group is within a 'pool' of light, whose size and boundaries correspond to those of the group, this will enhance the definition, cohesiveness, and even the phenomenological existence of the group.
2. If such a group is in an area of uniform illumination, so that there are no light gradients corresponding to the boundary of the group, then the definition, cohesiveness, and 'existence' of the group will be weakened.

We know of no experimental evidence which supports this conjecture directly. However, everyday experience bears it out in hundreds of ways.

Every good restaurant keeps each table as a separate pool of light, knowing that this contributes to its private and intimate ambience. In a house where family members live, a truly comfortable old chair, 'yours', has its own light, in dimmer surroundings — so that you retreat from the bustle of the family to read the paper in peace. Again, house dining tables often have a single lamp, suspended over the table — the light seems almost to act like glue for all the people sitting round the table. In larger situations the same thing seems to be true. Think of the park bench, under a solitary light, and the privacy of the world which it creates for a pair of lovers. Or, in a trucking depot, the solidarity of the group of men sipping coffee around a brightly lit coffee stand.

One on-the-spot observation supports this conjecture: at the International House, University of California, Berkeley, there is a large, dark room which is a general waiting and sitting lounge for guests and residents. During winter, at a time when the room was half dark, just dark enough for the lamps to be lit, we counted the people who sat near lamps.

There are 42 seats in the room, 12 of them are next to lamps. At the two times of observation we counted a total of 21 people sitting in the room; 13 of them chose to sit next to lamps.

These figures show that people prefer sitting near lights ($X^2 = 11.4$, significant at the 0.1% level). Yet the overall light level in the room was high enough for reading. We conclude that people do seek 'pools of light'.

One possible explanation for the phenomenon, is suggested by the experiments of Hopkinson and Longmore, who showed that small bright light sources distract the attention less than large areas which are less bright. These authors conclude that local lighting over a work table, allows the worker to pay more attention to his work than uniform background lighting does. It seems reasonable to infer that the high degree of person-to-person attention required to maintain the cohesiveness of a social group is more likely to be sustained if the group has local lighting, than if it has uniform background lighting. (See R G Hopkinson and J Longmore, 'Attention and Distraction in the Lighting of Workplaces', *Ergonomics, 2,* p.321 ff, 1959. Also reprinted in R G Hopkinson, *Lighting,* pp. 261-268, HMSO, 1963.)

It is also known that uniform lighting tends to obscure texture gradients and other visual cues, and may in this way also act against group members efforts to communicate with one another. (See for instance, *Elektisk Lys Klasserum,* Copenhagen, 1958; H L Logan, *Lighting and Wellbeing,* Holophane Company, New York, 1961; H L Logan and E Berger, 'Measurement of Visual Information Cues', *Illuminating Engineering,* 56, pp. 393-403, 1961.)

One word of caution. It might be possible to object to this pattern, on the ground that pools of light, and the consequent brightness gradients, will create glare. The subject of glare is complex; since glare depends on many factors, including not only the ratio of source brightness to background brightness, but also on their absolute brightnesses, the size of the source, the angle subtended at the perceiver's eye, and the angle of viewing.

Warm colours (64)

Pattern

If:

There is any space where people spend more than a few minutes at a time

Then:

The primary sources of illumination, in combination with the colours of floors, walls, ceilings, and furnishings, should be chosen to give a *warm light,* throughout the space. Essentially, this must be achieved by the dominant use of floors, walls and ceilings, in the red-brown range.

In detail, suppose we choose an arbitrary small surface with arbitrary position and orientation at any point in this space.

Under fixed illumination conditions, the light incident on this surface has a fixed spectral energy distribution. (We may obtain this spectral energy distribution either by direct measurement with a spectro-radiometer, or by calculation based on the known energy distribution of the primary light sources, and the reflectance characteristics of the surrounding surfaces.) Define this spectral energy distribution as $p(\lambda)$. Now any given $p(\lambda)$ may be plotted on the two-dimensional chromaticity diagram, for the 1931 CIE standard observer, by means of the standard colour matching functions given in Gunter Wyszecki and W S Stiles, *Colour Science,* pp. 228-317, New York, 1967. The coordinates of a plot in this colour space define the *chromaticity* of any given energy distribution.

We may now identify a region on the chromaticity diagram, which we shall call the warm region. It is shown hatched on the drawing.

We require that the light incident on any plane surface, at any point within 5 feet of the floor, in the space defined, have chromaticity within the warm region. In order to meet this requirement, it will be necessary for the floor, and most of the walls, to be in the red-brown range. Detailed computations on any given surface to estimate the chromaticity of the light in the room, as a function of the spectral distribution of the primary sources, and the reflection characteristics of floor, walls, and ceiling, may be made according to the methods described in P Moon and D E Spencer, *Lighting Design,* Cambridge, 1948, and summarized in Warren B Boast, *Illumination Engineering,* pp. 197-221, New York, 1953.

Problem

Typically, people like the inside of redwood houses, wood-panelling, the interior of a sunlit courtyard,

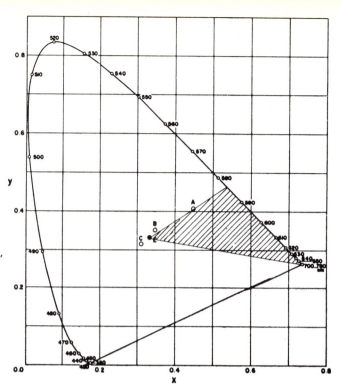

Fig. 3.10. 1931 CIE (x, y)-chromaticity diagram with spectrum locus, purple line, the chromaticity points of CIE standard sources *A, B, C,* and the equal-energy stimulus *E.*

especially towards evening.

Typically, they dislike the interior of offices equipped with fluorescent lighting and standard steel furniture.

We know that people have a clear subjective impression of the relative warmth, or coldness, of different spaces. See, for instance, Committee on Colorimetry of the Optical Society of America, *The Science of Colour,* p. 168, New York, 1953.

Individual observer stability in such judgements is high. Thus, one study gives reliability coefficients of 0.95 for warmth and 0.82 for coolness — N Collins, 'The Appropriateness of Certain Colour Combinations in Advertising', Master's Thesis, Columbia University, New York, 1924.

The most obvious origin of 'warmth' is in the spectral characteristics of the light sources. There has been considerable study of the spectral characteristics of different light sources — and it is now accepted that these light sources should have fairly 'warm' spectra.

However, even when 'warm' light bulbs and tubes are used in offices and factories, subjective judgements of coldness seems to persist. Apparently, the warmth of a space depends on other characteristics of the space beyond the light sources. (See F J Langdon 'The Design of Mechanised Offices, *Architects Journal,* May 1 and May 22, 1963. Amos Rapoport, 'Some Consumer Comments on a Designed Environment', *Arena,* January, 1967, pp. 176-178. Pilkington Research Unit, *Office Design: A Study of Environment,* Department of Building Science, University of Liverpool, 1965, p. 51 and 89. Peter Manning and Brian Wells, 'CIS: Re-Appraisal of an Environment', *Interior Design,* May-June, 1964.)

We make two conjectures:

1. The perceived 'warmth' of a room depends directly on the spectral distribution of the light incident on various things in the room (particularly faces, hands, clothes, work surfaces, etc.). The perceived colour of each of these things, regardless of its own reflec-

tance characteristics, is transformed by the spectral characteristics of the incident light. Since the various things in a room are all subject to these transformations equally, it is reasonable to suppose that the perceived warmth or coldness of a room depends on the nature of this transformation, i.e. on the spectral characteristics of the light in the room, as reflected from the walls and other surfaces.

2. Human comfort requires that the perceived chromaticity of the incident light, fall within the region shown on the diagram above.

Since the region shown as warm on the diagram, has been defined by guesswork, it is certain that it will need to be modified. The crucial part of this conjecture states that there *exists* such a region (whether or not it is the exact region defined above).

One study which attempts to identify the objective correlates of perceived 'warmth' is S M Newhall, 'Warmth and Coolness of Colours', *Psychological Record, 4,* pp. 198-212, 1941. This study revealed a maximum for 'warmest' judgements at dominant wavelength 610 millimicrons, which is in the middle of the orange range. However, the study concerned coloured chips; we cannot be certain that the result would be the same for light.

IV Buildings generated by the pattern language

We now describe the way that a designer might use the patterns to design a building.

A quick look though the list of patterns makes it clear that there are too many to grasp all at once. A designer who wants to make a building out of them, will not simply be able to read them through, and then design the building. They are too confusing.

To make a whole out of these many patterns, the designer needs to understand how they fit together. The pattern language, is a system which shows how the patterns fit together, and helps the designer make a whole of them. The cascade of drawings on the next page is a rudimentary picture of the language for the 64 multi-service centre patterns.

The language is intended to give the designer three specific kinds of help:

1. It gives him the opportunity to use the patterns in a way which pays full respect to the unique features of each special building: the local peculiarities of the community, its special needs, the particular service programmes the community intends to have, the particular administrative organization of the service centre itself, local peculiarities of location, site, and climate.

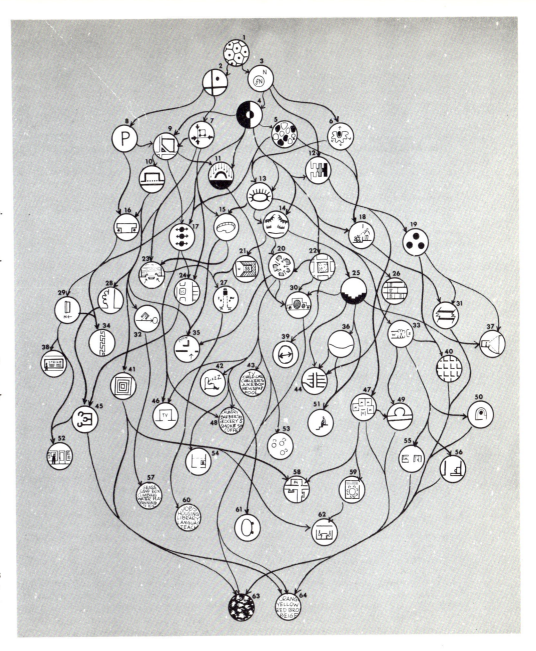

2. It tells him which patterns to consider first, and which ones to consider later. Obviously he wants to consider the biggest ones, the ones which have the most profound influence on the building, before he considers the details.

3. It tells him which patterns 'go together' — that is, which patterns refer to similar parts of the building, so that he knows which ones to think about at the same time, and which ones separately.

Before we try to explain exactly what this cascade of drawings means, we shall present eight worked examples which show it in use.

In each example we describe a hypothetical community, which needs a multi-service centre. We show a design for a multi-service centre building, appropriate for that community, which has been generated by the language. And we show, step by step, how the language helped to generate this design.

For each example, the steps are presented in sequence (A, B, C, D, . . .). Each step introduces new patterns into the design. At every step we mention the new patterns which have come into play and their interaction with local conditions, *in words*; we show the form of the building, as it has been formed up to that step, *diagrammatically*; and we show a miniature drawing of the *language cascade* so that we can see which part of the cascade is responsible for this step, and where this part sits in the cascade as a whole.

(One point must be heavily underlined. Although the evolution of these designs is presented in a step-by-step sequential manner, this is merely for convenience of presentation. It does not imply that the design process generated by the language, is, in any but the most general sense, itself sequential.)

HUNTS POINT

40,000 PEOPLE — STRONG COMMUNITY CORPORATION — LARGE BLOCK WORKER PROGRAM — 9 TO 12 SERVICES — SITE OPEN TO THREE SIDES — NEAR MAJOR INTERSECTION AND TRANSIT STATION.

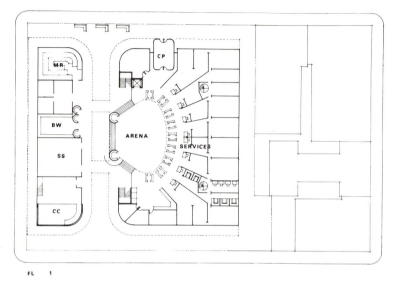

FL   1

1":60'

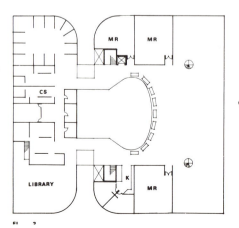

FL   2

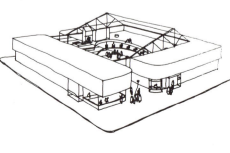

A. This multi-service centre is to service 40,000 people. According to Pattern 1 (Small Target Areas), this population is too large, but for political reasons, the decision stands and is irrevocable.

First a triangle site was selected, right on a major intersection (Pattern 2: Location). However other requirements made it clear that this site was too small (Pattern 3), and a larger, rectangular site was chosen, one-half block from the original site (thus still conforming to Pattern 2).

On this site there was room only for emergency parking, and so Pattern 8 (Parking) does not play a major role. Nor does 5, which had not been formulated prior to the Hunts Point design.

B. Pattern 16 (Necklace) calls for provisions for community projects around the 'live' edge of the building; hence we confine services to the 'dead' edge of the building, against other buildings.

C. Climate considerations made it clear that the arena could not be open (11: Enclosure), and so it was developed as an interior street. Orientation of this 'street' is given by local conditions in accordance with Pattern 7 (Entrance Location).

D. The size of the arena and its relationship to waiting and services is established by Patterns 13 (Services Off Arena), 14 (Waiting) and 15 (Overview); and the arena is shaped accordingly.

E. The arena is thus buried in the heart of the building, off the interior street. Since its ceiling had to be high (30), and since it was to be one of the things visible from outside (10), we gave it a huge, high truss. To enhance visibility further, and in accord with Patterns 23 (Entrance Shape) and 34 (Street Niche), the entrances were cut back, deep into the building.

F. With services taking up the north half of the building, the south was given over to core services and those things that need to be placed along the line of entry (Patterns 21: Self-service, 27: Self-service Progression, 28: Block Workers, 32: Child-Care).

Next, service layout is established (33 and 40); and the arena is raked back with a gallery at the second floor (25).

G. Finally 'pockets' in the arena are shaped and filled according to Patterns 20 (Activity Pockets), 35 (Information-Conversation), 43 (Waiting Diversions), and 42 (Sleeping).

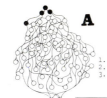

A

1. Small Target Areas
2. Location
3. Size Based on Population

B

16. Necklace

C

4. Community Territory
7. Entrance Location
9. Arena Thoroughfare
11. Arena Enclosure

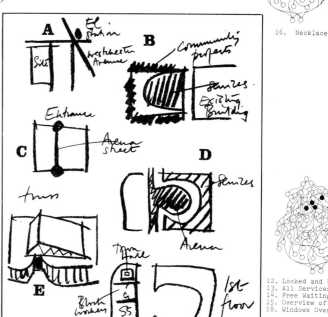

D

12. Locked and Unlocked
13. All Services off Arena
14. Free Waiting
15. Overview of Services
18. Windows Overlooking

E

10. Open to Street
23. Entrance Shape
30. Ceiling Heights
34. Street Niches

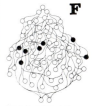

F

19. Core Service Adjacencies
21. Self-Service
27. Self-Service Progression
28. The Intake Process
32. Child-Care Position
27. Director's Overview

G

20. Activity Pockets
35. Information-Conversation
36. Dish-Shaped Arena
42. Sleeping OK
43. Waiting Diversions
51. Stair Seats

169

COMBINATION SERVICE AND RECREATION CENTER - MIL
CLIMATE - OUTDOOR ARENA - STRONG COMMUNITY ORGA
ZATION - CORNER SITE - OFF SITE PARKING PROVIDE

170

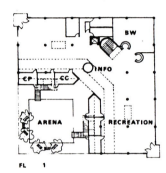

FL 1

FL 2

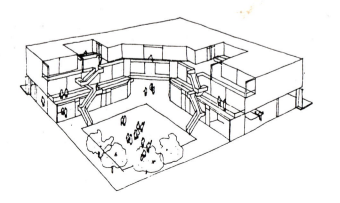

FL 3

A. To make the recreation part of the building highly accessible, the whole ground floor is devoted to recreation activity — this area will be open late, according to Pattern 12; also it is highly visible from the street (10), and provides a thoroughfare (Pattern 9). In this climate, the arena, which can be open to the sky (11) takes on an unusual character — it becomes a park. The whole ground floor becomes community territory (4).

B. The recreation area, which will become a hang-out for many members of the community, gives the building a natural base for community organization. It is therefore essential to put information, and community organizers and community projects at ground level. Patterns 17 (Community Projects Two-sided), 28 (Intake), 35 (Information-Conservation), and 16 (Necklace of Community Projects) put them in the positions shown.

C. If the recreation area is to occupy about one-third of the building and is to be at ground level, there will be two other stories for services. Since the services are not at ground floor, they cannot open directly off the arena. The next best thing, feasible in a mild climate, is to have them opening off a gallery which surrounds the arena. Self-service is placed in the centre of this gallery (21). The gallery steps back from the arena (Pattern 25). There are no corridors.

D. Since core service adjacencies (19) requires that community organizers be reasonably accessible to the rest of core services, there must be a stair inside the building; core services naturally go to the third floor, giving the director an overview (37). Since this stair opens from a 'late zone' downstairs, it is a natural path to meeting rooms; these rooms, clustered round a kitchen, are near the staff lounge, itself on the path to core services, and in easy reach of other services (Patterns 47 and 49).

E. To get windows overlooking life (18) for the interior spaces, there are holes from the second and third story, looking down into the recreation floor.

171

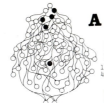

A
```
3.  Size Based on Population
4.  Community Territory
7.  Entrance Location
11. Arena Enclosure
43. Waiting Diversions
```

B
```
9.  Arena Thoroughfare
10. Open to Street
16. Necklace
17. Community Projects
23. Entrance Shape
24. Subcommittee Watchdogs
28. The Intake Process
29. Outdoor Seats
35. Information
```

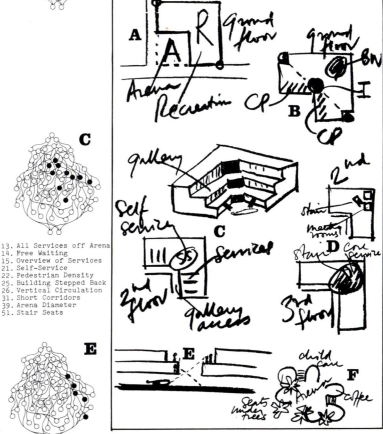

C
```
13. All Services off Arena
14. Free Waiting
15. Overview of Services
21. Self-Service
22. Pedestrian Density
25. Building Stepped Back
26. Vertical Circulation
31. Short Corridors
39. Arena Diameter
51. Stair Seats
```

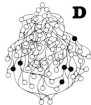

D
```
19. Core Service
41. Town Meeting
45. Block Worker Layout
47. Meeting Rooms
49. Staff Lounge
59. Square Seminar Rooms
```

E
```
18. Windows Overlooking Life
26. Vertical Circulation in Services
33. Service Layout
40. Office Flexibility
56. Informal Reception
```

F
```
20. Activity Pockets
27. Self-Service Progression
29. Outdoor Seats
32. Child-Care Position
38. Community Wall
42. Sleeping OK
48. Barbershop Politics
53. Form-Filling Tables
54. Accessible Bathrooms
57. Child-Care Contents
```

BROOKLYN

12,000 PERSONS - EXPANSION KEY ISSUE - STEEP
SITE - PARKING MUST BE PROVIDED - LAUNDROMAT
AND NEWS STAND ON SITE TO BE SAVED.

172

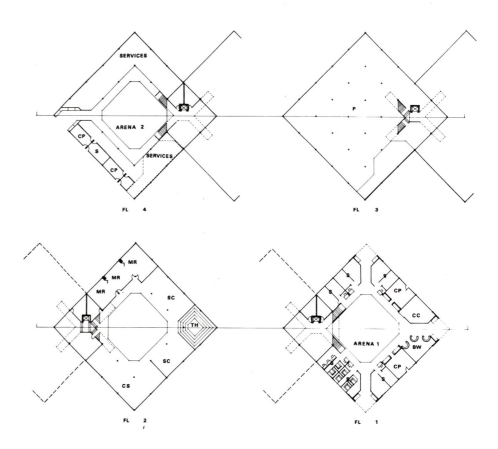

1":60'

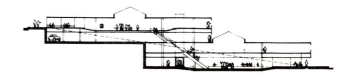

A. The community has acquired a corner lot, 12,000 square feet, at a major intersection (Pattern 2). In anticipation of expansion, the community has also purchased the lot in back (6: Expansion).
(The most striking feature of this building is that it has two arenas on two different levels. The need for expansion and the steep site, together with the square shapes of the lots and their relative positions, are the conditions which suggest this solution. The drawings show the entire development after expansion. At the first stage, only the lower lot is developed and the upper lot is used for parking.)

B. The most natural shortcut across the site (Pattern 9) cuts across the corner of the lower lot; another shortcut goes from the NE corner of the upper lot to the SW corner of the lower lot (in the first stage, this would be through the parking lot, into the building, down some stairs, through the first arena, out the main corner door).

C. The change of level from the NE corner of the upper lot to the SW corner of the lower lot, is approximately 40 feet. This suggests that the building when fully developed, should be stepped down four stories: the lower lot having two stories and the upper lot one story, with a basement for parking, and a core of four stories. In order to keep the shortcut through the two lots, the stairs connecting the two arenas will have to be very direct, with no backtracking. Thus, the stairs are in one long line.

D. Working toward the centre, from the two extreme entrances, first comes community projects, then the two arenas, and then the services; all functions which serve both arenas — the stair and elevator (44), core services (19), director's overview (37), and self-service (20) — are at the junction of the two arenas.

E. In order to keep the MSC as open to the street as possible (10), and still protect it from New York weather (11: Arena Enclosure), the necklace of community projects (15) is broken at intervals with glass doors which can be demounted during the summer. An existing laundromat and newspaper stand are left intact on the site, but made 'two-sided' (17). In addition, some of the 'store-front' spaces are services, some are community projects (5). Finally, block workers (28 and 45), and child-care (32) are arranged with respect to the shortcut path and the main entrance.

173

A

```
2.  Location
6.  Expansion
8.  Parking
```

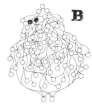

B

```
7.  Entrance Location
9.  Arena Thoroughfare
```

C

```
4.  Community Territory
10. Open to Street
12. Locked and Unlocked
13. All Services off Arena
16. Necklace
```

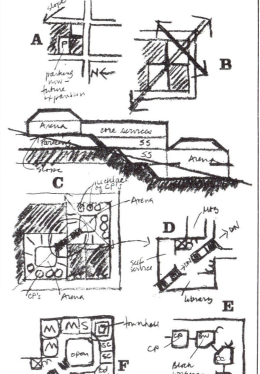

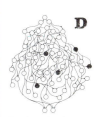

D

```
19. Core Service
21. Self-Service
37. Director's Overview
44. Elevator-Ramp
54. Accessible Bathrooms
```

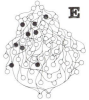

E

```
5.  Small Services
10. Open to Street
11. Arena Enclosure
15. Overview of Services
17. Community Projects
28. The Intake Process
32. Child-Care Position
45. Block Worker Layout
48. Barbershop Politics
```

F

```
24. Subcommittee Watchdogs
25. Building Stepped Back
41. Town Meeting
47. Meeting Rooms Clustered
58. Seats Outside Meeting Rooms
59. Square Seminar Rooms
```

PHOENIX

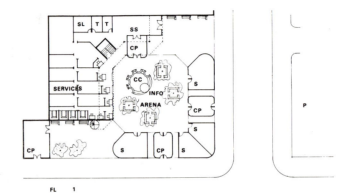

25,000 PERSONS - OPEN PARK ARENA - INTENSE
COMMUNITY ORGANIZATION PROGRAM - POSSIBLE
EXPANSION OVER THE YEARS - CORNER SITE -
LARGE CHILDCARE STATION.

174

FL   1

FL   2

1":60'

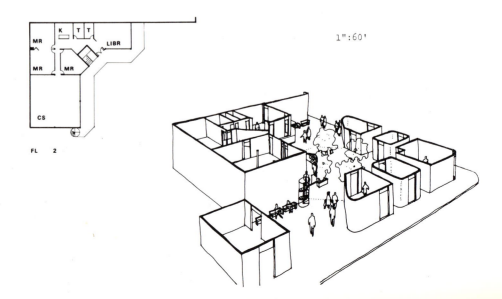

A. The Phoenix MSC is being built to serve 25,000 people. The programme is considered experimental, and so the Centre is being kept small, with the potential to expand. In the first phase the Centre will contain 18,000 square feet. The programme calls for parking, although this is not included in the 18,000 figure (there is a lot across the street from the site that the city is hoping to acquire).

The site is at the intersection of a main avenue and a slow residential street. Therefore the size, location and parking patterns (1, 2, 3, 8) are all appropriate.

B. First, the site is zoned according to Pattern 4 (Community Territory) and a thoroughfare is cut across the corner, the most natural shortcut (9: Arena Thoroughfare). Since this thoroughfare is meant to cut across community territory, the services are allocated to the back corner section of the site. The climate allows community territory to be almost totally open (11: Arena Enclosure).

C. The community is unorganized; there are no subcommittees. However, the Centre intends to launch a community organization effort. Consequently Patterns 16 (Necklace of Community Projects) and 24 (Subcommittee Watchdogs), while they will not be used immediately, will eventually come into play. Thus we surround the open arena with small spaces, for services and as a home base for organizers; and over time these spaces are turned into various community projects. (Pattern 5, No Red Tape, is thus partially solved.)

Expansion, if the programme is successful, will be toward the Northeast; Pattern 6 (Expansion) thus controls immediate considerations on the Northeast edge of the site: Arena and services must expand together.

D. Service-arena relationships are now generated by 13 (Services off Arena), 14 (Waiting), 15 (Overview) and 22 (Arena Density): The services get equal frontage on the arena, and the arena dips down a few feet, upon entry, to facilitate overview.

E. In the absence of block workers, intake is taken up by an enlarged information station (28 and 35), and is placed as shown. Child care (32) and self-service (21) are then placed near the information-intake hub.

F. An adjacent barbershop is open to the side of the arena, forming a natural alcove for outdoor seats and the community wall (29, 38, 48).

175

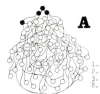

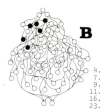

4. Community Territory
7. Entrance Location
9. Arena Thoroughfare
11. Arena Enclosure
16. Necklace
23. Entrance Shape

1. Small Target Areas
2. Location
3. Size Based on Population
8. Parking

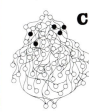

5. Small Services
6. Expansion
10. Open to Street
12. Locked and Unlocked
17. Community Projects

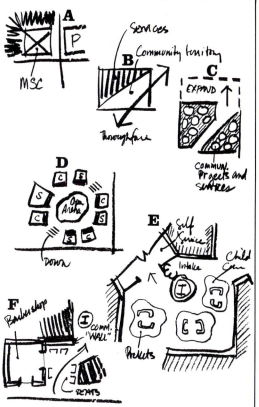

13. All Services off Arena
14. Free Waiting
15. Overview of Services
22. Pedestrian Density

20. Activity Pockets
21. Self-Service
24. Subcommittee
27. Self-Service
32. Child-Care Position
35. Information
43. Waiting Diversions
48. Barbershop Politics

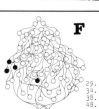

29. Outdoor Seats
34. Street Niches
38. Community Wall
48. Barbershop Politics

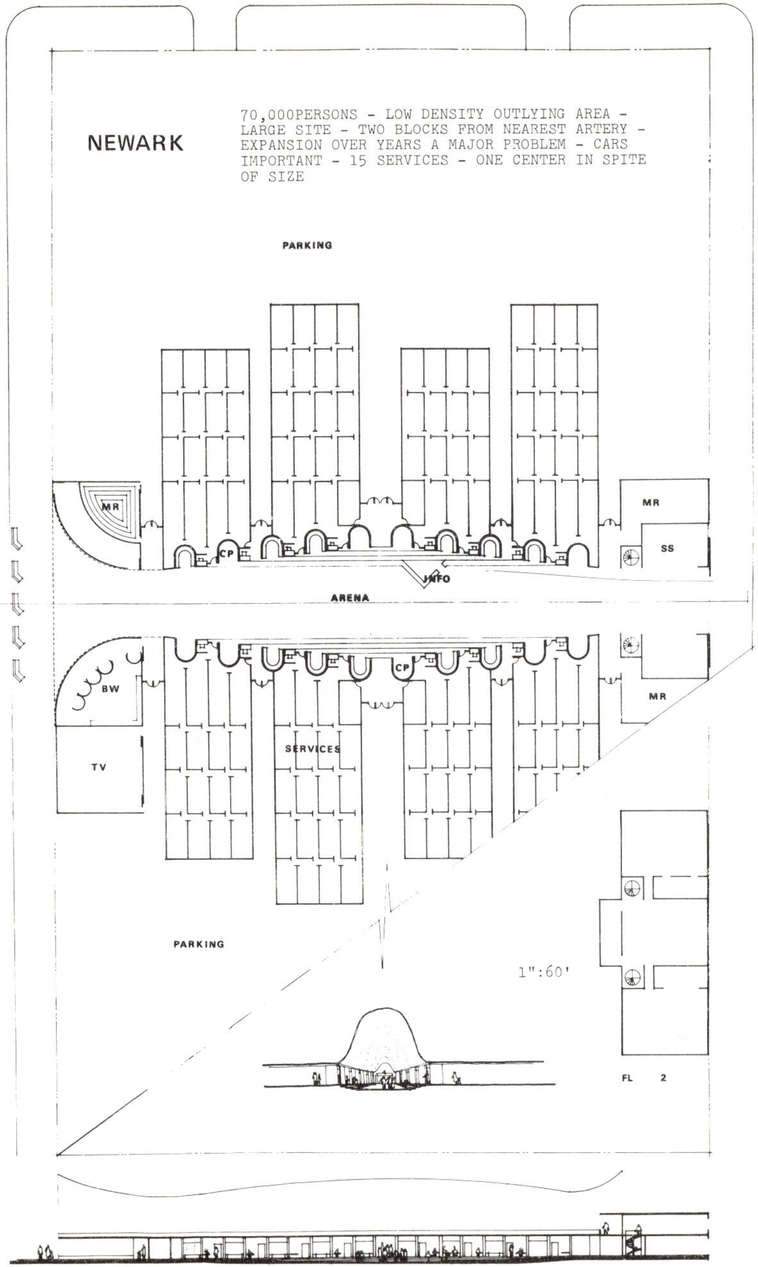

NEWARK

70,000 PERSONS - LOW DENSITY OUTLYING AREA -
LARGE SITE - TWO BLOCKS FROM NEAREST ARTERY -
EXPANSION OVER YEARS A MAJOR PROBLEM - CARS
IMPORTANT - 15 SERVICES - ONE CENTER IN SPITE
OF SIZE

PARKING

MR

MR

SS

CP

INFO

ARENA

CP

BW

MR

TV

SERVICES

PARKING

1":60'

FL 2

NEWARK

A. Small target areas (Pattern 1) is violated. To serve 70,000 people, the building will need 63,000 square feet (Pattern 3); since cars are a problem here, parking must be provided requiring another 35,000 square feet (Pattern 8). Land and construction costs dictate a one-storey building. For a one-storey building, the site needs to be 98,000 square feet — the chosen site is ample.

The form of this building is governed largely by the extreme importance of expansion (Pattern 6), and by the very large number of services required, calling for extra frontage in the arena (13: Services off Arena).

These patterns combine to give a spine-like arena, with services branching off it. Small services (Pattern 5) and windows overlooking life (Pattern 18) split the services into a series of branches, with paths from the parking lot coming in between them (Pattern 8).

B. Since parking is clearly on the outer part of the site, necklace of community projects (Pattern 16) suggests that the community projects grow round the edge of the site, in the direction shown by the arrows. As the community projects grow, the parking lot becomes internal and hidden. Access to parking lot is in the corners; the main entrance is placed centrally as shown (7).

C. In order to interrelate community projects and services (5), the community projects continue round the entrance (23) as shown, so they line the arena. Access to the services, is through the community projects, which alternate with services along the frontage.

D. To make the inside visible, the mouth of the arena is very wide and high, and the arena itself is high, to make it thoroughly accessible. There are no doors. It is an internal street. The close proximity of community projects and services, makes Pattern 24 (Subcommittee Watchdogs) easy to do.

E. Since waiting needs warmth, it cannot be out in the middle of the arena. Waiting must therefore be recessed in pockets (as defined by 20) — these can be formed naturally by the relation between community projects and services already indicated.

F. According to Pattern 36 (Dish-Shaped Arena) the arena has a gentle slope towards the centre giving at least a partial overview of services. If arena is deeper in the middle, steps from the parking lot will be longer — thus giving the arena elliptical form.

G. The self-service area must be placed smack bang in the middle of the street-arena — this puts it in the middle of waiting (21), and dead centre for people

entering. The entrance (23) is the obvious place for
the self-service menu. As a result, block workers and
information get placed to either side.

177

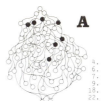

A

```
4.  Community Territory
6.  Expansion
7.  Entrance Location
9.  Arena Thoroughfare
18. Windows Overlooking Life
22. Pedestrian Density
39. Arena Diameter
```

B

```
6.  Expansion
8.  Parking
16. Necklace
```

C

```
5.  Small Services
12. Locked and Unlocked
13. All Services off Arena
15. Overview of Services
17. Community Projects
24. Subcommittee Watchdogs
```

E

```
14. Free Waiting
20. Activity Pockets
29. Outdoor Seats
34. Street Niches
42. Sleeping OK
```

D

```
10. Open to Street
11. Arena Enclosure
23. Entrance Shape
30. Ceiling Heights
```

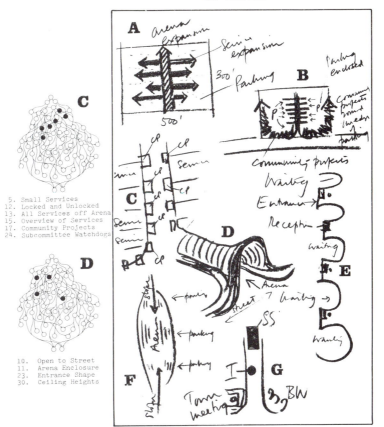

F

```
36. Dish-Shaped Arena
51. Stair Seats
```

G

```
21. Self-Service
23. Entrance Shape
27. Self-Service Progression
28. The Intake Process
32. Child-Care Position
35. Information-Conversation
41. Town Meeting
43. Waiting Diversions
46. Radio/TV Station
48. Barbershop Politics
```

A. Since this building is in the middle of the block, the most difficult problem is that posed by the arena thoroughfare. The arena is made to include the sidewalk, and thus becomes T-shaped. Size (3) tells us that at any given moment, there might be .0005N equals 4 interviews going on, and about the same number of people waiting. Pattern 22 then tells us that the arena should be on the order of 1200 square feet. The sidewalk must be open to through pedestrians. To shield it from the cold as much as possible, it can be roofed, and given a wall on the street side (10) — thus forming the community wall (38).
B. In this building, there is no distinction between community projects and services. The services are placed towards the back, to allow child-care (57), block workers (45), self-service (21), and a meeting room (47) to be in the unlocked (late) zone (12), which has to be in the front half of the building.
C. With this decision made, the problem now is to make the building community territory (4). A series of circular spaces are provided, which surround the arena and create places for people to sit down, even if they are only walking through. Some of these rooms might be used for non-service community projects.
D. We place the community organizers, meeting room, self-service and child-care behind these circular alcoves; and the information conversation station in one of the alcoves.

V: The language

We shall now discuss the nature of the pattern language, and the way in which it may be used to generate buildings. We wish to present it in such a way that anybody who wants to, can become a 'speaker' of the language — that is, he can use it, in his own way, to design multi-service centres in the various special circumstances which he faces. Let us establish one thing from the outset. The language, and the cascade, are two different things. The language contains far more structure than is captured in the cascade; the cascade is merely a partial representation of the language. However, we shall not discuss the additional structure in this report. Here, we confine ourselves, entirely, to those features of the language which are captured by the cascade.
Now we establish a second point. Although the cascade is a partial representation of the language, it is not intended that a person use this cascade

A

```
 4.  Community Territory
 7.  Entrance Location
 9.  Arena Thoroughfare
11.  Arena Enclosure
22.  Pedestrian Density
```

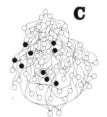

C

```
14.  Free Waiting
16.  Necklace of
20.  Activity Pockets
23.  Entrance Shape
29.  Outdoor Seats
34.  Street Niches
42.  Sleeping OK
48.  Barbershop Politics
53.  Form-Filling Tables
```

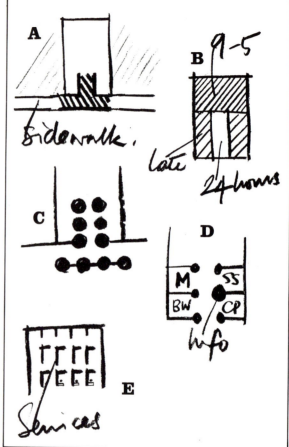

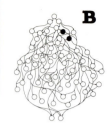

B

```
 5.  Small Services
12.  Locked and Unlocked
```

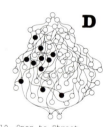

D

```
10.  Open to Street
17.  Community Projects
21.  Self-Service
24.  Subcommittee Watchdogs
27.  Self-Service Prog
28.  The Intake Process
32.  Child-Care Position
35.  Information
45.  Block Worker Layout
54.  Accessible Bathrooms
58.  Seats Outside Meeting
```

E

```
33.  Service Layout
40.  Office Flexibility
56.  Informal Reception
```

as a flow chart during the actual design process.

You cannot speak French by painstakingly following an open grammar book; in order to speak French, you must internalize the French grammer; when you have it in your head, and it has become automatic, then you can speak French.

Just so with the pattern language, You cannot design multi-service centres by painstakingly following the cascade with your finger; nor by following any other form of representation. In order to design with the language, you must internalize the structure of the language; once you have it in your head, and it has become automatic, then you can use it to design.

We must try to present the language in such a way, then, that the reader can internalize it, and make it his own. How is this to be done?

Let us imagine a large three-dimensional block of transparent space, which represents the building and its surroundings. Now imagine that the patterns are represented by transparent coloured clouds, floating within this block of space, interpenetrating and overlapping one another. The overall size and shape of each coloured cloud, corresponds to the 'domain of influence' of the pattern in question. Thus, Pattern 4 influences the whole building: it therefore has a very large cloud. The clouds for small services (5), office flexibility (40) activity pockets (20), and necklace of community projects (16) and others, are floating within this larger cloud. Then again, arena diameter (39) is floating within activity pockets (20); service layout (35) is floating within office flexibility (40). Some of the clouds have specific shapes, and specific geometrical relationships to one another. Thus, necklace of community projects (16) is a long necklace like cloud curled around the perimeter of community territory (4); activity pockets (20) is inside the circle defined by this cloud, but does not penetrate it at all.

Some clouds overlap; that is, a part of one cloud is identified exactly with a part of another cloud. Thus self-service progression (27) and intake (28) both contain 'entrance' and they both contain 'block workers' — to this extent they overlap. Since the entrance is detailed by entrance shape (23), and the block workers area is detailed by block workers layout (45), the clouds for 23 and 45 both fall within the overlap of 27 and 28.

Some clouds appear many times. Thus service layout (35) appears many times within small services (5); and interview booths (50) appears many times within the service layout cloud (35), and a few times within

block worker layout (45).

Although inclusion, and overlap, and some of the other geometrical relationships between clouds are clearly defined, we must be careful not to let our conception of these clouds become too rigid. It may be tempting to say that these clouds are no more than components of the building, nested inside one another. *But they are clouds, not components.* It is essential that we visualize them as loose, cloudy, and only partly formed; since it is just this fact which lets our picture stand for *all* multi-service centres, not for any single one of them.

We now make the following assertion:

A person understands the pattern language for multi-service centres, when he can completely visualize this system of clouds in three dimensions.

The two dimensional cascade of patterns, shown here, is a way of explaining this three dimensional system of clouds. An arrow drawn between two patterns, like this:

means that the cloud for pattern B falls within the cloud for pattern A.

Slightly more complicated, an arrow with multiple tails, like this:

means that the cloud for pattern C falls inside the union of the clouds for patterns A and B.

If we followed these definitions strictly, we should have to draw a very large number of arrows — so many, that the drawing would become utterly obscure. We have therefore chosen to draw some of the arrows, which seem to be particularly helpful; but have left many others out. And, of course, the cascade is drawn in such a way as to make the arrangement of the arrows as simple as possible. Two properties of the cascade follow at once:

1. The higher a pattern is, in the cascade, the 'larger' it is. Thus, Pattern 1, which refers to the city-wide

organization of target areas, is the largest pattern, and heads the cascade.

2. If two patterns have parts in common, they will be near each other horizontally — since there will be arrows going from both of them, to other 'smaller' patterns which detail this part.

Thus, it turns out that the cascade is an abstract two-dimensional picture of the system of clouds described above. The vertical dimension in the cascade represents the size of the clouds; and the horizontal dimension represents the distance between clouds, and the extent of their overlap.

It is now clear that the cascade may be used to help us visualize the abstract structure of multi-service centres. Now we see how the cascade may be used to help us design multi-service centres. Every designer knows that the most important feature of any form is the covariation among relationships. As we make minor changes in one relationship, other relationships have to change along with it. If we make the arena slightly larger, then it needs to be slightly higher, and there are more services around it; but there is less room for back-up services — which in turn have to be squeezed in behind the services, instead of opening directly off the arena as before.

To handle this kind of covariation, the designer strives constantly, to preserve a holistic, systemic, attitude towards the building; he is occupied with simultaneous interconnectedness. The pattern-language helps the designer to focus on more simultaneous interconnectedness than he could normally handle.

It does so by building on two simple rules of thumb:

1. He must work his way down the cascade, starting with the largest, most global, relationships, and moving gradually towards the details.

2. He must focus on clusters of patterns which are near one another in the cascade; since patterns which are near one another have parts in common, these clusters represent bundles of simultaneous relationships.

Both these rules of thumb are clearly visible in the examples in Chapter 3.

We finish by discussing the variety of buildings which the language can produce. The language is intended to generate an infinite variety of different buildings, each properly adapted to the unique local characteristics of any given community. Since the patterns define generic relationships, based on shared, recurrent problems, and are therefore, in a sense, standardized, we must ask how these standardized patterns can combine to give a unique local solution to an individual design problem.

First, not all the patterns are relevant to any given

building. Thus community territory (4) is not relevant in the Bowery building — old people need comfort, they do not need to be organized politically. Any given multi-service centre may use only forty or fifty of the sixty-four patterns. Since there are many, many ways of choosing fifty patterns from sixty-four, this creates a rich variety of combinations.

Second, each pattern allows all kinds of voluntary variation, over and above the relationships which it specifies. Thus activity pockets (20) says the arena must be surrounded by pockets of activity, alternating with points of access. It says nothing about the size of these pockets, nor their exact number, nor the exact geometry of their relationship to the arena. All these features may vary freely from building to building.

Third, many patterns are explicitly defined to vary according to specified conditions in the context. Thus, the size of the multi-service centre (3) varies according to the population of the target area. In cases like this, where the final specification of the patterns depends on the local context, each building gets different treatment from the pattern language.

In conclusion, we wish to emphasize the tentative character of the multi-service centre pattern language. We have already said that the individual patterns are tentative, that they are based on much conjecture, and that they need criticism and improvement. Here we underscore what the reader, no doubt, has already gathered:

The theory of the language is itself incomplete. The difficulty is largely one of representation; although we know a great deal about the structure of the language, and the varieties of connection between patterns, it is extremely hard to find a simple way of communicating this structure — the cascade, used in this report, is helpful, but it falls far short of what we need.

ADOLF LOOS IN VIENNA

AESTHETICS AS A FUNCTION OF RETAIL TRADE ESTABLISHMENTS

DIETRICH WORBS trs E W TEICHMANN

This study attempts to establish propositions about the effect of aesthetic elements and environments on retail distribution based on the functional and spatial analysis of an inner city shop for men's fashions.

The inner city functions as a district for the distribution of consumer goods. The places of distribution are the department stores, shops, arcades, and street and plaza markets. The retail shop constitutes the most useful model for the analysis of the exchange of consumer goods and of the design of the shell constructed for this economic event.

The discovery of the utility and effect of aesthetic factors (elements, environments) is useful in itself. However, even more important is the insight that here the *psychological* needs of the consumer to find satisfaction through elements of aesthetic communication in the shopping environment, are interlaced with the fulfilment of the *economic* needs of the retailer.

Historical context

At the turn of the century, 'English' outfitter shops existed in all the capital cities and retail centres of Europe. The interiors of the shops, and the fashions displayed there, were deliberately intended to imitate their British prototypes. Industrialization had begun in England and by this time was furthest developed there. An economy and commerce based on industrialization and imperialistic expansion secured for Britain the position of a leading world power. The British were admired for the social reforms into which they were forced. In the fields of housing and town planning, architecture and arts and crafts, their innovative ideas were widely published and discussed. English men's fashions were adopted not only be-

Entrance to the men's fashion shop today.

cause of their high quality, simplicity, comfort, and practicality, but also because other Europeans openly identified themselves with all that was English.

Furthermore, the European bourgeoisie considered this wave of English fashion as its own, contrasting strongly with the situation before the French revolution when the nobility set the fashion. And the bourgeoisie saw with pride that their fashions were being adopted by the nobility. Now, however, the needs of the rich bourgeoisie, as well as those of the remaining nobility, created a new type of service and an establishment to go with it: the famous 'tailor'.

In this shop, the purchaser could be sure of obtaining clothing which would be practical, elegant, and made according to the latest fashions because, of course, these outfitters had an economic interest in creating new styles. Moreover, the purchaser's attire indicated his status as a member of the ruling middle-class and set him off from the working class. Despite this, the designers managed to give their fashions the pretensions of middle-class egalitarianism which made 'every barber's apprentice equal to a duke.'[1]

The designers and cultural historians of the time who turned against nineteenth-century eclecticism often praised the Englishman's fashions and other products of craft and industry in the same breath. These included craftwork (bags, trunks, saddles), manufactured goods (plumbing fittings, coaches and light carriages), and industrial goods (machines). They were all seen as manifestations of the already existing style of the late nineteenth and early twentieth century, distinguished mainly by its efficiency, functionality, and lack of ornament — and they were also considered beautiful. The architects of early Viennese modern architecture used the products of craft and industry as an argument for breaking with traditional aesthetic concepts and developing functional aestheticism. Following the ideas of earlier American functionalism, Adolf Loos defined architecture (with the exception of tombs and monuments) as a 'useful object' which had to answer functional needs and be economically acceptable to its users.[2] His polemics against the wastefulness of newly invented ornaments and old styles, and his belief in the historical proof of the architect's inability to form ornaments, gave rise to the question of how a functional aesthetic can be articulated if function is to be transformed into

Above: Entrance with original lettering.

Left: View into the entrance.

space. He began his career as an architect building a men's outfitters' shop and did interiors for many more menswear shops between 1900 and 1930, in addition to designing private houses and office buildings. This analysis of one of his Viennese tailor's shops will try to describe the evolution of Loos' concept of functional aesthetic, how it allowed function to be absorbed in space, and the quality of spatial design which was then achieved by this new aesthetic.

The traditional English outfitters' and tailor's shop held strictly to a fixed pattern of interrelationships between different functional areas as follows:

— show-window and entrance zone which allowed one to look into the shop and exhibited the type and range of stock at a glance;
— salesroom, the walls lined with cupboards (drawers and shelves with sliding doors) in front of which were show-cases (counters around two or three sides of the salesroom or set up at angles to each other) above which was usually a peripheral
— gallery or mezzanine with cupboards, either open or closed, for storing materials and ready-made stock.

In the rear part of the salesroom further areas were divided by partitions as follows:

—fitting and changing rooms;
—cashier with book-keeping;
—staircase, corridor and circulation space to:
—upstairs salesrooms and changing rooms
—management offices
—workshop for outfitters, tailors, and seamstresses.

This type of interior design with its organization of the different functional areas can be found in most inner city outfitters' shops in Vienna. The spatial elements in this interior are simply added together and are thus easily comprehensible in themselves; they were not developed by a concept of space which goes beyond the mere functional arrangement of elements.

A different plan is found in a shop designed and built by Adolf Loos (1909-1913) for the renowned tailors and outfitters Knize & Co., in a classicistic inner-city building of palatial design typical of the end of the eighteenth century in Vienna. Loos was not able to create the kind of spacious interior the model prescribed because of the exterior constraints of the building. The Knize firm had been using the upper floor of the building for some time. Now they were expanding into the narrow ground floor salesroom.

183

Space Defining Elements / Spatial Areas

Legend:
- □ Bordering
- ⊥ Bisecting
- ✕ Connecting
- △ Directing

Space Defining Elements	Entrance	Salesroom Gr.Fl.	Fittingroom/Landing	Salesroom 1st.Fl.	Salesroom 2nd.Fl.	Manager's Office	First Salon	Second Salon	Fitting Cubicles
Wall Cupboards		▲		▲		□			□
Built-in Showcase	▲✕			▲✕□		✕□✕	✕□		
Cashier's Box		▲				□			
Stairs		▲✕▲✕▲	⊥						
Gallery						✕□✕ ▲			
Partition				□ □					
Wall Panelling	✕△✕	▲✕□✕△□		□	□		□✕□		
Ceiling		✕□✕□✕□✕□							
Stone Facing	▲			▲					
Sales Counter		▲		▲					
Free-standing Showcase						⊥			
Chairs						⊥	⊥	⊥	⊥
Mirror		▲ □ ▽		▲		□		□	□
Daylight		▲ ▲		▲		□		□	□
Artificial Light		□ ▲ □		▲		□		□	□

Activity / Spatial Areas

Legend:
- ● Some Minutes
- ⊕ ¼ Hour
- ◯ ½ Hour

Fitting Cubicles	Second Salon	First Salon	Manager's Office	Salesroom 2nd.Fl.	Salesroom 1st.Fl.	Fitting Room/Landing	Salesroom Gr.Fl.	Entrance	Activity
⊕	●	●	●	●	●		●	●	Customer Enquiring
	⊕			⊕	●		●		Selecting Item
⊕		⊕			●	●	●		Trying on
	●				●		●		Ordering
◯									Taking Measurements
	●						●		Paying
	⊕	⊕		⊕					Reading
	⊕	⊕		⊕					Waiting
⊕	⊕	⊕	●		●	●	●		Salesperson Info.
	⊕			⊕	●		●		Showing Goods
⊕									Fitting
	●				●		●		Ordering
◯									Taking Measurements
	●	●			●		●		Writing Bill
	⊕	⊙					⊙		Accounts
		⊙	⊕						Correspondence

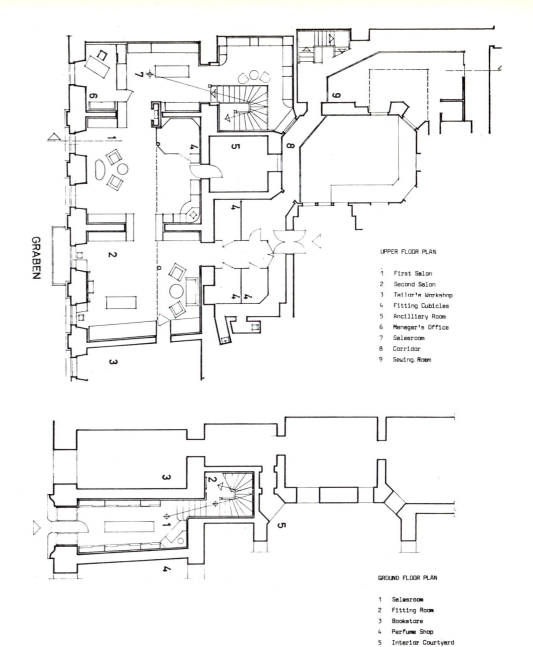

GRABEN

UPPER FLOOR PLAN

1. First Salon
2. Second Salon
3. Tailor's Workshop
4. Fitting Cubicles
5. Ancilliary Room
6. Manager's Office
7. Salesroom
8. Corridor
9. Sewing Room

GROUND FLOOR PLAN

1. Salesroom
2. Fitting Room
3. Bookstore
4. Perfume Shop
5. Interior Courtyard

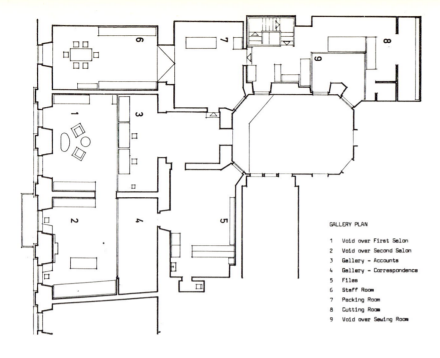

GALLERY PLAN

1 Void over First Salon
2 Void over Second Salon
3 Gallery - Accounts
4 Gallery - Correspondence
5 Files
6 Staff Room
7 Packing Room
8 Cutting Room
9 Void over Sewing Room

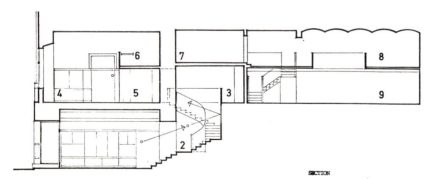

SECTION

1 Salesroom Gr.Fl.
2 Fitting Room
3 Salesroom 1st.Fl.
4 Salon
5 Fitting Cubicles
6 Gallery - Accounts
7 Packing Room
8 Cutting Room
9 Sewing Room

The limitations imposed by the site corresponded so closely to the spatial concepts Loos had developed during ten years of work as an architect, architectural theoretician and essayist (*Ornament and Crime,* 1908), that he easily consolidated the available space into a progression of rooms which are surprising to experience. The fact that his previous work was concentrated in renovation and redecoration of homes and shops probably greatly influenced the development of his ideas on functionalism, spatial economy, and spatial design.

Functional areas

The entrance to the Knize shop differs in its appearance and function from the typical shop front in the treatment of the display windows. Usually the entrance was framed with large windows placed in front of the building's supporting columns. In contrast the black granite entrance of the Knize shop emphasizes the columns it covers. The tall, narrow display windows are placed into the large clear lines of the entranceway so as to allow a view into the shop and to create a tall, narrow door. Attached to the column coverings, which curve back to the display windows in a convex-concave sweep, are small showcases at eye level.

The narrow, high-ceilinged salesroom on the ground floor, the walls of which taper inward toward the rear, is furnished like a typical Viennese tailor's shop. The side walls contain built-in drawers and cabinets with sliding glass doors; there is a long rectangular counter with squared ends made of glass fitted into a thin frame; in the right rear of the shop is a built-in cashier's cubicle. The side walls, the back of the display window and the wall behind the cashier culminate in a wooden architrave, a white frieze, and a carved wooden cornice. At the left of the cashier's cubicle, a stairway with six steps leads to a passageway which ends in a small fitting area. The stairway winds nineteen steps from this fitting area to the second floor of the shop. While the fitting room is only slightly above head height, above the landing the space is open to the second story ceiling. A mirror with shelf is set in the fitting room so that customers can look past the mirror down into the ground floor salesroom.

The artifically lighted stairway leads from the subdued daylight of the ground floor to the second floor. Next to the stairway is a sitting and display area, separated from the stairs by a railing. A mirror at the turning point of the stairway visually connects

the sales areas on both floors. The low-ceilinged sales room on the upper floor is windowless since the manager has his own office by the windows, separated from the rest of the room by wall cabinets and show-cases. A mirror built into the door-frame makes it possible for the manager to oversee the sales activity outside his office when the door is open. Electric bulbs, placed in the middle of the squares which pattern the dark ceiling, light the salesroom; the only full daylight in the upstairs salesroom comes through the passageway to the first salon to the left. The first salon, which is approximately square, is lit through two tall upper-floor windows. Across from the windows, a gallery projects into the room, divid-

Left: Original decor of ground floor salesroom.

Above: View of salesroom today.

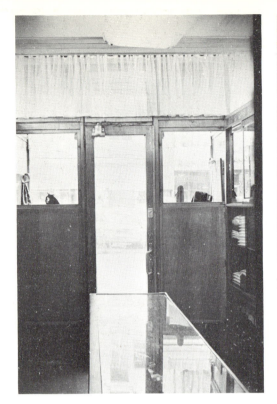

186

Above left: View back to entrance.

Above: Shelves with sliding doors.

Above right: Chest of drawers within the shelves.

Left: Ground floor cashier's desk.

ing it into a low-ceilinged area under the gallery and the gallery area above. The gallery itself contains the bookkeeping department; underneath are a fitting room, a door to a side room, and a cashier's cubicle. The cashier's cubicle is placed so that one can see it upon entering the room but not on leaving, an arrangement of the same discretion as on the ground floor.

The passageway to the second salon gives that room direction; simultaneously it serves to separate a bay-

like waiting area with chairs next to the windows from the rest of the room; a high free-standing show-case serves the same purpose. The passageways to both salons, but especially to the second, have the effect of being rooms in themselves because of the display cases which line their sides.

The second salon, of about the same dimensions as the first, concludes the sequence of rooms. As in the first salon, a gallery juts into the second, partitioning the room into three areas: a low-ceilinged region under the gallery, containing a quiet corner for reading and waiting, and a passageway, leading to the three changing rooms and to the workshops of the shirt tailors and the custom tailors; the gallery itself containing the assistants' desks; and the full-ceilinged portion of the salon with shelves for fabrics, a display table and a stand for men's fashion journals.

The short corridor to the changing rooms goes into an arcade with glass walks that leads to the shirt tailors' workshop. A vestibule connects the corridor and the sewing room; also a three-flight stairway with fourteen steps leads from the vestibule to an open gallery above the sewing room. This gallery extends around three sides of the room and is where the cutting is done. Both the sewing room and its gallery are lit by a courtyard window on the fourth side.

The galleries in the first and second salons are reached by going from the sewing room gallery through staff and side rooms over the upper floor salesroom. From the salon galleries, one can look both into the salons and into Grabenstrasse below.

Spatial analysis of the room sequence

The uninterrupted sequence of rooms, from the entrance area on the ground floor to the second salon on the upper floor, is developed as a spatially ascending spiral in accordance with the functions they serve within the structure of the classicistic Palais.

The individual rooms, except for side rooms such as changing rooms and the manager's office, are not separated by doors but are integrated beyond mere addition by connecting elements in the passage and transition areas. The entrance in itself is a transition zone from the exterior space of the street to the interior space of the shop.

The fashion goods salesrooms on the ground floor and upstairs are connected by the stairway with a fixed lifting area. The upstairs salesroom is bound to the first salon by a similar passage area as is the first salon with the second.

The entrance, which connects the exterior with the interior, attracts passers-by to the show window with the inward-swinging, convex-concave curve of its framing columns. This is in contrast to the form of the column bases, which holds the passer-by at a distance from the show window before leading him into the entrance with quarter-circle curves.

Loos reapplies the motif of the quarter-circle curve as a guide to motion in the interior at the base of the stairway, which connects the sales room downstairs to the fitting area on the landing and continues to the upstairs sales room. The stairs themselves are a spatial connecting element for these areas.

In the Goldman shop (1898) the curved stairway is separated off from the rest of the shop in a box-shaped room; as a spatially conceived and realized connecting element, it has no significance for the sale of fashion goods, or for the rooms on the upper

Above: Landing with fitting room to the left.

Above right: Mirror in the curve of the stairs.

floor, other than to serve its function as a vertical circulation link. In the Knize shop, on the other hand, the stairway serves to integrate the salesrooms on both floors vertically.

Loos understood this kind of circulation link to serve as preparation and introduction to what was to come, e.g. vestibules to main rooms: '. . . walking distances inside should be as short as possible since economical use should be made of area and distance. Nevertheless introductory passages that are longer than absolutely necessary offer the user many advantages. It is good for them to be curved. It is easier to climb stairs if they have turns rather than ascending in a straight line a floor at a time'.[2]

In order to differentiate the 'introductory passages' more vividly, he expanded the stair landings to make them into further spatial areas: '. . . . in the ground plan the stairways should be placed so that the landings serve also as entrances to those parts of a room which are at different levels.'

Loos conceives the fashionwear salesrooms on both floors, and the stairway between, as 'vestibules' or 'anterooms' to the salons or 'main rooms'; 'One should not pass suddenly into the main room. One should be gradually prepared for it but nevertheless, be *surprised* by it. It is inconceivable to have main rooms without anterooms.'[2]

The visitor's 'surprise' is prepared systematically; the long salesroom on the ground floor, illuminated by daylight, panelled and furnished in light cherry wood, flows into the stairway, fitting area, and upstairs salesroom. Daylight extends only to the fitting area on the stairway; beyond and throughout the upper

Above: View towards ground floor through mirror.

Above right: Staircase, landing and fitting room from upper floor.

salesroom is artificial light. The light cherry wood is continued on the upper floor to the point where the stairway ends; there walls project on both sides to form a passageway. On the other side, the wood used for panelling and furniture is dark-stained oak. This, combined with the dim electric lighting on the low ceiling, tones down the light to such an extent that passing into the high salons, each lit by two windows, is indeed a 'surprise'. This 'surprise' is 'prepared' by the daylight that comes in through the open door of the manager's office.

The daylight entering the high salons clearly sets off the high-ceilinged parts of the rooms from the gallery zones. The built-in elements of the salons (galleries, cabinets, shelves), the panelling and furniture, all made of dark-stained oak, appear quite severe in the full daylight which comes in from the direction of the street outside; nevertheless, the wood does not seem as dark as in the upstairs salesroom before entering the salon. The salons, square in plan, are oriented by an *enfilade* in the passageways; in the rooms themselves, the gallery railings, which seem to continue from one through the other, extend this directionality.

The continuous spatial sequence culminates in a large open area next to the windows of the second salon: '. . . as a result of Japanese influence, room plans today are centrifugal. . . there is no emphasized centre. . .'[2]

This building of Loos, by its arrangement of spatial elements and spatial areas, by its successions of materials and lighting, contains within it '. . . a free way of conceiving space, and rooms which are planned by arranging them on different levels rather than fixing them to a single floor with continuous passageways; rooms which are composed into an inseparable, harmonic whole which has a structure that is spatially economic.'[2] These principles became manifest in the dwellings he designed.

In the preceding section, an attempt is made to analyse, singly and collectively, the rooms that make up the Knize fashion tailor's shop, to show that Loos employed all the means available to constitute spaces to 'articulate the room through their use'[4] in order to produce an integrated sequence of rooms. Visitors experience this sequence as a preparation, introduction, transformation, and surprise in space; they directly encounter the dimension of time 'as a sum of successively experienced relationships between localities.'[6]

Above: Top of stairs and salesroom on the upper floor.

Above right: Upper floor salesroom and view of manager's office.

Propositions about the function and effect of spatial design

1 A sequence of rooms is functionally articulated to achieve a psychological effect so that a customer passing through it will experience an adventurous spatial drama:

The architect possesses the possibility of preparing a main room by an introduction. . . by designing anterooms and passageways with suitable proportions and materials to reach that effect. . Entered from a low-ceilinged room, a moderately high one seems higher . . . Materials can evoke . . . joy or sadness, fear or cheerfulness. [2]

This spatial drama influences the way in which individuals involved in it decide to act through its arrangement of spatial elements and configurations of them, and through its gradations of light intensity and differentiations in space stereometry. The customer is presented with walking directions but he is offered a choice among alternatives including rest areas, turning points, even possibilities for turning back; new domains for action open constantly. The 'alternatives' offered in this spatial drama, this decision game, are of course more or less fictitious since they are designed to serve one and only one purpose: selling. All decisions (toward movement, rest, or directionality) are meant to result in the decision to buy.

2 The elaboration of an otherwise simple and mechanical selling process opens the possibility that psychological needs of the customer can be satisfied. These needs include being able to make

choices in a playful manner while moving around, resting, or being momentarily distracted by the latest fashions; furthermore these needs are influenced by an individual experiencing constantly changing impressions of rooms with continuously varying stereometric spatial configurations, differentiated spatial structures, materials, and graded lighting — both qualitatively and quantitatively — which all contribute to impressively enhancing or unexpectedly changing these spatial impressions.

Moreover, it is possible to interpret the spatial sequence of this men's fashion shop in terms of unconscious symbolism, transformed by the designer into a configuration of rooms; this symbolism being that of a 'place of retreat.' It would be beyond the intention of this study (and beyond the competence of the author) to formulate an extended psychoanalytic interpretation of the spatial sequence. However, several discussions with psychologists revealed the

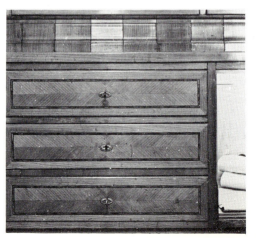

190

Far left: Sales area.

Centre left: Salesroom, glazed cupboards, and staircase.

Left: Corner of salesroom with built-in shoe cabinets and panelled ceiling.

Far left, below: Narrowing room divider between the two functional areas.

Below: Veneered design of drawers.

idea that this extended cavity, winding, narrowing, and widening at various places, symbolizes a vagina, which in turn symbolizes a place of retreat. (It should be possible to test the validity of the above statements with the help of tests and interviews administered by social psychologists.)

3 The effect of such places of retreat is ambivalent. On the one hand they can be used for an unconscious symbolic perception of spatial elements and structures; similarly they can be used for a conscious aesthetic reading of the spatial design concepts involved. (These concepts are readily available to anyone competent in aesthetics.) On the other hand, tapping this kind of regressive psychological activity can be done to influence the customer to buy. 'The display of merchandise and its viewing along with the sum of motives involved in and around the process of buying, all serve to promote the conception of a theatrical work of art, complete in itself, with the aim of influencing the public's willingness to buy. Thus, the selling place is made into a stage, the function of which is to convey experiences to the public which stimulates it to buy more.'[9] Thus the fulfilment of psychological needs (sublimating the needs of basic drives) and economic manipulation (compensation by buying goods) are ambivalently intertwined in the effects of spatial design.

4 This attempt to intertwine economic manipulation with psychological need-fulfilment — done unwittingly before Loos' time, but deliberately since — employs spatial design not only to stimulate buying, but also to make the prices of goods seem plausible, to distract buyers from considering their usefulness and to value goods in response to a mood evoked during the buying transaction. As a consequence, spatial design becomes a commodity which can be (and is in fact) sold, because it meets psychological needs and opens the possibility that interior environments be libidinously cathartic, something that does not usually happen in urban streets or public buildings. Thus the opposition between usefulness and uselessness is resolved in a different way than Loos intended. He considered himself an emancipated functionalist who would resolve the opposition by expanding the notion of functionalism; which was indeed realized in designing this shop. The only thing is that he was not far-sighted enough to take seriously the idea that the ambivalence involved in fulfilling libidinous needs could be used in spatial design to manipulate consumers; for him it only had a quality of playful irony.

5 It is not possible to 'resolve' the commercial and manipulative character inherent in spatial design either by a 'revolution in architecture' — as each new system of aesthetic means would possess new possibilities for manipulation — or by changing the social system. Rather it is necessary to initiate a process aimed at making conscious the ambivalent character of aesthetic complexes as well as of spatial design. Being aware of these complexes must be understood as a process of reflection about 'the objective analyses of the structural and specific mechanisms by which effects [of spatial design] are reached' and about 'those subjective contents [in relation to it] which can be recorded.'[7] The result should be a political understanding of the process of aesthetic communication. This latter phenomenon should be thought of as the subjective experience of the effects of objective spatial structures as well as reflections on them.

Conclusions

This study undertook to show that a spatial and functional analysis of an inner city Viennese men's fashion shop reveals that the design of the building

Far left: Entrance to manager's office.

Left: View into manager's office through mirror.

Left: High-ceilinged sales salons 1 and 2.

Top: Built-in cabinets in the 1st salon.

Above: Cashier in the 1st salon.

shell as well as its interior, where the transaction of business takes place, does not follow formally merely as an expression of its function but that the shell itself has an expressive content that fulfills psychological needs. The organization of the functional areas into a coherent sequence of rooms represents an operative symbolic system; beyond that it serves as a designative symbol which represents a 'place of retreat'. The emotional meaning of this sequence of rooms with its obligatory social value is used to influence the buyer and so becomes an immaterial commodity itself.

These insights into the interpenetrating parameters of spatial design may be formulated as the following themes for discussion:

1 Spatial design is used to guide individuals through sequences of signs and symbols;

2 Psychological needs are satisfied by designing spaces so that they serve as sequences of symbols intended to

193

Below left: Original decor of 1st salon.

Right: Fitting cubicle under the gallery.

Below right: Free-standing showcase.

manipulate these needs;

3 The psychological needs of the consumer and the economic needs of the entrepreneur interpenetrate in spatial design;

4 Spatial design creates a commodity in that it definitely influences the experience of buying (the sale of immaterial commodities);

5 Attempts to eliminate the commodity aspect of spatial design are possible only by reflective insight into this and also into the idea of a process of manipulation and the transition to a process of aesthetic communication.

Above: Passage between salesroom and 1st salon.

Above left: Connecting element between 1st and 2nd salon.

Far left: Vista from 2nd salon through 1st salon to salesroom.

Notes

1 A Loos, 'Die Herrenmode' (1898), 'Wasche' (1898), 'Ornament und Verbrechen' (1908) in *Samtliche Schriften,* Vol I., (Ed) F. Gluck, Vienna, 1962, p. 19-25; p. 113-120; p. 276-288.
2 H. Kulka, *Adolf Loos — Das Werk des Architekten,* Vienna, 1931.
3 L. Munz, G, Kunstler: *Der Architekt Adolf Loos,* Vienna, 1964.
4 Th W Adorno, 'Funktionalismus heute' in *Ohne Leitbild — Parva Aesthetica,* p. 104-127, Frankfurt, 1967.
5 D Worbs, 'Knize — Herrenmodegeschaft von A Loos (1909)', Lehrstuhl Grundlagen der Modernen Architektur, University of Stuttgart, 1968.
6 J Joedicke, 'Vorbemerkungen zu einer Theorie des architektionischen Raumes', in *Bauen + Wohnen,* p. 341-344, 9/1968.
7 Th W Adorno, 'Thesen zur Kunstsoziologie', in *Ohne Leitbild — Parva Aesthetica,* p. 94-103. op. cit.
8 A Lorenzer *Kritik des psychoanalytischen Symbolbegriffs,* Frankfurt, 1970.
9 W F Haug, *Kritik der Warenasthetik,* Frankfurt, 1971.

195

Left: Gallery visually connecting 2nd and 1st salon.

Above: Window wall in 2nd salon.

Above: Waiting area under gallery.

Above right: Original decor of 2nd salon.

MENTAL STRATEGIES IN ARCHITECTURAL DESIGN

PETER F SMITH

197

There is much talk of a need for a tool to assist the process of architectural design. Now available to nearly all architects is the most versatile tool conceivable, the human brain. Admittedly it has long been in the background in man's historic search for a design method, sometimes so merging with the background as to be indiscernible.

As a design instrument the brain has enormous potential, and before architects abdicate their role to an array of allied trades or alien computers, it is worth speculating how some of this potential can be realised. The task facing the architect is indeed formidable as he contends with the need for escalating performance standards both from himself and his architecture. But before capitulating to the prospect, it is sensible to tap the residual capacity which may be more than enough to meet today's and tomorrow's needs.

A good deal has been written about design processing and methodology. This article is an attempt to relate this activity to mental mechanisms and to suggest ways whereby the business of creativity can be supported by certain cerebral strategies. Being a summary of a course of lectures, many generalisations and assertions must remain unsupported owing to limitations of space. However, reference to the bibliography may provide partial compensation. The procedure will be first to describe the mental system, giving a very brief appraisal of the varied capacities of the brain. The second section will consider methods of exploiting the system, and proposes optimal strategies.

Description of the system

The brain has been described as a 'special universe',[1] that is, it is a system with its own rules. By understanding these rules, it should be possible for the architect to exploit the system more effectively. This will not inevitably produce better design, it will merely release potential. Nothing can make up for the absence of design capacity. So, these random thoughts are designed to help the architect with talent to do even better (and perhaps encourage the architect without talent to recognise the fact and become an administrator).

The brain possesses a number of specialised characteristics:

(1) It is a system for recording events. Memory operates on two levels, short-term and long-term, the latter almost certainly involving structural changes between cells.

(2) Input is analysed and recognised against categoric patterns or sub-schemas, and then attached to the appropriate memory patterns, e.g. 'church' or 'shopping street' sub-schemas.

(3) It operates a system of recall which is able to regard memory data as a unitary mass which cuts across time. Prominence within the memory system is a matter of repetition or singularity of the experience, not serial position in the time-scale.[2]

(4) The brain is also a learning system. In this respect it operates on two levels. First, on the level of the primary space schema, the principal brain instructs the 'lower brain' or cerebellum, by a cunning method of eavesdropping, to react correctly to the complicated cues of environment. This way the cerebellum learns to act automatically and generate the necessary motor responses.[3]

Beyond this there is the secondary space schema which involves cognitive appreciation of environment, relational perception, and symbolism. This is the level on which occur value judgements of built environment. The mind learns to recognise environment, and build its complex urban models. This is the sphere in which aesthetic relationships are learnt and appreciated.

(5) The brain operates a system of executive control, whereby purposive thought makes use of memory schemas to formulate conclusions or strategies of behaviour.

(6) In certain respects the performance of the brain is most efficient when it is not inhibited by the verbal, logical matrices of conscious thought. Many testify to the creative and problem-solving capacity of the unconscious and part-conscious mind. Thus on the unconscious level, executive controls still operate, but under non-rational rules; cabbages get linked up with kings.

It is important to point out that the brain is not merely a simple recording system. It is highly selective and even prejudiced. Selection is determined by two factors; individual needs and individual experience.

The individual needs may be determined by physical or psychological desires, preferences and prejudices. Input may be filtered, or perception orientated towards satisfaction of these needs, or reinforcement of myths. Otto Klineberg lists four ways in which information may be screened:

'*Selective inattentions:* noticing only what fits our prejudices and ignoring what does not.
Distortion of imagery: misperceiving what we cannot avoid attending to.
Making exceptions: shrugging-off as atypical what we cannot misperceive.
Reinterpretation: choosing from alternative ways of looking at the self-same facts.'[4]

Secondly, individual experience can interpose a selective filter, perhaps through certain patterns having pleasant or unpleasant associations.

However, the most important filtering process arises out of a physical characteristic of the brain. It is widely conceded that the brain achieves long-term storage by means of making patterns of connections between cells. As there are 10,000 million cells each capable of about 5,000 separate connections, the storage potential is impressive.

Cells are related to each other by 'switches,' and each time a switch is activated it henceforth has a lower threshold for activation. This is an immensely important characteristic because it determines so much of the style of perception and thought. This has been called the 'self-maximising principle' of the brain.[5]

If memory patterns are analogous to indentations in a surface which are deepened each time they are used, and thought and perception are regarded as a liquid, it illustrates this important mental principle. As a liquid will automatically flow to the deepest indentations, so attention gravitates to the most firmly established mental patterns. This means that one tendency of the brain is to be increasingly biased in favour of the familiar. This aspect of mentation is analogous to the biological principle of homeostasis since it opts for equilibrium between internal models and external reality. This aspect of the system is kept in check by the teleological, tensile, anti-cliché, curiosity-orientated side of the psyche, which corresponds to the 'activist' principle inherent in the central nervous system.

Returning to the mechanics of the mental system,

this principle of self-maximisation applies to perception as well as thought. In the former case, the brain opts for rapid categorisation, and the more it is allowed to practice this vulgar habit, the less it is sensitive to subtleties and variations.

This tendency gathers momentum with time, and when the age of forty is achieved, the mind may be in serious peril. The metaphor of the rut is all too appropriate, except that it is a wide range of ruts that dominate the system, resulting in a growing blindness to detail. The mechanical characteristic of the mind is to search for similarities, thus tending to evade differences.

As stated, the antidote is the curiosity drive which seeks to discover differences rather than similarities. Architects above all other species should have an insatiable appetite for novelty and variety. Not only does this keep the system flexible, it also enlarges the mental library of information from which new designs emerge.

This introduces the problem of creativity, which is a function both of memory and thought or executive control. Inventiveness is still sometimes regarded as a matter of inspiration, which, by definition means an idea or image implanted by an external agency. Whilst not wishing to tread on any theological toes, there are other views of creativity, not quite so mystical, which concern activity within the mind.

Memory comprises patterns of cell connections with 'pathways' between them. With constant use the pathways become increasingly efficient. This results in a particular way of seeing the world. Because of its low-threshold, high-probability state, this structure of patterns and connections becomes increasingly difficult to modify in any significant fashion. The system may be revised by extension but not usually by redistribution of pathways. Re-routing of connections is outside the scope of the normal memory-thinking system. This all means that there is an automatic tendency for the mind increasingly to work against inventiveness and originality. It opts for the cliché both in thought and perception. This fact has considerable bearing on the design process.

Design strategy

This has been a very brief description of the mode of operation of the system of the brain. The next problem is to decide how the system, with its positive and negative attributes, can most usefully be exploited by the architect and designer. But before suggesting an approach to design which fully exploits the various capacities of the mind, it will be helpful to give it a context. Architects tend to be biased towards one of three design strategies which may be called:

(a) Inertia method
(b) Scientific method
(c) Intuitive method.

In practice, design procedure involves all three; however, the style of strategy is determined by whichever is dominant, like the resultant of a force system.

The Inertia Method is a design strategy which involves the minimum of effort. It is a system of solving new problems with old answers. In a period of overload it is a tempting way for architects to save in time and production costs. Respectability is given to this system by paternalistic Governments who offer all kinds of 'advice' to architects with metric shells, mandatory dimensions and grids, etc. Local authorities who repeat their council house types *ad nauseam* are the greatest exponents of the Inertia method.

The Scientific Method is a design theory which became coherent in the sixties. It was carried to extremes by Christopher Alexander, and still exercises a fascination for those who adopt a rationalist view of science. Scientific method is a means of tackling a problem by logic, and proceeding in a straight line towards a predictable solution. Logic works to strict rules, utilising a faculty of the mind called the 'consistency demand'. Components of the design are regarded as individual problems to be solved. When each element is developed it is added to the design equation, and the new 'whole' is tested for illogicalities. Design in this context is based on synthesis: components rationally designed, such as plan, structure, services, elevations, are integrated into the scheme at the appropriate stage.

Scientific design method is committed to a mental strategy called 'momentum processing'. It avoids the facsimile reproduction of the Inertia Method. Nevertheless it is equally dependent upon the past, using it to provide the *system* by which future design is organised. Under the rules of rational thinking it is impossible to achieve any radical breakthrough in design. Logic is incompatible with innovation.

This is a useful method for people heavy in technology and light in imagination, but it has inherent dangers. One is that it can induce in the designer a false sense of security. Having been totally obedient to

SCIENTIFIC DESIGN METHOD

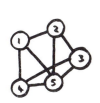

Stage 1

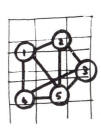

Stage 2

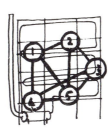

Stage 3

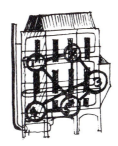

Stage 4

the Method, there is a temptation to expect architecture to emerge as if by right.

Secondly the logical thinker tends to be weak in self-criticism and possibly impervious to external criticism, with the result that periodically logical design produces some masterpieces of illogicality. Thirdly, there is danger such a designer (to adapt a McLuhanism) will proceed, by avoiding making small mistakes, to the grand fallacy. Urban environment now boasts more than its fair share of grand fallacies, and this is being written on the seventeenth floor of one of them.

The basic weakness of **scientific** method is that it confuses efficient building with architecture. Conscious, scientific design procedure can organise material excellently — it cannot make discoveries. Logical thinking is compelled to move in a straight line towards a specific goal. Attention cannot be multi-dimensional, because of what some psychologists call 'focal awareness'. At any one time attention covers a minute area analogous to the visual field which is in sharp focus on the retina. So thought can only move in a linear fashion. It is restricted either to inertia processing or momentum processing. Scientific design method is committed to the rules of the game, and even at its most sophisticated it is nevertheless governed by the self-maximising characteristic of the mind.

Certainly these are hard days for the architect who must contend with rising performance standards, litigation-happy contractors and mean governments. In face of all this and the explosion of technical information he is urged to become more 'scientific' in his approach. Some are a little uneasy about this because of their suspicion that certain ancillary technological 'experts' work to tolerances of roughtly ±100%. However, this can be dismissed as prejudice born of nostalgia for less complicated times. We are in a maelstrom of essential data, and a scientific approach to design is offered as the only chance we have of producing a rational building out of it all. This is all right provided rational building is not confused with architecture.

The Intuitive Method is superficially the antithesis of the Scientific Method. Amongst some intellectuals this design mode is unacceptable because it is supposed to be unscientific. Allegedly it is confined to certain

Left: Intuitive design method — 'deficient in those areas which call for logical processing'.

paleolithic members of the profession who refuse to acknowledge the post-machine age. What is more, a good number have the indecency to be successful and sometimes rather rich. That alone is enough to discredit the method.

The image of the intuitive designer is of one in communion with his muse, who receives the flash of insight, and *eureka* Ronchamp! Clearly some architects do believe themselves favoured in this way. But this charismatic view of design is unconvincing in such demythologized times. It was excusable for Abbot

CHARISMATIC METHOD

Suger of St Denis as an operational principle, but today we know a little more about the functioning of the mind.

The intuitive designer is one who allows unconscious information processing to dictate a conscious solution. Alvar Aalto is said to conceive a design at very high velocity. It coheres rapidly in his mind as he traverses the site having first digested the brief. What happens in his case is that a lifetime of experience, together with information relevant to the precise job, interact in a creative way, with minimum conscious executive control, to produce an answer. Because of his talent his answers are usually good.

Intuitive design methodology is sometimes vulnerable to the charge that it results in buildings which are deficient in those areas which call for logical processing. Against this charge many of the more exotic and idiosyncratic of contemporary buildings have no defence. The intuitive designer, because of his very facility, is tempted to reach premature three-dimensional conclusions. On his side he is a little contemptuous of technology, believing that

it is the job of the technologist to adapt to the demands of the architectural maestro. So intuitive designers have been known to be light on input, but this does not negate the importance of unconscious processing.

Unquestionably the unconscious strata of the mind are where man's real creative potential resides. The list of great discoveries and innovations which have been conceived quite unexpectedly, or through dreams or reverie, is endless. When the mind is allowed to freewheel it covers an astonishing amount of ground.

The intuitive designer exploits this problem-solving capacity of the unconscious mind. The mode is not without its hazards since there is a temptation to regard the product of intuitive processing as having some mystical infallibility. Solutions that have the mark of inspiration are sometimes invested with a semi-religious authority. To criticise certain architects is to commit heresy; understandably, since they have access to a transcendental pool of information.

Both scientific and intuitive processing have vital contributions to make to design strategy in architecture. It now remains to propose a policy which makes use of their positive aspects, whilst being alert to to those facets which are 'counter-productive'.

To distinguish it from inferior imitations this policy may be defined as the *Iterative Method.* This term is used to highlight the developmental nature of the method. The solution is conceived as an embryonic totality and developed by progressive input and feedback.

The Iterative Method has five stages, some of which correspond with classic design methodology. They are:

(a) Input or assembly of the brief
(b) Incubation
(c) Conceptualisation
(d) Development
(e) Appraisal

(a) Input

Two spheres of information comprise the input, the specific agenda and the non-specific agenda. The former consists of all the factors which are relevant to the one-off problem. This involves input from local authorities regarding planning constraints: a factor designed to test the ingenuity of every architect. There is also, of course, the client's agenda, which is usually something provided by the architect for the client. Specific input can have its lighter moments.

The non-specific agenda is made up of all information relevant to the problems common to architecture as a whole: building practice and building regulations, etc. Its efficiency increases with experience and feedback.

Much has been written about methods of assembling information and establishing relationships and hierarchies. Decisions made at the stage of the brief provide the design datum; therefore it is important that these decisions are right. Every building reveals a hierarchy of values. These may be consciously or

SPECIFIC CLIENT INPUT

"We must show that the Church is being up-to-date."

SPECIFIC INPUT

"Can we have a religious emblem on the main road?" Town Planning Condition.

unconsciously applied. An architect who relentlessly pursues a particular image, say in glass and concrete and in the process is subjecting his consumers to great discomfort, is advertising his own hierarchy of values. He is saying things about himself and his attitude to people.

Many of the complaints about contemporary environment may be pointing to the fact that certain archi-

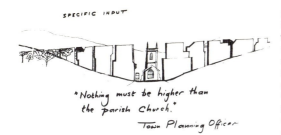

SPECIFIC INPUT

"Nothing must be higher than the parish Church."
Town Planning Officer

tects are deficient in their respect for people. The first factor which should decide the whole order of priorities in functional matters is a profound concern for human beings.

(b) Incubation

There should be no mistake about the fact that architecture is *discovery.* Every new building comprises a unique set of criteria, which call for a new solution. We are concerned with creativity. Certainly, logic and scientific analysis have a vital role to play. They are particularly valuable in testing the answer which has emerged by so-called intuition. The concept has to be developed and then passed through the sieve of criticism. But these are subservient to the creative skill which is a matter of establishing new connections, and relating hitherto disparate memory patterns: a cabbage with a king to produce the 'cabbing', a now familiar mutation.

In the last decade there has been a good deal of literature concerned with problems of creativity and innovation. Pre-eminent must be Arthur Koestler's *The Act of Creation.*[6] He leaves one in no doubt that creativity is a faculty monopolised by the unconscious mind. It is a matter of entirely new connections between schemas of memory; something which Koestler calls the 'bisociative act'. Logical, conscious processing is incapable of initiating a radical arcing across the cortex to produce an innovatory answer to a problem. Edward de Bono (*The Mechanism of Mind*) is quite adamant that any significant rearrangement of patterns of memory and pathways connecting them is outside the scope of conscious, rational thought. Basic rerouting of connections is the prerogative of non-rational thought which is active below the level of consciousness.

Why the unconscious is so efficient at innovation and creativity is still a matter of conjecture. Certainly it has something to do with the fact that it is not committed to the high-probability, logical, verbalised

matrices which govern conscious mentation. Released from focal constraint, attention can roam at will among the crevices of memory, discovering unlikely affinities and unique analogies. If there is a particularly obstinate problem on the mental agenda, it seems that the unconscious mind is capable of purposive activity in answer to the needs of that agenda. Since focal acuity has been relaxed and the 'beam' of attention greatly broadened, all manner of new relationships or bisociations can be shown up. Impetus is given to this activity by the stress induced by the very nature of the problem — 'the blocked matrix'.

In design theory, insufficient attention has been paid to the role of the unconscious mind. The idea of *inspiration* arose out of the manner of creative experience. Many artists and scientists have attested to the 'eureka' nature of inventive insight.

The originator of this phenomenon conveyed by that debased Greek word experienced the answer to a problem whilst taking a bath. The problem concerned the authenticity of the metal comprising a crown. It was ostensibly silver. He knew the specific weight of silver and the means of finding its volume came to him dramatically as he saw the water rise while stepping into his bath. Thus by measuring the water displaced by the crown he would know its volume — so, *heurisko!*

This story demonstrates how the problem was under constant scrutiny by his unconscious mind which was consequently ready to make the bisociative leap when the other half of the equation presented itself.

When released from the straight-jacket of rational thought, the mind can do remarkable things. So it is that some of the most dramatic discoveries have come through dreams.[7] Frequently the most creative time is the period between sleeping and waking when the mind is still uninhibited by logic but there is sufficient consciousness to recognise a good answer and capture it. Time should be allocated for the brain to perform its own alchemy.

It does this job all the better if the system is under stress. This may be induced by the desire to extract a good solution from an extremely complex brief. The architect who imposes upon himself apparently impossible standards of excellence is subjecting himself to stress. But he is the one to watch; great architecture comes from great expectations.

Purposive incubation is not a universal facility. For the fruits of unconscious gestation to be exploitable by the conscious mind, certain conditions are neces-

sary. The creative mind is one which is flexible and able to accommodate radical shifts in its frames of reference. It quickly tires of clichés and searches for the unexpected in the seemingly obvious. At the same time it avoids unyielding commitment to a particular design philosophy. Provided the self-maximising tendency is resisted early enough the mind can remain malleable, and indeed develop its creative propensity throughout life.

As a final thought it must be pointed out to those who regard all this as incompatible with scientific method, that a vast number of scientific and mathematical discoveries have all the appearance of accident. This is because they are the outcome of unconscious processing. Indeed it is from scientists that we get the best descriptions of the fruitfulness of the unconscious. The famous chemist, Friedrich von Kekulé, was particulary indebted to this facet of his mind, having made his major discoveries through dreams and reverie. He concluded an address to a group of most rational colleagues thus: 'Let us learn to dream, gentlemen.'

(c) Conceptualisation

Unconscious or subconscious incubation can only be exploited for a limited time. Busy practitioners soon have to switch over to conscious or directed executive control. Indeed gestation has to be accelerated by purposive thought. In this context the mode of giving birth can have an immense influence upon the shape of the product. Basically, there are three styles of thought or methods of processing which are relevant to design.

(1) Natural processing

This is all too common, and accounts perhaps for some of the gigantic mistakes which happen across the spectrum of people and nations. Natural thinking follows the undirected *modus operandi* of the brain. Thought freely follows the natural pathways which were often established at a pre-rational stage of mental development. The kind of conclusion drawn under this style of thought is that 'tall men are important or clever men.' If this seems foolish, consider that remarkable piece of anonymous research which found that the average height of professors is 4½ inches greater than the national average! Natural thinking is at the root of myths and prejudice and is something against which the architect, as the most social of all artists, must be on his guard.

(2) Logical processing

Solutions to present and future problems are synthesised from past answers. Development is by extension, using the past as its datum.

This kind of executive control works on the principle of deduction. De Bono calls it 'vertical thinking', the tendency of the mind, due to the self-maximising principle, to proceed in logical steps along established pathways to a precise goal. Logical processing tends to inhibit inventiveness for reasons stated; therefore it is desirable to find another method of processing which is not imprisoned in established patterns of schemas and pathways. If the mind is most fruitful when it is detached from logical and verbal thought matrices, so a style of processing which is equally uninhibited is likely to extract the best results from the system. One way in which the prevailing system can be changed is by the introduction of an external element which provides a new frame of reference.

(3) Heuristic processing
Both Koestler and de Bono come to a similar conclusion that an oblique or sideways approach to a problem may produce the best solution. Creativity cannot take place within the context provided by the current arrangement of information. Development is inevitably conditioned by the status quo producing at best a momentum solution. It is necessary to break free from the existing frame of reference to create the new thing. Creative thinking must by-pass the selective filters of logical thinking. In the latter, information which is not strictly relevant is excluded to produce a high probability solution. With the heuristic style of processing, nothing is irrelevant. All information is stored for its potential value, even though it may have an extremely low probability.

This kind of executive strategy has been called 'thinking sideways'; for de Bono it is 'lateral thinking'. Both imply that diverting attention away from a problem may be the best way of solving it.[8] An extension of this idea is the contention that the way to escape the momentum frame of reference to a problem is to relate it to a quite different frame of reference. This way new bisociations are thrown up. Hidden potential within the problem is released by the unconventional method of approaching it. This is called 'heuristic processing', since it is primarily concerned with discovery.

The oblique, new ingredient may stimulate creativity in three ways:-
(a) If there is a slight degree of logical correspondence between the lateral ingredient and the existing frame of reference, then it may act both as a *bridgehead* to the new concept and comprise its essence; in

biblical terms, both the way and the truth. This verges on a momentum solution.
(b) The lateral element may behave as a *catalyst*. It stimulates the interaction of memory patterns which would otherwise have no reason to combine under the self-maximising, high probability rules of the system. In this case the catalyst is not involved in the new state of affairs; it has acted like a symbol, exposing hidden affinities. Because it has no obvious connections with the problem and its consequent illogicality, it is able to spark off an interaction which logical thought would inhibit.
(c) Perhaps the greatest possibility of fertile interaction lies in the element of *chance*. This is a means of introducing ideas into the system which have no logical connection with it, in the hope that they may contain a hidden component of a bisociative interaction. When it is injected into the system the unconscious mind commences its scanning operation, searching for the hidden bisociative factor with which to establish the new affinity.

Certain techniques for providing the catalyst or the chance element are now widely recognised. Most common are gaming simulation and brainstorming. Alternatively the introduction of deliberate irrelevance may provide liberating illogicality. A change in the whole frame of reference, for example reversing the roles of figure and background, may prove fruitful. Some may be able to simulate a penumbral, dreamlike state in which attention flows freely across unconnected patterns, but in the context of a firm agenda. It is not suggested that this state should be artificially induced, despite such exemplars as Samuel Taylor Coleridge.

All these techniques are useless unless there is a sufficiently wide and varied matrix of stored information. Furthermore the matrix should be in a constant state of expansion. The more there is a rich and diverse input, the greater is the possibility of chance bisociation producing significant novelty. These observations are designed to help where there is already creative potential. The mind that is too committed to a logical organisation of data will never be creative. There is nothing so infertile as the strictly logical mind which is always right. De Bono offers a text for all architects:

'It is better to have enough ideas for some of them to be wrong than to be always right by having no ideas at all.'

Equally important as these liberating techniques is the ability to recognise a good idea when its shape

begins to assume coherence. All discoveries depend on the prepared mind, and architecture is as much a process of discovery as anything in art or science. The solution must be recognised at the right time and it must be sufficiently well-developed to survive the process of birth.

(4) Development
The basic concept which has materialised through incubation and purposive thought has to be capable of development into a physical building which works. From this stage there is the sequential, reciprocal procedure of decision and feedback. Development work in this design strategy is analogous to a helix. As decisions are taken and their implications on all other aspects of the building assessed, so the helical movement ascends towards the apex.

This is the time for the exploitation of the 'consistency demand'. As it implies, this describes the tendency of the mind to fit data into patterns of internal affinity; hence the concern is with the rules of the game. The consistency-demand operates largely on the unconscious level applying the rules which are relevant to the system under consideration.

One of the most demanding things about architectural design is that all decisions have innumerable repercussions throughout the structure and services. This requires mental skills equivalent to the computer, and perhaps it is the stage at which the computer has greatest potential.

To make the most of this facility of the mind, the rules of the game have to be firmly implanted, which is one important role of architectural education. When this is achieved the mind operates its own feedback system, testing the whole design complex for consistency whenever new decisions are made. Incompatibilities are thrown up, possibly in a coherent form, or sometimes through a sense of unease in the mind. The red warning light flashes, leaving conscious executive control to discover the precise point of inconsistency.

The design conceived after incubation through conceptualisation, has to be 'worked-up' into both a thing of elegance and an efficient machine for modifying micro-climate. The process of development and feedback is repeated many times until the required level of visual and mechanical performance is achieved.

(5) Appraisal
Maybe the most difficult skill for an architect is the facility to criticise the product of his creative mind

ASSESSMENT

I hate you!

Notes

1 Term used by E de Bono, *The Mechanism of Mind,* London, 1969.
2 The idea that memory data, though serially organised, act as a unitary mass was first proposed by F C Bartlett in *Remembering.*
3 This is very well explained by N Calder, *The Mind of Man* pp. 150-155, London, 1970.
4 Ibid.
5 A term used by de Bono and excellently explained by analogy in *The Mechanism of Mind.*
6 In *The Act of Creation,* London, 1964, a book which well repays the year or so it takes to read.
7 Koestler and de Bono, op. cit.
8 The truth of this is often experienced in relation to memory recall. Persistent thought may be unable to capture a particular memory. If attention is directed away from the problem for a time and then suddenly refocused on it, the elusive memory pattern is revealed. What in fact has happened is that the problem has remained on the agenda of the unconscious, which isolates the solution ready for capture by executive thought.

with true objectivity. He must achieve what T S Eliot regarded as impossible, the ability to be both artist and critic. Throughout the design sequence, the critical faculty is never dormant. Even so, the final product must be subjected to holistic appraisal. Others have written at some length about this, but one further thought is worth adding to current ideas about analytical techniques.

Architects are sometimes accused of illiteracy, which is a pity because critical ability is linked with semantic capacity. In this context, thoughts rely on words to give them life. Words are the vehicles for ideas. Sophistication in the realm of analysis or criticism is a matter of distinguishing subtleties and almost imperceptible shades of variation. It concerns the ability to verbalise the quality of relationships, and the essence of formal coherence. But this is an immense subject at present being tackled by one of my PhD students. I hope to be able to write about it with much greater authority in two years time, without, of course, acknowledging the source!

In such a rapid excursion through the design process it has only been possible to exemplify in the briefest way how certain attributes of the mind can support the operation. Apollo and Dionysius are present in all of us, and an efficient design strategy should exploit the qualities of each at the appropriate time.

Above: Typical operational view of a land-use gaming simulation exercise (see next article).

< REALITY   **INCREASING   ABSTRACTION >**

JOHN L TAYLOR

CASE STUDY	<->	IN·BASKET OR IN·TRAY METHOD	<->	INCIDENT PROCESS	<->	ROLE PLAYING	<->	GAMING SIMULATION OR GAME SIMULATION	<->	MACHINE OR COMPUTER SIMULATION

OBSERVATIONS ON THE REAL WORLD	NON-INTERACTING ONE TO ONE REPRESENTATION	INTERACTING ONE-TO-ONE REPRESENTATION	INFORMALLY STRUCTURED GROUP PORTRAYAL	STRUCTURED GROUP REPRESENTATION	ALL DATA & DECISIONS EMBEDDED IN A MATHEMATICAL REPRESENTATION

AFTER DUKE & BURKHALTER (1966 p.2)

204

The earliest widely publicised instructional simulation systems employing a gaming procedure to examine urban environmental problems were developed, in the United States, by Hendricks (1960). This prototype gaming experiment soon stimulated a considerable amount of discussion regarding the relevance of gaming-simulation approaches to professional training and, more importantly, activated the architectural and planning professions, as well as related disciplines, to undertake similar research efforts. It is such investigations that are the concern of these notes.

Definition of Terms

Hartman (1966, p.4) has defined 'simulation' as 'the development and use of models for the study of the dynamics of existing or hypothesized systems.' In this general sense, the term covers a range of dynamic representations that employ substitute elements to replace real or hypothetical components. To be useful, this definition has to be qualified according to certain specified criteria. For example, it is possible to classify simulation techniques in terms of particular objectives or according to their degree of abstraction from the real life system, operation or procedure. If, for illustrative purposes, the latter classification system is adopted, as in the figure *above right,* a single scale is established with the following major elements.

(a) Case studies
These exercises involve detailed descriptions or histories of selected problem situations which the student is required to analyse and discuss. The approach was very largely pioneered by the Harvard Law School and was subsequently developed and popularised by the staff and students of the Harvard Graduate School of Business Administration (MacNair, 1954).

(b) The 'in-basket' or 'in-tray' method
A method whereby an individual is called upon to play

Some related simulation techniques.

one specific role and must, in isolation, act on a number of hypothetical issues raised by the morning post. The participant is given a set time to make decisions arising out of each item of correspondence and each letter or memorandum is the basis for an individual decision-making exercise. The technique was pioneered and has been highly developed by the Educational Testing Service, Princeton, New Jersey, as a test for use in selecting American Air Force Officers (Zoll, 1966). The main feature of the test is the presentation of realistic problems in such a way as to elicit what might be termed reasonable responses. Records of these responses thus provide a basis for the assessment of performance. The objective of the exercise is to produce behaviour of the sort expected on the job. Consequently, interest not only rests on what is done, but also on the manner of execution.

(c) The 'incident' process
This technique is a modification of the case study method and it has been developed and described by Paul and Faith Pigors (1961) of MIT. In the incident process, the student is not given the entire case material and thus, throughout the exercise, must seek additional information by question and answer. In this way, the incident approach adds a data collection task to the case study process of analysis and discussion.

(d) Role-playing
A process requiring spontaneous mock performances from a group of participants. The people involved act out problems of human relations and discuss the development with other role players and observers. It is a technique which is used to gain insight into human interaction in the context of a safe learning environment and relies on spontaneous enactments to illustrate and dramatise human problems or actions. It should be noted that role-playing, socio-drama and psychodrama are closely related techniques and the terms are sometimes used interchangeably (Moreno, 1947).

(e) 'Gaming-simulation' or 'game-simulation'
Rauner and Steger (1961, p.3) have indicated that RAND adopted the latter expression to describe studies which incorporate both the free, explanatory, relatively unstructured characteristics of business or war games and the rigid, controlled, well structured qualities of traditional computer simulations. Such RAND studies customarily consist of human decision-makers interacting with a simulated environment; this environment is represented by other humans in combination with various models of the real world. The participants are then confronted with varied situations in order to facilitate the study of human behaviour or the development of particular processes.

(f) 'Machine' or 'computer' simulation

This species of simulation, as the name suggests, is used to identify operational models that have been programmed for high speed computing equipment. Here, the model is operated by manipulating the various symbols and programmes which replicate the variables and components of the system. Consequently, in these simulations, all data and decisions are embedded in the machine.

Before trying to establish a deeper understanding of gaming-simulation in particular, it should be emphasised that the preceding treatment of related simulation techniques is in no way comprehensive. There is, of course, considerable overlap amongst the preceding groups and the continuum presented here does not claim to be a complete taxonomy of simulation types but hopes to serve as a simple ordering device to clarify the ensuing discussion.

Basic Gaming-Simulation Elements

A clearer appreciation of gaming-simulation procedures can perhaps best be obtained by outlining the sequence of events which often constitutes an academic game. Prospective participants (players) are familiarised with the details of the actual exercise (the game). Certain objectives are usually described and actual play begins with an ordered system of decision-making. Decision outcomes (pay-offs) are almost immediately fed back to the players for evaluation. The cycle of decision-making, feedback and evaluation is repeated to allow the equivalent of many years of decisions to be completed in a single day. During this time, administrators closely observe all proceedings to enable further feedback, on the players' actions and performance, to be presented at the end of the game. At that stage, a post-mortem or critique session is held to discuss the gaming process and the development of particular strategies. The players have an opportunity for reviewing their performance and discussing the recurrent effect of continuous feedback. Finally, actual results and human interactions are analysed by the administrators to clarify and reinforce lessons learnt during play.
Simulation games, as used by urban planners and those in related disciplines, vary widely in their details, but they appear to share the following core features:

(1) They are principally used for learning how systems react under continually changing conditions.
(2) They are in essence simple abstractions of

relatively complex aspects of hypothetical or real world situations.
(3) They achieve their simplicity very largely through reducing complex operations into a series of simply expressed actions controlled by explicit rules.
(4) They expose participants to certain pre-selected features under relatively controlled and risk-free circumstances.
(5) They allow the concerted use of physical models, mathematical representations and human operators.
(6) They require participants to assume roles involving various degrees of co-operation, competition and conflict between players or teams and to make decisions which reflect their understanding of key features of the model.
(7) They produce certain decision 'pay-offs' — rewards or deprivations — determined by chance, by reference to human assessments or by the use of predetermined rules and formulae.
(8) They provide varied experience in controlling the course of events over time where the state of the simulated environment is continuously altered in response to the quality of accumulated decision-making.
(9) They generally compress 'time' and, as a result, are able to provide rapid feedback on the results and consequences of decisions.
(10) They progress in predetermined stages or periods and each period represents an allotted 'time' span.

In summary, simulation games are gross operational replicas that endeavour to provide insights into the dynamics of an on-going system. The participants are provided with decision-making experience over an extended period of simulated time, within a controlled and risk-free environment. The game replaces the complexity of the real world with a simplified abstraction which allows certain representative features to be easily understood and readily manipulated. There is quick feedback on all decisions and the games are structured into periods which force participants to consider repeatedly the development cycle of a series of interrelated problem issues. The technique provides a synthetic experience which allows players to profit from being directly exposed to, and personally involved with, pre-selected features of an evolving simulated system.

Urban Gaming-Simulation

Urban planning and development games are, in essence, dynamic representations of selected aspects of the human settlement; they describe, simply, the milieu

within which the architect and planner work. They collapse space and time, and are relatively unsophisticated mechanisms for studying urban phenomena which by other means might be expensive, difficult, or perhaps impossible to consider realistically. The adaptation of these instructional simulation systems to the study of urban phenomena owes much to American planners. As noted earlier, Hendricks (1960) was one of the pioneers in this field. His experimental gaming model was followed by two more complex urban-development games constructed independently by Duke (1964) and Feldt (1965). Encouraged by enthusiastic reports from these authors, representatives of similar professions and related disciplines are increasingly undertaking similar exploratory studies. As a result, various games are being used experimentally, on an international scale, by universities, colleges, research organisations and environmental practitioners.
All of these prototype games are, in many ways, derivatives of business games, which in turn are a direct outgrowth from war games. The latter type of game has been used for some considerable time by the military (Young, 1956) but business games are a comparatively recent addition to management training (Greenlaw et al, 1961). Both endeavours have benefited from, amongst other things, recent advances in computer technology, the continued development of a theory of games and a widespread interest in operational research. However, the impetus gained from these associated developments in no way overshadows the importance of the pioneering American work carried out by Hendricks, Duke and Feldt.

British Initiatives

Springing from such American pioneering efforts several forms or types of environmental simulation activity are discernible in the United Kingdom. A selection of these simulation groupings will now be reviewed in turn:

(a) The school system
Environmental simulationists owe much to schools and colleges. Not only have they been quick off the mark in recognising the existence of the technique but they have been in the forefront of much of the innovative and experimental work in progress in Britain. For example the 'project' tradition has allowed games and simulations to be integrated unselfconsciously into the classroom. In this context a low cost/high involvement format has been evolved

which puts to shame many of the more commercial or promotional models intended for similar settings yet at a much higher cost in terms of both finance and resources. The invigorating wind of change springing from such endeavours has been felt outside the school and college system and has helped to improve relationships with other educational sectors as well as with the world at large (see for example the extensive work documented by Tansey and Unwin, 1969, and Taylor and Walford, 1972).

(b) Extramural grass roots involvement
As a direct consequence of the school initiatives, a variety of charitable organisations, pressure groups and community action volunteers have employed the technique in a variety of settings. Liverpool's Educational Priority Area Project produced a game called 'Streets Ahead' to help children face and understand city life. Community Service Volunteers include 'Spring Green Motorway' — a simulation exercise on the advantages and disadvantages of building a motorway — and 'Mental Health' — a simulation involving the introduction of a hostel for mentally-subnormal young people into a community — all as part of their 'sack' of teaching materials. OXFAM have two simulations designed to teach young people about developing countries and SHELTER has a Tenement Simulation dealing with problems of families living in a multi-occupied house. In themselves, all such efforts appear very modest. Certainly they look very homespun in relation, for example, to the burgeoning products of American Evangelist groups. However, the real point of their significance in this context is their diverse range and comprehensive coverage. As a total effort it is impressive for this writer because of its uninhibited and yet unpretentious use of resources.

(c) Closing the gap between teacher and student in higher education
The structure of higher education in Britain, particularly the fragmentation of scarce resources for environmental studies, has done much to hinder the build-up of strong centres of excellence in terms of teaching, practice and research. As a consequence, smaller institutional units are common and very informal learning relationships tend to predominate. It seems that experiential approaches to many aspects of environmental studies have, in part, benefited from direct contact with 'coffee break' research which often remains unsanctioned by large foundation grants and sundry seals of approval. In an era where one man, one dog and a piece of string have been the rule rather than the exception in post-war Britain, all available hands

206

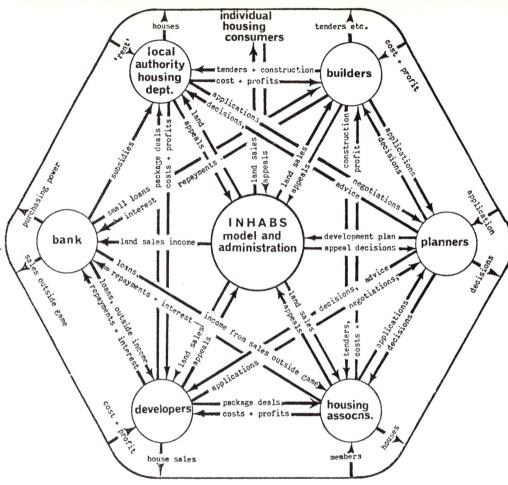

SOURCE: GREEN (1970)

have been frequently called to man the pumps regardless of status or departmental affiliation. What is being discussed here is a cottage-industry approach to fashioning new tools for learning. Excitement and ingenuity have become the order of the day and writing about such initiatives is very much second best to actual involvement.

Role relationships inside INHABS.

Examples of this type of work have been produced by Bracken (1970 and 1972) and Green (1971) who have both made significant contributions to the evolution of simulations catering for the needs of architects and planners. Bracken's Instructional Urban Simulation (INURBS) simulates the development of an urban community, mainly in physical and economic terms. The game is played on a large baseboard where various building types and land usages are presented in three-dimensional modular units to a specified scale. Players represent groups in both the public and private sectors of the community and are required to act out their roles within an overall financial framework. As a consequence, costing and financial justification must be made for each piece of proposed development irrespective of whether it be public or privately sponsored. The game has built-in facilities for such elements as economic studies related to density, location, accessibility, urban renewal, population growth and so on, in addition to allowing a variety of planning control mechanisms to be manipulated and the resultant consequences continuously displayed for public scrutiny. In essence INURBS is one of the more successful attempts designed to retain the immediacy and physical clarity of basic land-use games whilst at the same time incorporating the physical and economic impact of urban form.

A similar concern for urban form is to be found in Green's Instructional Housing and Building Simulation (INHABS). This model focuses on housing problems and consists of three games: SQUAT, SPRAWL and SPIRAL which are differentiated by their starting conditions in terms of site, player and economic condition. The games will accommodate between ten and forty players, whose primary goal is to find a 'home', but who may adopt roles concerned with the provision of housing as indicated *(opposite left)*. SQUAT reproduces the conditioning when land is occupied by low-income families and there is no form of planning control or publicly subsidised housing. SPRAWL is, as its name suggests, a suburban game concerned with the consumption of space in relation to familiar British land-use planning controls. SPIRAL reproduces the conditions found in the central housing areas of cities — high land costs, a demand for mixed development, mixtures of high and low income players, etc. In summary it must be stated that these games are not intended to classify the spectrum of housing problems into three self-contained categories, but merely to provide three defined starting points from which games may

Some of the results of the Instructional Housing and Building Simulation designed by Cedric Green.

develop. New starting points can be selected and sets of real conditions which apply to an actual site may be reproduced.

Such projects have an immediacy which defies simple description. Links to higher levels of complexity and other technologies are optional, for example, video tape, film, slides, graphic displays and three-dimensional models can be used if required but the predominant impression is very much of a low-cost and high-involvement approach to simulation. Above all, at an operational level such games do much to minimize the familiar accounting, administration and book-keeping problems which have bedevilled so many simulation procedures.

(d) Problem perception, identification and mapping Gaming-simulation as a process for thinking through urban problems still awaits serious development but there are signs that efforts to place the remote or passive subject into more actively involved learning situations is having some impact in a variety of spheres. For example, the work of Wilson (1962) and Hoinville (1968, 1971) in examining community attitudes and public perception of planning prob-

lems has broken new ground in employing simulations as a piece of social technology. A popular by-product of these efforts has been the use of 'priority evaluators' as aids to public participation and as an alternative to the overworked questionnaire. At the research frontier, Manchester University Institute of Science and Technology has been noticeably ambitious in defining experimental approaches to socio-technical problems. In particular Forque (1969), Platt (1969) and Roy (1971) have each in turn examined the position of the public services in the future. Feo (1971) has considered the practical use of simulation as a tool for community action groups. Finally, Warshaw, Levy and Talbot (1971) have evolved and set up an informal testing network for a set of linked games and simulations which permit groups to identify planning problems and possible design solutions. Space does not permit more than a passing reference to the tip of the iceberg, already presented above, but the speculations of writers such as Armstrong and Hobson plus Goodey (1970), all at the University of Birmingham, leads one to be exceptionally hopeful about the potential of simulation when related to what has been termed the art of contextual mapping and long-range forecasting.

General Education Features

Few validation studies of urban gaming simulation systems in use have been published and, as one might expect, it is the older, more mature American models which have been subjected to more detailed study. METROPOLIS and CLUG are two of the pioneering models which have outgrown constant up-dating procedures and these have been the focus of some evaluative attention; consequently it is assessments of these two games which are now considered. However, before going on to outline these findings it should be remembered that the authors concerned regarded both evaluation attempts as pilot studies and as demonstrations of the type of evaluation which could be employed in more extensive long-range studies. For example, the researchers did not fully investigate areas such as: the role and significance of the instructor or the appropriate selection of a game model, its length of use, its juxta-position with other material and its optimum utility in relation to age levels and academic attainment. Such neglected factors were made manifest and were identified as obvious areas for further research.

In the METROPOLIS study (Duke 1964), the performance of two gaming groups was compared with that of a control group; in all cases the students concerned were Michigan State University 'seniors', enrolled in a terminal course on city and regional plan design. After testing to establish a base line, 30 students were separated into the three groups, two of the gaming groups were given a three-hour briefing and a nine-hour exposure to METROPOLIS. Meanwhile, the ten members of the control group maintained the 'normal' lecture and studio work pattern which had been established for the course. Within a fourteen-day period all groups which played the game showed a marked improvement from the control team. In addition, approximately one month after the terminal examination was given an attitude questionnaire was distributed to reveal all the groups' reactions to METRO-POLIS. All replies were anonymous and students were encouraged to be frank. The response to this questionnaire indicated that: three-quarters of the total class had a desire to play METROPOLIS at a future date; two-thirds of those who had already participated in the game wished to repeat the experience and eighty per cent of those in this category considered their commitment in the experiment worth the time and effort.

A more recent and more detailed study of some of the educational aspects of another pioneering planning game has been provided by Margaret Warne Monroe (1968). Using the CLUG 1 model with three experimental groups and lecture course presentations with three control groups, she compared the performance of these six matched groups of students in a Human Ecology course at Cornell University in the autumn of 1967. Although limitations of time and numbers involved in the investigation restrict any generalisations from the findings, this research does provide some interesting insights into CLUG's teaching effectiveness and potential usefulness as well as providing a case study of a commendable methodology for testing planning games.

The experimental design of this pilot study was concerned primarily with a test of the hypothesis: will a gaming-simulation model (CLUG I) teach the same body of material as effectively as a lecture course with associated reading assignments, given equal amounts of time for instruction in both methods? To test this hypothesis, matched groups were evaluated as either CLUG players or as lecture and reading-course students. Three types of learning and retention tests were given to the total sample, which numbered thirty-two at the outset and twenty-four at the completion. The evaluation comprised: a factual test given twice, once immediately after the experimental application and once at the end of the academic term; an opinion rating; and a continuous participant and observer assessment. The results of this comparative study indicated at least three things. First, while the CLUG model can teach facts, it is not particularly effective for teaching factual or theoretical material. However, the game did incorporate an additional form of learning which was testable in terms of the dynamics of systems and more precisely in terms of how theory is affected by practice. Here it is of interest to note that perhaps the most important aspect of the research for Monroe was the implication that games have the ability to introduce a new dimension to the world of facts and theory by adding the pragmatism of experience (Monroe, 1968, p.ix). Second, confirming the observations commonly found in the literature, games motivate most students in a way not achieved by other teaching tools. Third, the nature of the learning which took place over time, and beyond the actual gaming sessions, indicated that there is a positive interaction between games and lecture materials, and a sufficient correlation to emphasize that games should not stand alone but should be integrated with lectures to constitute a broader form of course presentation.

In contrast to this limited validation material the literature is a rich source for a multitude of claimed benefits which can be summarised broadly under three main headings, connected with the design, operation and evaluation stages of gaming procedures. The actual task of designing games is seen by many as being an instructive activity which requires detailed data collection, systematic analysis and an ability to recognise essential and important relationships. Even when a satisfactory model is not achieved, the investigators are led to believe that they have obtained a considerable insight into the nature of the phenomena under study. For example, the model building process for the instructor is a means of demonstrating how little he knows about his teaching objectives in terms of the value of each academic task, its associated response and its relationship within the general educational framework. In other words, the formulation of a precise statement of objectives and the level of clear thinking required makes it necessary to consider the whole range of the designer's concepts, assumptions and tenets concerning his subject matter. Participation in a gaming situation allows players to experiment in a risk-free learning environment with alternative strategies and to witness immediately the resultant behaviour of a dynamic system. The simulation is seen generally as a low-cost substitute for experience where players are exposed to selected forces parallel to those found in the real world. Participants are, amongst other things, introduced to: a variety of interests in conflict; a varying degreee of stress; a number of sequential decisions where they are not in complete control; and a quick and repeated feedback on the adequacy of their performance. Through endeavouring to manipulate the simulated system and by experiencing consequences attached to their actions, and the actions of others, the players are expected on a trial and error basis to test out their understanding of an analogue central to a real life process. Implicit in this involvement is a widespread belief that the participant is being educated rather than trained; that is to say that he is improving his general orientation to problems, as distinct from perfecting his skill in particular techniques.

Post-operative discussion and evaluation enable the student to review systematically what he has or has not learnt and to correlate this with what he was expected to learn. Therefore, it is incumbent upon the teacher in his critique of the play, and to some extent throughout the administrative process, to compare the development of the simulation with the appropriate theory. He must indicate to the players how and when events take place in accord with theory. In sum, this stage, in addition to focusing attention upon critical and meaningful aspects of the experience, is a final check to ensure that erroneous learning is quickly corrected and that the lessons learnt during play are adequately reinforced.

Over and above these 'area' claims, a number of initial reactions from the author's own experience may be useful and relevant. But before presenting these comments, it must be appreciated that this experience is very largely limited to using games at the undergraduate level over the last five academic years. Their use can not claim to be fully integrated within the curriculum and, so far, they have occupied a minute position in the students' timetable. Obviously, instructional simulation systems must eventually be viewed as an integral part of a properly structured course. Meanwhile, it must be noted that reactions are likely to differ from individual to individual, from model to model and from situation to situation. Despite these difficulties, the experience seems to be sufficiently in accord with the literature and other researchers' personal observations to justify description at this stage.

In terms of student appreciation, instructional simulation systems employing gaming procedures are seen primarily as enjoyable experiences. All the models used by the author appear to be able to arouse and sustain a high level of interest and enthusiasm. The majority of students are favourably disposed toward the experience and very willing to take part in lengthy and experimental runs outside normal academic hours. The results of simple follow-up surveys together with volunteered opinion and reports from impartial observers confirm the popularity of the activity and the high level of student involvement. Whether a technique which is enjoyable is more conducive to learning than when the reverse is the case is a contentious issue. Suffice it to say that Beard (1967, p.27) has pointed out that:

'It is a well known principle in physics that the less the resistance the greater the effect for the same effort, in other words the greater the efficiency. This is a principle which holds in learning as well as in physical phenomena: if something which students enjoy doing can be introduced relevantly into the learning, the resistance is reduced and efficiency is likely to be maximised.'

By way of further comment on this point it can be noted that the game environment seems to reduce the so-called traditional instructor/learner polarisation. During operating sessions no judgment on the students' performance is generally needed since short-comings are very largely self-evident. The instructor can often stand aside and allow the participant to look upon the effects of his own behaviour. Team progress is invariably monitored according to a pre-determined scale and so most games are free from a type of subjective teacher assessment which, in some instances, might inhibit involvement or learning. The value of such a receptive learning situation is best seen when experienced professionals and junior students participate together; they take part readily and harmoniously on an equal footing not easily achieved in other forms of professional/student instructional interaction. In addition, reactions from both these parties suggest that the benefits, from this type of confrontation, accrue equally to both groups.

Finally it is important to appreciate that gaming-simulation procedures have certain properties not combined in other techniques. Here they attempt to fill a much needed gap by collapsing time and space whilst reducing human and irrational involvement to a degree of abstraction which is meaningful to many academic levels. Thus, dynamic urban systems can be transformed into relatively simple sequential processes where the momentum of time and the characteristics of scale can be repeatedly observed and manipulated, free from considerable background noise. The process is able to handle, broadly, both physical and social systems so that quantitative, qualitative and irrational elements in decision-making assume an appropriate real world relationship. In Meier's and Duke's (1966) terms, a novel hybrid form of simulation is being evolved which employs a mixed strategy to cope with ubiquitous human intangibles as well as with the more readily definable tangible elements of physical phenomena.

It is difficult to elaborate on these very general claims as so much in this new field remains to be identified or substantiated. As a result, it is only possible to conclude this section on general educational features by acknowledging that instructional gaming takes cognisance of at least *four* seemingly important educational trends which value —

(a) *active and extensive student involvement* in the process, with considerable emphasis placed on guided self-discovery;

(b) *decision-making experience* in realistic settings with rapid and repeated feedback; the feedback indicating the consequences of actions and the adequacy of performance;

(c) *conducive environmental conditions* with, for example, opportunities to experiment with little at stake and situations where the role of teacher as critic or judge is partly suppressed by self-pacing and self-monitoring instructional procedures;

(d) *diversity of presentation* through differing combinations of media with methods and materials which call upon the full range of auditory, manipulatory, verbal and visual skills.

Some Cautionary Notes

One of the most commonly cited faults concerns the possible substantial cost involved in designing and developing any game. It is to be regretted that no meaningful cost estimates for game construction in specific situations appear to be available. However, Feldt (1967, p.4) has argued that design costs are a very small fraction of those involved in the development of many urban models and probably no more than one or two man-years' work have been invested in the majority of today's planning games. He points out that costs required for a particular game depend, of course, upon the degree of detail used, the system it is intended to represent, and the amount of previous work upon which the game construction may be based. Although a considerable commitment in terms of time and effort is, at present, required to design and run a gaming exercise, it does appear that once a body of games is constructed and popularised then operating costs are likely to decrease continuously as experience increases.

As with any technique, care is needed; gaming-simulations may obviously be employed either efficiently or inefficiently. To achieve satisfactory results requires not only a willingness to integrate them into the educational system but also discernment and a high degree of expertise. The dangers of erroneous transfer and abuse can to some extent be mitigated by careful model construction and skilful operational control. In its ability to teach the 'right' rather than the 'wrong' things, gaming appears to be no more foolproof than any other technique.

A number of cautions have been voiced about the emotional problems which may occur in a gaming situation. For example, initially some participants find it difficult to accept a simple yet highly formalised game as a substitute for a system of complex environmental relationships. This scepticism is at present understandable when viewed against the novelty of the technique and the educational background of the players. It is not too much to hope that this attitude may be modified, over time, as a freer and more experimental approach to education becomes more commonplace. In addition, the widespread usage of academic games in the school system plus advances in the technique at a professional level will bring publicity and familiarity which *may* dispel unjustifiable inhibitions. It is then likely that a greater problem will arise from conflict between games as entertaining devices and as educational instruments. Already, there are those who feel that games produce more enjoyment than learning.

One final qualification follows this brief survey of claimed advantages and limitations. Such a collection of assertions is built on a growing consensus of opinion rather than a well documented catalogue of proved successes and failures. Since learning situations differ one from another, what is a satisfactory combination of human and technical resources in one case may not necessarily be an appropriate 'mix' in another. Much rests upon the quality of the game itself and the skill of the administrator in directing all efforts toward the assigned objectives. It must be acknowledged that few validation studies on gaming techniques are available to shed any real light on the efficacy of particular simulation procedures in specific educational settings. Thus, the case for or against this form of simulation as a learning technique stands very largely unproven.

Expectations and Opportunities

If it is considered that certain British gaming-simulation approaches to environmental problems have any value or potential then it is possible to speculate about several avenues of development which seem particularly promising in their own localised context. Some of these opportunities are itemised briefly below:

(a) Wider and more varied employment of what is already on the shelf seems likely to be particularly rewarding — the only barrier to progress here seems to be the availability of better directories, operational manuals and introductory learning systems.

(b) In crossing the credibility threshold and leaving behind a preponderance of half-hearted commitment, the role of radio, television and film seems likely to

be of increasing importance. The use of such media in monitoring and analysis is already acknowledged but its value as a primer for *'simulating the simulation'* is barely explored beyond the superficial Madison Avenue image building.

(c) From the above, it follows that an improved orientation toward the consumer ought to be developed. However, many still view games and simulations primarily as psychologically satisfying intellectual devices for a select groups of academics rather than as instructional tools for an army of players. This self-indulgence has to give way if a better match and balance is to be struck between designers' ambitions, the available technology, as well as consumer needs and resources.

(d) The need for better packaging and distribution outlets seems clear and a move away from the cottage-industry production line must be more realistically explored. It may well be that one of the better multi-media packages may still turn out to be a book — but in a format very much in tune with simulation's needs. Commercial exploitation of the technique in Britain is almost non-existent. This point has to be recognised if entrepreneurial initiatives are to be shaped by more than basic market forces. Whatever transpires it is possible to take comfort in the fact that even pale simulations of reality might provide a degree of instructional stimulus in much the same way as a pot egg sets the wayward hen laying!

(e) Finally it is possible to take comfort in such small beginnings if one subscribes to the view that there may be something to be gained from the logical motor progression of crawl — walk and run! Here the concern is not with the need to reinvent the wheel but for more practitioners to be better aware of *existing* models and experience. Certainly in coming to terms with the administrative and accounting problems attached to many simulations the hard won experience of military and business exponents of the technique seems to be very largely ignored. If these opportunities to improve the performance of instructional systems are accepted, it is possible to see games and simulation as very much more powerful tools in the future. Clearly their use in inner city problems could be very much extended in identifying how people perceive problems, generate different courses of action and evaluate chain reactions.

Concluding Remarks

In summary it is possible to be excited by a small

number of new 'homespun' simulation approaches to urban problems which are crystallising very slowly in Britain. But by any standards it must be acknowledged that this work is obviously embryonic and far from complete. There is a modest degree of enthusiasm and vigour associated with developments in hand but few signs of widespread support or many discriminating consumers. In short, the absence of systematised and rationalised communication and co-operation networks largely defines the current state of the art. On the one hand, a high degree of 'isolationism' has left the individual free to plough his own distinctive furrow quietly, whilst on the other hand it has thwarted efforts to foster, disseminate and up-grade the expertise at the fingertips of the very few at 'the frontier'.

References

Armstrong, R H R and J L Taylor, *Instructional Simulation Systems in Higher Education,* Cambridge Institute of Education: Cambridge Monographs on Education No. 2. 1970.
Armstrong, R H R and J L Taylor, *Feedback on Instructional Simulation Systems*, Cambridge Institute of Education: Cambridge Monographs on Education No. 5. 1971.
Beard, R M, 'Using Tests to aid Learning' in *Teaching for Efficient Learning.* A report of the proceedings at the second conference organised by the University Teaching Methods Research Unit held at the Institute of Education, London, 6th January. 1967.
Bracken, I, *INURBS: Instructional Urban Simulation — A Manual for the Introductory Version,* Cardiff: Department of Town Planning, University of Wales, Institute of Science and Technology. 1971.
Cole, J P and N J Beynon, *New Ways in Geography,* Oxford: Basil Blackwell. 1968.
Crean, P, *A House Purchase Exercise,* Sheffield: Department of Town and Regional Planning, University of Sheffield. 1971.
Dalton, R et al, *Simulation Games in Geography,* London: Macmillan. 1972.
Dimitriou, B, *Video Tape Recording in Gaming Simulation,* Second Symposium on Instructional Simulation Systems in Higher Education, University of Birmingham, 6-8th January 1970. 1970.
Dimitriou, B, 'System Alphaville' in *Bulletin of Environmental Education* B13 May. 1972.
Duke, R D, *Gaming Simulation in Urban Research,* Institute for Community Development, Michigan State University, East Lansing, Michigan. 1964.

211

Duke, R D and B R Burkhalter, *The Application of Heuristic Gaming to Urban Problems,* Technical Bulletin B. 52 Institute for Community Development and Services, Michigan State University, East Lansing, Michigan. 1966.

Feldt, A G, *The Community Land Use Game,* Ithaca, New York, Miscellaneous Papers No. 3, Division of Urban Studies, Centre for Housing and Environmental Studies, Cornell University (mimeo.). 1965.

Feo, A, *Operation Games: Their Application to Socio-Technical Problems,* M.Sc. Dissertation, Design Research Laboratory, Institute of Science and Technology, Manchester University. 1970.

Glasson, J, C Minay and J Minet, *Politics and Planning an Education Game,* Oxford Working Papers in Planning Education and Research No. 6. 1971.

Goodey, B, *Perception, Gaming and Delphi: Experiential Approaches to Environmental Education.* Paper prepared for Architectural Psychology Conference, Kingston Polytechnic, Kingston upon Thames, Surrey, 3rd September. 1970.

Graves, N J, *Geography in Secondary Education,* Sheffield: The Geographical Association. 1972.

Graves, N J (ed.), *New Movements in the Study and Teaching of Geography,* London: Temple Smith. 1972.

Green, C W, *INHABS 2 Instructional Housing and Building Simulation: Operating Manual,* Cheltenham Papers 4, Gloucestershire College of Art and Design. 1970.

Greenlaw, P S, L W Herron and R H Rawson, *Business Simulation in Industrial and University Education,* Englewood Cliffs, N J: Prentice Hall Inc. 1962.

Hartman, J J, *Annotated Bibliography on Simulation in the Social Sciences,* Rural Sociology Report No. 53, Iowa State University, Ames, Iowa. 1966.

Henderson, R, *Gaming as a Teaching Vehicle.* Paper presented at the Heriot-Watt University and Edinburgh College of Art Department of Town and Country Planning Seminar on 'Teaching Methods in Scottish Planning Schools' 30th November. 1968.

Hendricks, F H, *Planning Operational Gaming Experiment.* Paper presented to the North California Chapter of the A.I.P. Meeting on 'New Ideas in Planning' 19th November. 1960.

Hoinville, G. *Economic Evaluation of Community Priorities.* Paper prepared for the 'Research for Social Policy Seminar', February 1970.

Longley, C, *Games and Simulations,* London: British Broadcasting Corporation. 1972.

Mackie, A D, *Free Gaming in Urban Design.* A paper prepared for the R.I.B.A. Forum on Gaming Simulation held at the Institute of Advanced Architectural Studies, University of York, 12-14th July 1971. 1972.

Mallen, G L, *Ecogame,* Computer Arts Society, Bristol Computer Society Specialist Group Announcement. 1970.

Massey, D, *Problems of Location: Game Theory and Gaming Simulation,* Centre for Environmental Studies, London, Working Paper 15, August. 1968.

Meier, R L and R D Duke, *Gaming Simulation for Urban Planning,* American Institute of Planners Journal XXXII (1) January pp. 3-16. 1966.

Monroe, M W, *Games as Teaching Tools: An Examination of the Community Land Use Game.* Papers on Gaming Simulation No. 1, Centre for Housing and Environmental Studies, Division of Urban Studies, Cornell University, Ithaca, New York, p. 133. 1968.

Moreno, J L, *The Theatre of Spontaneity,* translated from the German, 'Das Stegreiftheater', New York, Beacon House. 1947.

Mchale, J, *The World Game,* Architectural Design XXXVII February. 1967.

Macnair, M P (ed.), *The Case Method at the Harvard Business School,* Cambridge, Mass., Harvard University Press. 1954.

Pigors, P and F Pigors, *Case Method in Human Relations: the Incident Process,* New York, McGraw Hill. 1961.

Rae, J, *Games,* Architects' Journal No. 15, Vol. 149 9th April, pp. 977-983. 1969.

Rae, J, *Use of games in architectural education: I, Educational Strategy,* Architects' Journal, 13th October, pp. 827-830. 1971.

Rauner, R M and W A Steger, *Game-Simulation and Long-Range Planning,* p. 2355 Rand Corporation Santa Monica, California, 22nd June. 1961.

Roy, R, 'Studying the future of public services by simulation' in *Feedback on Instructional Simulation Systems,* Armstrong and Taylor. 1971.

Sarly, R M, MIKEGASIMO *The Milton Keynes Gaming Simulation Model,* London: Department of Town Planning, Central London Polytechnic. 1971.

Tansey, P J (ed.), *Educational Aspects of Simulation,* London: McGraw-Hill p. 274. 1971.

Tansey, P J and D Unwin, *Simulation and Gaming in Education,* London: Methuen. 1969.

Taylor, J L, *Instructional Planning Systems: a gaming simulation approach to urban problems,* London and New York: Cambridge University Press, p. 190. 1971.

Taylor, J L and R Walford, *Simulation in the Classroom,* Harmondsworth, London: Penguin Education. 1972.

Tidswell, W V, *Geography in Primary Schools,* Sheffield: Geographical Association. 1972.

Walford, R, *Games in Geography,* London: Longmans. 1969.

Ward, C and A Fyson, 'Environment Education: classroom games' in *Town and Country Planning* 39 (6) pp. 324-326. 1971.

Warshaw, L D, R Levy, and R J Talbot, *GRIPS 1: Gaming, random interfacing and problem structuring.* A paper prepared for the Design Research Society Conference on Design Research Society Conference on Design Participation at the University of Manchester, September. 1971.

Yeomans, D T, 'Teaching Simulation to Architects', *SAGSET News* Vol. 2, No. 2, April, pp. 36-42. 1972.

Young, J P, *A Brief History of War Gaming,* Washington D.C. Operations Research Office, the Johns Hopkins University. 1956.

Zoll, A A, *Dynamic Management Education,* Seattle, Washington: Management Education Associates. 1966.

Acknowledgement

This article results from the author's studies into the development of instructional simulation systems in higher education and draws on a series of progress reports which have been issued in connection with aspects of this work. As a consequence the writer is indebted to many long suffering students and colleagues for their generous co-operation, encouragement and guidance. Last, but by no means least, the author would like to thank the Department of Town and Regional Planning, University of Sheffield, The Sheffield Centre for Environmental Research, the Royal Institute of British Architects and the Nuffield Foundation for their continuing support and financial assistance.

'U-DIG' GAME: A TOOL FOR URBAN INNOVATION

ERVIN J BELL

212

This is a study of a study of a process. The environment of the *design decision-making process* exerts a very strong influence on the form of the city. The more we as designers or we as city dwellers understand this process the better are the possibilities of improving the quality of our urban living. The various 'actors' in the process of the development of the environment have been isolated from each other for many reasons such as specialization, the academic division of disciplines, and the complexity involved.

The contractor is concerned about completing the building with a good profit margin, the architect is concerned about the building's publishability, the banker is concerned about the building's loan, the building commissioner is concerned about compliance to a set of legal regulations and so on, until finally we reach the occupant who is concerned about adapting the building to his specific needs.

This process has slowly evolved into its present form. The slow development and partitioning of the activities of design decision making have resisted and discouraged serious study.

One relatively recent method to study a complex process is through operational gaming. When answers can't be given because the variables are too numerous and interdependent, the process may yield understanding through simulation or gaming.

U-DIG Game is a study of the process of the development of city form. It is frankly only an entry and not an exhaustive study. The entry is the attempt to simulate and simplify the financial environment so that it can be a comprehensible component in the game. With this complex but relatively well-definable component designed, the other components can be studied for inclusion in the game. The development of the brute force of the computer has made this type of study more possible.

If such a study can lead to the elimination or lowering of barriers, so that the architect understands the influence of the financial structure on the physical structure, so that the banker understands the relationship of his financial decisions to the quality of living in his community, so that the building speculator sees the long-lasting effect of short-term decisions and the law-maker understands his role in the inhibiting **port**ions of the building code and the zoning laws — then their attention might turn to innovative ways to attain a higher quality of living for all. I proceed from a naive belief that all the 'actors' in the environmental design process would genuinely wish to work to improve the quality of life if they were able to break out of their narrow interest constraining cells by understanding their vital roles in attaining a better life.

The objectives of U-DIG are:

(a) *Pedagogical* — to teach university students and others about real-estate investment and the building process.

(b) *Research* — to investigate better ways of living through manipulation of various factors in the game environment.

The basic design objective in developing the U-DIG Game was:

To be simple, directly comprehensible, yet still contain significant parallels to the real world and to provide a basis of knowledge for further understanding of the process.

Functional objectives were:

(a) To have a visual display of the progress of the community upgrading in the course of the game.

(b) To keep the accounting procedures as simple as

possible in playing the game, using prepared tables (but not to depend on the availability of a computer).

(c) To provide opportunities for using strategies similar to those used in real life.

(d) To incorporate consideration by the players for the *form* of new community buildings and for the site.

(e) To be a structure or tool for innovative future research.

The game was designed with a six-block neighbourhood using a Lego base with one Lego block representing two rental units. Red blocks represent all new construction after the start. Zoning has been established to control density, and height limitations could be added.

When a blackboard is available, the neighbourhood blocks are drawn on it and after each change in property ownership, the title is 'recorded' by writing the owner's name on the lot.

In Version One, three to five teams of one to four players play in multiple sessions of three to four hours each. A board illustrating a neighbourhood plan is used. When an opportunity to purchase occurs to a team, computer developed investment tables are consulted for aid in the decision to buy. Buying, selling, building and bidding all may take place in the course of play. Year end pay-offs are made after income tax in a simple bookkeeping procedure. Interest rates and occupancy rates fluctuate. Mortgages are available at the current interest rate. Thus the economic rules are closely patterned after the real world. After an initial period of play, the players become familiar with the dynamics of real estate economics and the basis for decisions that determine the urban form.

In Version Two, a news item is distributed that announces the elimination of property lines. Property owners own a proportional share of a block. They can now build dwelling units on top of units owned by others in a common structure that crosses streets within the same density limitations as the first version. Rules are set that establish ground coverage and the relationship on each level above ground. This is one version in which an experiment with a change in one factor in urban form determination is varied to result in a new form. The 'quality-of life' merits of this can then be debated. Other rules may easily be changed to study the effects, thus the research possibilities exist.

The value of U-DIG lies in its worth as a tool for

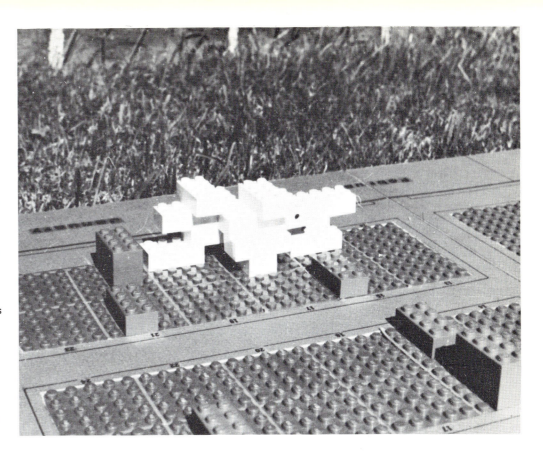

understanding existing urban situations (Version One) and as a research device to help develop a better quality of urban life (an example is Version Two). In Version Two, the game sessions indicate some of the problems of planning, phasing and blending a growing megastructure with an existing urban fabric.

Investments or playing strategies can be devised based on the predicted rates of return given in the tables. Some possible strategies are:

(a) Investing with little concern for a rate of return much greater than that possible to receive from the cash in the bank.

(b) Investing with great discrimination, that is, waiting for the best rate of return which means waiting for the lowest rate of interest in a year of high occupancy.

(c) 'Trading Up' or always being alert for opportunities of selling older property so one can have the same equity in a much larger project.

(d) Hoarding cash in order to be secure at a 5% increase each year.

(e) Bidding always below offering price, and building and buying most heavily during years with a low interest rate.

Rigorous testing of strategies has not been done. Such testing would require many runs for a period of time to simulate fifteen or twenty years, about ten to fifteen playing hours. In order to test strategies, the game might be programmed so that one person could play the game on a computer time-sharing console. This would return basically to the simulation programme modified for input by one person. It suggests another possible modification of U-DIG; to play with the computer doing the computations during the game. To do so would open up many more options such as, a change in the rent by the owner, bids at any over minimum price.

The game can be used in a variety of university classes in various ways:

(a) A single playing session: to demonstrate a limited number of ideas such as the effect of the financial environment on the forms of the city, or how a mortgage actually functions.

(b) Several playing sessions: to demonstrate and experiment with limited modifications of the variables of the game. Version One might be played with different ranges of rents and gross multipliers and interest rates by changing the variable values in the computer programme. Version Two could be modified by adding building requirements to provide for many building patterns, such as a diamond-shape building in plan that spans three adjacent blocks.

(c) The structure might be presented to a class in architecture in a quarter or semester project. The investigation of existing parameters of play (or of construction in real life) would be the task of the students. With the existing conditions outlined, the student's ideas on 'ought to be' or revised conditions can become the basis for new rules to be tested by incorporating them in a game that is then played. The student's basis of investigation would be in four components outlined in the final section of this paper and the development of 'new rules' would be an opportunity (and obligation) to understand their values in order to express them in drawing up the new set of rules. The debates would centre around improvement of the 'quality of life' and how to attain it.

(d) A variation on (c) to challenge the class to devise a set of minimal rules that would require agreements by players to decide on their own rules, especially on the arrangements allowable in the Version Two game.

In (c) and (d) the class would investigate ways to evaluate the resulting forms. Among the factors of evaluation would be the amount and quality of natural light that is allowed into the various living areas, the density, the amount of open space for play and interaction, and the relationship of areas and activities. As a learning experience, this would tend to focus the attention of the student on the most relevant factors of architecture that relate to the quality of living. As this is done with stylized blocks to represent the building shape, the student

thinking is pushed into the conceptual level of design.

In the above, the teacher's role should be a minimal one, with the responsibility for the decisions that affect the environment being on the game decision-maker's shoulders. The board could be rebuilt allowing street and other city patterns to be redesigned and the game would encourage class interaction and critique.

The structure of U-DIG is meant to be flexible in order to provide for innovative learning and research goals. As a background for considering further developments, the major components of the U-DIG Game are identified.

First, an *economic component* is represented in the prepared tables and their understanding and use. This is the financial environment of the growth of the community.

Second, a *technological component* is embodied in the Lego block and its rules of combination. The Lego block represents two dwelling units and a part of a corridor. It is a structurally complete unit that has been designed to be combined as described by the rules of combination. The plumbing, mechanical and other architectural considerations have been assumed to be resolved.

Third, a *legal component* is the set of rules that parallel the legal requirement affecting the development of the community. It includes the zoning codes, building codes and property ownership laws.

Fourth, a *social component* is the most evasive one to simulate. Presently it is represented by the attitudes and agreements between players and underlies the other components. In Version Two, the social interaction is increased by the need to coordinate construction in order to consider the quality of living.

Each of these components might be an area of further development:

The *economic component* is a relatively well-defined area. The tables can be simply altered to change the range of any one or more of the financial variables. Before playing the game in a specific neighbourhood, the existing factors can be 'in-put'ed to make the tables and hence the game's operation more relevent to that neighbourhood. Another use of the game is to investigate the effects of government subsidies in privately owned rental dwelling units by printing tables to reflect the subsidy, such as a lowered mortgage rate and a lowered down payment.

The *technical component* could reflect innovations in building systems. For instance, a newly designed

building unit in a hexagonal form could be modelled and used in the game. Its development within the constraints of the game would be the result of decisions by each of the teams.

The *legal component* may be altered in order to test its effects on the form of the city. Version Two, the mega-neighbourhood, is an example of this. The private property lines concept was modified: property lines were eliminated thus allowing a new building form to emerge. Height, density, open space are other legal requirements that might be modified in order to view the form resulting from a 'run' of the game.

The *social component* is the most ill-defined element as it represents the total diversity of human experience. This area of experiment might include playing of the game by members of a ghetto so that they might not only learn about some of the factors in community development, but also may better understand those unreachable owners of ghetto property so that they may better communicate with them. Coalitions or ways of cooperating to own and develop their community may be run in the game. Innovative means of ownership might be devised and tested.

Combinations of modifications of two or more of the components may be chosen to be studied in the game. Another direction of the game may be to add more playing components. An enlargement of the number of blocks to a small town with several neighbourhoods of different character, a commercial area, public areas, schools, parks, civic buildings, etc. Politicians, planners, school officials, architects and others involved in decisions that affect the form of the city might be added. In order to simulate the formulation and operation of zoning laws, a limited functioning planning commission and city council might be added.

U-DIG, the study of an urban process, is never ending. The game is a tool to help in the understanding of parts of the urban labyrinth.

A COMMUNITY DETERMINES
WHAT ITS CENTRE IS

DAVID LEWIS

Because of the recent interest in ordinary citizens participating in the architectural and planning processes which directly affect their lives, the editors of *The Inner City* have invited me to make some remarks on the work which my firm has done during the last nine or ten years in community-based projects in cities in the United States.

During this period we have been involved in a number of projects, each of which — except the very first — has a community participation model designed specially for it by the participants themselves.

How does such a project get started? It is difficult to generalize. Some projects begin in an atmosphere of crisis, confrontation and violence. Others begin peacefully and rationally. Perhaps one should just say that some critical issue of public interest arises which defies traditional methods of problem solving.

And at some point a person or a group, the mayor or a community leader or a community group, calls an open meeting to which citizens and representatives of government agencies, colleges, health and religious institutions, and the private sector are invited to come together in the realization that the only intelligent way to resolve the city's most urgent problems and to shape its future is not through confrontation, but to work together and to pool resources in a comprehensive plan of action.

Although this seems at once obvious and reasonable, it represents a profound departure from the way things are usually done. Most public schemes are in the hands of bureaucracies set up specifically for them. There are dozens of separate bureaucracies in the USA to deal with housing, education, health, recreation, traffic, and so on. Some of these bureaucracies are at the local level. Others are at county or state levels. And yet others, particularly those involving national programmes, are even more remote. And each bureaucracy has its own specialist staffs, budget lines, priorities, timetables, and administrative rules and constraints.

But communities are extremely complex. It has been said that communities resemble nets, or, more precisely, overlapping nets, and I think that this is true. You take action on one issue and it affects the entire network. Problems cannot therefore be resolved one at a time. Yet this is precisely the way most public, subsidised programmes are set up.

For example, housing seldom, if ever, exists by itself. Housing means families. And families are not only very individual collections of people but include three or more generations, from children to grandparents. A community of families therefore contains a great variety of people, with a variety of cultural and recreation needs, and employment and health needs, and with an enormous richness of detailed experience and creative resources. As a result, housing means a lot more than just houses; and education means a lot more than just schools.

Holistic concepts of planning are by no means new. During the past thirty or forty years there have been a number of bureaucratic mechanisms set up to dovetail programmes in terms of comprehensive planning goals and policies. The problem however is that these mechanisms have traditionally involved only the bureaucracies themselves, working within an established political power structure. They scarcely, if ever, involve ordinary people. It is hardly surprising that decisions tend to be remote, over-simplified, insensitive to precise local configurations and values and at best 'second guesses'. We miss out on a great deal of wisdom and concern in not enfranchising the man-in-the-street. After all, no one knows local problems and local needs better than he does.

The situation is often extremely frustrating not only to the people whose lives are directly affected by this kind of planning, but also to the local administrators of public programmes. The executive director of a housing authority or the principal of a school may know local needs and aspirations extremely well as a result of day-to-day contacts with the people of his community. But critical decisions which affect his work at the local level are seldom made locally at all but in some remote office at the state or national level by bureaucrats who have not the slightest contact with the lives of the people they are affecting.

When we first began, rather timidly and amateurishly, nearly ten years ago, to work in the way we do now, there was little or no room in the design process for the people who actually use the buildings and streets. It was unheard of at that time to involve typists and personnel managers and janitors in, say, the design of a multi-story office block beyond perhaps just filling out some questionnaires (the impact of which on the ultimate design is of course unknown to these consumers because there are no monitors), any more than planners and architects involve mothers and fathers and children and grandparents, even today, in the design of multiple housing projects.

Our concern was partly for a richness which we knew was missing, not only in our own work, but in the city all around us. Cities seemed to have become compilations of fragments. 'Good' buildings, 'bad' buildings, 'beautiful' buildings by famous architects with eloquent vocabularies of form which the glossy magazines could get breathless over, or 'ugly' buildings by hack architects which lacked eloquence or originality of form — they were all fragments.

And we found ourselves wondering why the coherence of so-called primitive environments, the hill towns of Italy or Greece, the villages of the Dogon, the walled cities of the Sahara, or the *barriadas* of Peru and Venezuela appealed to us so much, urban environments in which the vernacular architecture does not depend on individual form-inventiveness for its richness but rather on a cultural and social appropriateness which finds formal utterance in precisely the opposite way, in coherence and belonging.

But our concern did not really take shape until we were asked to become involved in a planning programme, the basis of which was social fragmentation in which the disenfrachised were beginning to riot in the southern cities and to burn the buildings of the establishment, the banks, the schools and the chain stores. It then became clear that the appeal of popular environments was not nostalgia for things past or other, but something real and pertinent to our work in modern cities today. It became clear that all of the old and traditional places which are so admirable to us were held together by a common and extremely sophisticated culture of popular expression — an expression which without exception sprang from an awareness of belonging and social wholeness among ordinary people, a responsibility for community values which is not necessarily entirely conscious or declared but which finds sensitive utterance in form and scale, colour, incident and continuing dialogue.

And we began to realise that the creation of urban coherence by formal means, by self-conscious design, in the absence of social coherence would perhaps be less true and less meaningful than fragmentation, until we found a way of involving ordinary people again and of providing a means in contemporary attitudes and approaches which has since remained constant.

Pittsburgh

In February 1964 I was asked to be the physical planning consultant in a city-wide effort to integrate the schools. The main thrust of the project was racial integration; but in Pittsburgh integration came to mean many other things as well.

Pittsburgh is a very diverse city. It has steep hills and valleys, and broad rivers. In its nineteenth-century industrial expansion steel mills and railroads were built in the valleys, and the houses were built on the hillsides and the higher elevation plateaus. As a result the city is really a series of residential neighbourhoods separated by steep topographies and formidable man-made barriers.

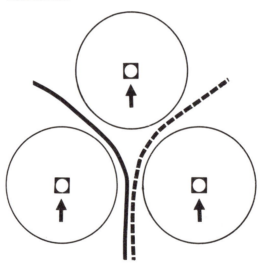

Since they have always been cut off from one another, it is hardly surprising that these neighbourhoods are introverted in character. Each has its own commercial centre, usually in the form of a traditional high street, and its own churches, parks, schools, and clubs. Add to this infrastructure the fact that Pittsburgh's industries, during their period of rapid growth, relied heavily on immigrant labour for its steel mills, Poles, Russians, Italians, Serbs, Irish, Germans and Jews, and it is easy to see how the neighbourhood form became a perfect vehicle for articulating and entrench-

ing cluster in terms of ethnic, religious, linguistic and cultural traditions.

Several neighbourhoods in the city still have great charm and local richness. Russian churches with onion domes painted gold and blue stand among white frame houses; and along tree-shaded streets are the delicatessens and the bakeries, the restaurants and the taverns with their pool tables, and the places where you can still buy special clothes and books and antiques.

But powerful forces are destroying the neighbourhoods. The new residential areas are suburban one-acre lots, on which the domestic architecture is toted by real estate agents as 'ranch houses'. Pedestrian scale has been replaced by automobile scale. The high street of the suburbs is an air-conditioned mall, an island in an ocean of parked cars. Suburban neighbourliness is automobile range. 60 mph is its scale, and freeways are the link.

Meanwhile the older in-city neighbourhoods, built all at once, are growing obsolete all at once. Their narrow streets, not designed for big American cars with their marvellous fins and lights, are filled with fumes, noise, dirt and crime, and are no longer pleasant or safe for pedestrians. The inner city neighbourhood has become the area you escape from if you can afford it. And the destruction of the older neighbourhoods is supported insidiously, and with tragic results, by education. This may seem to be a curious charge, but it is nevertheless true. Education, we are told, is the road out of the ghetto. But where to? To the suburbs, of course. Universalist education in a technological world is a linear progression from kindergarten to PhD by annual increments. From neighbourhood to university to the national technocrat employment market and the middle class. This prescription, for the immigrant family keen for the success of its sons, is mandatory. Education is the road out of the ghetto, and it is a one-way street.

As planners we inherit a number of significant factors as a result of this out-migration from the older neighbourhoods to the suburbs. In the suburbs there are decentralizing industries eager to be attractive to young managers and technocrats; shopping centres eager to capitalize on mobile affluent shoppers with the young look; young teachers eager to work in bright new schools, and with a homogeneous student body without the complications of social, racial, class and cultural mixes. and smart real estate men eager to facilitate the transience that is the inevitable result of an international technocracy.

Pittsburgh, USA: steel mills, railroads and highways fill the river valleys. The residential areas of the city are hilltop islands.

terms for their expression of social wholeness, of local environmental belonging and responsiveness. Our process therefore does not start with programmes, clients or bureaucracies. It begins with people, places and issues. And it assumes that bureaucrats and clients are people and citizens too, in the same way that everyone is. The process is truly holistic, and therefore works against polarization. It does not serve special interests, nor does it take sides, whether community or establishment, and it is therefore rather different from 'advocacy' planning. It deals with issues, bureaucracies and people as wholes. Unfortunately in a short article there is not enough room for more than three examples. And even these have to be treated in such a generalized way that I know I will be guilty of over-simplification. And in the interests of continuity I am choosing only projects in which the major component is education. I am starting with an early example, 1964-67. Although its community participation was extremely weak, it set in motion a series of

And then there are the suburban jurisdictions, the new local governments, not only in competition with the inner city for new industries and commercial areas and other forms of attractive tax-paying settlement, but keen to protect themselves against any form of in-migration from the inner city which they might consider undesirable. By irony, the first-generation children of migrant families who have 'made it' are now conservatively protective against migration!

As this process continues year by year, the capacity of the city to renew itself is weakened through loss of tax-base, and the skills and leadership of the young. And with the out-migration of young families, gradually only the ageing remain, in large houses which they have difficulty in keeping up on pensions or fixed incomes; so cultural continuity is eroded and will ultimately crumble.

But as the older ethnic neighbourhoods have declined, it seemed that another kind of neighbourhood was growing stronger in its identity and cultural richness, and this is the black ghetto. Black in-migrants from the south are not new to Pittsburgh; but cultural identity, the establishment of urban neighbourhoods culturally different from every other kind in the city, is relatively new, and to begin with not generally perceived by white society. Where most people in the city, and particularly in the bureaucracies, saw dirt, poverty, violence and unemployment, some were beginning to see neighbourhood richness, colourful clothes, music and dance, a tremendous revitalization of language through the colour of 'ghetto talk' and the powerful quest for identity which has expressed itself through the civil rights movement, the Black Panther movement, and in Afro-Americanism.

Much has changed since 1964. The riots in the Watts section of Los Angeles, the assassination of Martin Luther King and the subsequent riots in Washington, DC, Detroit and Pittsburgh have galvanized black pride and white recognition. And much celebration of blackness, and black identity, has occurred. But each celebration of blackness alone, each emphasis on one part of the city or one culture as separate from the whole, increases the danger of introvertism. As I have already pointed out, I was asked in 1964 to assist in planning a city-wide effort to integrate schools. The Board of Education was prepared to demolish every high school in the city, located as they were in the old neighbourhoods and reinforcing neighbourhood patterns, and replace them with four or five educational centres so large that their

service areas, covering a whole quadrant of the city, would automatically produce integration. In my view the argument in favour of these centres was false in one basic concept.

Integration was seen as numbers. It was seen only as an acceptable mix of black faces and white faces. Once the mix was obtained universalist curricula took over. Equal opportunities and equal options for all. The road out of the ghetto is through education. Unfortunately there are no *equal* opportunities or *equal* options, because people start from different points. It seemed to me that education, and a number of other programmes as well, required to be restructured to produce, not equal opportunities but opportunities, not equal options but options. It seemed to me that education should respond, not to a technocratic universalist goal, but to the personal and social needs of highly differentiated peoples, cultures and neighbourhoods.

At the time there was a lot of talk about the 'plural society'; but I felt that very few people, especially planners, had thought pluralism through. Whether I did or not I don't know; but I saw these education centres as an opportunity to express pluralism instead of integration, and thus to express the vitality of differentiation at major points of confluence, meeting and exchange in the city. I put a team together, which has since become a permanent firm, Urban Design Associates, to explore the possibility of treating the Board of Education's capital budget as investment, not

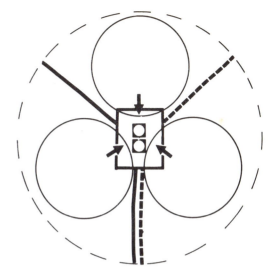

in schools in the traditional sense, however large and modern, but in a more total **piece** of city. The idea was to coalesce around education's investment all the public investment in other programmes which could be brought together; in housing, parks, transit, health, cultural facilities and so forth; and then to see what additional private investment — in commercial facilities, market housing, service industries, and so forth

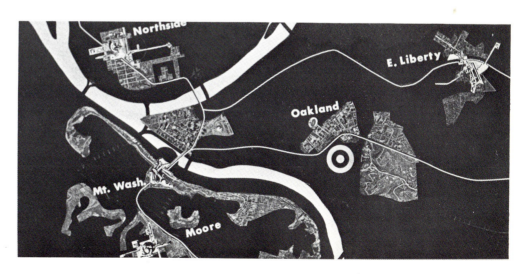

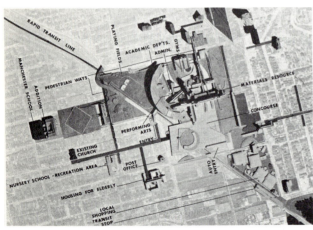

Two designs for multi-usage community centres in Pittsburgh. Although each scheme includes housing, shops, entertainment and recreation its major component is education. (Urban Design Associates: David Lewis and Geoffrey Copcutt, 1964-67)

— could be attracted by this public investment magnet.

From 1964 to 1967 four centres were designed; but they were never built. They were conceived as a federation of cores in the inner city, so located that they would be linked to one another by the highways and proposed rapid transit routes which presently encourage suburban expansion and the death of the older neighbourhoods.

They were seen as an opportunity to restructure the inner city to compete successfully with suburban expansion. Each centre included shopping malls, light industries, schools, cultural facilities, and so forth. Besides their relationship to highways they were also located on sites which would serve a number of hitherto separate and introverted neighbourhoods. New housing and pedestrian greenways fingered outwards into the neighbourhoods, linking them to the new centres and to each other. Most of all the centres were designed to celebrate multiplicity; to celebrate the unique resources of all the inner city communities, their food and music, their cultures and languages; and to interface education, as a learning experience, with this incredible richness. The concept of 'school' as a separate institution is thus replaced by a piece of city in which education, along with many other things, occurs.

But as I look back I see, not the forms, but the failure; the magnitude of our lost opportunity; our inexperience in putting bureaucracies together in a single plan of action; and our failure to canalize into our project the rich creativity of the communities. We did not make these mistakes again.

Pontiac

In the summer of 1967 when we first went to Pontiac, the home of two of the largest automobile industries in the US, the riots in Detroit and other cities had recently flared up with shootings and arson; and Pontiac was full of tension and the threats of public violence between blacks and whites.

The city was polarized not only racially but in many other ways as well. In Pontiac's black ghetto were the city's worst pathologies of poverty, crime, slum housing, unemployment, drop-outs, and transience. There was also a Spanish-speaking population; a ghetto-within-the-ghetto; Puerto Ricans and 'chicanos' (Americans of Mexican origin), separated by language, culture and religion. Yet containing the ghetto on two sides were extremely affluent exclusively white residential areas. And on yet another

side lay a white blue-collar area, a bastion of trade unionism. Segregation in Pontiac thus had many layers of meaning; for segregation by race was also segregation by class, income, culture, restrictive employment practices, and neighbourhood.

In this tense situation the Board of Education wanted to build a school, dedicated to the idea of bringing the children and parents of all the divided sections of the population together. We suggested the Board go one stage further.

Working on our Pittsburgh experience, we suggested that instead of talking about a school in the traditional institutional sense, the Board should challenge the citizens of Pontiac to view its capital budget as an equity investment in the social and physical future of the city which the citizens themselves should help to design.

If present-day society is in a state of confrontation and violence, is this the urban world in which we want our children to grow up? If the answer is no, then the challenge is to impel into being a place which will bring all sections of the city together voluntarily, and in terms of their own recognition; a centre which would provide the sense of meeting and spontaneity of a public plaza; yet would also provide a series of specialist facilities directly related to the community's needs and in which everyone could share; a centre which would also act as a catalyst to other schemes and projects in other parts of the city; indeed to design, not a community centre, but the centre of a community. We recommended an open and public design process in which anyone and everyone could participate freely. Dr Dana Whitmer, who is the superintendent of

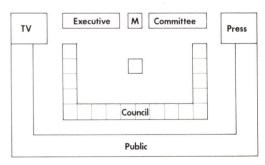

Seating plan for the Pontiac Area Planning Council, USA. This was an early example of a citizen-participation planning process (1967), and the council was directly responsible for the community centre now known as the Human Resources Centre.

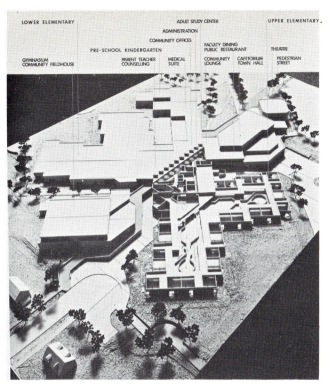

LOWER ELEMENTARY   ADULT STUDY CENTER   UPPER ELEMENTARY
ADMINISTRATION
COMMUNITY OFFICES
FACULTY DINING
PRE-SCHOOL KINDERGARTEN   PUBLIC RESTAURANT   THEATRE
GYMNASIUM   PARENT TEACHER   MEDICAL   COMMUNITY   CAFETORIUM   PEDESTRIAN
COMMUNITY FIELDHOUSE   COUNSELLING   SUITE   LOUNGE   TOWN HALL   STREET

*The site for the Human Resources Centre in Pontiac,
USA, was selected by the citizens. They decided that
it should be adjacent both to City Hall and to the
city centre which lies immediately west of City Hall.
The pedestrian street which runs through the complex will ultimately connect by a bridge to the new
multi-level city centre now being built. (Urban Design Associates: David Lewis, Raymond L Gindroz,
and James N Porter.)*

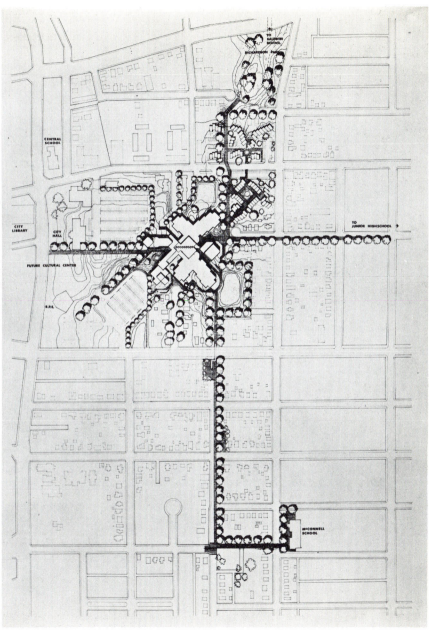

schools in Pontiac and widely acknowledged as one
of the most courageous educators in the nation, readily
agreed; and the Pontiac Area Planning Council was
born.
The council contained representatives of all sections,
races and interests in the city — from executive
directors of General Motors to Black Power youth,
from the trade unions to the banks, from the chamber of commerce to religious leaders and politicians.
It was chaired by the mayor; and sitting on its execu-

tive committee were the directors of every public agency in the city. Meetings were held every three weeks and were open to the public for full participation. The press and TV/radio stations were always invited, and usually present. In fact sound reporting was one of the main constituents of the success of the process.

Fundamentally the process was simple. The public was asked to draw up inventories of need and of aspiration. The executive committee was asked to respond with explanations of available resources in programmes, funds and priorities. In this way the planning process moved forward, step by exploratory step, from goals and ideas through alternative site and building design studies to construction and realisation.

Although the process was simple it was not easy. Hostility and suspicion ran deep. And the realities of public programming were often idiosyncratic and contradictory. But the desire to overcome the mistakes of the past was a constant force. Today the Human Resources Centre, as it came to be known, is built and occupied. It is different from any other centre in the USA. That is perhaps inevitable since its design responds to local needs as articulated by the people themselves.

A street runs through the complex. Along the street are theatres, libraries, social services, a day-care centre, a public restaurant, a health centre, and a major indoor recreation centre. Threading through the building are facilities for 3500 adults and for 1800 children. Many of these facilities are intermixed or shared. For the adults there are workshops, studios, a language centre, an ethnic centre, a food co-op, extension courses by three universities and a community college, cultural and social facilities, and special programmes and services for the elderly. For the children there are resource centres, mini-theatres, and learning spaces where education through team teaching and ungraded continuous progress occurs.

In many ways the centre is a piece of city rather than a separate building. The street which runs through the centre is the culmination of a system of pedestrian greenways which radiate out into the neighbourhoods. Within the centre there is also an internal street system. The centre is thus the confluence of several communities which in the past have been traditionally separate and introverted, and is the link between the neighbourhoods to the east, north and south and the centre of the city.

At the urging of the people in the public meetings, the linkstreet is covered and skylit like a shopping

mall with as many of the social and cultural facilities as possible, such as the library, the theatres and exhibition areas, the public restaurant, the informal lounges and terraces, and the offices of the social agencies opening directly from it. Colour, light and glass are everywhere, inviting people to come in and out at any time and in complete freedom.

After two years in operation the Human Resources Centre can now be seen in retrospect to confirm that when citizens and bureaucrats participate in a comprehensive and action-oriented project together not only will there be new, surprising and unexpected design forms but a new spirit of identity will develop. One of the curious things about the process was that dichotomies between citizens and bureaucrats, even at the national level, began gradually to break down in much the same way as the hostilities and fears that existed between various sections of the community. They all became simply people working together, even though many of them were hundreds of miles apart. And while the community worked on programmes and monitored plans, federal, state, county and city officials bent or combined the very regulations and policies about which in the past they had been so protective, and congressional representatives even

Black is beautiful.
Red is beautiful.
White is beautiful.
Yellow is beautiful.

changed state law to make the Centre happen.
What emerged is the first joint-usage complex in the USA to be funded comprehensively, on a multi-agency basis, from federal, state, county, city and Board of Education resources. And today the consumers who

helped to design it have an equal voice in its governance. As a result the spirit of exploration and inventiveness which went into its programming and design has led to many changes. The centre is not only very different already in its content, but it has expanded into adjacent buildings. Thus the process continues; all of which proves that if architects and bureaucrats will relax a little it can be done.

Gananda

Since Pontiac began we have been involved in several community-based projects. In some of these, schools have been the beginning of the process. In others, a hospital or housing have been the starting-points, and in another scheme it is a city-centre. All of them, until Gananda, have been in the inner city; and they have all been what one might call neighbourhood phenomena in that they are at once part of a metropolitan whole yet they represent a spirit of revolt among relatively compact and coherent communities of people who have responded to an opportunity to participate publicly and responsibly in the political and planning and architectural discretions which affect the quality of their lives at an utterly local level. And none of them has sought architectural innovation. Rather they have sought environmental forms which are directly and honestly appropriate to local concerns and values and which have within them the capacity to be modified and to evolve, since obviously needs and values in the future will change.

The whole experience therefore becomes extremely salutory, for the architect is not asked to invent but to respond, to be acutely aware of human mutation, to create in colour and scale, mass, void and continuity environments which will celebrate, not the architect's genius, but the human worth and belonging of the people who will use them; and we are perpetually reminded of the fact, which we like to ignore, that those urban environments from other cultures from which we so often draw sustenance were seldom the work of planners and architects at all, in the studio or professional sense, but of people, ordinary anonymous citizens, who were in direct dialogue with the historical processes and pressures and crises of their time and place. It is our culture only which has separated the role of planner and architect from his function as a citizen and it is our mistake, and also our conceit, if we believe that citizens are any less capable of discretion now than they were in the past.
The extent to which architects and planners have overlooked this truism is borne out by the sameness of

modern cities throughout the world. You see exactly the same buildings in Boston as in Buenos Aires, Seattle or Sydney. Yet in a city-centre project in Cincinnati in which we are involved there is a citizen's non-profit corporation which is a prominent component of the otherwise usual mix of bureaucracies and developers; the citizens in this case are ordinary working people, street people, black and 'blue grass'/ white; and without any loss of technical efficiency, the result is not likely to be confused with Boston, Buenos Aires, Seattle or Sydney.

But Gananda posed a special problem. Gananda is the name of a new city of 80,000, and this city is still in its planning stages. The gently rolling fields, woodlands and streams where it will be built are in upper New York State, twenty miles southeast of Rochester, the home of Kodak and Xerox, and one of the fastest growing metropolitan regions in the country. We have been asked to design the first community centre; and the question which we immediately asked ourselves was how can a community centre containing education, cultural facilities, social services, recreation and the rest, properly reflect what the community wants and needs when the community does not yet exist?

The answer, of course, is that the community does exist. Just ask the market people! And that is only one part of the community, the future residents. Other parts also exist. For example there are the people who live in the area now, the farmers and the people who live in the rural towns and hamlets whose lives will be directly and enormously affected by the new city; there are the officials, the people who sit on the local and metropolitan planning commissions, and on the library boards, and the education people, the health people, and the social services people at local, state and federal levels; and there are the clients, the developers, the investors, and their staffs and planners and engineers. That is quite a list of people. But while the number and assortment of people is one thing, their purposes and interrelationships within the whole are another. Gananda is to be a new city which differs from the English new towns in somewhat the way that Columbia, Maryland, did. The main developer and his investors act as land planners. They are in the private sector, and are not a government department. They will put in the physical infrastructure of roads, sewers, water and utilities, and the formal and informal open spaces and pedestrian links; and they will designate densities and building types, and set basic but stringent design guide-lines. Within these parameters they will sell comprehensive development packages

to individual builders on a bid or negotiated basis. But as part of the infrastructure, the main developer also puts in the public buildings, such as the community centre which he has asked us to design. At first he is the outright owner of the public buildings; but as the community begins to generate a tax base it will progressively pay off the capitalization and amortization until, in fifteen years, the community is the owner. And parallel with this process the community sets up a government structure which over the same period assumes progressively greater control and responsibilty for the policies and quality of its public life.

Of course it would be possible to design and build a community centre in the traditional way. You, Mr or Ms super intelligent reader, could draw up a programme as well as or better than I, so what the hell are we waiting for? The repudiation lies of course in the tensions and confrontations not only in our old cities but in our new cities as well, all new and polished and completely expressed by developers and planners, architects and landscapers, who don't even live there, in which the disenfranchised surprise us by being in conflict with our institutions. The problem, then, was to devise an open and inclusive participatory planning process for these diverse people; and this is what we did.

In a way what we devised was a series of planning games, and we only called them games for want of a better word; but they are rather different from computer games, and should not be confused with the them. For one thing our process is not a simulation; it is the real thing; what came out of the process will be built; and will be used by and belong to the players. Secondly, in most computer games the players assume roles — the mayor, the developer, the school superintendent, and so forth. In our process no one assumes any roles. In real life we all have particular skills and experiences; we all, as they say, come from somewhere. But we are not so much concerned with the identification of roles and the sharpening of particular skills in our process as we are with concentrating on developing a sophisticated programme for and an understanding of the most critical aspect of any new community — why should people want to cluster and live together in Gananda, what are the common preoccupations and values of this community, how does one create in environmental terms a centre which celebrates the idea of being an individual and yet belonging together, belonging to a place, identifying with a people who become your people. Ours therefore was a process which was as deeply involved in values as it was in things. And in

222

GAME 1: DEVELOPING AN INVENTORY

INVENTORY OF SPACES	HOW THE SPACE IS USED	HOW THE SPACE IS SERVICED FOR THOSE USES

URBAN DESIGN ASSOCIATES
3508 FIFTH AVE
PITTSBURGH PA

fortable seating, carpeting, adjustable lighting, etc. and by the time a few dozen types of spaces have been named and discussed by the participants it becomes clear that their usage is so fraught with overlap of every kind that only the most specialised uses can remain institutionalized in the traditional sense. Time for the game: 2 hours.

223

such a process no one has a name-tag role; but everyone has an individual contribution to make, and all discussions are anonymous. Therefore, at the door as you enter, you pick up a name-tag with a false first name on it, Sally or John or Betty or Raymond, and nothing else; and you are simply you.

Approximately two hundred people participated in the games to begin with; and all of them, plus any others who want to get involved are periodically reconvened to act as monitors as the programming and design process continues. And in between these rather large public sessions smaller workshops and task forces are working on particular parts of the total programme. It should be borne in mind, of course, that these groups are also not only the nascent governance of the community, but also they are nascently its social and cultural groups and its conservationists; and also they are the public officials at metropolitan and state levels with whom this governance will have to deal long after the buildings are built and the population is there.

GAME 1. *Developing an Inventory.* The first game is devoted entirely to inventories of the uses and facilities which can properly be described as central, public or common in a community. These are considered in three columns *(see above)*:

As an indication of how the three columns were filled here are some brief indications:

Inventory of spaces:

Library; the resource centre of a school; a theatre; etc.

How the space is used:

Reading, writing, sitting, listening, dozing, whispering, acting, speaking, viewing, just being there, courting, working in a group, being with others, browsing, visiting, etc.

How the space is serviced for those uses:

Administration, storage, janitorial and custodial assistance, heating, air conditioning, water, com-

GAME 2: BASIC ACTIVITIES

1. Self Identity

2. Self Expression

3. Self-Place

4. Skill Development

5. Colloquia

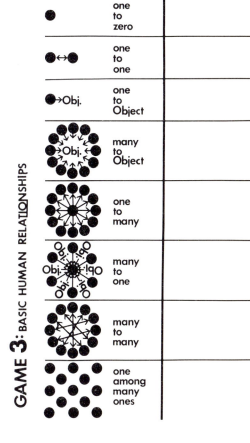

GAME 3: BASIC HUMAN RELATIONSHIPS

	one to zero	
	one to one	
→Obj.	one to Object	
	many to Object	
	one to many	
Obj.	many to one	
	many to many	
	one among many ones	

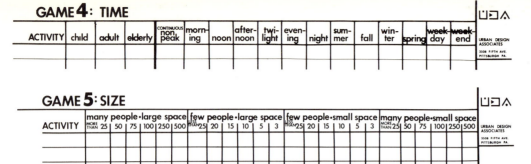

GAME 4: TIME

ACTIVITY	child	adult	elderly	CONTINUOUS non peak	morn-ing	noon	after-noon	twi-light	even-ing	night	sum-mer	fall	win-ter	spring	week-day	week-end

URBAN DESIGN ASSOCIATES
3508 FIFTH AVE
PITTSBURGH PA.

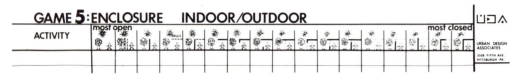

GAME 5: SIZE

ACTIVITY	many people · large space MORE THAN 25	50	75	100	250	500	few people · large space MORE THAN 25	20	15	10	5	3	few people · small space LESS THAN 25	20	15	10	5	3	many people · small space MORE THAN 25	50	75	100	250	500

URBAN DESIGN ASSOCIATES
3508 FIFTH AVE
PITTSBURGH PA.

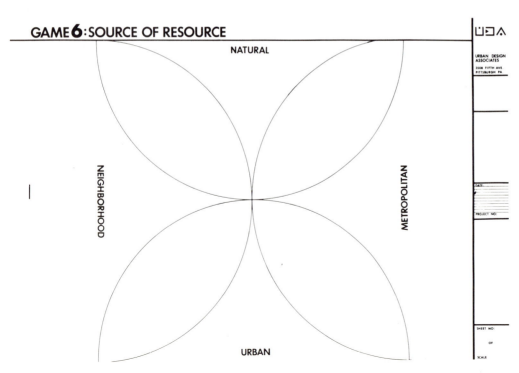

GAME 5: ENCLOSURE   INDOOR/OUTDOOR

ACTIVITY   most open .... most closed

URBAN DESIGN ASSOCIATES
3508 FIFTH AVE
PITTSBURGH PA.

GAME 6: SOURCE OF RESOURCE

NATURAL

NEIGHBORHOOD

METROPOLITAN

URBAN

URBAN DESIGN ASSOCIATES
3508 FIFTH AVE
PITTSBURGH PA.

DATE:
PROJECT NO:
SHEET NO:
OF
SCALE

224

GAME 2. *Basic Activities.* For the second game the multitudes of words and phrases which fill up the *second* column of Game 1 *(How the space is used)* are now examined for repetition and reduced to approximately a hundred. Players are asked to form groups of three or four and to apply these words and phrases in the appropriate column on a large sheet of paper. The columns are headed by the following words, which are intended to describe why anyone might want to go to the centre at all:

Self-identity; self-expression; self-place; skill development; colloquia.

Although what these words mean is intended to be self-evident, we found that self-place (physical identity with a centre, physically being there, knowing that a physical centre to the community exists) and colloquia (meeting people, discussing, gossiping, attending formal and informal occasions) needed explanation.

This game demonstrated to the players that simple spaces and simple activities can be rich with personal and individual meanings, and assisted to condition the players, many of whom come from highly specialised and/or bureaucratized daily backgrounds, to think more openly, freely and creatively in the games which followed. Time for the game: ½ hour.

GAME 3. *Basic Human Relationships.* In this game the same one hundred words and phrases as those used in Game 2 are used again, only they are spelled out twice this time, in caps and lower case. The same groups and teams are asked to place them according to first and second preferences against the following categories of basic human relationships: Time for the game: ¾ hour.

GAME 4. *Time.* The players are now asked to form eight equal groups, one for each of the categories of basic human relationships identified in Game 3. Each group then deals in this game only with the activities which in Game 3 were identified by all the players in its particular category: viz. the group *many to object* deals with all the results in that category; and so on. The group then responds on the following gaming sheet, by writing in the activity and drawing a horizontal line across the appropriate column. (Where activities are continuous the horizontal lines will form a continuous line.) Time for the game: ½ hour.

GAME 5. *Size: Enclosure.* The process for this game is the same as Game 4 and is conducted on the following gaming sheet:

NATURAL

NEIGHBORHOOD

METROPOLITAN

URBAN

source centres were in the middle of the teaching wings, and they too became their most public place. The edges of buildings are often the most private place. Yet a person seated by a window, in thought or reading or quiet observation, is separated from a public space by a transparent pane of glass. And a person in nature, under trees and stars, is sometimes the most secluded of all. In this game, players are provided with a large target. At the centre of the target is the word PUBLIC and at the edge is the word PRIVATE. Players are asked to cluster activities in what they consider to be appropriate interrelationships on the target. Time for the game: ½ hour.

Throughout the games there is a secretary for each team who makes notes on the discussions which are usually continuous and sometimes heated, sometimes humorous, sometimes extremely inventive. At the end of the games the players are asked to enter into a general discussion, and this will last for an hour or more and is tape-recorded. The Gananda series of games were played on three separate occasions, with approximately sixty-five people playing on each occasion.

The games have had an important bearing on programming and design. In the first place they have developed a climate of understanding — not only of the problem, but also among the players themselves — without role playing. This is crucial, since most of the people are not only going to be discretionary as the design proceeds, but also later, once the centre is built and operational.

Secondly, the games have illustrated both to the players and to the designers a series of new possibilities and realisations which grow out of the analysis of overlap in terms of function, space, time, size, location, cluster and interrelationship.

Thirdly, these overlaps have illustrated at once the enormous range of uses and subtlety of quite simple spaces if they are designed with knowledge and understanding, but they have also illustrated the considerable economies of usage and personnel that can be achieved by de-institutionalizing a whole series of uses which traditionally have been the purview of separate institutions (library; school; health centre; etc.). By separating out only those few activities which are completely specialised, and treating all the others in multi-usage clusters according to activities, sizes, and peaks, one arrives not only at new concepts of space but also at new concepts of administration, staffing, and capital and operational funding.

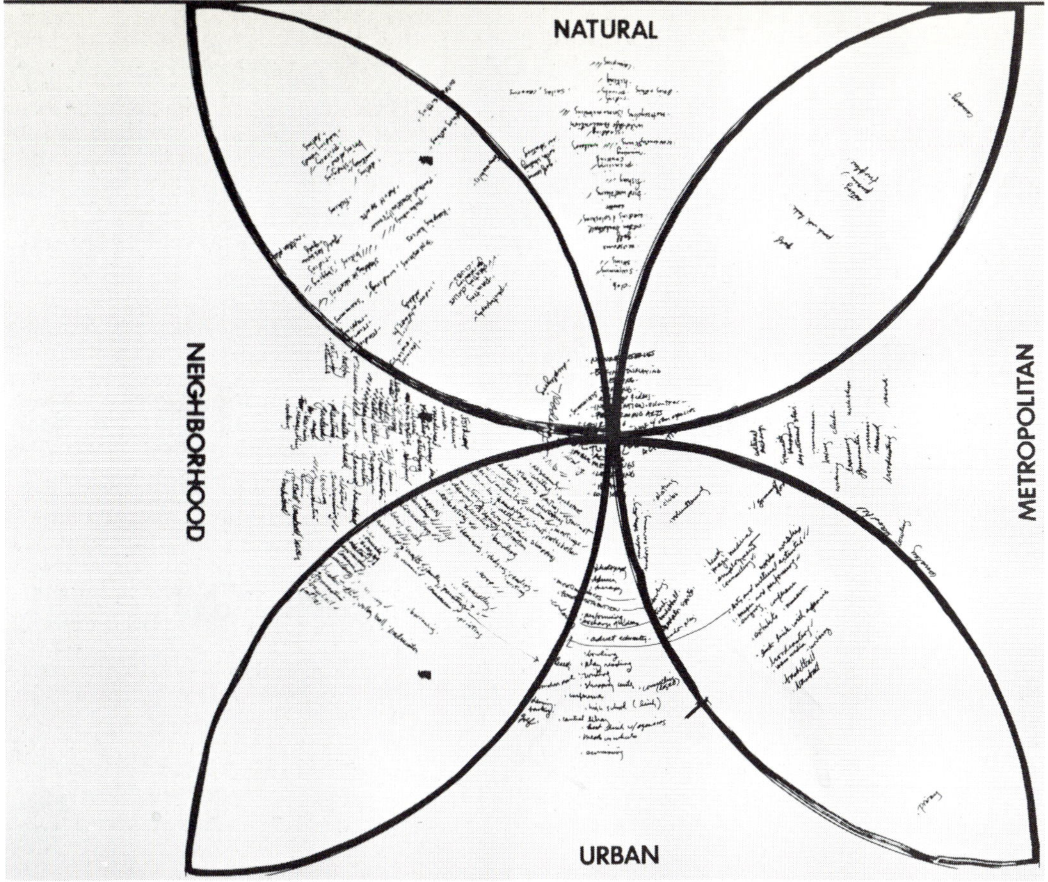

Players of Game 5 were also asked to set out the same list of activities on the following sheet:
Time for the game: ¾ hour.

GAME 6. *Source of Resource.* The previous game indicated the relationships of indoor activities to the outside, and relative degrees of seclusion. Game 6 is an attempt to increase that sense of inside/outside interrelationship by indicating that some activities within the centre may have special relationships with resources outside it. Players are asked to write the activities with which they have been dealing in previous games wherever they

think appropriate on the following gaming sheet and to draw a line in coloured pencil around these activities which they think, as a result of their experiences in the previous games, should be clustered, irrespective of where they are placed on the sheet. Time for the game: ½ hour.

GAME 7. *Cluster: Public/Private.* This is also a cluster game, and is played in the same way as Game 6. The basis of this game is a series of ironies which we began to observe in the Pontiac design. In Pontiac the street ran through the building; and the heart of the building became its most public place. The re-

225

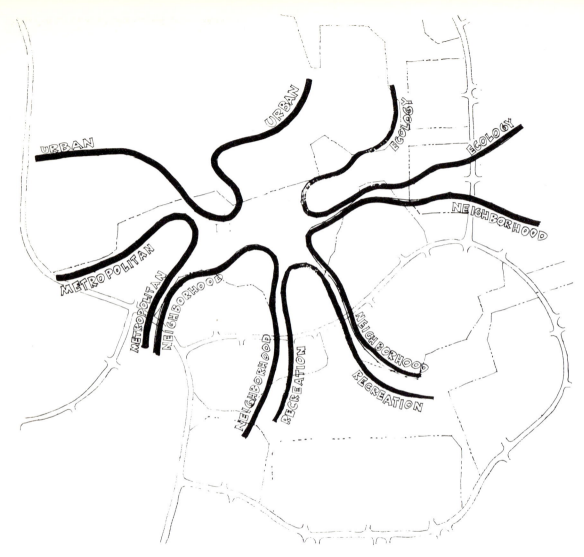

Why a non-conclusion?

Because the processes we are talking about here are designed to be responses to local and creative situations, open-ended and unpredictable.

As this goes to press, the design of the community centre has been completed and construction has just begun. The accompanying illustrations show how directly the design grew out of the games. For the architects, the process is therefore almost at an end. But for the future inhabitants of Gananda it has only just begun.

In terms of administration the centre could become a bureaucratic nightmare if its multi-usage were to be set up in the traditional way. But we have long since recognized that architects are singularly ineffective in bringing about bureaucratic change; quite the contrary, bureaucrats always win! One of the objects of the games was to get the bureaucrats themselves, as people, to join with the citizens in determining community goals and values, and then to realize that these can never be achieved without new inter-agency administrative forms.

A positive result of the games is that new administrative forms are now being invented by the agencies and the developers themselves. In Gananda a Community Facilities Corporation will be responsible for the centre and will collect revenues for its administration and maintenance from all the agencies, societies, religious groups and so forth which use it. In this way the citizens themselves and not the bureaucracy of tradition will become directly responsible for the centre's governance.

A governance of this kind guarantees, you can be sure, that programmes and usages in the centre will be perpetually changing.

One thing above all others that the games established is that the world of adults and the world of children are becoming inextricably interwoven. Reading, playing, painting, eating, acting, meeting and talking, are shared experiences; all part of a common life together. And as far as the centre is concerned, it will be a life of richness, variety, options, creativity and change.

This says important things to the designer. The drawings indicate how we moved forward. First the results of the games were tabulated and analysed. Then clusters of use and overlap were established in scale and applied to the sloping site which commands a superb view of rolling hills. Pedestrian networks were designed to link the site with housing of varying densities and sub-community characteristics, woodlands, a lake, and to the commercial centre of the new city.

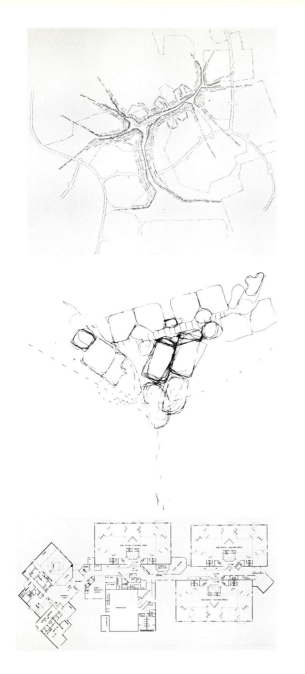

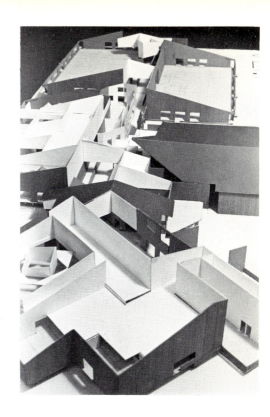

As a design programme began to emerge, we worked closely with task forces in education and community facilities, drawn from the participants in the planning games. And from the design programme a building evolves which includes learning centres, libraries, theatres, art workshops, food services, formal dining and a street café, indoor and outdoor recreation, and a health centre. All of these are multi-usage facilities; a series of agencies will use the spaces at different times, and their rentals and administrative responsibilities are negotiated on time/space ratios.

The people were deeply concerned that although the building is large it should not conflict with residential scales and that it should be if possible in a rural vernacular. The result is a group of barnlike structures with wide-span shed roofs, within which there are a number of enclosures rather like small pavilions, several of which are built to be temporary and changeable.

Certainly the use of a computer in tabulating and analysing the results of the games might have reduced the time frame. But the Gananda experience is different in every respect from traditional computer simulations; its most basic difference being, of course, that it is not a simulation of anything, but something new and real.

In terms of time and cost, the facts are interesting. The process began in November 1972. The games were played in December. In January 1973 the results were tabulated and analysed. In February basic programmes were drawn up and site boundaries were finalized. March and April were design months. May and June were devoted to construction drawings. July was for specifications and construction contracts. August — construction began. Size of the complex: approximately 70,000 sq ft. Cost: 30 per cent lower than the New York State average for elementary education buildings.

There is no doubt in our minds that this short time frame and cost effectiveness, together with the richness of the building, would not have been possible in the absence of a continuing process in which citizens, officials, developers, planners, architects and engineers all participated with a unity of purpose and, at an important level, simply as people. But cuts in cost do not represent the essential achievement of the Gananda programme.

Architects and planners are prone to believe that they are responsible for every detail of the environments they create. This is a far cry from the urbanism of the old cities which we admire so much, the cities with streets and squares which utter, if nothing else, the vitality and scale of generations of social interaction.

The programmes described here are an attempt to show that the interpersonal responsibility and creativity of citizens can be put back into design processes.

Basic to building

LONDON BRICK COMPANY LIMITED
12 York Gate, London NW1 4QL   **Tel. 01- 487 4321**
District Sales Offices at AYLESBURY, BIRMINGHAM, BRISTOL, BURY ST. EDMUNDS,
HODDESDON, LEEDS, LONDON, NOTTINGHAM, SEVENOAKS, SOUTHAMPTON.

PHORPRES

LBC clay products are fundamental to good building. Infinitely
flexible in use and aesthetically attractive, their initial cost is low,
they are quick to erect, and maintenance free.
LBC bricks and blocks, available throughout the country.

Choose your own Shower

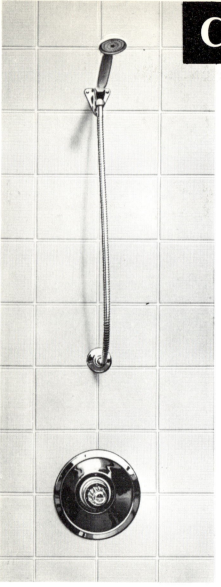

Safemix

Completely thermostatic, 'Safemix' can be preset at a maximum temperature which cannot be exceeded. Anti-vandal socket screw secures control knob. Differing pressures and temperatures are fully compensated— avoiding shower acrobatics. 'Safemix' gives immediate shut-off if cold water fails. The most thorough tests have proved 'Safemix' beyond all doubt. No sign of failure or fatigue after 100,000 tests. A minimum pressure of 3 ft. head is acceptable.

Blendamix

The 'Blendamix' is a non-thermostatic mixer, with a single control acrylic knob for flow and temperature. It can be used with pressures as low as 3 ft. head. Supplies must be from equal pressures which are normally available. 'Blendamix does not require check valves or outlet stop cocks. A comprehensive choice of shower fittings, for either exposed or recessed pipework is available.

Complete with the trendy elegance of acrylic control knobs

MEYNELL VALVES LTD., BUSHBURY, WOLVERHAMPTON
Tel: 20297

ARCHITECTS YEAR BOOK

URBAN STRUCTURE

VOLUME 12

edited by **DAVID LEWIS**

This volume explores the many facets of the 'urban revolution' which is taking place throughout the world. One series of articles is concerned with population, with the impact of urban forms of new systems of movement, and with new technologies of building. Another deals with new approaches to planning as cities expand to unprecedented geographic and population sizes and complexities, and a third series shows the impact of these forces on old cities. Other contributions reveal the social problems which have arisen during this difficult period of massive urbanization. Over 500 illustrations include examples of the work of sculptors and graphic artists whose explorations of form relate to the new architectural vocabularies. 284 pages   £7

Contents

PAUL ELEK Ltd
54-58 Caledonian Road
London N1 9RN

THE GROWTH OF CITIES

VOLUME 13

edited by **DAVID LEWIS**

Throughout the world man is rapidly becoming urban; major cities are expanding at alarming rates. Volume 13 examines the economic and sociological forces which cause cities to grow and the forms which these cities take. For example, one series of articles examines the overnight mushrooming of shanty settlements on the edges of major South American cities. Another contrasting series shows how the rehabilitation of metropolitan areas and the building of new towns have become pressing necessities in more affluent societies like France, England and the United States. Another series analyses the impact of these modern patterns of growth on historic cities such as Germany's medieval Regensburg, the walled cities of the Sahara, and the ancient cities of Aegean Greece. A final round-up gives a working report on the planning of Thamesmead, a site and a concept which has called for bold architectural solutions. 256 pages   £9

Contents

the teamworkers

If you would like to know more
about us please contact
Edward W. M. Page
Taylor Woodrow Construction Limited
345 Ruislip Road, Southall
Middlesex UB1 2QX
Telephone : 01-578 2366. Telex : 24428.
Or for overseas Emil R. S. Coppock
Taylor Woodrow International Limited
Western House, Western Avenue
London W5 1EU
Telephone : 01-997 6641. Telex : 23503

Taylor Woodrow

1972
Taylor Woodrow
International Ltd.

**The world-wide team of engineers
constructors and developers.**